computer sciences

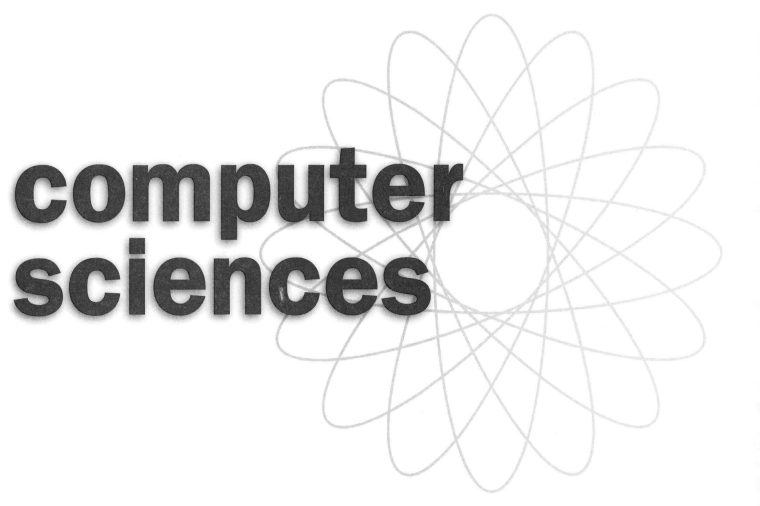

computer sciences

VOLUME 3
Social Applications

Roger R. Flynn, Editor in Chief

**MACMILLAN
REFERENCE
USA™**

GALE

New York • Detroit • San Diego • San Francisco • Cleveland • New Haven, Conn. • Waterville, Maine • London • Munich

Macmillan Reference USA
300 Park Avenue South
New York, NY 10010

Gale Group
27500 Drake Rd.
Farmington Hills, MI 48331-3535

Library of Congress Cataloging-in-Publication Data
Computer sciences / Roger R. Flynn, editor in chief.
        p.   cm.
          Includes bibiographical references and index.
          ISBN 0-02-865566-4 (set: hardcover : alk. paper) —
          ISBN 0-02-865567-2 (Volume 1: Foundations: Ideas and People : alk. paper) —
          ISBN 0-02-865568-0 (Volume 2: Software and Hardware : alk. paper) —
          ISBN 0-02-865569-9 (Volume 3: Social Applications : alk. paper) —
          ISBN 0-02-865570-2 (Volume 4: Electronic Universe : alk. paper)
          1. Computer science. I. Flynn, Roger R., 1939-
QA76 .C572   2002
004—dc21
                                                        2002000754

Printed in the United States of America
1 2 3 4 5 6 7 8 9 10

Preface

The science of computing has come a long way since the late 1930s, when John Vincent Atanasoff and Clifford Berry began work on the first electronic digital computer. One marvels to see how the science has advanced from the days of Charles Babbage, who developed the Difference Engine in the 1820s, and, later proposed the Analytical Engine. Computer science was and continues to be an intriguing field filled with interesting stories, colorful personalities, and incredible innovations.

Ever since their invention, computers have had a profound impact on society and the ways in which humans conduct business and financial matters, fight wars and maintain peace, provide goods and services, predict events (e.g., earthquakes, the weather, global warming), monitor security and safety, and a host of other applications too numerous to mention. Plus, the personal computer revolution, beginning in the 1980s, has brought computers into many homes and schools. This has helped students find new ways to prepare reports, conduct research, and study using computerized methods. In the new millennium, the role that computers play in society continues to grow.

The World of Computer Science

In preparing this encyclopedia, I came across references to the early work on the IBM System/360 series of computers, which featured capacities of 65,000 to 16 million bytes (4 byte-words) of main storage and disk storage of several million to tens or hundreds of million bytes. At the same time, I opened the Sunday paper in February of 2002 and scanned the ads for personal computers, announcing memories of several hundred million bytes and disk storage of gigabytes. The cost of the 360 series ranged from fifty to several hundred thousand dollars to more than a million. Prices for the computers advertised in my Sunday paper ranged from several hundred dollars to a few thousand. The IBM 360 series was released in 1964. If a similar breakthrough occurred in education or automobile manufacturing (a factor of 1000, on the conservative side), a year in college would cost $20, as would a good model car! This, of course, is not the case.

However, computer hardware is not the entire story. Machines all need software, operating systems, applications software, and the like. While a person was hard pressed to get a line drawing or a bar chart on the screen 25 years ago, someone today has a choice of presentation software (slides or projections of the computer screen), desktop publishing, spreadsheets, and the like, much of which comes bundled with the system.

In fact, today one can purchase, for a few thousand dollars, more equipment and software than the Department of Information Science and

Telecommunications at my school (the University of Pittsburgh) or, for that matter, the entire university, could buy, when I first arrived in 1974. This is, indeed, an extraordinary era to have been a part of and witnessed. However, this does not happen in a vacuum. In this encyclopedia we aim to detail the people, activities, products, and growth of knowledge that have helped computer science evolve into what it is today.

Volume Breakdown

The organization of this encyclopedia reflects the history and application of the field. Our first volume in this series is dedicated to the history of computing. Its subtitle is *Foundations: Ideas and People*. The second volume describes *Software and Hardware*, while the third addresses *Social Applications*. The fourth is appropriately subtitled the *Electronic Universe* as it looks at such developments and inventions as the Internet, ubiquitous computing (embedded computing), and miniaturization.

While the intent is to give an exhaustive view of the field, no encyclopedia of this size, or, for that matter, ten times its size, could provide a complete rendering of the developments, events, people, and technology involved. Hence, the four volumes provide a representative selection of the people, places, and events involved. The encyclopedia was developed from a U.S. point of view, but we trust that the articles herein are not intentionally biased and, hopefully, do justice to innovations and contributions from elsewhere in the world. A brief look at each volume of the encyclopedia follows.

Volume 1

Volume I discusses the foundations of computer science, including computing history and some important innovators. Among the people are American inventor Herman Hollerith (1860–1929), the designer of punched card and punched card equipment; English mathematician Charles Babbage (1791–1871), the inventor of the Difference Engine and the proposed Analytical Engine, a precursor of the stored program computer; English noblewoman Ada Byron King, the Countess of Lovelace (1815–1852), the first "computer programmer"; American executive Thomas J. Watson Sr. (1874–1956), early chief of the IBM Corporation; and American mathematician Grace Hopper (1906–1992), who helped in the development of COBOL (COmmon Business Oriented Language) and developed one of its predecessors, FLOW-MATIC, and is the person who allegedly coined the term "computer bug."

Within Volume 1, various groups and organizations are discussed. These include the Association for Computing Machinery (ACM), which brings together people from around the globe to exchange ideas and advance computer science; the Institute of Electrical and Electronic Engineers (IEEE), which serves as the world's largest technical professional association, with more than 350,000 members; and the IBM Corporation, Apple Computer Inc., and the Microsoft Corporation, which all contributed to the start of the personal computer (PC) revolution. Among the more general articles the reader will find those concerning topics such as early pioneers, featuring primarily American and European scientists and their work; language generations, focusing on the evolution of computer languages; and computer generations, discussing early machines such as the ENIAC (Electronic

*Explore further in Hollerith, Herman; Babbage, Charles; Lovelace, Ada Byron King, Countess of; Watson, Thomas J., Sr; and Hopper, Grace.

*Explore further in Association for Computing Machinery; Institute of Electrical and Electronic Engineers (IEEE); IBM Corporation; Apple Computer, Inc.; Microsoft Corporation; Early Pioneers; Generations, Languages; and Generations, Computers.

Numerical Integrator and Computer) and the EDVAC (Electronic Discrete Variable Automatic Computer).

Finally, other articles of general interest in Volume 1 concern the history and workings of supercomputers; the development of the mouse; the question of computer security; the beginnings of the Internet; and the basics of digital and analog computing. The government's role is explained in articles on the U.S. Census Bureau and funding research projects. In addition, mathematical tools such as the binary number system and the slide rule as well as innovations such as France's Minitel are also featured.

*Explore further in Supercomputers; Mouse; Security; Internet; Digital Computing; Analog Computing; Census Bureau; Government Funding, Research; Binary Number System; Slide Rule; Minitel.

Volume 2

Volume 2 describes software and hardware. Articles cover topics from system analysis and design, which is the cornerstone of building a system, to operating systems, compilers, and parallel processing, which discuss some of the technical aspects of computing. Telecommunication subjects range from network design to wireless technology to ATM transmission, while application-oriented articles include pattern recognition, personal digital assistants (PDAs), and computer music. Essays concerning software products include object-oriented languages, client/server technology, invasive programs, and programming.

*Explore further in System Analysis; Systems Design; Operating Systems; Compilers; Parallel Processing; Network Design; Wireless Technology; ATM Transmission; Pattern Recognition; Personal Digital Assistants; Music, Computer; Object-Oriented Languages; Client/Server Systems; Invasive Programs; and Programming.

Among the people featured in Volume 2 are John Bardeen (1908–1991), Walter H. Brattain (1902–1987), and William B. Shockley (1910–1989), inventors of the transistor; English mathematician George Boole (1815–1864), developer of Boolean logic; and Alexander Graham Bell (1847–1922), inventor of the telephone. Rounding out Volume 2 are the technical aspects of hardware-related topics, including coding techniques, digital logic design, and cellular technology.

*Explore further in Bardeen, John, Brattain, Walter H., and Shockley, William B.; Boole, George; Boolean Algebra; Bell, Alexander Graham; Coding Techniques; Codes; Digital Logic Design; and Cellular Technology.

Volume 3

In Volume 3, the emphasis is on social applications. From fashion design to meteorology, the use of computers impacts our everyday lives. For example, computer technology has greatly influenced the study of biology, molecular biology, physics, and mathematics, not to mention the large role it plays in air traffic management and aircraft flight control, ATM machines and magnetic stripe cards for shopping and business. Businesses, large and small, have significantly benefited from applications that track product growth, costs, and the way products are managed. Volume 3 essays also explore the computer's role in medical image analysis and legal systems, while our use of computers in everyday life and our means of interacting with them are addressed in subjects such as library applications and speech recognition.

*Explore further in Fashion Design; Weather Forecasting; Biology; Molecular Biology; Physics; Mathematics; Aircraft Traffic Management; Aircraft Flight Control; ATM Machines; Magnetic Stripe Cards; Project Management; Economic Modeling; Process Control; Productivity Software; Integrated Software; Image Analysis: Medicine; Legal Systems; Library Applications; Speech Recognition.

Volume 3 addresses our aesthetic and intellectual pursuits in areas such as composing music, playing chess, and designing buildings. Yet the advancements of computer sciences go much further as described in articles about agriculture, geographic information systems, and astronomy. Among the people featured in the volume are American inventor Al Gross (1918–2001), the "father of wireless"; Hungarian mathematician Rózsa Péter (1905–1977), promoter of the study of recursive functions; and American author Isaac Asimov (1920–1992), famed science fiction writer who wrote extensively about robots.

*Explore further in Music Composition; Chess Playing; Architecture; Agriculture; Geographic Information Systems; Astronomy; Gross, Alfred J.; Péter, Rózsa; Asimov, Isaac.

*Explore further in Internet: History; Internet: Applications; Internet: Backbone; Molecular Computing; Artificial Life; Mobile Computing; Cryptography; E-banking; E-books; E-commerce; E-journals and E-publishing; Information Access; Information Overload; Ethics; Copyright; and Patents.

*Explore further in Photography; Art; Cybercafe; Social Impact; Data Mining; Data Warehousing; Java Applets; JavaScript; Agents; Visual Basic.

*Explore further in Marconi, Guglielmo; Shannon, Claude E.; Glushkov, Victor M.

*Explore further in Zuse, Konrad.

*Explore further in Data Processing; Nanocomputing; Mainframes; E-mail; Abacus.

Volume 4

Volume 4 delves into our interconnected, networked society. The Internet is explored in detail, including its history, applications, and backbone. Molecular computing and artificial life are discussed, as are mobile computing and encryption technology. The reader will find articles on electronic banking, books, commerce, publishing, as well as information access and overload. Ethical matters pertaining to the electronic universe are also addressed.

Volume 4 extends our aesthetic interest with articles on photography and the use of computers in art. Readers will learn more about how cybercafes keep friends and family connected as well as the type of social impact that computers have had on society. Data gathering, storage, and retrieval are investigated in topics such as data mining and data warehousing. Similarly, Java applets, JavaScript, agents, and Visual Basic are featured.

Among the people highlighted in Volume 4 are Italian physicist Guglielmo Marconi (1874–1937), inventor of wireless communications; American engineer Claude E. Shannon (1916–2001), a pioneer of information theory; and Soviet mathematician Victor M. Glushkov (1923–1982), who advanced the science of cybernetics.

The Many Facets of Computer Science

Computer science has many interesting stories, many of which are told in this volume. Among them are the battle between John Atanasoff and John Mauchley and J. Presper Eckert Jr. over the patent to the electronic digital computer and regenerative memory, symbolized and embodied in the lawsuits between Sperry-Rand (Mauchley-Eckert) and Honeywell (Atanasoff) and Sperry-Rand (Mauchley-Eckert) and CDC (Atanasoff). The lawsuits are not covered here, but the principal actors are. And there is Thomas J. Watson's prediction, possibly apocryphal, of the need ("demand") for 50 computers worldwide! Plus, Ada Byron King, Countess of Lovelace, became famous for a reason other than being British poet Lord George Gordon Byron's daughter. And German inventor Konrad Zuse (1910–1995) saw his computers destroyed by the Allies during World War II, while Soviet mathematician Victor M. Glushkov (1923–1982) had an institute named after him and his work.

Scientific visualization is now a topic of interest, while data processing is passé. Nanocomputing has become a possibility, while mainframes are still in use and e-mail is commonplace in many parts of the world. It has been a great half-century or so (60 some years) for a fledgling field that began, possibly, with the Abacus!

Organization of the Material

Computer Sciences contains 286 entries that were newly commissioned for this work. More than 125 people contributed to this set, some from academia, some from industry, some independent consultants. Many contributors are from the United States, but other countries are represented including Australia, Canada, Great Britain, and Germany. In many cases, our contributors have written extensively on their subjects before, either in books or journal articles. Some even maintain their own web sites providing further information on their research topics.

Most entries in this set contain illustrations, either photos, graphs, charts, or tables. Many feature sidebars that enhance the topic at hand or give a glimpse into a topic of related interest. The entries—geared to high school students and general readers—include glossary definitions of unfamiliar terms to help the reader understand complex topics. These words are highlighted in the text and defined in the margins. In addition, each entry includes a bibliography of sources of further information as well as a list of related entries in the encyclopedia.

Additional resources are available in the set's front and back matter. These include a timeline on significant events in computing history, a timeline on significant dates in the history of programming and markup and scripting languages, and a glossary. An index is included in each volume—Volume 4 contains a cumulative index covering the entire *Computer Sciences* encyclopedia.

Acknowledgments and Thanks

We would like to thank Elizabeth Des Chenes and Hélène Potter, who made the project possible; Cindy Clendenon; and, especially, Kathleen Edgar, without whose work this would not have been possible. Also thanks to Stephen Murray for compiling the glossary. And, I personally would like to thank the project's two other editors, Ida M. Flynn and Ann McIver McHoes, for their dedicated work in getting these volumes out. And finally, thanks to our many contributors. They provided "many voices," and we hope you enjoy listening to them.

Roger R. Flynn
Editor in Chief

Measurements

Data Unit	Abbreviation	Equivalent (Data Storage)	Power of Ten
Byte	B	8 bits	1 byte
Kilobyte	K, KB	$2^{10} = 1{,}024$ bytes	1,000 (one thousand) bytes
Megabyte	M, MB	$2^{20} = 1{,}048{,}576$ bytes	1,000,000 (one million) bytes
Gigabyte	GB	$2^{30} = 1{,}073{,}741{,}824$ bytes	1,000,000,000 (one billion) bytes
Terabyte	TB	$2^{40} = 1{,}099{,}511{,}627{,}776$ bytes	1,000,000,000,000 (one trillion) bytes
Petabyte	PB	$2^{50} = 1{,}125{,}899{,}906{,}842{,}624$ bytes	1,000,000,000,000,000 (one quadrillion) bytes

Time	Abbreviation	Equivalent	Additional Information
femtosecond	fs, fsec	10^{-15} seconds	1 quadrillionth of a second
picosecond	ps, psec	10^{-12} seconds	1 trillionth of a second
nanosecond	ns, nsec	10^{-9} seconds	1 billionth of a second
microsecond	μs, μsec	10^{-6} seconds	1 millionth of a second
millisecond	ms, msec	10^{-3} seconds	1 thousandth of a second
second	s, sec	1/60 of a minute; 1/3,600 of an hour	1 sixtieth of a minute; 1 thirty-six hundredths of an hour
minute	m, min	60 seconds; 1/60 of an hour	1 sixtieth of an hour
hour	h, hr	60 minutes; 3,600 seconds	
day	d	24 hours; 1,440 minutes; 86,400 seconds	
year	y, yr	365 days; 8,760 hours	
1,000 hours		1.3888... months (1.4 months)	$1{,}000 \div (30 \text{ days} \times 24 \text{ hours})$
8,760 hours		1 year	$365 \text{ days} \times 24 \text{ hours}$
1 million hours		114.15525... years	$1{,}000{,}000 \div 8{,}760$
1 billion hours		~114,200... years	$1{,}000 \times 114.15525...$
1 trillion hours		~114,200,000 years	$1{,}000 \times 114{,}200$

Length	Abbreviation	Equivalent	Additional Information
nanometer	nm	10^{-9} meters (1 billionth of a meter)	~ 4/100,000,000 of an inch; ~ 1/25,000,000 of an inch
micrometer	μm	10^{-6} meter (1 millionth of a meter)	~ 4/100,000 of an inch; ~ 1/25,000 of an inch
millimeter	mm	10^{-3} meter (1 thousandth of a meter)	~ 4/100 of an inch; ~ 1/25 of an inch (2/5 × 1/10)
centimeter	cm	10^{-2} meter (1 hundredth of a meter); 1/2.54 of an inch	~ 2/5 of an inch (1 inch = 2.54 centimeters, exactly)
meter	m	100 centimeters; 3.2808 feet	~ 3 1/3 feet or 1.1 yards
kilometer	km	1,000 meters; 0.6214 miles	~ 3/5 of a mile
mile	mi	5,280 feet; 1.6093 kilometers	1.6×10^3 meters

Volume	Abbreviation	Equivalent	Additional Information
microliter	μl	1/1,000,000 liter	1 millionth of a liter
milliliter	ml	1/1,000 liter; 1 cubic centimeter	1 thousandth of a liter
centiliter	cl	1/100 liter	1 hundredth of a liter
liter	l	100 centiliters; 1,000 milliliters; 1,000,000 microliters; 1.0567 quarts (liquid)	~ 1.06 quarts (liquid)

Base 2 (Binary)	Decimal (Base 10) Equivalent	Approximations to Powers of Ten
2^0	1	
2^1	2	
2^2	4	
2^3	8	
2^4	16	
2^5	32	
2^6	64	
2^7	128	10^2; 100; one hundred; 1 followed by 2 zeros
2^8	256	
2^9	512	
2^{10}	1,024	10^3; 1,000; one thousand; 1 followed by 3 zeros
2^{11}	2,048	
2^{12}	4,096	
2^{13}	8,192	
2^{14}	16,384	
2^{15}	32,768	
2^{16}	65,536	
2^{17}	131,072	
2^{18}	262,144	
2^{19}	524,288	
2^{20}	1,048,576	10^6; 1,000,000; one million; 1 followed by 6 zeros
2^{21}	2,097,152	
2^{22}	4,194,304	
2^{23}	8,388,608	
2^{24}	16,777,216	
2^{25}	33,554,432	
2^{26}	67,108,864	
2^{27}	134,217,728	
2^{28}	268,435,456	
2^{29}	536,870,912	
2^{30}	1,073,741,824	10^9; 1,000,000,000; one billion; 1 followed by 9 zeros
2^{31}	2,147,483,648	
2^{32}	4,294,967,296	
2^{33}	8,589,934,592	
2^{34}	17,179,869,184	
2^{35}	34,359,738,368	
2^{36}	68,719,476,736	
2^{37}	137,438,953,472	
2^{38}	274,877,906,944	
2^{39}	549,755,813,888	
2^{40}	1,099,511,627,776	10^{12}; 1,000,000,000,000; one trillion; 1 followed by 12 zeros
2^{50}	1,125,899,906,842,624	10^{15}; 1,000,000,000,000,000; one quadrillion; 1 followed by 15 zeros
2^{100}	1,267,650,600,228,229,401,496,703,205,376	10^{30}; 1 followed by 30 zeros
2^{-1}	1/2	
2^{-2}	1/4	
2^{-3}	1/8	
2^{-4}	1/16	
2^{-5}	1/32	
2^{-6}	1/64	
2^{-7}	1/128	1/100; 10^{-2}; 0.01; 1 hundredth
2^{-8}	1/256	
2^{-9}	1/512	
2^{-10}	1/1,024	1 /1000; 10^{-3}; 0.001; 1 thousandth

Base 16 (Hexadecimal)	Binary (Base 2) Equivalent	Decimal (Base 10) Equivalent	Approximations to Powers of Ten
16^0	2^0	1	
16^1	2^4	16	
16^2	2^8	256	2×10^2; 2 hundred
16^3	2^{12}	4,096	4×10^3; 4 thousand
16^4	2^{16}	65,536	65×10^3; 65 thousand
16^5	2^{20}	1,048,576	1×10^6; 1 million
16^6	2^{24}	16,777,216	
16^7	2^{28}	268,435,456	
16^8	2^{32}	4,294,967,296	4×10^9; 4 billion
16^9	2^{36}	68,719,476,736	68×10^9; 68 billion
16^{10}	2^{40}	1,099,511,627,776	1×10^{12}; 1 trillion
16^{-1}	2^{-4}	1/16	
16^{-2}	2^{-8}	1/256	
16^{-3}	2^{-12}	1/4,096	$1/4 \times 10^{-3}$; 1/4-thousandth
16^{-4}	2^{-16}	1/65,536	
16^{-5}	2^{-20}	1/1,048,576	10^{-6}; 1 millionth
16^{-8}	2^{-32}	1/4,294,967,296	$1/4 \times 10^{-9}$; 1/4-billionth
16^{-10}	2^{-40}	1/1,099,511,627,776	10^{-12}; 1 trillionth

Base 10 (Decimal)	Equivalent	Verbal Equivalent
10^0	1	
10^1	10	
10^2	100	1 hundred
10^3	1,000	1 thousand
10^4	10,000	
10^5	100,000	
10^6	1,000,000	1 million
10^7	10,000,000	
10^8	100,000,000	
10^9	1,000,000,000	1 billion
10^{10}	10,000,000,000	
10^{11}	100,000,000,000	
10^{12}	1,000,000,000,000	1 trillion
10^{15}	1,000,000,000,000,000	1 quadrillion
10^{-1}	1/10	1 tenth
10^{-2}	1/100	1 hundredth
10^{-3}	1/1,000	1 thousandth
10^{-6}	1/1,000,000	1 millionth
10^{-9}	1/1,000,000,000	1 billionth
10^{-12}	1/1,000,000,000,000	1 trillionth
10^{-15}	1/1,000,000,000,000,000	1 quadrillionth

Sizes of and Distance to Objects

Sizes of and Distance to Objects	Equivalent	Additional Information
Diameter of Electron (classical)	5.6×10^{-13} centimeters	5.6×10^{-13} centimeters; roughly 10^{-12} centimeters
Mass of Electron	9.109×10^{-28} grams	roughly 10^{-27} grams (1 gram = 0.0353 ounce)
Diameter of Proton	10^{-15} meters	10^{-13} centimeters
Mass of Proton	1.67×10^{-24} grams	roughly 10^{-24} grams (about 1,836 times the mass of electron)
Diameter of Neutron	10^{-15} meters	10^{-13} centimeters
Mass of Neutron	1.673×10^{-24} grams	roughly 10^{-24} grams (about 1,838 times the mass of electron)
Diameter of Atom (Electron Cloud)	ranges from 1×10^{-10} to 5×10^{-10} meters;	$\sim 10^{-10}$ meters; $\sim 10^{-8}$ centimeters; $\sim 3.94 \times 10^{-9}$ inches (roughly 4 billionth of an inch across or 1/250 millionth of an inch across)
Diameter of Atomic Nucleus	10^{-14} meters	$\sim 10^{-12}$ centimeters (10,000 times smaller than an atom)
Atomic Mass (Atomic Mass Unit)	1.66×10^{-27} kilograms	One atomic mass unit (amu) is equal to 1.66×10^{-24} grams
Diameter of (standard) Pencil	6 millimeters (0.236 inches)	roughly 10^{-2} meters
Height (average) of Man and Woman	man: 1.75 meters (5 feet, 8 inches) woman: 1.63 meters (5 feet, 4 inches)	human height roughly 2×10^{0} meters;
Height of Mount Everest	8,850 meters (29,035 feet)	1/804.66 miles; 10^{-3} miles ~ 5.5 miles; roughly 10^{4} meters
Radius (mean equatorial) of Earth	6,378.1 kilometers (3,960.8 miles)	$\sim 6,400$ kilometers (4,000 miles); roughly 6.4×10^{6} meters
Diameter (polar) of Earth	12,713.6 kilometers (7,895.1 miles)	$\sim 12,800$ kilometers (8,000 miles); roughly 1.28×10^{7} meters (Earth's diameter is twice the Earth's radius)
Circumference (based on mean equatorial radius) of Earth	40,075 kilometers (24,887 miles)	40,000 kilometers (25,000 miles) (about 8 times the width of the United States) (Circumference = $2 \times \pi \times$ Earth's radius)
Distance from Earth to Sun	149,600,000 kilometers (92,900,000 miles)	$\sim 93,000,000$ miles; ~ 8.3 light-minutes; roughly 10^{11} meters; roughly 10^{8} miles
Distance to Great Nebula in Andromeda Galaxy	2.7×10^{19} kilometers (1.7×10^{19} miles)	~ 2.9 million light-years; roughly 10^{22} meters; roughly 10^{19} miles

Timeline: Significant Events in the History of Computing

The history of computer sciences has been filled with many creative inventions and intriguing people. Here are some of the milestones and achievements in the field.

c300-500 BCE	The counting board, known as the ancient abacus, is used. (Babylonia)
CE 1200	The modern abacus is used. (China)
c1500	Leonardo da Vinci drafts a design for a calculator. (Italy)
1614	John Napier suggests the use of logarithms. (Scotland)
1617	John Napier produces calculating rods, called "Napier's Bones." (Scotland)
	Henry Briggs formulates the common logarithm, Base 10. (England)
1620	Edmund Gunter devises the "Line of Numbers," the precursor to slide rule. (England)
1623	Wilhelm Schickard conceives a design of a mechanical calculator. (Germany)
1632	William Oughtred originates the slide rule. (England)
1642	Blaise Pascal makes a mechanical calculator, which can add and subtract. (France)
1666	Sir Samuel Morland develops a multiplying calculator. (England)
1673	Gottfried von Leibniz proposes a general purpose calculating machine. (Germany)
1777	Charles Stanhope, 3rd Earl of Stanhope, Lord Mahon, invents a logic machine. (England)
1804	Joseph-Marie Jacquard mechanizes weaving with Jacquard's Loom, featuring punched cards. (France)
1820	Charles Xavier Thomas (Tomas de Colmar) creates a calculating machine, a prototype for the first commercially successful calculator. (France)
1822	Charles Babbage designs the Difference Engine. (England)
1834	Charles Babbage proposes the Analytical Engine. (England)
1838	Samuel Morse formulates the Morse Code. (United States)
1842	L. F. Menabrea publishes a description of Charles Babbage's Analytical Engine. (Published, Italy)

1843	Ada Byron King, Countess of Lovelace, writes a program for Babbage's Analytical Engine. (England)
1854	George Boole envisions the Laws of Thought. (Ireland)
1870	William Stanley Jevons produces a logic machine. (England)
1873	William Thomson, Lord Kelvin, devises the analog tide predictor. (Scotland)
	Christopher Sholes, Carlos Glidden, and Samuel W. Soule invent the Sholes and Glidden Typewriter; produced by E. Remington & Sons. (United States)
1875	Frank Stephen Baldwin constructs a pin wheel calculator. (United States)
1876	Alexander Graham Bell develops the telephone. (United States)
	Bell's rival, Elisha Gray, also produces the telephone. (United States)
1878	Swedish inventor Willgodt T. Odhner makes a pin wheel calculator. (Russia)
1884	Dorr Eugene Felt creates the key-driven calculator, the Comptometer. (United States)
	Paul Gottlieb Nipkow produces the Nipkow Disk, a mechanical television device. (Germany)
1886	Herman Hollerith develops his punched card machine, called the Tabulating Machine. (United States)
1892	William Seward Burroughs invents his Adding and Listing (printing) Machine. (United States)
1896	Herman Hollerith forms the Tabulating Machine Company. (United States)
1901	Guglielmo Marconi develops wireless telegraphy. (Italy)
1904	John Ambrose Fleming constructs the diode valve (vacuum tube). (England)
	Elmore Ambrose Sperry concocts the circular slide rule. (United States)
1906	Lee De Forest invents the triode vacuum tube (audion). (United States)
1908	Elmore Ambrose Sperry produces the gyrocompass. (United States)
1910	Sperry Gyroscope Company is established. (United States)
1912	Frank Baldwin and Jay Monroe found Monroe Calculating Machine Company. (United States)
1914	Leonardo Torres Quevado devises an electromechanical calculator, an electromechanical chess machine (End Move). (Spain)
	Thomas J. Watson Sr. joins the Computing-Tabulating-Recording Company (CTR) as General Manager. (United States)

1919	W. H. Eccles and F. W. Jordan develop the flip-flop (memory device). (England)
1922	Russian-born Vladimir Kosma Zworykin develops the iconoscope and kinescope (cathode ray tube), both used in electronic television for Westinghouse. (United States)
1924	The Computing-Tabulating-Recording Company (CTR), formed in 1911 by the merger of Herman Hollerith's Tabulating Machine Company with Computing Scale Company and the International Time Recording Company, becomes the IBM (International Business Machines) Corporation. (United States)
1927	The Remington Rand Corporation forms from the merger of Remington Typewriter Company, Rand Kardex Bureau, and others. (United States)
1929	Vladimir Kosma Zworykin develops color television for RCA. (United States)
1931	Vannevar Bush develops the Differential Analyzer (an analog machine). (United States)
1933	Wallace J. Eckert applies punched card machines to astronomical data. (United States)
1937	Alan M. Turing proposes a Theoretical Model of Computation. (England)
	George R. Stibitz crafts the Binary Adder. (United States)
1939	John V. Atanasoff devises the prototype of an electronic digital computer. (United States)
	William R. Hewlett and David Packard establish the Hewlett-Packard Company. (United States)
1940	Claude E. Shannon applies Boolean algebra to switching circuits. (United States)
	George R. Stibitz uses the complex number calculator to perform Remote Job Entry (RJE), Dartmouth to New York. (United States)
1941	Konrad Zuse formulates a general-purpose, program-controlled computer. (Germany)
1942	John V. Atanasoff and Clifford Berry unveil the Atanasoff-Berry Computer (ABC). (United States)
1944	The Colossus, an English calculating machine, is put into use at Bletchley Park. (England)
	Howard Aiken develops the Automatic Sequence Controlled Calculator (ASCC), the Harvard Mark I, which is the first American program-controlled computer. (United States)
	Grace Hopper allegedly coins the term "computer bug" while working on the Mark I. (United States)
1946	J. Presper Eckert Jr. and John W. Mauchly construct the ENIAC (Electronic Numerical Integrator and Computer),

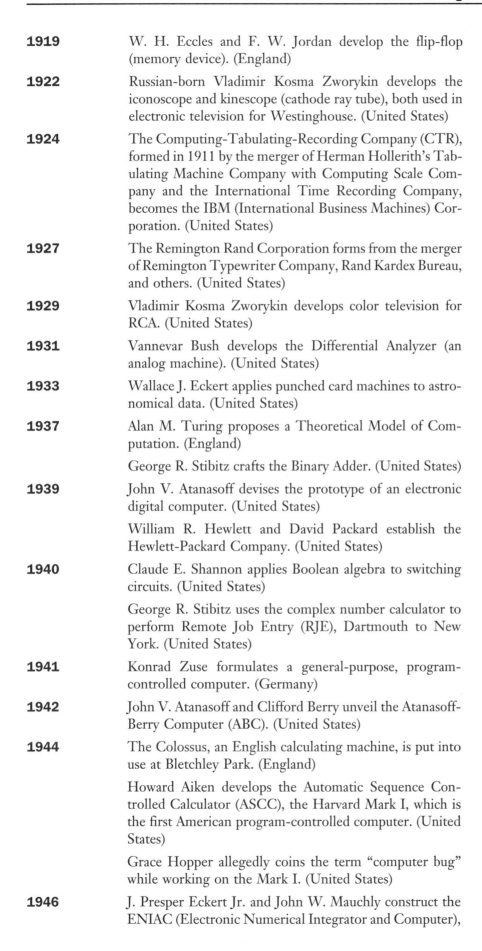

the first American general-purpose electronic computer, at the Moore School, University of Pennsylvania. (United States)

J. Presper Eckert Jr. and John W. Mauchly form the Electronic Control Company, which later becomes the Eckert-Mauchly Computer Corporation. (United States)

1947 John Bardeen, Walter H. Brattain, and William B. Shockley invent the transistor at Bell Laboratories. (United States)

J. Presper Eckert Jr. and John W. Mauchly develop the EDVAC (Electronic Discrete Variable Automatic Computer), a stored-program computer. (United States)

1948 F. C. Williams, Tom Kilburn, and G. C. (Geoff) Tootill create a small scale, experimental, stored-program computer (nicknamed "Baby") at the University of Manchester; it serves as the prototype of Manchester Mark I. (England)

1949 F. C. Williams, Tom Kilburn, and G. C. (Geoff) Tootill design the Manchester Mark I at the University of Manchester. (England)

Maurice V. Wilkes develops the EDSAC (Electronic Delay Storage Automatic Calculator) at Cambridge University. (England)

Jay Wright Forrester invents three dimensional core memory at the Massachusetts Institute of Technology. (United States)

Jay Wright Forrester and Robert Everett construct the Whirlwind I, a digital, real-time computer at Massachusetts Institute of Technology. (United States)

1950 J. H. Wilkinson and Edward A. Newman design the Pilot ACE (Automatic Computing Engine) implementing the Turing proposal for a computing machine at the National Physical Laboratory (NPL). (England)

Remington Rand acquires the Eckert-Mauchly Computer Corporation. (United States)

1951 Engineering Research Associates develops the ERA 1101, an American commercial computer, for the U.S. Navy and National Security Agency (NSA). (United States)

The UNIVAC I (Universal Automatic Computer), an American commercial computer, is created by Remington Rand for the U.S. Census Bureau. (United States)

Ferranti Mark I, a British commercial computer, is unveiled. (England)

Lyons Tea Co. announces Lyons Electronic Office, a British commercial computer. (England)

1952 UNIVAC I predicts election results as Dwight D. Eisenhower sweeps the U.S. presidential race. (United States)

Remington Rand Model 409, an American commercial computer, is originated by Remington Rand for the Internal Revenue Service. (United States)

Remington Rand acquires Engineering Research Associates. (United States)

1953 The IBM 701, a scientific computer, is constructed. (United States)

1954 The IBM 650 EDPM, electronic data processing machine, a stored-program computer in a punched-card environment, is produced. (United States)

1955 Sperry Corp. and Remington Rand merge to form the Sperry Rand Corporation. (United States)

1957 Robert N. Noyce, Gordon E. Moore, and others found Fairchild Semiconductor Corporation. (United States)

Seymour Cray, William Norris, and others establish Control Data Corporation. (United States)

Kenneth Olsen and Harlan Anderson launch Digital Equipment Corporation (DEC). (United States)

1958 Jack Kilby at Texas Instruments invents the integrated circuit. (United States)

1959 Robert N. Noyce at Fairchild Semiconductor invents the integrated circuit. Distinct patents are awarded to both Texas Instruments and Fairchild Semiconductor, as both efforts are recognized. (United States)

1960 The first PDP-1 is sold by Digital Equipment Corporation, which uses some technology from the Whirlwind Project. (United States)

The UNIVAC 1100 series of computers is announced by Sperry Rand Corporation. (United States)

1961 The Burroughs B5000 series dual-processor, with virtual memory, is unveiled. (United States)

1964 The IBM/360 family of computers begins production. (United States)

The CDC 6600 is created by Control Data Corporation. (United States)

1965 The UNIVAC 1108 from Sperry Rand Corporation is constructed. (United States)

The PDP-8, the first minicomputer, is released by Digital Equipment Corporation. (United States)

1968 Robert N. Noyce and Gordon E. Moore found Intel Corporation. (United States)

1969 The U.S. Department of Defense (DoD) launches ARPANET, the beginning of the Internet. (United States)

1970 The PDP-11 series of computers from Digital Equipment Corporation is put into use.(United States)

The Xerox Corporation's Palo Alto Research Center (PARC) begins to study the architecture of information. (United States)

1971 Ken Thompson devises the UNIX Operating System at Bell Laboratories. (United States)

Marcian E. (Ted) Hoff, Federico Faggin, and Stanley Mazor at Intel create the first microprocessor—a 4-bit processor, 4004. (United States)

1972 Seymour Cray founds Cray Research Inc. (United States)

Intel releases the 8008 microprocessor, an 8-bit processor. (United States)

1974 Intel announces the 8080 microprocessor, an 8-bit processor. (United States)

Motorola Inc. unveils the Motorola 6800, its 8-bit microprocessor. (United States)

Federico Faggin and Ralph Ungerman co-found Zilog, Inc., a manufacturer of microprocessors. (United States)

1975 Bill Gates and Paul Allen establish the Microsoft Corporation. (United States)

The kit-based Altair 8800 computer, using an 8080 microprocessor, is released by Ed Roberts with MITS (Model Instrumentation Telemetry Systems) in Albuquerque, New Mexico. (United States)

MITS purchases a version of the BASIC computer language from Microsoft. (United States)

The MOS 6502 microprocessor, an 8-bit microprocessor, is developed by MOS Technologies, Chuck Peddle, and others, who had left Motorola, (United States)

1976 Gary Kildall creates the CP/M (Control Program/Monitor or Control Program for Microprocessors) Operating System of Digital Research; this operating system for 8-bit microcomputers is the forerunner of DOS 1.0. (United States)

Steven Jobs and Stephen Wozniak found Apple Computer, Inc. and create the Apple I. (United States)

Seymour Cray devises the Cray-1 supercomputer. (United States)

Commodore Business Machines acquires MOS Technologies. (Canada)

1977 The Commodore PET (Personal Electronic Transactor) personal computer, developed by Jack Tramiel and Chuck Peddle for Commodore Business Machines, features the 6502 8-bit Microprocessor. (Canada)

The Apple II personal computer from Apple Computer, Inc., is released featuring a 6502 microprocessor. (United States)

The TRS-80 personal computer from Tandy Radio Shack, equipped with the Zilog Z80 8-bit microprocessor from Zilog, is unveiled. (United States)

1978 Intel announces the 8086 16-bit microprocessor. (United States)

Digital Equipment Corporation launches the VAX 11/780, a 4.3 billion byte computer with virtual memory. (United States)

1979 Intel presents the 8088 16-bit microprocessor. (United States)

Motorola Inc. crafts the MC 68000, Motorola 16-bit processor. (United States)

1980 Tim Patterson sells the rights to QDOS, an upgrade operating system of CP/M for 8088 and 8086 Intel microprocessors, 16-bit microprocessor, to Microsoft. (United States)

1981 The IBM Corporation announces the IBM Personal Computer featuring an 8088 microprocessor. (United States)

The Microsoft Operating System (MS-DOS) is put into use. (United States)

The Osborne I, developed by Adam Osborne and Lee Felsenstein with Osborne Computer Corporation, invent the first portable computer. (United States)

1982 Scott McNealy, Bill Joy, Andy Bechtolsheim, and Vinod Khosla found Sun Microsystems, Inc. (United States)

1984 The Macintosh PC from Apple Computer Inc., running with a Motorola 68000 microprocessor, revolutionizes the personal computer industry. (United States)

Richard Stallman begins the GNU Project, advocating the free use and distribution of software. (United States)

1985 The Free Software Foundation is formed to seek freedom of use and distribution of software. (United States)

Microsoft releases Windows 1.01. (United States)

1986 Sperry Rand and the Burroughs Corporation merge to form Unisys Corporation. (United States)

1989 SPARCstation I from Sun Microsystems is produced. (United States)

1991 Tim Berners-Lee begins the World Wide Web at CERN. (Switzerland)

Linus Torvalds builds the Linux Operating System. (Finland)

Paul Kunz develops the first web server outside of Europe, at the Stanford Linear Accelerator Center (SLAC). (United States)

1993	Marc Andreesen and Eric Bina create Mosaic, a web browser, at the National Center for Supercomputing Applications (NCSA), University of Illinois-Urbana Champaign. (United States)
1994	Marc Andreesen and James H. Clark form Mosaic Communications Corporation, later Netscape Communications Corporation. (United States)
	Netscape Navigator is launched by Netscape Communications Corporation. (United States)
1995	Java technology is announced by Sun Microsystems. (United States)
1996	World chess champion Garry Kasparov of Russia defeats Deep Blue, an IBM computer, in a man vs. computer chess matchup, four to two. (United States)
1997	IBM's Deep Blue defeats world chess champion Garry Kasparov in a rematch, 3.5 to 2.5. (United States)
	An injunction is filed against Microsoft to prohibit the company from requiring customers to accept Internet Explorer as their browser as a condition of using the Microsoft operating system Windows 95. (United States)
1998	America OnLine (AOL) acquires Netscape. (United States)
	Compaq Computer Corporation, a major producer of IBM compatible personal computers, buys Digital Equipment Corporation. (United States)
	America OnLine (AOL) and Sun form an alliance to produce Internet technology. (United States)
1999	Shawn Fanning writes code for Napster, a music file-sharing program. (United States)
	The Recording Industry Association of America (RIAA) files a lawsuit against Napster for facilitating copyright infringement. (United States)
2000	Zhores I. Alferov, Herbert Kroemer, and Jack Kilby share the Nobel Prize in Physics for contributions to information technology. Alferov, a Russian, and Kroemer, a German-born American, are acknowledged for their contributions to technology used in satellite communications and cellular telephones. Kilby, an American, is recognized for his work on the integrated circuit. (Sweden)

Timeline: The History of Programming, Markup and Scripting Languages

The history of computer sciences has been filled with many creative inventions and intriguing people. Here are some of the milestones and achievements in the field of computer programming and languages.

CE c800	al-Khowarizmi, Mohammed ibn-Musa develops a treatise on algebra, his name allegedly giving rise to the term algorithm.
1843	Ada Byron King, Countess of Lovelace, programs Charles Babbage's design of the Analytical Engine.
1945	Plankalkul is developed by Konrad Zuse.
1953	Sort-Merge Generator is created by Betty Holberton.
1957	FORTRAN is devised for IBM by John Backus and team of programmers.
	FLOW-MATIC is crafted for Remington-Rand's UNIVAC by Grace Hopper.
1958	LISP is produced by John McCarthy at Massachusetts Institute of Technology.
1960	ALGOL is the result of work done by the ALGOL Committee in the ALGOL 60 Report.
	COBOL is formulated by the CODASYL Committee, initiated by the the U.S. Department of Defense (DoD)
1961	JOSS is originated by the RAND Corporation.
	GPSS (General Purpose Simulation System) is invented by Geoffrey Gordon with IBM.
	RPG (Report Program Generator) is unveiled by IBM.
	APL (A Programming Language) is designed by Kenneth Iverson with IBM.
1963	SNOBOL is developed by David Farber, Ralph Griswold, and Ivan Polonsky at Bell Laboratories.
1964	BASIC is originated by John G. Kemeny and Thomas E. Kurtz at Dartmouth.
	PL/I is announced by IBM.
	Simula I is produced by Kristen Nygaard and Ole-Johan Dahl at the Norwegian Computing Center.
1967	Simula 67 is created by Kristen Nygaard and Ole-Johan Dahl at the Norwegian Computing Center.

	LOGO is devised by Seymour Papert at the MIT Artificial Intelligence Laboratory.
1971	Pascal is constructed by Niklaus Wirth at the Swiss Federal Institute of Technology (ETH) in Zurich.
1973	C developed by Dennis Ritchie at Bell Laboratories.
	Smalltalk is invented by Alan Kay at Xerox's PARC (Palo Alto Research Center).
1980	Ada is developed for the U.S. Department of Defense (DoD).
1985	C++ is created by Bjarne Stroustrup at Bell Laboratories.
1986	SGML (Standard Generalized Markup Language) is developed by the International Organization for Standardization (ISO).
1987	Perl is constructed by Larry Wall.
1991	Visual Basic is launched by the Microsoft Corporation.
	HTML (HyperText Markup Language) is originated by Tim Berners-Lee at CERN (Organization Europeene pour la Recherche Nucleaire).
1993	Mosaic is created by Marc Andreesen and Eric Bina for the National Center for Computing Applications (NCCA) at the University of Illinois-Urbana Champaign.
1995	Java is crafted by James Gosling of Sun Microsystems.
	A written specification of VRML (Virtual Reality Markup Language) is drafted by Mark Pesce, Tony Parisi, and Gavin Bell.
1996	Javascript is developed by Brendan Eich at Netscape Communications co-announced by Netscape and Sun Microsystems.
1997	VRML (Virtual Reality Modeling Language), developed by the Web3D Consortium, becomes an international standard.
1998	XML (Extensible Markup Language) is originated by a working group of the World Wide Web Consortium (W3C).

Contributors

Tom Abel
Penn State University, University Park, PA

Martyn Amos
University of Liverpool, United Kingdom

Richard Archer
Pittsburgh, PA

Pamela Willwerth Aue
Royal Oak, MI

Nancy J. Becker
St. John's University, New York

Mark Bedau
Reed College, Portland, OR

Pierfrancesco Bellini
University of Florence, Italy

Gary H. Bernstein
University of Notre Dame, Notre Dame, IN

Anne Bissonnette
Kent State University Museum, Kent, OH

Kevin W. Bowyer
University of Notre Dame, Notre Dame, IN

Stefan Brass
University of Giessen, Germany

Barbara Britton
Windsor Public Library, Windsor, Ontario, Canada

Kimberly Mann Bruch
San Diego Supercomputer Center, University of California, San Diego

Ivan Bruno
University of Florence, Italy

Dennis R. Buckmaster
Pennsylvania State University, University Park, PA

Dan Burk
University of Minnesota, Minneapolis, MN

Guoray Cai
Pennsylvania State University, University Park, PA

Shirley Campbell
University of Pittsburgh, Pittsburgh, PA

Siddharth Chandra
University of Pittsburgh, Pittsburgh, PA

J. Alex Chediak
University of California, Berkeley, CA

Kara K. Choquette
Xerox Corporation

John Cosgrove
Cosgrove Communications, Pittsburgh, PA

Cheryl L. Cramer
Digimarc Corporation, Tualatin, OR

Anthony Debons
University of Pittsburgh, Pittsburgh, PA

Salvatore Domenick Desiano
NASA Ames Research Center (QSS Group, Inc.)

Ken Doerbecker
Perfection Services, Inc.; WeirNet LLC; and FreeAir Networks, Inc.

Judi Ellis
KPMG, LLP, Pittsburgh, PA

Karen E. Esch
Karen Esch Associates, Pittsburgh, PA

Ming Fan
University of Notre Dame, Notre Dame, IN

Jim Fike
Ohio University, Athens, OH

Ida M. Flynn
University of Pittsburgh, Pittsburgh, PA

Roger R. Flynn
University of Pittsburgh, Pittsburgh, PA

H. Bruce Franklin
Rutgers University, Newark, NJ

Thomas J. Froehlich
Kent State University, Kent, OH

Chuck Gaidica
WDIV-TV, Detroit, MI

G. Christopher Hall
PricewaterhouseCoopers

Gary Hanson
Kent State University, Kent, OH

Karen Hartman
James Monroe Center Library, Mary Washington College, Fredericksburg, VA

Melissa J. Harvey
Carnegie Mellon University, Pittsburgh, PA

Albert D. Helfrick
Embry-Riddle Aeronautical University, Daytona Beach, FL

Stephen Hughes
University of Pittsburgh, Pittsburgh, PA

Bruce Jacob
University of Maryland, College Park, MD

Radhika Jain
Georgia State University, Atlanta, GA

Wesley Jamison
University of Pittsburgh at Greensburg

Sid Karin
San Diego Supercomputer Center, University of California, San Diego

Declan P. Kelly
Philips Research, The Netherlands

Betty Kirke
New York, NY

Mikko Kovalainen
University of Jyväskylä, Finland

Paul R. Kraus
Pittsburgh, PA

Prashant Krishnamurthy
University of Pittsburgh, Pittsburgh, PA

Marina Krol
Mount Sinai School of Medicine, New York, NY

Susan Landau
Sun Microsystems Inc., Mountain View, CA

Nicholas C. Laudato
University of Pittsburgh, Pittsburgh, Pennsylvania

George Lawton
Eutopian Enterprises

Cynthia Tumilty Lazzaro
Pinnacle Training Corp., Stoneham, MA

Joseph J. Lazzaro
Massachusetts Commission for the Blind, Boston, MA

John Leaney
University of Technology, Sydney, Australia

Robert Lembersky
Ann Taylor, Inc., New York, NY

Terri L. Lenox
Westminster College, New Wilmington, PA

Joyce H-S Li
University of Pittsburgh, Pittsburgh, PA

Michael R. Macedonia
USA STRICOM, Orlando, FL

Dirk E. Mahling
University of Pittsburgh, Pittsburgh, PA

Cynthia J. Martincic
St. Vincent College, Latrobe, PA

Michael J. McCarthy
Carnegie Mellon University, Pittsburgh, PA

Ann McIver McHoes
Carlow College, Pittsburgh PA

Genevieve McHoes
University of Maryland, College Park, MD

John McHugh
CERT™ Coordination Center, Software Engineering Institute, Carnegie Mellon University, Pittsburgh, PA

Donald M. McIver
Northrop Grumman Corporation, Baltimore, MD

Maurice McIver
Integrated Databases, Inc., Honolulu, HI

William J. McIver, Jr.
University at Albany, State University of New York

Trevor T. Moores
University of Nevada, Las Vegas

Christopher Morgan
Association for Computing Machinery, New York, NY

Bertha Kugelman Morimoto
University of Pittsburgh, Pittsburgh, PA

Tracy Mullen
NEC Research Inc., Princeton, NJ

Paul Munro
University of Pittsburgh, Pittsburgh, PA

Stephen Murray
University of Technology, Sydney, Australia

Carey Nachenberg
Symantec Corporation

John Nau
Xceed Consulting, Inc., Pittsburgh, PA

Paolo Nesi
University of Florence, Italy

Kai A. Olsen
Molde College and University of Bergen, Norway

Ipek Özkaya
Carnegie Mellon University, Pittsburgh, PA

Bob Patterson
Perfection Services, Inc.

Robert R. Perkoski
University of Pittsburgh, Pittsburgh, PA

Thomas A. Pollack
Duquesne University, Pittsburgh, PA

Guylaine M. Pollock
IEEE Computer Society; Sandia National Laboratories, Albuquerque, NM

Wolfgang Porod
University of Notre Dame, Notre Dame, IN

Anwer H. Puthawala
Park Avenue Associates in Radiology, P.C., Binghamton, NY

Mary McIver Puthawala
Binghamton, NY

Sudha Ram
University of Arizona, Tucson, AZ

Edie M. Rasmussen
University of Pittsburgh, Pittsburgh, PA

Robert D. Regan
Consultant, Pittsburgh, PA

Allen Renear
University of Illinois, Urbana-Champaign

Sarah K. Rich
Pennsylvania State University, University Park, PA

Mike Robinson
Sageforce Ltd., Kingston on Thames, Surrey, United Kingdom

Elke A. Rudensteiner
Worcester Polytechnic Institute, Worcester, MA

Frank R. Rusch
University of Illinois at Urbana-Champaign

William Sherman
National Center for Supercomputing Applications, University of Illinois at Urbana-Champaign

Marc Silverman
University of Pittsburgh, Pittsburgh, PA

Munindar P. Singh
North Carolina State University, Raleigh, NC

Cindy Smith
PricewaterhouseCoopers, Pittsburgh, PA

Barry Smyth
Smart Media Institute, University College, Dublin, Ireland

Amanda Spink
Pennsylvania State University, University Park, PA

Michael B. Spring
University of Pittsburgh, Pittsburgh, PA

Savitha Srinivasan
IBM Almaden Research Center, San Jose, CA

Igor Tarnopolsky
Westchester County Department of Laboratories and Research, Valhalla, NY

George A. Tarnow
Georgetown University, Washington, DC

Lucy A. Tedd
University of Wales, Aberystwyth, Wales, United Kingdom

Umesh Thakkar
National Center for Supercomputing Applications, University of Illinois at Urbana-Champaign

Richard A. Thompson
University of Pittsburgh, Pittsburgh, PA

James E. Tomayko
Carnegie Mellon University, Pittsburgh, PA

Christinger Tomer
University of Pittsburgh, Pittsburgh, PA

Upkar Varshney
Georgia State University, Atlanta, GA

Jonathan Vos Post
Webmaster <http://magicdragon .com>

Tom Wall
Duke University, Durham, NC

Brett A. Warneke
University of California, Berkeley, CA

Patricia S. Wehman
University of Pittsburgh, Pittsburgh, PA

Isaac Weiss
University of Maryland, College Park, MD

Martin B. Weiss
University of Pittsburgh, Pittsburgh, PA

Jeffrey C. Wingard
Leesburg, VA

Victor L. Winter
University of Nebraska at Omaha

Charles R. Woratschek
Robert Morris University, Moon Township, PA

Peter Y. Wu
University of Pittsburgh, Pittsburgh, PA

William J. Yurcik
Illinois State University, Normal, IL

Gregg R. Zegarelli
Zegarelli Law Group, P.C.

Table of Contents

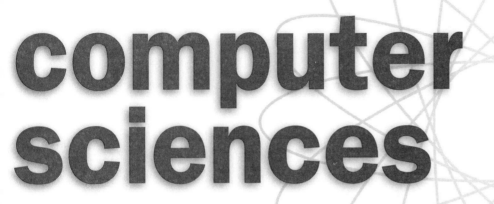

computer
sciences

Accounting Software

Computers were developed to perform routine tasks over and over based on a set of instructions and data provided by the user. Accounting and bookkeeping consists of a series of routine tasks (transactions) performed over and over with new data. Given the automation provided by computers and the routine nature of accounting, it was inevitable that the two would match up. In fact, the earliest applications of computers were for accounting purposes. American inventor Herman Hollerith's original tabulating machine was used to count the U.S. Census population numbers in 1890.

The first computer software designed for accounting purposes dealt with basic computations and accumulation of numbers. The large early computing systems added and subtracted numbers to help companies keep track of their financial information. As capabilities advanced, more complex systems were used for tracking customer transactions and related calculations.

Typical Applications

Accounting consists of some basic calculations and accumulation of numbers. Items such as loan interest computations, loan payment amounts, and tax due can be calculated with accounting software. In addition, there are several categories of general accounting tasks that any accounting software should support. These include general ledger, accounts payable, accounts receivable, payroll, inventory, job cost estimating, fixed assets, sales orders, and budgeting.

General Ledger.   The general ledger is the final accumulation of financial data for an organization. It allows the organization to view the overall status of all accounting data.

Accounts Payable.   The accounts payable area handles payments to be made to vendors or others who provide goods or services to an organization. Data such as vendor information, payment amount, and related items are tracked by this software. Summaries of payments are posted to the general ledger on a periodic basis.

Accounts Receivable.   The accounts receivable area processes money due to an organization from customers or other parties. Data related to the reason for money due and the due date are contained in accounts receivable

Accounting software is designed to help people and businesses make sense of their monthly bills and payments.

demographic statistical data pertaining to a population

records. The accounts receivable software posts summaries of the data to the general ledger on a periodic basis.

Payroll. Payroll deals with the calculation and payment of money to employees for work performed for the company. In addition, payroll records may also house **demographic** information related to employees (human resources data). Payroll accounting involves a series of calculations for taxes, benefits, and other payroll items. The accumulation of payroll data is posted to the general ledger on a periodic basis.

Inventory. Inventory software tracks the goods and supplies an organization keeps on hand to either supply customer needs or for internal use. The basic calculations handle additions and subtractions from the quantity in stock at any given time.

Job Cost Estimating. Job costing helps project managers and others deal with the process of analyzing and estimating data to provide a cost estimate for a given project. Job costing software analyzes costs such as labor, equipment, supplies, and materials.

Fixed Assets. Fixed assets are the physical components of an organization—property, plant, and equipment. The purchase costs associated with each item, along with any improvements made to the item, would be tracked by accounting software. Also, depreciation of the item over the years would be calculated. The accumulation of fixed asset and depreciation data is posted to the general ledger on a periodic basis.

Sales Orders. Sales orders can be tracked and credited to individual salespersons in an organization. Each order is entered to show details such as the quantity ordered, price, and other financial data. The accumulation of sales data is posted to the general ledger on a periodic basis.

Budgeting. Budgeting software allows the organization and its managers to accumulate data on projected revenues and expenditures for a future time period. Usually, this period is a one-year look into the future. Budgeting software allows actual revenue and expenditure data to be posted so that fluctuations between budget and actual values can be reported.

Accounting software is available for use on various operating systems and for a wide variety of computer types, from stand-alone computers used for small business or home accounting needs to **mainframe computers** that process accounting data for multinational corporations. Selecting the appropriate software for an organization is a matter of carefully matching the needs of the organization with an accounting software package that provides the functions and features needed by the organization at a price that is in proportion to the benefit to be gained. SEE ALSO IBM CORPORATION; OFFICE AUTOMATION SYSTEMS; TABULATING MACHINES.

Richard Archer

mainframe computers large computers used by businesses and government agencies to process massive amounts of data; generally faster and more powerful than desktop computers but usually requiring specialized software

Bibliography

Atrill, Peter, and Eddie McLaney. *Accounting and Finance for Non-Specialists.* New York: Prentice Hall, 1996.

Boutell, Wayne S. *Accounting for Anyone.* Englewood Cliffs, NJ: Prentice-Hall, 1982.

Internet Resources

Collins, J. Carter. "Accounting Software News." <http://www.accountingsoftwarenews.com/>

"Enterprise and Accounting Software Products." 2020Software. <http://www.2020software.com/>

"CPAOnline." Inphinet Interactive Communications, Inc. <http://www.cpaonline.com/>

Agriculture

Agriculture is a vast industry that includes plant and animal production, comprehensive support and infrastructure systems, and food and fiber processing. Key application areas of computers in agriculture include record keeping, decision-making, control, and research. The diversity of agricultural enterprises and associated products requires a variety of computer hardware and software solutions, from specialized software packages to computerized components for traditional machinery and equipment. A particular challenge to designers and manufacturers of computerized agricultural machinery is to make computers, analog/digital (A/D and D/A) converters, terminals, and connections unaffected by environmental conditions. Agricultural equipment experiences extremes of dust, rain and high humidity, vibration, and temperatures.

Recordkeeping

Recordkeeping is vital in any business. Agricultural enterprises use computers for common financial and business tasks such as inventory, payroll, accounting, and taxes. Because there are many differences between agricultural businesses and other businesses (with regard to tax structure, labor management, insurance, and inventory, for example), software packages have been tailored specifically for agriculture. Spreadsheet and database templates are common, but specific application programs also exist.

Livestock and crop production farms have unique needs for records. For example, crop production fields have numerous descriptors and variables that should be recorded (e.g., soil type, drainage, slope, pH, nutrient status); databases have been developed to deal with this information. Precision agriculture (sometimes called site-specific farming) requires such data to be recorded not only for fields, but for locations within fields. Because they provide a combination of database and drawing functions, Geographic Information Systems (GIS) are needed to handle the large amount of data. Global Positioning Systems (GPSs) work with computerized machinery in the field to correlate crop and soil conditions with exact locations on the Earth's surface. Because soil and crop conditions can vary tremendously within fields, this capability can improve the environmental friendliness of farming and improve profitability.

Similarly, livestock farms track individual animals, storing and evaluating information such as age, growth rate, milk production, health records, offspring productivity, and reproductive cycle status. Unlike with large corporations that employ computer scientists, farmers generally do not have or cannot hire the expertise to customize relevant software; therefore, there is a market for software products suitable for those who are mostly novice computer users.

Decision-Making

Computers can be used to assist agricultural decision-making through such tools and techniques as optimization, simulation, **fuzzy logic**, expert systems, and computer aided drafting (CAD). A common problem to be solved on crop farms is the selection of the optimal field machinery set. Equipment that is too large will result in poor use of capital and labor; equipment that is too small may result in poor timing of operations and consequential loss of crop value. The equipment must function as an interdependent set; operations must flow in a sequential and timely manner. Simulations can model farm and machine events over time to predict what would happen if particular machinery sets were chosen. Important factors include weather, soil type, and desired field operations. Optimization techniques such as linear or non-linear programming that minimize cost subject to reasonable constraints (e.g., labor availability, frost dates) can help improve profitability.

Increasing regulations require that nutrient management plans be developed, implemented, and monitored. While much of this is recordkeeping in nature, decision tools are used to project future impact and profits, given past performance and conditions. Integrated pest management (IPM) also takes a **holistic** view of production and optimizes the timing and rates of chemical application (if necessary) or the use of alternative measures. IPM

fuzzy logic models human reasoning by permitting elements to have partial membership to a set; derived from fuzzy set theory

holistic looking at the entire system, rather than just its parts

requires projection of consequences with various strategies so that the optimum strategy can be implemented. IPM models include simulation of pest population dynamics and rule-based expert systems techniques.

A farmer uses his laptop to access WeedCast computer software. The program provides information on weed management strategies that will help the farmer control the spread of pigweed in his soybean crops.

In poultry and livestock production, a major cost of production is feed, often exceeding 35 percent of gross receipts. Minimizing feed cost is a classic linear or non-linear optimization problem. Optimization methods can help determine the least costly ingredient package in a diet subject to constraints including energy, protein, intake limitations, minerals, and fiber requirements.

Landscape design and construction, which is also an agriculture-related enterprise, can benefit from computer aided drafting and drawing packages that help designers generate and illustrate concepts to clients. By providing projection of individual plant growth, good packages can show how plants on a site will look years after installation.

Control

Control of machinery by computers can provide consistency and reliability unmatched with human operation. Controller area networks (CANs) are common on tractors and self-propelled equipment; these CANs reduce wiring complexity and allow one or more on-board chips to control machine functions such as engine controls, transmission, and hydraulic power output. CANs use serial communications like other networks, but they have

algorithms rules or procedures used to solve mathematical problems—most often described as sequences of steps

a specific data structure to facilitate interchange among vendors of CAN compatible devices and diagnosis of problems.

Computers are used increasingly to control seeding or chemical application rate automatically in fields. This requires GIS and GPS data input, computer **algorithms** to generate control signals (rule or formula based), and relays and amplifier cards to power mechanisms that perform the desired functions.

Support industries for inputs to production agriculture include manufacturing and delivery of machinery, feed, and fertilizer. After the farm production of raw products, there is food and fiber manufacturing. Programmable logic controllers (PLCs) are used in all of these agricultural industries, as well as on farms. PLCs can perform intelligent on/off and proportional control on machines that meter, grind, weigh, blend, cut, and weld.

Research

Research in agriculture requires some uses of computers not used in other aspects of agricultural work. Very sophisticated simulation models address issues such as crop growth, animal nutrition, water flow in soil, thermal and physical behavior of agricultural products, machinery performance, and integrated farm systems.

As with most areas of research, good agricultural research requires computers for statistical analysis of data, generation of mathematical models, and control of research devices. Instrumentation to measure temperature, flow, pressure, electrical conductivity, and strain also requires computers or data loggers. SEE ALSO Biology; Geographic Information Systems; Molecular Biology; Weather Forecasting.

Dennis R. Buckmaster

Bibliography

National Research Council. *Precision Agriculture in the 21st Century: Geospatial and Information Technologies in Crop Management.* Washington, DC: National Academy Press, 1998. Also available at <http://www.nap.edu/catalog/5491.html>.

Siemens, J.C. "A Farm Machinery Selection and Management Program." *Journal of Production Agriculture* 3, no. 2 (1990): 212-219.

Zazueta, Fedro S., and Jiannong Xin, eds. *Computers in Agriculture.* St. Joseph, MI: American Society of Agricultural Engineers, 1998. Also available at <http://wcca.ifas.ufl.edu/>.

Internet Resources

Agricultural Software Page. Agri-Publications, Inc. <http://www.agdownload.com>

FEEDING MADE EASY

Computer-based feeding systems can feed individual animals precisely what they need. Tags identify individual animals, then controllers dispense a customized feeding plan controlling feed type, quantity, and time of day. In addition to controlling the action of feeding, the program can also keep track of how much feed is used.

Aircraft Flight Control

Aircraft in flight require adherence to a specific course for long periods of time, which can be tiring for the pilot. Likewise, steering ships on the water for hours is tedious and leads to crew fatigue. For more than a century, ships have had auto-pilots or devices that maintain a heading without human operators. Controlling an aircraft is similar but more complex because an aircraft operates in three dimensions and travels at considerably higher speeds. In the air, small deviations can become large errors more quickly.

The automatic control of aircraft was not considered until aircraft were capable of practical long distance flight. In the 1920s when radio navigation became available for aircraft, air travel became practical, eventually leading to the development of auto-pilot systems for aircraft. The first aircraft auto-pilots were based on **gyros** and were similar to those found in a ship. Such simple auto-pilots were capable of maintaining a set heading, but did not ensure the aircraft would follow a specific course. Heading is just what the word implies, the direction the aircraft is heading, which is not always the same as the path the aircraft actually flies. That path is called its "track." Its "course" is the desired path for the aircraft to fly. Because the medium in which aircraft fly, air, is not still, winds will blow the aircraft around in a somewhat unpredictable manner and the track and course may not agree. Flight crews needed to determine how much to change the heading in order keep the aircraft on course. The crew also had to adjust the power, **ailerons**, and elevators to prevent the aircraft from gaining or losing altitude as well as keep it flying level.

When radio navigation and its accompanying electronics came along, auto-pilots became more sophisticated, allowing the auto-pilot to follow a radio beam. Auto-pilots could keep the aircraft at a constant altitude and keep the wings level as well.

Auto-Pilot Operation

An aircraft is said to have six degrees of freedom—up-down, left-right, forward-aft—and can rotate around three axes—roll, pitch, and yaw. Roll is rotation around the forward-to-aft line of the aircraft. Pitch is around the axis of the wing, and yaw is around the vertical. Auto-pilots used for en route travel can completely control an aircraft by changing only three of the six degrees of freedom: roll, pitch, and yaw. The most capable auto-pilots can actually land an aircraft, control engine power, and manipulate all six degrees of freedom.

An auto-pilot requires input information to control the motion of an aircraft. Gyros are used to sense motion while an altimeter senses altitude. Radio receivers provide information relative to the desired course of an aircraft. When the more sophisticated long distance navigation information is available, an aircraft may be controlled on a course to a specific point called a waypoint. Essentially, an aircraft could be programmed with a destination and automatically flown to that destination. When an auto-pilot reaches this level of sophistication it is called a "flight management system" (FMS). At the heart of an FMS is a "flight management computer" (FMC).

Microprocessors in Auto-Pilots

Although many auto-pilots existed before the introduction of the microprocessor, they were difficult to implement and required each aircraft type to have its own model auto-pilot. This is because each aircraft has its own characteristics and the auto-pilot reacts differently for each aircraft type. A programmable auto-pilot was the ideal solution and a perfect application of the microprocessor.

With the introduction of the microprocessor, an auto-pilot or FMS could be found even in small, private aircraft. However, the microprocessor

gyros a contraction of gyroscopes; a mechanical device that uses one or more spinning discs which resist changes to their position in space

ailerons control surfaces on the trailing edges of the wings of an aircraft—used to manage roll control

Pilots and navigators undergo extensive training to learn how to maneuver aircraft. A sea of instruments, buttons, and switches line the airplane's cockpit, such as that found in this Bombardier Aerospace CRJ700.

also brought new challenges. The microprocessor must perform a series of operations, some of which jump from one address location to another and then return while keeping track of the entire process in what is called a stack. On some occasions, because of a software or hardware problem, the computer loses track and executes a bogus program. This situation can have catastrophic results. Just as personal computers sometimes "hang up," requiring a reboot, aircraft computers can similarly hang up, potentially leading to a disaster.

Therefore, every piece of equipment that is installed in an aircraft registered in the United States must be certified by the Federal Aviation Ad-

ministration (FAA) and similar agencies in other countries. All automatic flight control equipment must demonstrate that it is "fail-safe." This means that if the computer has a failure, the auto-pilot does not place the aircraft in a dangerous situation. It was difficult for the early microprocessor-controlled auto-pilots to demonstrate this characteristic.

Aircraft certification, until the introduction of the microprocessor, meant hardware. However, when microprocessor-based equipment appeared in aircraft, it became clear that software, like hardware, could also fail with serious consequences. Something needed to be done to insure the integrity of the software. The FAA developed certification procedures for software, one of the first organizations to recognize this need.

Until then, while the microprocessor was revolutionizing the world, **analog** auto-pilots were the mainstay in aircraft. Eventually, the new procedures adopted by the FAA to certify software were implemented and digital auto-pilots using microprocessors became common. The first microprocessor auto-pilots introduced in the late 1970s were programmed using **assembly language**. This was necessary because of the small size of read-only memories of the time. It was not uncommon to find memories as small as 4K bits (not bytes). It was not long before 64K-bit **ROMs** were available, but by modern standards that is very small. Also, many of the functions performed by the microprocessor involved switching the state of one bit of a **port**. Assembly language provided the closest connection to the actual inner workings of the hardware.

analog a quantity (often an electrical signal) that is continuous in time and amplitude

assembly language the natural language of a central processing unit (CPU); often classed as a low-level language

ROM read only memory

port logical input/ output points on computers that exist in a network

Flight Management Systems

In the late 1970s, the long range navigation system LORAN-C became fully operational. This navigation system provided aircraft position in latitude and longitude. The desired course was set by entering waypoint information, and deviation from the selected course was provided to the auto-pilot. This development led to the integration of the auto-pilot and the long distance navigation computer into one unit, and later, the integration of other navigation systems, such as short distance navigation and landing systems, into the auto-pilot as well. This is the concept behind a flight management system or FMS.

The FMS controls the aircraft and the navigation equipment. It contains databases for airways, airports, radio frequencies, and radio navigation aids. With the FMS, a desired course is entered and the FMS will automatically select the navigation equipment and radio frequencies. With so much stored data, changes occur regularly. Therefore, it is necessary to update the databases periodically to reflect the changes using a CD (compact disc), floppy disk, or a notebook computer. SEE ALSO AIRLINE RESERVATIONS; NAVIGATION; SATELLITE TECHNOLOGY; TELECOMMUNICATIONS.

Albert D. Helfrick

Bibliography

Billings, C. E. *Aviation Automation: The Search for a Human-Centered Approach.* Mahwah, NJ: Lawrence Erlbaum Associates Publishers, 1996.

Garrison, Paul. *Autopilots, Flight Directors, and Flight-Control Systems.* Blue Ridge Summit, PA: TAB Books, 1985.

Tischler, Mark B., ed. *Advances in Aircraft Flight Control.* London: Taylor and Francis, 1996.

Aircraft Traffic Management

In the early days of aviation, airplanes were mostly used as joy rides, in air shows, and for just general "barnstorming." Even into the 1920s, debate occurred regarding whether the airplane had a useful purpose, and one of the main concerns was the inability of planes to fly in bad weather. With the development of radio navigation aids, which would eventually lead to the flight instruments of today, radio landing aids were installed at larger airports. These airports became the first hubs for successful air travel and were connected to each other via airways, which are similar to highways that connect large cities. However, just as highways funnel traffic into a city, causing traffic congestion and possible collisions, airways also experience similar problems near airports, making methods of controlling air traffic necessary.

In the beginning, air traffic control (ATC) was mostly implemented via such tools as colored lights and flags. However, while lights and flags work well on the ground and therefore seem obvious choices for use at airports, they are only good for operations very close to airports and then only when the aircraft has a clear view of the airport. A system was needed to control the entire airway.

Early air traffic control systems were based on ensuring safe separation—that is, an aircraft departing an airport reported its position by radio. If the airplane was flying under poor visibility conditions, it would be difficult to determine its position with the crude radio navigation equipment of the time; the aircraft's altitude, which could be measured with reasonable accuracy even in poor visibility, was an important part of position reports. Other departing aircraft would then be held at the airport until the previous plane was sufficiently far from the airport to ensure that no collisions would occur. The key person in such ATC was the "air traffic controller," who was in constant radio contact with the aircraft's crew. The problem with this type of ATC is that the required separation is so great, often more than 37 kilometers (20 nautical miles), that the capacity of the airport is diminished.

Primary and Secondary Radar

radar the acronym for RAdio Direction And Ranging; a technique developed in the 1930s that uses frequency shifts in reflected radio waves to measure distance and speed of a target

With the advent of **radar**, aircraft could be located from the ground even in clouds, and accurate position reports were not required from the aircraft. The required amount of separation was reduced significantly and the airport was used at a higher capacity. However, radar alone was not enough to ensure flight safety. The controller saw only anonymous green "blips" on the radar screen, denoting the aircraft. Secondly, the radar screen, which is called a plan position indicator, or PPI, is a two-dimensional display and aircraft are flying in a three-dimensional world. In order to control planes more accurately, a way was needed to identify the blips and to show their altitude. The system used is called a "secondary radar" system, a communications system that operates in concert with the radar.

With these two tools, primary and secondary radar, air traffic controllers could monitor more aircraft in less airspace and increase the amount of aircraft on the airways. The air traffic controllers noted the pertinent information about an aircraft such as its flight number, aircraft ID number, assigned altitude, and destination on a small card. This card was placed in a holder called a "shrimp boat" because of its shape; it held the card so that the data were easily visible to the controller. These data were a part of the flight plan, which was filed with ATC before the flight. As with the first ATC systems, constant communication with the aircraft was vital for safe separation.

Even with long distance radar, the controller can only handle a limited area of airspace, called a sector. When an aircraft goes from one controller's sector into another, the shrimp boat is pushed along a track to the next sector's controller. This process is called "handing off."

Computers in ATC

ATC involves a large number of radar sites, information from flight plans, and controller-entered information. One of the first uses of large computers was gathering and displaying these data. Radar sites are connected to an en route air traffic control center, which is responsible for tens of thousands of square kilometers (or miles) of air traffic. Smaller centers serve airports and are called "terminal radar control centers" or TRACONs.

Air traffic controllers monitor radar screens to help aircraft reach their intended destinations safely. A specialist views the ASDE3 digitized ground radar system at Chicago's O'Hare Airport.

high-speed data links digital communications systems that permit digital data to be reliably transferred at high speed

cathode ray tube (CRT) a glass enclosure that projects images by directing a beam of electrons onto the back of a screen

algorithm a rule or procedure used to solve a mathematical problem—most often described as a sequence of steps

Radar data require reliable **high-speed data links**. Data from several radar sites are combined and distributed to the sector displays. Even though air traffic control is accomplished with many controllers using data obtained from many radar sites, the entire system needs to be "seamless"; that is, there can be no gaps or areas not covered by ATC.

Historically the controller's PPI display would update in synchronism with the radar in real time. The image was not stored in a computer only displayed on the screen. The PPI **cathode ray tube (CRT)** had a very long "persistence," meaning the image would fade away very slowly, allowing the controller to view it for a few seconds. Before the image faded completely, the radar would make another sweep and refresh the image. Because the image grew dim as it faded, it was necessary to make the radar room dark.

Modern air traffic control systems store the images digitally. The display is much brighter, can contain color, can be zoomed in or out, and can be scanned with a trackball or mouse. This improves the controllers' working conditions.

In the early part of the twenty-first century, air traffic control began a massive change to a totally different philosophy called "free flight." The existing air traffic control system funnels aircraft onto airways and then controls them from the ground. If aircraft were to choose their flight plan without using airways, the preferred route would be a direct route from departure to destination; separation would be automatic. Of course there is a chance that routes would cross and cause a collision. In a free flight system, aircraft choose a direct flight path and enter that flight path into a computer. A software **algorithm** called a "conflict probe" compares the flight plan to those of other aircraft, looking for potential collisions. If a potential collision does exist, the flight plan will be rejected and the aircraft will be requested to make a change.

The computer also receives data from the air traffic radars and predicts future paths of aircraft already airborne. If the path of any aircraft projects a collision, the air traffic manager contacts the aircraft in question and requests a change of course. With this system, air traffic control becomes air traffic management or ATM.

The key to this system is a massive networked computer system with data from flight plans, en route radar data, and aircraft. Just as important as the computer is a network of data links, including air-ground-air links. A much smaller staff of air traffic managers would be able to ensure a higher level of safety for future air traffic. SEE ALSO Aircraft Flight Control; Global Positioning Systems.

Albert D. Helfrick

Bibliography

Illman, Paul E. *The Pilot's Air Traffic Control Handbook.* New York: McGraw-Hill, 1999.

Jane's Air Traffic Control. Alexandria, VA: Jane's Information Group, 1994.

Nolan, Michael S. *Fundamentals of Air Traffic Control.* Pacific Grove, CA: Brooks/Cole, Wadsworth, 1999.

Airline Reservations

Airline reservation systems originated in the mid-1950s as relatively unsophisticated internal systems to help with tasks such as seat assignments, maintenance scheduling, and aircraft loading. Modern airline reservation systems are multi-faceted, full-service systems that assist with a variety of airline management tasks and service customer needs from the time of initial reservation through completion of the flight

First Computerized Systems

American Airlines, an early pioneer in the use of commercial computer technology, developed a semi-automated customer reservation system called Reservisor by 1960. It required considerable manual intervention and had a reservation error rate of eight percent, which was the lowest in the industry at the time. Recognizing that semi-automatic systems would not be capable

Airline ticket agents access computerized reservation systems to make flight arrangements, view current reservations, and check passenger lists, among other things. Secure and stable systems are vital to the airline industry.

of handling the rapidly increasing demand for air travel, American Airlines had already begun working with IBM, in the late 1950s, to develop the first automated, online, real-time computerized reservation system (CRS). The joint project would use interactive, real-time computing technology developed for a U.S. government air defense project referred to as Semi-Automatic Ground Environment (SAGE).

In 1964 the Semi-Automated Business Research Environment (Sabre) System was introduced. Sabre, a coast-to-coast telecommunications network, was the largest, private, online, real-time data processing system in the United States. Only the U.S. government had a larger working system. Most of the computing systems that existed in the 1960s were **batch processing** systems, but Sabre was an early example of a **transaction processing** system. It modified the content of the large databases containing flight and passenger information as a direct result of information entered directly from data terminals. For the first time, an airline was able to track passenger names on all connections of their flights.

batch processing an approach to computer utilization that queues non-interactive programs and runs them one after another

transaction processing operations between client and server computers that are made up of many small exchanges that must all be completed for the transaction to proceed

In the early years, American Airlines invested more than $350 million in this project, with $40 million spent for initial development. By comparison, a new jet cost $4.5 million during this time period. The immediate impact of the Sabre System implementation was a reduction in the reservation error rate to less than one percent, and a 30 percent savings on investment in personnel.

After investing $250 million in system development, United Airlines entered the CRS market in 1976 with the Apollo Reservation System. Other well-known traditional reservation systems originally developed by individual airlines include Worldspan LP, Galileo International Inc., which purchased Apollo in May 1997, and European competitor Amadeus Global Travel Distribution SA.

In 1976 Sabre and Apollo began placing their computerized reservation systems in travel agencies. Through office automation offered by the systems, travel agents could print both tickets and boarding passes for their customers. Travel agents were transformed into an extension of the airline industry, which significantly streamlined the ticketing process.

Expanding Reservations Services

deregulation the lowering of restrictions, rules, or regulations pertaining to an activity or operation (often commercial)

Following **deregulation** of the airline industry in 1978, the major computerized reservation systems such as Sabre and Apollo began listing airline reservations for all competing major carriers as well as for their host airlines. This networked a large number of travel agents with the major airlines and yielded a very profitable per ticket booking fee for the host airline.

Accusations of favoritism toward the host airline, based on the order in which available flights were listed on terminal screens, surfaced early in the 1980s. Since studies reveal that 90 percent of flights are booked from the first reservation screen, a favorable position can dramatically affect ticket sales. The U.S. Department of Transportation investigated this allegation and issued a ruling to prohibit favoritism toward the host airline by requiring that flight information be presented in a neutral order. Because of the prohibitive cost of developing their own computerized reservation systems, the airlines ultimately agreed to pay the per ticket booking fee to the major computerized reservations providers, and a code-sharing scheme was developed to help alleviate the screen order bias. Sabre, one of the most widely recognized information systems ever developed, was spun off as a private company by AMR Corporation in 2000.

Full-Service Travel Management

Computerized reservation systems have grown in sophistication and are able to offer customer services such as electronic tickets, wireless database access, hotel room reservations, rental car reservations, frequent flyer program mileage, and provision for special meal requests. The systems also provide airline management assistance by addressing financial, administrative, and staffing issues. These include crew management, flight operations, planning and scheduling airplane maintenance, loading aircraft to maintain balance, baggage tracking, decision support for control of overbooking, discount seat allocations, and yield management programs that dynamically adjust the number of special fare seats based on the number of reservations.

Enhancements are made to computerized reservation systems with the understanding that interruptions in service are not acceptable. To be successful, a reservation system must be reliable with a very low failure rate. Hardware and software redundancy for immediate backup in the event of a failure is an absolute necessity.

Impact of the Internet

In the mid-1990s an increasing number of consumers began purchasing airline tickets and other travel needs online. To meet rising customer interest in booking online air travel reservations, computerized reservation systems have evolved into convenient, user-friendly systems that are available via the Internet twenty-four hours per day. The long-established computerized reservation systems are experiencing a gradual technology migration away from traditional **mainframe**-based systems and large databases in favor of client server systems with effective web-based interfaces. Search results that previously required an individual to interpret complex codes are now presented in straightforward, easy to understand notations.

In 1996 Sabre launched Travelocity.com, the first of the major comprehensive Internet travel sites. Travelocity.com and other systems, such as Expedia.com, allow consumers to gather information about flights using search criteria such as airline, lowest price, shortest flight, and departure and arrival times. Many airlines offer their own online ticket purchasing services. Also joining in the quest for online reservations is an airline collaborative called Orbitz.com, sponsored by American, United, Delta, Northwest, and Continental Airlines. Many online systems also allow for selection of hotels, rental cars, and other travel necessities.

The wealth of customer data collected by these systems is used to target marketing and incentive programs that appeal to specific consumer interests. Internet-based systems offer many of the capabilities of the traditional computerized reservation systems, but in a customer-friendly format that is easy to use and understand. SEE ALSO AIRCRAFT FLIGHT CONTROL; INTERNET; OFFICE AUTOMATION SYSTEMS.

Thomas A. Pollack

IMPACT OF 9/11

The terrorist attacks on the United States on September 11, 2001, have affected all aspects of the airline industry, including airline reservation systems. The U.S. Department of Transportation is considering security measures that involve red-flagging a suspected terrorist's name in an airline reservation system. Such queries and retrievals from long-established mainframe-based systems would represent a very costly system overhaul. In addition to resolving technical and cost issues, various local, state, federal, and international government agencies must resolve privacy and data ownership issues associated with information sharing.

mainframe large computer used by businesses and government agencies to process massive amounts of data; generally faster and more powerful than desktop computers but usually requiring specialized software

Bibliography

Bly, Laura. "Virtual Voyager." *USA Today*, January 26, 2001, p. D9.

Carr, Houston H., and Charles A. Snyder. *The Management of Telecommunications: Business Solutions to Business Problems.* Boston: McGraw-Hill Companies, 1997.

Koller, Mike, and Jeffrey Schwartz. "American's Life After Sabre." *Internet Week*, January 15, 2001, pp. 1, 49-50.

O'Toole, Kevin. "Surfing for Value." *Airline Business*, July 1999, p. 68.

Internet Resources

Expedia.com Web Site. <http://www.expedia.com>

Orbitz.com Web Site. <http://www.orbitz.com>

Sabre, Inc. Web Site. <http://www.sabre.com>

Travelocity.com Web Site. <http://www.travelocity.com>

Architecture

Architecture, which is generally defined as the art and science of designing and constructing edifices of any kind for human use, is one of the main design activities humankind has developed to modify its environment. Architecture is often cited among the oldest existing professions on Earth. Indeed, the way architects have approached their design problems, realized their designs through construction, and practiced their profession had not changed significantly over many centuries until the emergence of computers.

Computers typically allow architects to create, store, and retrieve data describing design; to generate design solutions automatically; to test prospective solutions for their applicability; and to collaborate and communicate with clients, constructors, engineers, and other designers during design and construction processes. The early uses of computers in architecture and design did not come directly from the discipline itself, however.

The introduction of computer graphics commenced in the late 1940s through the U.S. Navy's Whirlpool project, a general-purpose flight simulator. However, incorporating computer graphics and usage with design activities took speed only after 1963 when American engineer Ivan E. Sutherland developed the Sketchpad system for his Ph.D. thesis at Massachusetts Institute of Technology (MIT). Sketchpad allowed a mechanical engineer to generate designs by sitting at an interactive graphics terminal. The tool manipulated drawings displayed on the screen by use of a keyboard and a light pen—a selecting tool with a light sensing device, such as a photocell, which generates an electrical pulse to identify the portion of the display being pointed to. Sketchpad cleaned up rough drawings by straightening and connecting lines and constructing geometric patterns; therefore, it was conceived as the first computational drawing assistant.

Although Sketchpad's major application domain was mechanical design, it opened the way to the development of computer-aided design (CAD) tools for architecture and other design disciplines. Most of the early CAD systems were applications for engineering design. Architecture lagged considerably behind, primarily due to economic reasons. As computers developed and the costs became more affordable for architectural firms and university-based research groups, utilization of the technology became an increasingly widespread reality for architects.

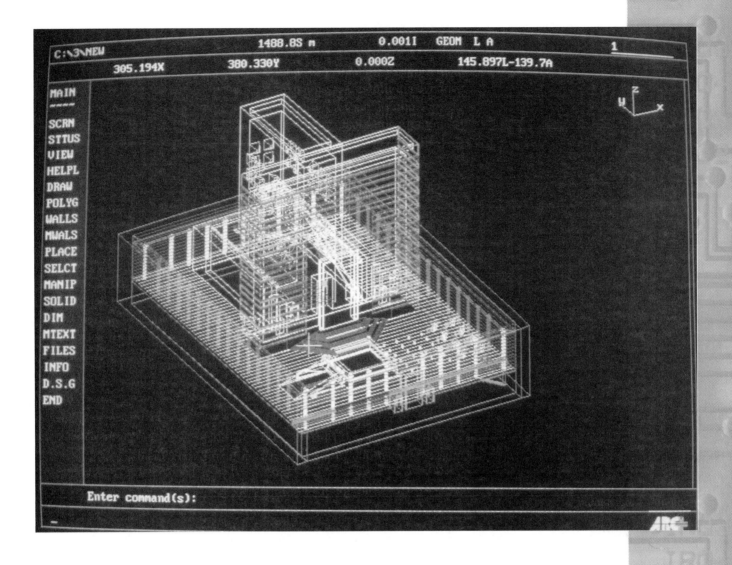

Software for Architects

The first milestone applications specifically developed for architectural usage were designed to help with planning and research of a project, using basic **algorithms** to draw shapes, to calculate engineering formulas involved in building design both correctly and automatically, and to help manage conflicting constraints. These computer tools mostly focused on the following areas of architectural design:

- Structural and mechanical calculations, such as those needed to determine what capacity of heating and ventilating equipment should be used;

- Cost estimation to determine the cost impact of design, materials, and construction decisions before the building is constructed;

- Documentation of building specifications (specs) that outline specifically which materials should be used, and how, and in what order for each building component;

- Automatic layout generation to figure out how spaces, equipment, or furniture should be allocated in a given area.

Architects use computers to display their designs in 3-D. This plan of the Temple Institute in Jerusalem, Israel, was designed in accordance with the ancient laws of the Talmud.

algorithms rules or procedures used to solve mathematical problems—most often described as sequences of steps

The widespread availability of personal computers starting in the early 1980s marks the beginning of the boom in commercial CAD software for architects. The major impact of these developments has been in the daily routines of how architects work in the office. Computerized drawing, three-dimensional modeling, and graphics editing applications have replaced paper, pen, and rulers, the traditional tool set of an architect. Architectural software offers speed, accuracy, ease of revision-making, and the ability to create rapid **prototypes**. Moreover, some allow multiple users to work simultaneously on the same file, facilitating teamwork.

Computer-aided architectural design is a technology intensive field that is strongly dependent on processor capabilities, display technologies, and software and algorithm capabilities of the tools developed. Hardware technology has been capable of answering these demands for architects in their office environment with the introduction of devices such as high resolution and color printers, scanners, plotters, and advanced processors.

On the construction site, tools increasing accuracy also help advance the quality of building design. For example, hand-held computers make it possible for users to access a central building database, whether they are architects on the building site or in the office. Increased and accurate communication via networked computers means that efficient revision management strategies can be employed to deal with worksite issues. Similarly, laser-scanning technology is used to collect data from existing buildings, which used to be done manually. Very high-resolution three-dimensional models are created using these data; the resulting drawings are used for renovation projects.

Specialized Tools

Architectural design is a special kind of problem-solving process with unique research and analysis needs. Computer-based research can help architects by providing automated decision-making tools. Generative systems, case-based design systems, and performance analysis tools are among the most popular application areas that aim to enhance an architect's design thinking pattern with the use of computer tools. A generative system explores alternative ways of solving the design problem by assembling various design elements in different combinations. Case-based design tools retrieve previously stored design information when a new problem is encountered. They function like a digital library where a previous design becomes the base for solving a new problem. Performance analysis tools complement these design tools by computationally supporting the evaluation of various design solutions according to how they behave under certain conditions such as daylight, noise, weight loads, and more.

Architectural software designers are now focused on developing computational tools and methods that are more streamlined and easier for architects to use. New sketching tools and applications that seamlessly handle the collection, processing, and dissemination of information take the lead in research and development. The pace of change in the computer industry often means that software applications are outdated before disciplines with unique problems such as architectural design can modify the programs to suit their needs. For that reason, there is always a considerable need for new software and devices to serve the needs of the ar-

prototypes working models or experimental investigations of proposed systems under development

---

SOFTWARE FOR ARCHITECTS

Examples of software commonly used by architects include FormZ by AutoDesSys Inc., for architectural three-dimensional modeling and drawing; ProjectBank by Bentley Inc., for versioning and real-time file sharing; AutoDesk 3D Studio Viz by AutoDesk Inc., for visualization, modeling and rendering; and Adobe Photoshop by Adobe Systems Inc., for graphics editing.

chitectural profession. SEE ALSO CAD/CAM, CA ENGINEERING; GRAPHIC DEVICES.

Ipek Özkaya

Bibliography

Akin, Ömer. *Psychology of Architectural Design.* London: Pion Ltd., 1986.

Carrara, Gianfranco, and Yehuda Kalay, eds. *Knowledge Based Computer-Aided Architectural Design.* New York: Elsevier, 1994.

Mitchell, William J., and Malcolm McCullough. *Digital Design Media*, 2nd ed. New York: Van Nostrand Reinhold, 1995.

Asimov, Isaac

American Science Fiction Writer
1920–1992

Isaac Asimov.

Isaac Asimov was arguably the single most important fiction author to treat the subject of computers. Also one of the preeminent science writers in America during his lifetime, he applied discipline, intellect, smooth storytelling, and insight to all of his work. He wrote or edited more than 500 books and innumerable articles. His novels and stories dazzled the public with a visionary glimpse of the future of computing. He also changed forever the way that robots were imagined as a positive influence in human society.

A paradox in person, he was a gentleman who pretended to be a playboy, a witty and entertaining "life of the party," who led a fairly solitary writer's life—typing 90 words per minute, 10 hours a day, 363 days per year, and selling every word. He was a loving and loyal man, who became estranged from his son and his first wife. He had a profound understanding of the world, rarely traveled, and, though his fiction is filled with spaceships, he never once flew in an airplane.

Asimov was born January 2, 1920 (some sources cite October 4, 1919), in Petrovichi, Russia. He emigrated to the United States with his parents when he was three, and taught himself to read at the age of five. He exhibited an early interest in science and would later write voluminously on the topic. As an academic, Asimov earned a B.S. in chemistry from Columbia University in 1939, an M.A. in 1941, and a Ph.D. in 1948. He taught at Boston University School of Medicine in 1949, was associate professor of biochemistry from 1955 to 1979, and became full professor in 1979, although he stopped teaching full time in 1958.

In his work, Asimov was influenced by science writer, historian, and science fiction author H.G. Wells and by Jules Verne, whom he admired as one of the first writers able to make a living while specializing in science fiction. Asimov sought knowledge and success in multiple fields of interest. He almost majored in history, but settled on chemistry. He later published books on history, and his historical view colored both his nonfiction and fiction, especially in the fields of computers and robotics. Asimov's "Foundation" series, with a future human culture spanning 25 million planets, was explicitly modeled on Edward Gibbon's *The Decline and Fall of the Roman Empire*. His fictional "Psychohistory" proposes mathematical prediction of future human events; but his final stories show that he was skeptical of this idea.

WELLS AND VERNE

H.G. Wells (1866–1946) is remembered for many works of fiction, including *The Invisible Man, The Time Machine,* and *The War of the Worlds.* His contemporary, Jules Verne (1828–1905), is also remembered for numerous works of fiction such as *Around the World in Eighty Days* and *Twenty Thousand Leagues Under the Sea.*

Asimov ended his biochemistry professorship to become a full-time writer. As a nonfiction author, he covered dozens of fields, including astronomy, biology, chemistry, math, poetry, music, Sherlock Holmes, the Bible, and William Shakespeare. As a fiction author he concentrated on science fiction and on the mystery/detective genre, sometimes combining both in the same story.

Asimov wrote stories that are as thought-provoking today as they were when he wrote them. Among them is the 8,600-word short story, "A Feeling of Power," first published in 1958. In the work, Asimov predicted widespread use of a handheld programmable calculator, multicolored for civilians, blue-steel for the military. But he set the scenario 400 years in the future, after the art of doing arithmetic by pencil and paper had been lost. In the story a lone genius re-invents manual math, and then commits suicide when the military takes over his research. Interestingly, Asimov's prediction concerning the advent of handheld calculating hardware and software was flawless. But the technology was available within two decades, rather than in 400 years.

The "Multivac" stories of Asimov spin ideas about the infinite future of computing. Among several examples are: "The Last Question," a 5,400-word story from 1956, in which a computer ponders humans' ultimate question, and eventually merges with humanity, acquires god-like power, travels back in time, and creates the universe; "The Machine that Won the War," a 2,100-word story from 1961; and "The Life and Times of Multivac," published in 1975 by the *New York Times Magazine.* In the latter, the Multivac computer benignly takes control of all government and economic power, to save people from themselves.

Asimov once described science fiction as "that branch of literature which is concerned with the impact of scientific advance upon human beings." Asimov took that definition seriously, and wrote many millions of words to prove his point. He is credited with coining the word "robotics" from the word "robot," which was itself coined by the Czech playwright Karel Capek from the Slavic root for "worker," in the 1923 play "R.U.R." (Rossum's Universal Robots). The word "robotics" is the accepted name for an actual academic and industrial discipline that focuses on the study, design, manufacturing, and application of robots in a variety of settings.

Numerous anthologies of computer and robot stories were published during the 1950s, including Isaac Asimov's *I, Robot,* 1950; Henry Kuttner's *Robots Have No Tails,* 1952; Martin Greenberg's *The Robot and the Man,* 1953; Groff Conklin's *Science Fiction Thinking Machines,* 1954; and Lester del Rey's *Robots and Changelings,* 1957. Yet today, it is Asimov more than any author who comes to mind when the word "robot" is spoken, in fiction or otherwise.

Asimov received numerous awards, including several Hugo Awards and multiple Nebula Awards. His novel *The End of Eternity* (1955) was selected and praised in *Science Fiction: The 100 Best Novels,* by David Pringle.

Asimov's Three Laws of Robotics

Asimov is arguably most famous and influential for what has become known as Asimov's Three Laws of Robotics, with credit to editor John Campbell, who codified them from Asimov's fiction. These edicts are as follows:

1. A robot may not injure a human being or, through inaction, allow a human being to come to harm.

2. A robot must obey the orders given it by human beings, except where such orders would conflict with the First Law.

3. A robot must protect its own existence as long as such protection does not conflict with the First and Second Laws.

Asimov explored the implications of these three laws in clever and meaningful ways, in at least twenty-nine short stories, spread over five short story collections, and in several novels. *The Caves of Steel*, which appeared in 1954, was a murder mystery that sketched a fascinating speculation on the utopian sociology of an automated future. In the 1945 story "Paradoxical Escape," everything people know about physics, astronomy, and "space warp theory" is input to a mechanical computer called the Brain. This robotic "character" invents Faster Than Light travel, but since it would be fatal to humans, the robotic computer wipes blank its memory. Other computers (robots) had also discovered this, as well, but Asimov's First Law of Robotics prohibited them from telling this to humans, as the knowledge—or rather, the likelihood that they would use it—would harm them. They burned out, rather than pass on the dangerous secret.

Isaac Asimov was not an inventor or creator of computer hardware or software. Nevertheless, his fictional portrayals of the relationship between computers and human beings had an impact on the development and integration of computer technology in modern society. His commentaries on the sociological and psychological effects of computerization on human society will, in all likelihood, continue to influence computer science scholars and enthusiasts. SEE ALSO ARTIFICIAL INTELLIGENCE; FICTION, COMPUTERS IN; ROBOTS.

Jonathan Vos Post

Bibliography

Asimov, Isaac. *Asimov on Science Fiction*. Garden City, NY: Doubleday, 1981.

Asimov, Isaac. *In Joy Still Felt: Autobiography of Isaac Asimov, 1954–1978*. Garden City, NY: Doubleday, 1980.

Asimov, Isaac. *In Memory Yet Green: Autobiography of Isaac Asimov, 1920–1954*. New York: Doubleday, 1979.

Asimov, Isaac. *Understanding Physics*. New York: Walker, 1966.

Bretnor, Reginald. *Modern Science Fiction; Its Meaning and Its Future*. Chicago: Advent Publishers, 1979.

Internet Resources

Rothstein, Mervyn. "Isaac Asimov, Whose Thoughts and Books Traveled the Universe, Is Dead at 72." *New York Times*. <http://www.nytimes.com/books/97/03/23/lifetimes/asi-v-obit.html>

Astronomy

Astronomy is the scientific study of the universe as a whole and of objects that exist naturally in space, such as the Moon, planets, stars, and galaxies. The Sun is a rather typical star moving around the center of the Milky Way at a distance of 20,000 light years. This Milky Way, our galaxy, is made of

MUTUAL ADMIRATION SOCIETY

It is reported that Isaac Asimov once shook hands on a "treaty" in a New York City cab with Arthur C. Clarke, author of *2001: A Space Odyssey*, in which they agreed that each would tell the public that Isaac Asimov was the world's number one science writer, and Clarke was the world's number one science fiction writer. In truth, the two rank side by side in both fields.

three-body problem an intractable problem in mechanics that involves the attempts to predict the behavior of three bodies under gravitational effects

stellar pertaining to the stars

radio telescopes telescopes used for astronomical observation that operate on collecting electromagnetic radiation in frequency bands above the visible spectrum

NUMERICAL COSMOLOGY

Structures in the universe such as stars, galaxies, and clusters of galaxies are thought to arise from the collapse of initially diffuse matter via gravity. Regions in space, which were slightly more dense in the early universe than the average density, started to contract as early as 100 million years after the Big Bang—the beginning of the universe. Small objects formed first and merged into larger and larger galaxies. Cosmologists have been using supercomputers to follow this origin of cosmic structure in sophisticated, three-dimensional modeling. These models follow how gas and the mysterious dark matter, which is thought to constitute 90 percent of all the mass in the universe, clump into galaxies. The model universes are remarkably successful in matching observations, and they give novel insights into the sequence of events that occurred before the universe attained its present complexity.

hundreds of millions of stars with vast empty regions and diffuse gas in between all held together by gravity. There are at least another hundred billion galaxies in the observable universe.

Every day and night astronomers collect data on these objects in all bands of the electromagnetic spectrum of light. From radio waves through X-rays, small and large telescopes on the ground and in space record immense amounts of data. Analyzing these data is one of the major challenges of modern astronomy. Sophisticated time-dependent, three-dimensional models of astronomical objects and the universe as a whole are now routinely constructed to help astronomers interpret their observations.

In 1823 the president of the Royal Astronomical Society presented the society's gold medal to British mathematician Charles Babbage (1791–1871) for the invention of the first digital calculating machine. The president remarked: "In no department of science or of the arts does this discovery promise to be so eminently useful as in that of astronomy. . . . The practical astronomer is interrupted in his pursuit, is diverted from his task of observation, by the irksome labour of computation;. . ." Before the first electronic computers became available to astronomers, many observatories employed humans referred to as computers for this "irksome labour of computation."

In the 1950s theoretical astronomers began tapping the potential of programmable computing systems. Their first programs derived the solution of the restricted **three-body problem** (the gravitational interaction of three massive bodies) and also the solution to the equations of **stellar** structure. Model stellar atmospheres were also constructed from atomic data to be compared with observations of stellar spectra. The first practical applications were computations of precise apparent star positions and analysis routines transforming photoelectric observational data into meaningful scientific quantities.

By the 1960s computers had become an integral part of research in astronomy. In particular, progress in the theoretical understanding of stellar structure and evolution was driven largely by results of numerical investigations.

Astronomical research stimulates new advances in computing. A prime example is SETI@home, a project that uses the computing power of idle home and office computers. SETI, which stands for Search for ExtraTerrestial Intelligence, involves the analysis of the many gigabytes of data collected daily at **radio telescopes**. A freely distributed screensaver connects to a central data server and collects a small part of these data. When the home computer is otherwise idle, its processing power is used to look for extraterrestial signals. Upon completion of the analysis, the results of the computation are relayed back to the central server. Although no alien life has been found to date, millions of SETI@home users are contributing to this scientific endeavor.

The rapid growth in computing technologies also enables new areas of astronomical research. The data obtained at telescopes are now all stored in large databases that can be accessed by astronomers around the globe. These archived data repositories act as virtual observatories. Scientist can retrieve

(observe) data on the same astronomical objects in many different wave-bands in a very short time without even having access to a telescope. Any relevant scientific studies are cross-referenced with the observed objects and are readily accessible on the Internet worldwide.

Supercomputers play an important role in astronomy today. Perhaps one of the most important uses of supercomputers is the physical modeling of the origin and evolution of astrophysical objects. Computational astrophyics has become a mature science in the past decades, driven not only by the ever-increasing power of computers but especially by new **algorithmic** breakthroughs. Novel techniques allow scientists to capture the vast space and time scales that astronomical objects span. It has become possible to study in detail such difficult problems as the collision of black holes; the formation of planets, stars, and galaxies; and the large-scale structure of the universe.

In detailed three-dimensional models, computational astrophysicists follow the time evolution of magnetic fields, radiation, gas dynamics, chemistry, gravitational interactions, cosmic ray interactions, and many more physical processes. Physicists can experiment in laboratories to test their theories. Only numerical experiments allow the astronomers and astrophysicists to test their theories in the quest to understand the nature of astronomical objects.

Rapidly evolving computing technologies and their uses in astronomical research will continue to lead to profound new insights into the nature,

In the desert near Socorro, New Mexico, twenty-seven radio telescopes form a Y-shape configuration. Called the Very Large Array (VLA), they are used by astronomists and scientists to monitor and record sounds in space.

supercomputers very high performance computers, usually comprised of many processors and used for modeling and simulation of complex phenomena, like meteorology

algorithmic pertaining to the rules or procedures used to solve mathematical problems—most often described as a sequence of steps

origin, and evolution of the cosmos and the complex structures within. SEE ALSO NAVIGATION; PHYSICS; WEATHER FORECASTING.

Tom Abel

Bibliography

Duffett-Smith, Peter. *Astronomy with Your Personal Computer.* New York: Cambridge University Press, 1990.

Foust, Jeff, and Ron LaFon. *Astronomer's Computer Companion.* San Francisco: No Starch Press, 2000.

ATM Machines

It is your money and you want immediate and easy access to it. Can you imagine a time, way back in the 1970s, when people had to wait in line during a bank's limited hours to get money from their own accounts? The advent of the automated teller machine (ATM) changed the way consumers

As technology allows in the future, ATM machines will likely be used for purposes beyond dispensing cash.

handle their money. The ATM also shows how technology can change traditional business and consumer practices.

The evolution of the ATM reflects the technology of the time. As personal computers (PCs) and networks became more sophisticated, the ATM followed. The first ATMs were proprietary (i.e., the private property of a single individual or institution) and stand-alone (i.e., independent devices that did not connect to a network). These original ATMs were not PC-based; they did not have a PC processor or hard drive. They were based on a proprietary processing chip that was developed by the ATM manufacturer. Because the first generation of ATMs were stand-alone devices, they had to be updated each day with account balances from the host bank. The magnetic strip on the back of the bank card recorded the customer's activity for the day to maintain an accurate account balance between updates from the host.

In the 1970s, the online network became part of the ATM. With a modem and phone line, the ATM could connect to the bank's computers to verify account balances. Banks realized they could reduce their hardware and expand their reach through shared networks (i.e., the once private networks of one bank communicated to another bank's network). Through the decade, these networks expanded regionally and later consolidated their interests into national networks, such as Cirrus and Plus.

Inside most ATMs in the early twenty-first century are PCs with an Intel processor chip running IBM's OS/2 Warp **operating system**. Software and hardware developed by ATM manufacturers connects all of the peripheral devices of the ATM: card reader, currency dispenser, receipt printer, depository, and optional equipment such as an electronic audit printer or camera. At the application or software level, however, ATMs remain proprietary. Vendors have their own transaction processing language to direct the interaction of customer and machine, pass messages to and from the host processor, and handle any errors.

The input device for an ATM is a card reader, which initially identifies the account. A keypad is used to enter passwords and select transactions. A depository allows the user to deposit cash or checks. Some ATMs have a camera to record transactions, a useful tool to combat fraud. The output devices include a currency dispenser, receipt printer, speaker, electronic audit printer, and display screen.

Displays on some early ATMs used plastic letter wheels that would spin and form words. By borrowing the **cathode ray tube (CRT)** technology from the television, text messages could direct a customer through the steps of a transaction. Early-twenty-first-century ATMs use a **graphical user interface (GUI)** with sophisticated color display and dialogue.

The latest movement in ATM technology is to use a browser-based **interface**, similar to what is seen on an Internet web page. This type of ATM connects to a host computer through a web server. The trend is moving away from proprietary application software to become more vendor independent.

Technology was not the only driving force behind the ATM phenomena. Two other changes created the incentive and opportunity. First, the

operating system a set of programs which control all the hardware of a computer and provide user and device input/output functions

cathode ray tube (CRT) a glass enclosure that projects images by directing a beam of electrons onto the back of a screen

graphical user interface (GUI) a technology whereby graphical objects are placed on a computer screen for interaction with the user—examples are icons, menus, and buttons

interface a boundary or border between two or more objects or systems; also a point of access

ATM CARD THIEVERY

Most people have not experienced problems using their ATM cards at automated teller machines. However, some ATM users have fallen prey to thieves who steal their information and raid their bank accounts. One of the ways that criminals gain access to bank accounts is by placing hidden cameras near ATM machines and recording people as they enter their PINs (personal identification numbers). Then the thieves use a device to record data from the magnetic stripe on their victims' ATM cards in order to create fake cards. Armed with the replica cards and PINs, the criminals gain access to accounts and withdraw funds.

two largest regional networks changed operating procedures in 1996 and permitted surcharges on foreign transactions (i.e., transactions initiated on ATMs not owned by your bank could be charged with a service fee). Second, a federal law in the same year eliminated the requirement of a federal bank charter to establish an ATM. This allowed independent service organizations (ISOs) to enter the market.

Credit card companies introduced a new product, the "debit card," to add utility for bank customers that, in effect, worked against the ATM. The debit card, like a credit card, allows one to purchase a product or service. Unlike the credit card, however, the funds for the purchase move immediately from the user's account to the merchant's account. Debit card users can also request additional cash at the time of purchase. The use of credit and debit cards and shopping on the Internet do not require constant trips to the ATM for physical currency.

How have these changes affected the number of ATMs and the volume of activity? The numbers are not exact, but the trend is clear. In 1995 there were around 120,000 ATMs in the United States. By 1999 the estimate was 220,000. That number is expected to approach 300,000 by 2003. While the number of machines is increasing, the overall volume of transactions has steadily decreased since 1999 and is expected to decline further while the debit card flourishes.

So what is an ATM to do when its primary function of dispensing cash is challenged? It can offer new features, such as selling stamps or display advertising. New software features created by ATM vendors along with the development of web-enabled ATMs will make ticket purchases for concerts, theater, or sporting events possible through the ATM. An ATM receipt could be exchanged at the box office for the actual tickets. A web-enabled ATM could execute electronic trades over the Internet. But do consumers really want to manage their portfolios from an ATM? With Internet access so available, does this add value to the ATM?

ATMs in convenience stores have already started to issue money orders, wire money, pay bills, print maps, deliver stock prices, and arrange video rentals. The applications that power the ATM continue to evolve. Perhaps the ATM will replace the old voting booth. So, while technology and legislation spurred the growth of ATMs, technology, new applications, and a trend toward a cash-less society will certainly change and enhance their utility in the future. SEE ALSO IBM CORPORATION; INTERACTIVE SYSTEMS; USER INTERFACES.

Paul R. Kraus

Internet Resources

Bowen, Jim. "How Automated Teller Machines (ATMs) Work." <http://www.howstuffworks.com/atm.htm>

Biology

What role do computers play in the study of biology? Most people understand that computers produce spreadsheets, help analyze data, graph results of experiments, and prepare final reports for presentations. Although computers are workhorses in these areas, computers and the Internet are considered vital in other ways to many different fields of biology and research. In some cases, computer science and biology (along with chemistry, physics, and mathematics) are woven so tightly together they have become inseparable.

Scientific Organizations

The Centers for Disease Control and Prevention, or CDC, is a U.S. government agency headquartered in Atlanta, Georgia. The goal of the CDC is to protect the health and safety of U.S. citizens at home, work, and abroad through the detection, treatment, and prevention of health-related issues. The CDC has an integral role in the tracking of infectious diseases and uses computers in a multitude of ways.

This is illustrated by the Division of Parasitic Diseases (DPD), a branch of the CDC. The DPD extends knowledge and control of parasites and parasitic diseases primarily through the use of the Internet and extensive computer databases. At the agency's Internet web site, thousands of known parasites can be viewed (including microscopic slides). This aids in the identification of parasitic organisms and the diseases they cause.

Through the web site, the DPD supplies information to health care workers on how to recognize and treat possible cases of parasite-caused disease. Health care professionals can also find out how to get and submit samples for a diagnosis. Experts at the DPD will answer e-mailed questions and review digital images of slides of suspected parasites. Confirmed cases of parasitic infection are reported back to the DPD and are added to its extensive databases. Through the use of statistical analysis, trends of parasitic infections are tracked. Armed with this information, experts at the CDC are able to identify populations vulnerable to parasites. Steps can then be taken to find infected individuals for treatment and limit exposure to others, keeping people healthy.

Originally, the CDC was founded to eliminate malaria. It now tracks a multitude of infectious diseases, from AIDS to the common flu. In 2001, the CDC was engaged in building a National Electronic Disease Surveillance System, which through the Internet creates a broad-based and comprehensive system linking local and national health departments regardless of differing computer platforms and software. This new system will allow faster detection of and more rapid intervention against public health threats.

The National Institutes of Health, or NIH, is another U.S. agency that extensively uses computers and the Internet in its collection and application of biological information. The National Center for Biotechnology Information (NCBI), a subdivision of the NIH, maintains expansive databases on their computers, including known gene sequences, for molecular biology researchers all over the world. The largest biomedical research facility in the world, the NIH is headquartered in Bethesda, Maryland.

Bioinformatics

One field that has proved essential to gene sequencing is *bioinformatics*. Researchers in this field develop **algorithms** and software to allow enormous amounts of biological information to be processed. Bioinformatics is essential to molecular biologists working on "breaking" genetic codes.

CALL TO ACTION

In the fall of 2001, bioterrorists sent letters containing deadly anthrax spores through the U.S. Postal Service to government and media employees. To bring authoritative information to the public as quickly as possible, the CDC put its web site into action. It posted information, including: facts and frequently asked questions about anthrax, smallpox, antibiotics, and vaccines; fact sheets on other types of biological and chemical agents; articles on treatment options and research findings; and instructions on how to handle mail. In addition, the web site offered the medical community information on how to test for anthrax exposure, what treatment options are available, and how to create a bioterrorism readiness plan. <http://www.bt.cdc.gov>

algorithms rules or procedures used to solve mathematical problems—most often described as sequences of steps

Computer simulations can help researchers learn more about viruses and other diseases. This model of the common cold virus helped scientists at Purdue University learn more about how the virus infects human cells.

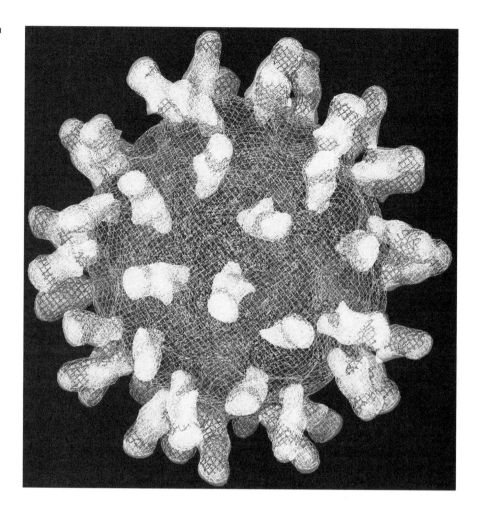

With only ten percent of the world's bacteria identified, gene sequencing is also being used to examine the DNA (deoxyribonucleic acid) of various bacteria. Scientists expect to use this method to identify previously undiscovered bacteria in what have always been considered inhospitable environments around the world, such as thermal springs, oil fields, or areas deep under the Earth's crust. Research on this amazing diversity of life contributes to humankind's knowledge of biological processes, and holds much promise for future researchers.

Bioengineering and Biomedical Engineering

Bioengineering is a new study that brings the science of engineering into the science of cell and molecular biology. Bioengineers use computers to study the structure and processes of living cells and organisms. The advances from bioengineering are seen in fields as diverse as manufacturing, chemical industries, defense industries, electronics, and agriculture. For example, through bioengineering one can detect harmful pollutants in the environment and harmful microorganisms in food.

Biomedical engineering, however, draws from many fields of engineering, such as electrical, mechanical, and chemical engineering. It is used to advance medicine and health care. Computers are used to analyze the functions of cells, and then to design mechanical reproductions to master that function. Computers are needed to use the components that result. One well-known example of biomedical engineering is the artificial heart.

Another result of biomedical engineering is the mechanization of lab tests. Routine lab tests used to be conducted by hand. The process of, for instance, checking a complete blood cell count required several time-consuming steps. Frequently the test was repeated to rule out possible lab error. Through biomedical engineering, the testing processing is done quickly, efficiently, and with very little likelihood of lab error. A blood sample is marked with the patient's **bar code** moments after the blood is drawn from the patient. Once it is put in the automated machine, the computer takes over the processing. In some tests, computerized image analysis is used for a definitive diagnosis. The computer then directs the test results where needed. The use of automated lab tests lowers costs while vastly increasing efficiency, speed, and accuracy.

bar code a graphical number representation system where alphanumeric characters are represented by vertical black and white lines of varying width

Environmental Biology

Computers are also valuable in environmental studies. Conservation agencies, such as the U.S. Fish and Wildlife Service, use computers in several ways. One key to successful conservation efforts is effective communication with local conservation groups, state officials, and local legislative bodies (who frequently decide upon important zoning issues). Through the Internet, a variety of educational materials are easily accessible.

Although the U.S. Fish and Wildlife Service's goal is to standardize equipment and provide reference material and electronic communication within the service, particularly to remote field offices, these efforts are seriously hampered by lack of funding for equipment upgrades. In other conservation efforts, computers are being used to model natural ecological systems for study. Satellite remote sensing, such as imagery and **telemetry**, make regional and landscape mapping easier, more accurate, and cost effective. This helps environmental biologists gather information more effectively.

telemetry the science of taking measurements of something and transmitting the data to a distant receiver

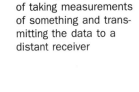

With the growing sophistication of research needs and resources and the increased use of the Internet to gather, share, and analyze scientific data, evidence suggests that computers will continue to play a vital part in the study of biology in its many applications. SEE ALSO MOLECULAR BIOLOGY; PHYSICS; SCIENTIFIC VISUALIZATION.

Mary McIver Puthawala and Anwer H. Puthawala

Internet Resources

Centers for Disease Control and Prevention Web Site. <http://www.cdc.gov>

"DPDx—Identification and Diagnosis of Parasites of Public Health Concern." Centers for Disease Control and Prevention. <http://www.dpd.cdc.gov/dpdx/HTML/Aboutdpdx.htm>

Massey, Adrianne. "What Is Biotechnology?" *Biotechnology Industry Organization.* <http://www.bio.org/aboutbio/guide2000/whatis.html>

CAD/CAM, CA Engineering

At first a seemingly indecipherable collection of symbols, these acronyms are fairly easy to understand once one realizes that each "CA" stands for

Use of computer-aided design tools through the life-cycle of a design process has taken the place of building physical models. Boeing airplane designs were developed and tested using CAD/CAM technology.

CRT the acronym for cathode ray tube; a glass enclosure that projects images by directing a beam of electrons onto the back of a screen

Computer-Aided (or Assisted). Thus, CAD is Computer-Aided Design; CAM stands for Computer-Aided Manufacturing; and the last acronym denotes Computer-Aided Engineering. Although presently interrelated technologies, they evolved separately.

The earliest to develop was CAD, originally termed Computer-Aided Drafting, a terminology still in use by approximately half the users of this technology mainly in the architectural, consulting, construction, mapping, and public utility fields. In many instances, the acronym is presented as CADD, signifying both applications. Invented by American engineer Ivan Sutherland, CAD was outlined in his seminal 1961 Ph.D. dissertation. Sutherland described a computerized sketchpad in which he used a **CRT** display and light pen to construct basic geometric entities such as points, lines, and arcs. Sutherland's initial concept resulted in the first commercially available CAD systems in the mid 1970s—systems which have evolved, over the following decades, developing into the CAD software in use today.

In computer-aided drafting, the mouse, or "puck," on a digitizing tablet attached to the computer is used to trace or draw lines that are stored in the computer as graphic primitives. Combined with a digitizing tablet, which is basically an electronic drafting board, CAD represents the primary means for entering paper map documents into the computer. It should be noted that an alternative means is a scanner—basically a large, spatially accurate fax machine. However, the digital data produced by these two techniques is quite different. Digitizing (or drafting) with CAD produces **vector** (points and lines) digital data while a scanner provides **raster** data, which is essentially an accurate digital picture.

The basic drafting capabilities of CAD were supplemented through the addition of software tools allowing for the production of precise engineering drawings of intricate designs, such as complex machine parts or electronic circuit boards. A key development in CAD was the introduction of the graphic display terminal, which not only offered dramatically real displays of objects but also allowed the designer to interact graphically rather than through the keyboard or digitizer. In such a manner, designers could concentrate on decisions concerning the objects represented on the screen rather than focusing on the drawings. Indeed, the development of computer graphics is closely linked to that of CAD. Thus, in the manufacturing arena, CAD became an integral part of the design process, offering efficient and accurate creation, modification, analysis, and optimization of designs.

Computer-aided design applications enabling precise two-dimensional and three-dimensional designs to be implemented and graphically displayed are now routine parts of the manufacturing process for a wide variety of products in many fields, such as aerospace and automotive engineering. They are employed by such companies as Boeing, Ford, Toyota, and Volvo. AutoCAD and Microstation software are two of the standard products for industrial strength CAD for both two-dimensional and three-dimensional drafting and design.

If a design exists in the computer, then the next logical step would be to have the computer drive machine tools to produce the object indicated by the design. This is how CAM, or computer-aided manufacturing, was created. Since the mid-1980s, CAM has been closely linked with CAD, and the union is represented by the single acronym CAD/CAM. Although CAM actually includes various applications in the manufacturing process, such as production scheduling and inventory control, it is best illustrated by the integrated CAD/CAM systems within which a design can be developed and the manufacturing process controlled. In such a union, CAD software creates CNC/NC (computer numeric control/numeric control) codes, which are coded numerical instructions for automated control of machine tools such as lathes and mills, and are similar to the programming codes that drive plotters. Originally, paper tapes were produced to drive the machine tools, but newer tools are connected directly to the computer, so that the design and manufacturing process is seamless and computer-aided. This has resulted in faster, more efficient, and more accurate procedures.

A good illustration of the versatility offered by an integrated CAD/CAM approach is the design and development of printed circuit boards. A **schematic** is created, using interactive graphics, to recall symbols from a database and place them in the appropriate locations. Once the design is completed, a circuit analysis program is used to test and verify the performance of the circuit board. The final step is to produce a photographic transparency directly from the CAD/CAM system, which is then used to manufacture the circuit board.

vector an abstraction used in the physical sciences to model a quantity that has a magnitude (size) and a direction of action

raster a line traced out by a beam of electrons as they strike a cathode ray tube (CRT)

schematic a diagrammatic representation of a system, showing logical structure without regard to physical constraints

This basic feat of engineering, integrating computer capabilities with manual design, has recently been perfected by the integration of complex mathematical functions or analyses, such as finite element modeling and analysis, computational **fluid dynamics**, boundary element analysis, and rigid body analysis, into the engineering design process, thereby establishing the field of computer-aided engineering.

CA engineering can basically be considered a set of numerical tools and processes to conduct numeric simulations. A good example is the **analytic simulation** of the **aerodynamics** of a body in a wind tunnel. Such an approach is used, for example, to make sure that a designed part is strong enough, or to simulate the operation of a designed feature before its manufacture. By providing analytic prototypes in the manufacturing process, CAE has reduced the need for physical prototypes, thereby speeding up the production process. Expert systems are also being added to extend the capabilities of the process. One such system presently under development is intelligent CAD, or IntCAD.

A practical application of these technologies occurred when the U.S. Civil War submarine *H. L. Hunley* was raised off the coast of Charleston, South Carolina, in October 2000. CAD and CAE techniques were used in this historic project to assess the submarine's structural weaknesses and to test and simulate various methods for raising the vessel. The final and successful method, fully tested in the system before application, was to place thirty-two nylon slings under the submarine, support it with a steel structure from above, and squirt foam along the side of the vessel to replace the sand that had supported it for more than a century. SEE ALSO DISPLAY DEVICES; GRAPHIC DEVICES; PROCESS CONTROL.

Robert D. Regan

Bibliography

Franken, Stephanie. "Ansys Quietly Builds Business in Computer Aided Design." *Pittsburgh Post Gazette*, May 31, 2001.

Visitainer, Randal, David Watts, et al. *CAE Methods and Their Application to Truck Design.* Warrendale, PA: Society of Automotive Engineers, 1997.

Zecher, Jack. *Computer Graphics for CAD/CAM Systems.* New York: Marcel Dekker, 1994.

Cell Phones

Among all consumer electronic devices ever invented, cellular telephones (cell phones for short) have been the most popular in terms of the number of devices sold as a function of time. Today, cell phones are almost as common as the wired telephone. In certain European countries, they exceed the total number of wired telephones, and in several Scandinavian countries, cell phones have become a way of life.

The concept behind the working of a cell phone is based on what is known as *frequency reuse*. There is only so much of available *electromagnetic spectrum*, or frequency band, available for transmitting a voice call with a cell phone and this has to be shared by many users. Each voice conversation requires a certain amount of **bandwidth**, which is a chunk of the avail-

---

HUNT FOR THE HUNLEY

Scientists were eager to raise the Confederate submarine, the *H. L. Hunley,* from its watery grave near Charleston, South Carolina. Sunk in 1864 during the Civil War, the sub held the remains of eight sailors when it was raised in 2000. The *Hunley,* weighing 7.5 tons, disappeared after sinking the Union's *U.S.S. Housatonic* on February 14, 1864. The sub's location was discovered in 1995 and efforts began to recover the vessel in order to learn more about the people and technology of that era.

fluid dynamics the science and engineering of the motion of gases and liquids

analytic simulation modeling of systems by using mathematical equations (often differential equations) and programming a computer with them to simulate the behavior of the real system

aerodynamics the science and engineering of systems that are capable of flight

bandwidth a measure of the frequency component of a signal or the capacity of a communication channel to carry signals

able frequency band. In order to support the large number of subscribers, the service providers split the frequency band into smaller sub-bands and spread them over a given area. They install radio transmitters, called base stations, that serve an area called a cell. Each cell utilizes a sub-band of the spectrum. Two cells that are sufficiently far apart can use the same sub-bands because radio signals lose their strength with distance and do not interfere. Thus, frequency sub-bands are spatially reused by the creation of several cells supported by base stations. The name "cellular telephony" comes from this architecture.

Each base station is connected to a mobile switching center that handles cell phone calls and also performs a very important function called mobility management. If you make a phone call to a wired telephone, a telephone switch will know how to route your call because the telephone device is fixed. If you make a phone call to a cell phone, there must be a mechanism that keeps track of where the cell phone is and accordingly routes the call. This mechanism is called mobility management. It is performed by the mobile switching center, with the assistance of two databases called the home location register and the visitor location register.

Every cell phone is registered with a home location register in its home calling area. When you make a call to a cell phone, the telephone switch contacts the mobile switching center associated with the home location register. The home location register contains information about the visitor location register with which the mobile phone is currently registered while roaming. From this point, the call is routed to the mobile switching center associated with the visitor location register and handled from there. As the person with the cell phone moves, the cell phone constantly updates its location with the visitor location register, which in turn updates the home location register upon a change in location.

Another important aspect of managing mobility is what is known as the process of *handoff*. As users move with their cell phones, they cross the coverage of one base station and enter the coverage area of another—that is they cross cell boundaries. At this point, the cell phone should switch its connection from the old base station to the new base station. This procedure is called handoff and it involves measuring and comparing the received signal strengths from multiple base stations.

Within a cell, multiple users may simultaneously conduct phone conversations using the available frequency sub-band. They may do this in several different ways. The earliest technique was to further divide the sub-band into smaller chunks of frequency and use one chunk for one conversation. This is called *frequency division multiplexing* and was used in the analog cellular service first implemented in the early 1980s by AT&T. This was also adopted in Europe by several countries, each using its own standard. These systems were called the first generation cellular telephone systems. The frequency division multiplexing technique is inefficient and the resulting capacity to support subscribers is smaller than desired.

In the 1990s, there was a trend to move to *digital standards* to enhance the capacity of cellular systems. In Europe, all the countries agreed upon a common digital standard called the global system for mobile communications (GSM). In the United States, two major standards emerged called the

CELL PHONE HEALTH RISKS

Is your cell phone hurting your brain? Researchers are studying that very question in an effort to determine whether heavy and frequent cell phone use leads to an increase in brain cancer. Concern about cell phone safety centers on the device's built-in antenna, which emits electromagnetic waves. Thus far, various medical studies have yet to prove any significant increase in brain cancer among cell phone users. However, since widespread cell phone use is a relatively new phenomenon, such studies only cover short-term use. As such, the long-term effects have yet to be determined.

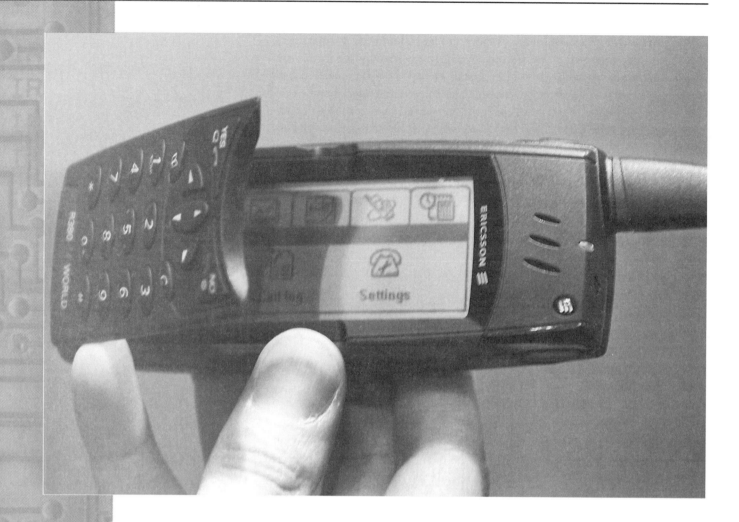

Cellular phone and PDA (personal digital assistant) technologies converge in this prototype unveiled by Ericsson in 2000. Combining the two electronic devices provides the powerful computing and large data-storage capabilities of the PDAs with the wide wireless access of cell phones.

IS-136 and IS-95 standards. These are the second-generation cellular telephone systems.

The GSM and IS-136 standards are based on *time-division multiplexing* where users appear to talk continuously, but their signals are transmitted one after another. That is, their signals are separated in time and these are commonly called the TDMA (Time Division Multiple Access) standards. The IS-95 standard employs *code-division multiplexing* where the signals of all users are simultaneously transmitted using the same frequency band. Each user is assigned a unique code that is designed to enable easy separation of signals with minimum interference. This is called the CDMA (Code Division Multiple Access) standard and it has proved to provide a significant increase in capacity and other additional benefits. Today, there is a global evolutionary trend toward third generation (3G) systems where cell phones in Europe and in the United States will all use some variation of CDMA.

Today, cell phones are becoming much more than simply tools used for voice conversations. The most modern phones are equipped with a micro-browser that can display whittled down versions of web pages using a *wireless application protocol* (WAP). In Japan, a different system called I-mode provides access to web pages on the cell phone display. In either case, a subscriber can get stock quotes, news, traffic, weather information, sports scores, and other personalized and customized information on a cell phone. In Europe, a service called short-messaging service (SMS) is extremely popular.

This allows almost instantaneous exchange of very short messages (up to 140 characters long) between two cell phones. This is very similar to computer-based instant messaging and is growing in popularity, especially with young adults. In summary, the cell phone is becoming a pivotal part of popular culture worldwide. There are also increasing trends toward integrating the cell phone with **personal digital assistants (PDAs)**, whether they run the PalmOS or WindowsCE operating systems.

Even as cell phones have become the single-most popular consumer electronic device, questions remain as to how safe electromagnetic signals are to the health of human beings. Studies relating cell phone usage to cancer are inconclusive, but manufacturers are gradually including transmit power and radiation information as part of cell phone specifications and documentation to alert consumers of potential hazards associated with long-term usage of cell phones. SEE ALSO INTERNET; TELECOMMUNICATIONS; WIRELESS TECHNOLOGY.

Prashant Krishnamurthy

personal digital assistants (PDAs) small scale hand-held computers that can be used in place of diaries and appointment books

Bibliography

Oliphant, M. W. "The Mobile Phone Meets the Internet." *IEEE Spectrum* 36, no. 8 (1999).

Sweet, W. "Cell Phones Answer Internet's Call." *IEEE Spectrum* 37, no. 8 (2000).

Chess Playing

The ancient, intellectually challenging game of chess originated in India and is played by two players on a checkerboard consisting of 64 squares, with 32 pieces divided equally by color. Each piece has its own role and ability to perform a unique function on the board. The game has enjoyed steady popularity and minor rule changes over centuries of time. With the development of computer technology, more and more players were able to improve their skills by playing against computers, using information stored in computer databases and even using computers as personal trainers.

How Chess Computers Work

There is no principal difference between a chess computer and a regular one. The computer programs evaluate chess positions on a virtual chessboard and select the best moves according to the specific criteria. Usually a computer calculates a numerical score for each position it evaluates, based on four variables. The highest score determines the move. These four variables include:

- *Pieces.* Each piece is assigned a value at the start of the game. For example, a pawn gets a value of 1; a queen 9. These values may also be modified later as the game progresses.

- *Position.* The computer observes all of the chess pieces on the chessboard and assigns them unit values based on how much territory they are able to attack.

- *King safety.* The computer evaluates both kings' positions and attempts to put its own king on a safer square and to force its opponent's king to a more vulnerable square.

Figure 1. Possible moves when starting a chess game.

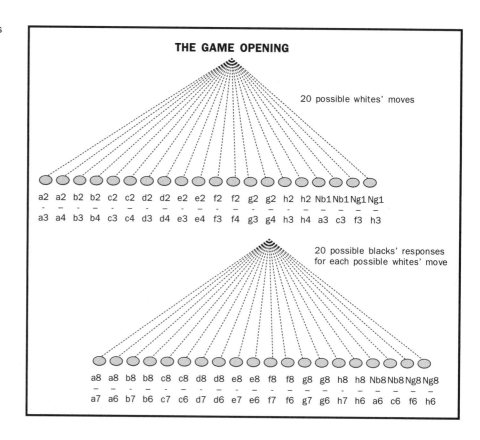

THE GAME OPENING

20 possible whites' moves

a2 a2 b2 b2 c2 c2 d2 d2 e2 e2 f2 f2 g2 g2 h2 h2 Nb1 Nb1 Ng1 Ng1
– – – – – – – – – – – – – – – – – – – –
a3 a4 b3 b4 c3 c4 d3 d4 e3 e4 f3 f4 g3 g4 h3 h4 a3 c3 f3 h3

20 possible blacks' responses for each possible whites' move

a8 a8 b8 b8 c8 c8 d8 d8 e8 e8 f8 f8 g8 g8 h8 h8 Nb8 Nb8 Ng8 Ng8
– – – – – – – – – – – – – – – – – – – –
a7 a6 b7 b6 c7 c6 d7 d6 e7 e6 f7 f6 g7 g6 h7 h6 a6 c6 f6 h6

artificial intelligence (AI) a branch of computer science dealing with creating computer hardware and software to mimic the way people think and perform practical tasks

minimax algorithm an approach to developing an optimal solution to a game or contest where two opposing systems are aiming at mutually exclusive goals

alpha beta pruning a technique that under certain conditions offers an optimal way to search through data structures called "trees"

supercomputer a very high performance computer, usually comprised of many processors and used for modeling and simulation of complex phenomena, like meteorology

• *Tempo.* The computer seeks to place its pieces on the intended squares to carry out its current plan faster than its opponent can counter.

The most popular opening chess move for the player of the white pieces is "e2-e4," which means the Whites move the pawn directly in front of the King 2 squares forward. This is only one of twenty possible first moves the Whites can make. Blacks' pieces have the same number of possible responses. So, there are 400 possible combinations for the first move alone. As the game continues, the number of possible positions keeps growing. All these possible moves may be presented in the form of a tree. (See Figure 1.)

It is impossible for any computer to calculate all possible moves by brute force. Therefore, a computer estimates positions for only several moves ahead. Today, computers are able to calculate up to 14 moves. Moreover, there are many well-developed **artificial intelligence (AI)** strategies, such as **minimax algorithm** or a technique called **alpha beta pruning**, that limit the search for the best move to an analysis of the most promising positions. In addition, computers use extensive databases of previous games for openings and endgames. For the endgames, when the number of pieces and thus the number of possible moves reduces significantly, computers are able to calculate all possible positions when five or fewer pieces are left on a chessboard.

First-class chess computers also require very powerful hardware. IBM's Deep Blue **supercomputer** uses a total of 512 microprocessors working in parallel to break down and analyze chess positions. Each processor simultaneously calculates and evaluates one possible sequence of moves, enabling the computer to examine 200 million positions a second!

History

The idea of a machine capable of playing chess was born long before computers. Historical annals mention Baron Wolfgang von Kempelen, who traveled around Europe in the eighteenth century with his Maezal Chess Automaton, nicknamed the Turk. The machine looked like a marionette that was able to make chess moves. The trick, of course, was that a tiny chess master was hidden inside the box.

The connection between modern computers and chess games began with a prophecy of British mathematician Alan Turing (1912–1954) that machines would compete in all purely intellectual fields including chess. He specified the first computer program for chess as early as 1947. Claude Shannon estimated the number of possible computer positions and proposed basic strategies for restricting the number of possibilities to be considered in a game of chess.

The first computer program for a full-fledged game of chess was written in 1957, and since 1966 computers have been playing in human chess tournaments, gradually increasing their rating and the level of tournaments over the years. Former world chess champion and scientist Mikhail Botvinnik (1911–1995) contributed to the development of computer algorithms for playing chess and to the creation of the KAISSA chess-playing computer program. KAISSA won the world computer chess championship in 1974.

As the result of a growing population of computer chess programmers the International Computer Chess Association (ICCA) was founded in 1977. The same year was marked with the first defeat of a grandmaster of chess by a computer. Since 1990 computers have occasionally beat the top players and even world champions Anatoly Karpov and Garry Kasparov. In 1997 the Deep Blue computer—coached by a research team of IBM scientists and engineers, and a grandmaster and U.S. chess champion Joel Benjamin— defeated the reigning world champion (Garry Kasparov) in a classic chess match against a computer for the first time. Kasparov had won a prior match in 1996. A number of computer programs now have a chess rating comparable with the top human players.

Recent Development: Internet and Chess

With the introduction of the Internet, millions of chess players and fans became a global chess community. Chess enthusiasts are able to play online with partners all around the world, browse through the latest chess news, download chess games from databases containing millions of games, and even play with the chess world champion. The "Kasparov versus the World" online chess tournament over the Internet lasted for more than four months from June to October 1999. More than 58,000 individuals from 75 countries submitted their move votes and were able to give a respectable fight to the world champion. The game lasted 62 moves and was observed by more than 3 million web site visitors. The quality of the chess played throughout the game has been recognized by chess experts around the world as one of the best public chess games ever documented.

Growing proliferation of computers and the Internet gave an opportunity to masses of chess devotees to improve their expertise and chess literacy and to widen horizons by providing easy access to chess databases and

---

COMPUTER GAMES

One of the founders of computer science and a leading scientist of Bell Laboratories, Claude Shannon (1916–2001), estimated the number of possible computer games as 10^{120}. How big is this number? In comparison, there are thought to be 10^{75} atoms in the entire universe.

other information. Used by grandmasters and novices alike, computers prove to be exceptionally handy tools to enjoy the ancient and popular game of chess. SEE ALSO ARTIFICIAL INTELLIGENCE; GAMES; IBM CORPORATION.

Marina Krol

Bibliography

Hamilton, Scott, and Lee Garber. "Deep Blue's Hardware-Software Synergy." *Computer* 30, no.10 (1997): 29–35.

Krol, Marina. "Have We Witnessed a Real-Life Turing Test?" *Computer* 32, no.3 (1999): 27–30.

Lawrence, Al, and Lev Alburt. *Playing Computer Chess: Getting the Most out of Your Game.* New York: Sterling Publishing Company, 1998.

Levy, David N. L., and Monty Newborn. *How Computers Play Chess.* New York: W. H. Freeman Company, 1990.

Newborn, Monty, and Monroe Newborn. *Kasparov Versus Deep Blue: Computer Chess Comes of Age.* New York: Springer-Verlag, 1997.

Pecci, Ernest F., and Edward Sheppie. *Chess: How to Beat Your Computer.* Walnut Creek, CA: Pavior Publishing, 1999.

Chip Manufacturing

Computer chips are at the heart of the modern technology revolution. But what are they made of and how are they made? They are made primarily of **transistors,** which act as electrical switches in digital circuits, and metal wires. The most significant type of transistor, from an economic perspective, is the complementary metal oxide semiconductor (CMOS) transistor. This is a three-terminal device consisting of a gate (metal), a source, and a drain. The gate is an electrical switch that controls the flow of electrons from the source to the drain. Applying a voltage turns "on" the gate, which directs an electric field across a thin silicon dioxide film, causing the semiconductor material to become conductive and thereby allowing electrons to flow. If the gate voltage is turned "off," the electrons go away. Transistors being "on" or "off" correspond to the binary "1" and "0."

So how are these transistors and wires made? The devices and wires on a chip are fabricated at the same time, alongside hundreds of other chips, using a process known as batch fabrication. It does not cost any more to fabricate 1,000 transistors than 100 transistors—or many million of transistors for that matter! This is known as batch fabrication and it results in substantial economies of scale that make chips inexpensive despite their complexity.

It all starts with **silicon**—the primary constituent of sand, and therefore abundant and inexpensive. The silicon is purified, and large cylindrical crystals one to two meters (three to six feet) long and up to one-third meter (twelve inches) in diameter are grown. These crystals are sliced into wafers 500–750 micrometers thick that form the substrate for the chips. The chip designer provides the chip manufacturer with a set of photomasks that contain a physical representation of the transistors and associated wires to be reproduced on the wafer. Photomasks are made of glass and chrome and define regions where light can penetrate (glass), and others where the light cannot penetrate (chrome), similar to a stencil. In a 0.18 micrometer, six metal layer process, up to twenty-five such photomasks are used.

transistors the plural of transistor, which is a contraction of TRANSfer resISTOR; semiconductor device, invented by John Bardeen, Walter Brattain, and William Shockley, which has three terminals, and can be used for switching and amplifying electrical signals

silicon a chemical element with symbol Si; the most abundant element in the Earth's crust and the most commonly used semiconductor material

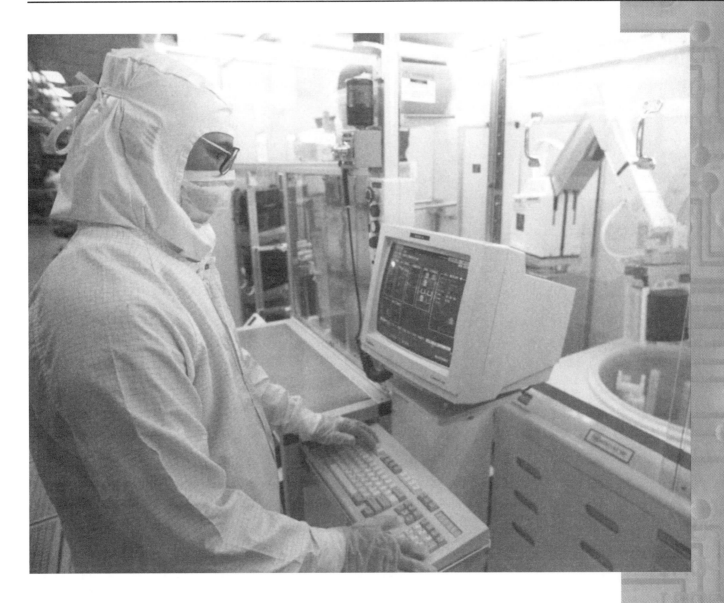

One set of photomasks is used to define where dopant elements will be added. What are dopants? They are elements—such as boron, phosphorus, and arsenic—added to the silicon that allow the charge-carrying characteristics of the material to be altered in a controllable fashion, facilitating the formation of transistors. Another set of photomasks is used in a set of successive steps whereby a thin film (typically less than one micrometer, or 1 μm) is deposited on the wafer, a thin photosensitive polymer film is placed on top, and the pattern from the photomask is transferred to the photosensitive polymer by shining light on the photomask. The thin film is etched where the photosensitive polymer has been removed, and finally the photosensitive polymer is removed. These steps are repeated to fabricate the transistor gate, the wires that connect the transistors together, and the insulating films that separate the metal wires from each other. After the circuits have been fabricated—a process that can take twenty to thirty days in a 0.18 μm CMOS production plant—the wafers are cut into small chips and individually packaged.

Now that these chips are ready, how fast will they run? The speed depends on the amount of time the transistors take turning on and off and the

Wearing a protective suit, mask, and gloves, this employee of a microchip manufacturing plant must keep the working environment sterile. Particles, including skin and dust, could cause a chip to malfunction, hence the need for workers to wear the so-called "bunny suits."

delay imposed by the wiring. The length of the gate determines the switching time of transistors: the shorter the gate, the faster the device can switch. Wiring delays come from two primary sources—the time it takes to charge the wire up to the necessary voltage and the time it takes for a signal to travel a given distance. The former is reduced when the size of the wire is shrunk, so as chip miniaturization progresses, this delay decreases. The travel time is set by the speed of light and the material properties. For typical materials, signals travel 15 centimeters (about 6 inches) in a billionth of a second, which means that it will take over a quarter of a clock cycle to travel across a 2 centimeter (about 3/4 of a inch) chip running at 2 GHz. Historically, the frequency at which microprocessors operate has doubled every two years!

The scaling of features to smaller dimensions (known as technology scaling) improves performance while decreasing cost. Technology scaling basically means more computing power is packed into increasingly smaller physical space. Scaling propels the semiconductor market growth, which in turn generates sufficient profit to develop increasingly aggressive technology generations—scaling begets scaling! This cycle fuels what is known as "Moore's Law," which states that the number of transistors per integrated circuit doubles every eighteen months. Since the length of the gate is a primary indicator of the speed of a process, it is associated with a generation of computer chip technology. Not only do microprocessors get faster as the gate length decreases, but if one is making memory chips, more memory can be packed on the chip.

Economics of Chip Manufacturing

Just as computer chips have decreased in size and increased in power in each generation, semiconductor sales as a percent of the Gross World Product (GWP) have doubled every three technology generations. The manufacturing capacity of the semiconductor industry is often measured in wafer starts per week, which is simply a tally of how many wafers are placed at the beginning of the manufacturing process. From 1998 to 2000, this figure increased by about 20 percent—from seven million to eight and a half million.

It is also important to understand that as miniaturization has occurred, the cost of the equipment necessary to fabricate the microelectronic devices has dramatically increased. This is because higher equipment quality is required to manufacture the increasingly small devices, as well as to control the dimensions of these devices within strict tolerances. Consequently, the cost of a factory has grown significantly each year, from ten million dollars in the 1980s, to almost two billion dollars in 1999. The expectation is that the cost of semiconductor manufacturing facilities will continue to increase—by about 3 percent per year due to productivity requirements and 5 percent per year for technology upgrades.

Chip making is all about packing as many transistors in as small an area as possible, to produce fast microprocessors and large amounts of memory. Chip making employs economies of scale, because most process operations are performed for many wafers at once, and each wafer contains many chips, and each chip contains many transistors. This has resulted in a tremendous return on investment for manufacturers that has far outweighed the rising manufacturing costs. It is anticipated that such trends will continue until

MORE ON MOORE

Moore's Law was a prediction made by Gordon Moore of Fairchild Semiconductor Corporation in 1965, and it has held remarkably true into the 2000s. In fact, rival companies, knowing Moore's Law, each set out to exceed it, making Moore's Law a self-fulfilling prophecy.

2030 or so. SEE ALSO CENTRAL PROCESSING UNIT; MICROCHIP; PROCESS CONTROL.

Brett A. Warneke and J. Alex Chediak

Bibliography

Jaeger, Richard C. *Introduction to Microelectronic Fabrication.* Menlo Park: Addison-Wesley Publishing Company, 1993.

Streetman, Ben G., and Sanjay Banerjee. *Solid State Electronic Devices.* Upper Saddle River, NJ: Prentice Hall, 1999.

Internet Resources

Moore's Law. Intel Corporation Web Site. <http://intel.com/research/silicon/mooreslaw.htm>

International Technology Roadmap for Semiconductors. ITRS Web Site. <http://public.itrs.net>

Semiconductor Industry Association Web Site. <http://www.semichips.org/stats/>

Computer Assisted Instruction

Computer Assisted Instruction (CAI) is defined as the use of computers and software applications to teach concepts or skills. IBM developed one of the first instructional computer systems in the 1960s using **minicomputers**. From the 1960s to the 1980s, IBM produced a handful of these 1500 series computers for the military and several universities. These units, contained in special trailers, consisted of complete workstations: one large **central processing unit (CPU)**, one instructor's station, and sixteen student terminals. The trailer was hauled from place to place as needed.

Pennsylvania State University and the University of Alberta (Canada) were two of the biggest advocates of the 1500 series stations and provided a great deal of early research on computer assisted instruction. Researchers from several universities, such as from the University of Pittsburgh's Learning Research and Development Center (LRDC), continue the effort to identify the best methods and tools for using interactive computer programs to enhance learning.

Computer assisted instruction has changed radically since the 1500 series. Computers are found in a growing number of homes and schools, and a variety of applications exist to use the computer to teach. The military has continued to be a significant advocate of computer assisted instruction to teach large numbers of trainees a multitude of jobs, including teaching pilots how to fly with the use of flight simulators. Without question, "e-learning" is a growing economic sector. In 2000, e-learning (electronic-learning) was a $2.2 billion dollar business. By 2003, it is expected to be worth $11.4 billion.

Learning Management Systems

One growing trend among schools is to use a powerful application called a Learning Management System (LMS). Some companies that sell LMSs provide a service to the schools. Students, using either the school-owned computers or computers in the schools provided by the company, connect to the service's web site to access a curriculum chosen by the faculty. The students access the educational resources for a specific period of time over a

minicomputers computers midway in size between a desktop computer and a mainframe computer; most modern desktops are much more powerful than the older minicomputers

central processing unit (CPU) the part of a computer that performs computations and controls and coordinates other parts of the computer

"Traditional" curriculum can be integrated into an electronic teaching platform. Changing the format of the information sometimes helps students access the material more easily.

specific number of weeks; the frequency and duration vary from program to program.

The advantages of using an LMS are compelling. Many students are eager to use such a site because of its "cool factor," which may motivate them to do well. The curriculum can be adjusted to focus on specific areas of weakness, whether for the entire class or for an individual. Any or all students can be monitored for progress.

Among the disadvantages to implement an LMS, schools must have a reliable Internet system installed, which can be a major and expensive project. Another disadvantage is that the programs themselves can cost up to $30,000, a price that might not include the cost of computers. The effectiveness of these programs, as compared to conventional instruction, is also still open to debate among critics and proponents of learning management systems.

A variety of LMSs are available from different manufacturers. Choosing among them can be quite difficult, as they have considerable variation of methodology and depth. They also work on several different hardware platforms. Construction of each course must be done on an individual basis, and so there are no "plug and play" options. Also, there are no universally accepted standards to compare programs. The Shared Content Object Reference Model, or SCORM (developed by the U.S. government), is one set of standards gaining acceptance.

Electronic Books

Electronic books, especially electronic textbooks, are another form of computer assisted instruction. E-textbooks offer several advantages over print textbooks. They can be updated quickly and easily at a far cheaper price than conventional textbooks. Complex images and concepts, such as molecular biology, can be illustrated in interactive, three-dimensional presentations, instead of traditional drawings or photographs on paper, to aid in understanding. A laptop computer, to which e-textbooks can be downloaded, weighs a fraction of several paper textbooks and occupies less space. Their use would address the growing concern about overweight backpacks for students of varying ages. Teachers could cut and paste curriculum text in a customized format for students. Assignments and homework could be posted on a server. Such a system would need little introduction or training for students, so many of whom are already media savvy and using online resources for learning-related activities.

There are drawbacks to using e-textbooks, however. The initial investment of computers and software can be costly. In some programs, graphics (such as maps, charts, graphs, and pies) might not be accessible. Compatibility of programs with other learning software might be a problem. However, despite these concerns, some experts predict that the sales of e-textbooks will net $3.2 billion in 2005, and will consist of 25 percent of all textbook sales by that time.

Electronic Performance Support Systems

Electronic Performance Support Systems, or EPSS, is another form of computer assisted instruction. Gloria Gery, an educational software expert in Tolland, Massachusetts, began developing EPSS in the early 1990s. The purpose of EPSS is to help automate a job. TurboTax is an example of an EPSS. Once the program is started, the user is prompted to answer a series of financial questions. When finished, the program computes the complete tax return for the user. The program can print out a copy of the results for the user, and if directed to do so, will even send an electronic copy to the Internal Revenue Service (IRS).

EPSS has found uses in many fields. Auto mechanics use an EPSS to diagnose car trouble. Travel agents make reservations with one. Cornerstone, an EPSS used by the NASD (a Wall Street self-regulatory organization) helps auditors do their jobs. The sale and leasing of cars is simplified with the help of an EPSS.

People often believe their jobs are too creative or complex for EPSS, but in many cases they are mistaken. In jobs that require human judgment, EPSS offers a series of alternatives to which the user can refer. As a result, employees can assume more complex job responsibilities after much shorter training periods and with significantly higher accuracy than would be likely with traditional training or job support structures. Hiring employees becomes cheaper. Because employees do not need to be so highly trained, the pool of applicants is much bigger, which is a benefit for employers. There is a downside to EPSS. The reduced need for better-educated individuals and shorter training periods could reduce the need for highly educated

ALTERNATIVE APPROACHES TO LEARNING

Learning management systems are also available that allow colleges and universities to construct their own courses for teaching non-traditional students. These include students who require flexible hours or live in distant locations. A professional team consisting of the subject matter expert (such as a faculty member), a curriculum expert, a graphics designer, and a programmer, usually works together to create these programs.

employees, resulting in lower salaries in many job categories. SEE ALSO EDUCATIONAL SOFTWARE; LIBRARY APPLICATIONS; LOGO.

Mary McIver Puthawala

Bibliography

Alexander, Steve. "Learning Curve—Uncertainty Surrounding Standards and Rising Costs Can Make Choosing a Learning Management System a Difficult Lesson." *InfoWorld* 23, no. 23 (2001): 59.

Sheppard, Robert. "March of the Laptops: Is Technology Overtaking the Classroom?" *MacLean's*, November 2, 1998: 86(1).

Windman, Russell. "Lessons Learned—eWeek Labs Grades Tools That Build Lessons for Distance Learners." *ZDNet; eWeek*, May 14, 2001: 28.

Internet Resources

"The IBM 1500: Historical Perspectives." University of Alberta Web Site. <www.quasar.ualberta.ca/EDIT572/572h3.html>

Computer Professional

As young people begin their search for a career, it is likely that many will consider one of the vast opportunities available in the computer industry. Skilled computer professionals are in steady demand, despite the normal fluctuations of the world economy.

Rise of the New Economy

At the beginning of the twenty-first century, widespread computerization of business, education, and entertainment meant that virtually all aspects of the global economy were dependent, in one way or another, on the fortunes of the computer industry. This effect was heightened during the late 1990s when the so-called "**dot.com**" market skyrocketed, boosting stock portfolios for investors worldwide. Young entrepreneurs backed with financing from **venture capitalists** created multi-million dollar Internet companies based on ideas that were often untested against traditional business standards of profit and loss projections. Stock prices soared as hopeful investors jumped at the chance to capitalize on the tremendous wealth being made as these start-up companies created the latest software and Internet products and services.

Soon it became clear that many, if not most, of these new economy companies would not become or remain profitable to their stockholders. When the standard measures of business success were applied to the high technology market, the entire U.S. economy began to feel the impact. High tech consulting firms went bankrupt. Telecommunications networks designed to support the once-growing demand for digital services collapsed overnight. News reports of layoffs in major computer industry companies became common. The future suddenly appeared less positive for "techies" who had come to expect high financial rewards in a short period of time. Economic analysts characterized this shift as a correction in the market; computer professionals considered it more of a disaster. However, the market for computer professionals remains strong, in part because every segment of the U.S. and world economy depends on fast, reliable computer

dot.com a common term used to describe an Internet-based commerical company or organization

venture capitalists persons or agencies that speculate by providing financial resources to enable product development, in the expectation of larger returns with product maturity

networks and equipment. Professionals are needed to create and maintain this infrastructure.

Choosing and Preparing for a Career

There is a need for people to design, build, connect, and maintain computers and computer networks; these jobs fall into the general category of hardware engineering. There is also a need for people who can conceptualize and create computer software; these jobs fall into the general category of computer programming. Within each broad type of computer-related work there are many specialized technical functions, as well as the kinds of industry support jobs common to other market segments, including administration, sales and marketing, and customer service and support. Computer professionals also include the men and women who teach and perform research in academic settings.

Education. Individuals interested in pursuing a career as a computer professional should generally plan to earn at least a four-year degree (bachelor's level) in computer science or computer engineering. Fluency in multiple computer programming languages is vital for anyone interested in software development; the more languages learned, the more valuable the prospective employee. A solid understanding of hardware infrastructure is important, as well, especially for those interested in network creation or administration.

Not all computer professionals have an academic background in computer science or engineering, however. Often, people with advanced degrees in business, education, or something as seemingly unrelated to the computer industry as music, art, journalism, or criminology will find a niche as a computer industry professional. These individuals may not be involved in the technical aspects of software development or network configuration. However, their expertise may help provide unique services such as computer training, Internet access company development, web site design, or the marketing of computer-based services to schools, governments, or nonprofit agencies.

Most American universities now offer a variety of academic programs that will prepare students to become computer professionals. Many well-known schools throughout the United States, such as the Massachusetts Institute of Technology (MIT), specialize in technology-related fields. There are also accredited certification programs available from industry giants such as Cisco Systems. As in all career fields, the selection of a training or preparatory program should be based on a match between student interests, strengths, and career goals, and the particular program and training options of any given school.

Hardware Engineers. Computer professionals who specialize in the hardware or **infrastructure** aspect of the computer industry are the ones who design, build, test, and improve the computers and networks that support the economy. From the design of a mouse to the building of a **supercomputer**, hardware engineers are needed to create the physical tools of the computer age. Some hardware engineers specialize in designing networks of computers. Others focus on creating computer peripherals to meet the unique requirements of special needs users. Hardware specialists

HOT HIGH TECH JOBS

As of 2002, one of the hottest high tech job prospects is in the field of bioinformatics. The discipline, which combines the fields of biology and computer science, seeks ways to improve medical advances using supercomputers, huge data depositories, and medical knowledge.

infrastructure the foundation or permanent installation necessary for a structure or system to operate

supercomputer a very high performance computer, usually comprised of many processors and used for modeling and simulation of complex phenomena, like meteorology

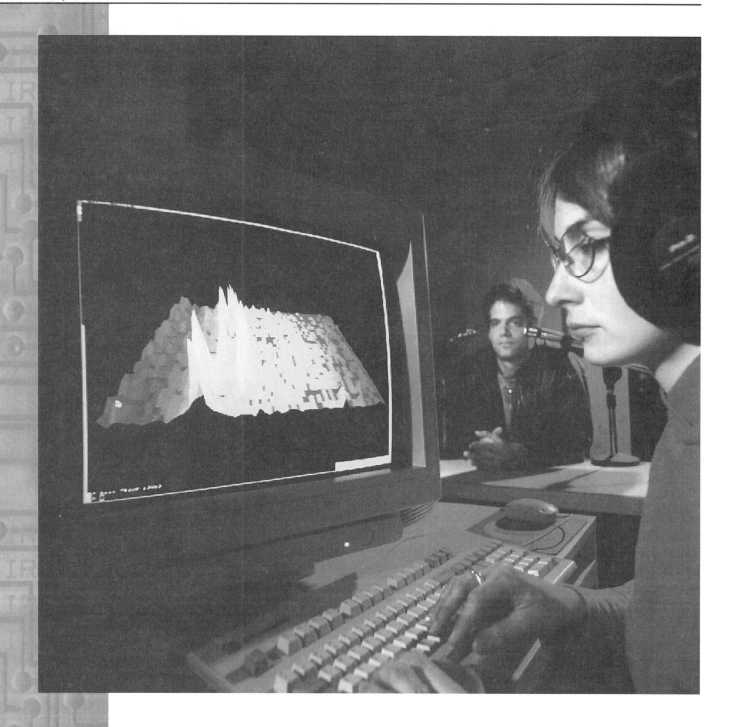

Career options for individuals comfortable with computer technologies are vast, ranging from systems development to jobs requiring expertise in specific applications.

are needed to repair and modify equipment. Computer hardware engineers need to understand the technical aspects of computer design and connection; ideally, they will also learn to understand how people use and interact with computers, as well, which can help them create better equipment.

Computer Programming Without software to operate the hardware, computer systems are useless. Computer programmers are charged with the duty of writing the code that creates user-friendly software. Programmers are responsible for conceiving, designing, and building software applications. Sometimes they work alone. Often, teams of programmers apply their skills in a shared effort to create complex software. Computer programmers need to work methodically and analytically. Many programmers specialize in writing software for particular business, education, or entertainment purposes; the most adept programming specialists learn that it is important to communicate with users about what they want their finished software to accomplish.

Jobs in the Computer Industry

In addition to the people who create the tools—hardware and software—that one calls computers, there are professionals whose job it is to help businesses figure out the most effective way to use these tools. Many companies now have something called an Information Technology (IT) department. Information technology specialists work with a company to identify the best combinations of hardware, software, and networking to meet the company's needs. In some cases this is done externally, on a consulting basis; in other companies this may be handled by in-house technology staff. The IT specialist must typically figure out how to use a company's limited resources to maintain a system of computer-based communications equipment from a vast array of vendors, always with an eye toward improving the firm's competitive edge in the market. Career paths for IT professionals start with entry-level positions and can lead to managerial and executive positions with titles such as information technology director, chief information officer, and chief technology officer.

Many other jobs are available for computer professionals with the right combination of technical and other skills. Since people need to learn to use their company's technology resources, from hardware to software, there is a steady need for educators and training personnel. Repair specialists who can troubleshoot hardware and software problems on very short notice are in high demand wherever there are complex networks to maintain. Software companies need knowledgeable personnel to staff their customer support departments and help personal computer owners fix their problems by phone or by e-mail. There will always be a place for creative thinkers who can create and fill market niches with specialized software and hardware products and services. SEE ALSO COMPUTER SCIENTISTS.

John Nau

Internet Resources

"Careers in Computer Science." *State University of New York Oswego Web Site.* <http://www.cs.oswego.edu/careers.html>

"Careers in Computer Science and Computer Engineering." *IEEE Computer Society Web Site.* <http://www.computer.org/education/careers.htm>

"DataMasters Salary Survey." *DataMasters IT Jobs, Resources, and Links.* <http://www.datamasters.com>

"Graduating Engineer and Computer Careers Online." CASS Communications, Inc. <http://www.graduatingengineer.com/>

Computer Supported Cooperative Work (CSCW)

Computer Supported Cooperative Work (CSCW) results from the connectivity provided by modern computers via **local area networks (LANs)**

local area networks (LANs) high speed computer networks that are designed for users who are located near each other

mainframe computers
large computers used by businesses and government agencies to process massive amounts of data; generally faster and more powerful than desktop computers but usually requiring specialized software

punched cards paper cards with punched holes which give instructions to a computer in order to encode program instructions and data

groupware a software technology common in client/server systems whereby many users can access and process data at the same time

teletype a machine that sends and receives telephonic signals

domain a region in which a particular element or object exists or has influence; (math) the inputs to a function or relation

or the Internet, that allows multiple users to work together. In the early days of computing during the 1950s and 1960s, **mainframe computers** executed business programs. They were given a stack of **punched cards**, processed for a while, and eventually printed out an answer on long strips of folded green computer paper. End users never even saw these machines. Only "operators" had access to the input and output devices. End users would usually hand a job request through a small window in the "computer center" to an operator, returning in a day or two to pick up the answer.

Then came the personal computer, or PC, which essentially did the same thing, except the computer center and the operators were no longer required. As a "personal" computer, this machine belonged to one individual, who no longer had to share processing time with others who also had access rights to the mainframe. Instead of punched cards and paper, keyboards and display screens became available. Ultimately WYSIWYG ("what you see is what you get") interfaces, such as Apple's Mac OS and the various releases of Microsoft Windows, became available, increasing the user's easy control of the machine's processes.

This focus on the solitary user changed with the development of the local area network (LAN), which allowed people to send e-mail around the office. It allowed people to access shared files and even to share applications. Chat and bulletin boards first appeared in these environments, and workflow programs and file servers started their lives on LANs. Many of these concepts have become the foundation for **groupware** and multi-user programs, as they have developed into the twenty-first century.

By 2002 the Internet boosted the idea of working together that was pioneered in the time of the LAN. One of the major influences for groupware and multi-user applications on the Internet was games. In particular, multi-user dungeons (MUDs) pioneered many of the concepts that are leveraged today for collaborative applications in business, research, communications, and other endeavors.

Computer Supported Cooperative Work (CSCW) draws on these concepts. The view of what a computer is changes with it. While early computers were mainly viewed as "tools," they were later also seen as "documents." A word processor, for example, turns the computer into a tool. The file that is created with the word processor exists eventually independently of the word processor. Still, it is "in the computer." The computer therefore also serves as a "document."

With the advent of LANs and the Internet, a third view of computers was introduced: the computer as communication device. Very much like a telephone or a **teletype**, the computer acts as the medium that transports messages. And although it is actually the network that transports the message, the computer is the terminal device, the access point to the communications network.

With these three perspectives on computers as tool, document, and communication device, one can start to look at the other issues that have an impact on groupware and multi-user systems.

Applications

CSCW and groupware can be categorized according to application **domain**. A meeting system used in education will differ from a meeting system used in a business context. Engineering tasks usually require different tools than administrative tasks. The following list of task and application domains will grow as new systems are built and applied to an ever-expanding set of domains:

- Engineering
- Administration
- Manufacturing
- Research and development
- Banking and insurance
- Logistics and warehousing
- Decision making
- Teaching and learning
- Authoring
- Drafting
- Entertainment
- Software engineering
- Project management
- Military planning and operations.

Technology

In order to build, deploy, and use groupware, a number of enabling technologies must be in place. Among the most important technologies for the design and implementation of CSCW systems are:

- Networks
- Connectivity
- Naming and name spaces
- Mail and other communication protocols
- Multimedia technologies
- Hypertext and hypermedia
- Video technologies
- **Cross-platform** development tools
- Large **bit mapped displays.**

Synchronous/Co-located Applications

One example of a CSCW system is a synchronous/co-located application. To support teams in negotiating, decision making, brainstorming, learning, and other activities, a number of systems have been built to enhance a meeting room. Examples of such *electronic meeting rooms* are the *Capture Lab* at Electronic Data Systems, the *Electronic Meeting Systems (EMS)* at the University of Arizona, a commercial system by IBM, and the CoLab at Xerox PARC (Palo Alto Research Center). These systems usually consist of a room with special furniture that can be rearranged. The furniture is also designed with the monitor under the surface of the desk. Users view the monitor

cross-platform pertaining to a program that can run on many different computer types (often called hardware platforms)

bit mapped displays computer displays that use a table of binary bits in memory to represent the image that is projected onto the screen

XEROX PARC'S COLAB

Short for "collaboration laboratory," the CoLab project was conducted at Xerox PARC between 1987 and 1992. In part, the project evaluated the difference between meetings held without computer technology and those held with high tech tools available. CoLab offered each participant a computer and included a main electronic white board on which notes, diagrams, and discussion ideas could be displayed.

Figure 1. Electronic meeting room setup.

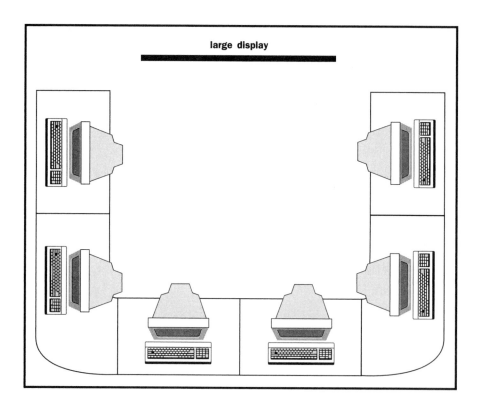

through a glass surface on the desk, thus having an unobstructed view of other participants. The tables either form a circle or a semi-circle. Sometimes a large bitmapped device is used instead of the whiteboard or chalkboard. All devices are connected by a LAN. Special software can be written to take advantage of a configuration such as in Figure 1.

The motivation to create such meeting rooms is rather obvious: Media such as overheads and flip charts influence the way people communicate and how well they remember what was said in meetings.

Meetings can be classified along their functions: exploration, information sharing, brainstorming, problem solving, decision making, morale building, negotiating, planning, or social structuring. This diversity creates a wide range of design issues concerning the layout of the room, the capability of the software, the performance of the hardware, the selection of user interfaces, and many others. SEE ALSO COMPUTER PROFESSIONAL; OFFICE AUTOMATION SYSTEMS.

Dirk E. Mahling

Bibliography

Haring-Smith, Tori. *An Introduction to Collaborative Learning.* New York: Harper-Collins College Publications, 1993.

Weber, Aaron, and Scott Weber. *The Book of Evolution: Groupware for Linux Users.* San Francisco: No Starch Press, 2001.

Computerized Manufacturing

Computerization aids in the design of products, their fabrication, and the planning of manufacturing processes. Computerization of manufacturing began with the advent of computers after World War II, mainly in military-related applications. Now it is common in many commercial applications as well. The aerospace, automobile, chemical, electronics, and biomedical industries are among many that rely on computerized manufacturing.

Computer-Aided Design

In contemporary applications of computerized manufacturing, the process often begins with computer-aided design, more commonly known as CAD. In CAD, instead of drawing with pencils and a few drafting tools on paper, an engineer uses lines and curves stored in computer memory to produce a drawing that appears on a screen. The finished drawing can also be stored in computer memory.

Sometimes it is not faster to produce a drawing with CAD than it is to draw it by hand, especially when the drawing is in its initial stage. Why use CAD then? There are several advantages. First, a CAD program allows an engineer to "copy and paste" portions of drawing, just as text can be manipulated in word processing, moving them and using them in as many locations on the screen as necessary. Secondly, just as changing numeric values in a spreadsheet cell alters the rest of the spreadsheet accordingly, an engineer can make size changes to a drawing without using pencil and eraser. Another advantage to using CAD even for preliminary drafts is that an engineer can recall previously drawn components from computer memory and use them in the drawing. Finally, CAD allows an engineer to transform a two-dimensional sketch into one that appears to be three-dimensional, and to rotate the image on the screen to evaluate it from different angles. For these reasons, using a CAD program is much more efficient than drawing with pencil on paper.

Computer-Aided Engineering

CAD drawings can be incorporated into a computer-aided engineering (CAE) process. In CAE many hypothetical questions about material behavior can be answered by means of a computerized mechanical analysis of the effect of conditions such as stresses and **deformations**. CAE also uses **visualization** techniques such as computer animation to simulate a product's performance under various loads.

Instead of building expensive **prototypes**, engineers can use CAE software to create numerous computer simulations that help them determine how machines and their parts will behave in different circumstances. CAE is used in many applications, but it is especially important in the aerospace and automobile industries where weight reduction is always a highly sought-after goal of engineering.

Computer-Aided Manufacturing

After the design and engineering processes are complete, manufacturing involves materials handling and product fabrication. These processes can also be automated by computerized technologies. In technical literature, these technologies are usually referred to as CAM, which is an acronym for computer-aided manufacturing. When computer-aided manufacturing also uses computer-aided design, this is referred to as CAD/CAM.

deformations mechanical systems where a structure is physically misshapen, e.g., dented

visualization a technique whereby complex systems are portrayed in a meaningful way using sophisticated computer graphics systems; e.g., chemical molecules

prototypes working models or experimental investigations of proposed systems under development

Prior to the computerization of complex machinery such as this textile mill, each of the steps required to make thicker yarns from the fine threads would have been supervised by a human. Allowing a computer system to "run" this mill makes the process of yarn production more efficient.

embedded computers computers that do not have human user oriented input/output devices; they are directly contained within other machines

Computerized materials handling focuses on automated storage and retrieval systems. These systems are automated warehouses where materials are stored on racks. The location of each stored material is registered in a database. Materials can be retrieved by conveyors, monorails, or computerized carts. The database keeps a continuous inventory of materials and their availability.

Product Fabrication

Fabrication of products and their components is automated by means of flexible manufacturing systems, robots, and **embedded computers**. The prevailing tendency in manufacturing is to shorten the time between conception of an idea and creation of a finished product so the consumer will get it as quickly as possible. Flexible manufacturing systems help achieve this goal. They often produce parts in small batches, just as they are needed for the rest of the manufacturing process.

Flexible Manufacturing Systems. A flexible manufacturing system comprises equipment workstations connected by parts delivery routes. Parts are directed along those routes and are treated at the workstations. Each batch of parts might follow a different set of routes and workstations, according to production needs. In this way a manufacturing enterprise can quickly respond to ever-changing market demands and be ahead of the competition.

Delivery routes may employ motorized carts on tracks, or they may use motorized carts that follow wires embedded in the shop floor. Equipment workstations are the islands along delivery routes where tools for parts fabrication, assembly, and inspection are located. Most of those tools are automated and can be reprogrammed if the need arises. Each workstation is usually dedicated to the treatment of groups of similar parts.

Robots.   Another approach to the automation of production is the use of industrial robots. Contrary to popular early images of robots, industrial robots do not and should not look like humans. Their main features are multifunctionality and reprogrammability. Paint-spraying robots in the automobile industry do not look at all human, but they help humans by doing their work in an environment that is hostile to human health.

Robots are also employed in the spot welding of automobile bodies. Because of the heat and bright light involved in spot welding, it is difficult for humans to perform this task with consistent quality. Not only is the job adaptable to robotics, it is better suited to computerization than to human performance. Other manufacturing processes suited to the multifunctionality of robots include the automated loading and unloading of heavy objects, the application of adhesives, the assembly of aircraft parts especially with rivets, the drilling and fastening of metal panels, and the sanding of missile wings, to name just a few.

The ability to reprogram a robot is an important advantage of using robots over other types of automated manufacturing equipment. A robot is made up of a controller, a manipulator, and sensors. The controller is a device through which a robot is programmed. Robots employ programs of varying complexity, from programs with multiple "if . . . then" conditions to **artificial intelligence (AI)**. An example of artificial intelligence is a program based on an expert system. Such a system is usually construed by gathering information from human experts. Out of this information, a program is developed. It encodes a set of rules mimicking human intuition. The robot is programmed to act according to this set of rules.

The robot's manipulator usually comprises electric, hydraulic, or **pneumatic** mechanisms that move an industrial robot's arms. An arm has a number of joints that determine its capability to fulfill the numerous functions the robot is designed to perform.

Not all robots are equipped with sensors, but the most versatile are. Of course, robots with sensors usually are much more expensive than those without. Sensors vary depending on tasks. If an industrial robot is used for inspection, its sensors may detect flaws in manufactured parts. A robot used to assemble electronic circuit boards is usually equipped with sensors that enable it to put components into proper places on the board.

Embedded computers are extensively used in many manufacturing applications, especially for the control of production processes. The most advanced of them are linked to sensors and have some kind of networking capability. They might receive remote commands and send this information to enterprise management system databases.

Computer-Aided Process Planning (CAPP)

Detailed planning is needed in order to implement a successful computerized manufacturing project. Once a design is finalized, an engineer prepares a detailed process plan. The plan comprises step-by-step instructions that

---

MULTIFUNCTIONALITY

What does multifunctionality mean? It means a robot can fulfill as many tasks as possible within the scope of its operation. For example, spray painting is a hazardous and monotonous job. It requires the consistent ability to follow various shapes and cover them with numerous protection layers. Using a paint-spraying robot reduces health risks to human beings, and it also provides a higher level of repetitive consistency than human beings can achieve.

artificial intelligence (AI) a branch of computer science dealing with creating computer hardware and software to mimic the way people think and perform practical tasks

pneumatic powered by pressurized air, supplied through tubes or pipes

include how to set up equipment, how to make a part, and last but not least, how to assure quality by inspecting the part after it is made. Routings between equipment workstations must also be determined. The plan is usually supplemented with drawings of the tools necessary to make the part and detailed instructions about how to operate the tools. Process planning is a tedious and time-consuming job. In a manufacturing environment, where it is always desirable to reduce time from idea to finished product, the computer-aided process planning (CAPP) can speed up the planning process and help ward off the competition.

There are two approaches to computer-aided process planning: variant and generative. The variant CAPP system is based on parts classification. As in biological classification, parts to be manufactured are combined into families. Parts that belong to a certain family have similar shapes, attributes, and parameters. They should also have similar production processes. This assumption is true in the majority of cases. The determination of which family a new part belongs to is made either manually by an engineer or by an appropriate artificial intelligence method. Once the family is established, a generic process description can be pulled from the program's database and an engineer may start modifying it to comply with the actual characteristics of the part.

One drawback of the variant CAPP is that the generic family process may not be suitable for a particular new part. The generative CAPP system does not have this drawback because it is based on an entirely different principle than variant CAPP. Instead of retrieving a generic family process and editing it, a process plan is created from scratch by using a set of decision rules that define the selection of proper operations, the sequence of operations, the treatments, the tools, and the delivery routes to be used in creating the part.

Computer Integrated Manufacturing (CIM)

The most advanced computerized manufacturing system is called Computer Integrated Manufacturing, or CIM. The goal of CIM is to combine **synergistically** all the computerized manufacturing technologies described earlier. At a slightly less comprehensive level, there are many manufacturing enterprises that include islands of automation—materials handling, for example—as well as manufacturing processes that are not automated. Integration of those islands into one system is another approach to CIM.

While integrating computerized manufacturing technologies into CIM, it is important to keep in mind that an enterprise might use different brands of equipment, process controllers, conveyors, robots, and other components. An engineer should always exercise common sense and evaluate profits versus costs while making a decision about what level of computerized manufacturing automation is appropriate in each particular case. SEE ALSO CHIP MANUFACTURING; IMAGE ANALYSIS: MEDICINE; PROCESS CONTROL; ROBOTICS; ROBOTS.

Robert Lembersky

synergistically relating to synergism, which is the phenomenon whereby the action of a group of elements is greater than their individual actions

Bibliography

Chang, Tien-Chien, et al. *Computer-Aided Manufacturing.* Upper Saddle River, NJ: Prentice Hall, 1997.

Owen, A. E. *Flexible Assembly Systems: Assembly by Robots and Computerized Integrated Systems.* New York: Plenum Press, 1984.

Rembold, U., B.O. Nnaji, and A. Sorr. *Computer Integrated Manufacturing and Engineering.* Reading, MA: Addison-Wesley, 1993.

Rietman, Edward A., and Ralph E. Smith. *Intelligent Manufacturing: Computerized Factories for the 21st Century.* Boca Raton, FL: CRC Press, 1998.

Singh, Nanua. *Systems Approach to Computer-Integrated Design and Manufacturing.* New York: John Wiley & Sons, 1995.

Zhang, Hong-Chao, and Leo Alting. *Computerized Manufacturing Process Planning Systems.* New York: Chapman & Hall, 1994.

Cormack, Allan
1924–1998

Hounsfield, Godfrey Newbold
1919–

Developers of Computer-Assisted Tomography

Allan McLeod Cormack and Godfrey Newbold Hounsfield won the Nobel Prize in physiology or medicine in 1979 for their work in the development of **computer-assisted tomography** (CAT).

Allan Cormack

Allan Cormack was born in Johannesburg, South Africa, in 1924. His parents had emigrated from Scotland to South Africa shortly before World War I (1914–1918); his father was a civil servant, who worked as an engineer for the post office. The family migrated through South Africa until 1936, when they settled in Cape Town after the death of Cormack's father. Cormack attended the Rondebosch Boys High School in Cape Town, and subsequently received both bachelor's and master's degrees in physics from the University of Cape Town. However, he initially studied electrical engineering in a department headed by B. L. Goodlet, who believed that engineers needed a good grounding in physics and math. Cormack was already interested in these subjects, having earlier studied astronomy, a field which requires a solid background in physics and math. Thus, he eventually abandoned engineering for physics.

After obtaining his degrees at Cape Town, he went to St. John's College, Cambridge, England, as a research student and worked in the Cavendish Laboratory under Professor Otto Frisch (1904–1979), a renowned physicist. Frisch, along with his aunt Lise Meitner, had performed fundamental work in the area of nuclear fission. Cormack later worked on problems connected with Helium-6 (He-6, Helium of atomic weight 6).

Cormack later married Barbara Seavey, an American, whom he had met at a quantum dynamics lecture. Cormack sought a teaching position in the physics department at the University of Cape Town. Offered a position as lecturer, Cormack returned to Cape Town with his wife in 1950. His first sabbatical, however, was spent at Harvard University, where he worked on the team connected with the **Harvard Cyclotron**. During his stay at

computer-assisted tomography the use of computers in assisting with the management of X-ray images

Harvard Cyclotron a specialized machine (cyclotron) developed in 1948 at Harvard University; it is used to carry out experiments in sub-atomic physics and medicine

Allan Cormack.

Harvard, Cormack was offered a position in the physics department at Tufts University, which he accepted in 1957, remaining there for the duration of his career. Having officially retired in 1995, Cormack continued working at Tufts.

While in Cape Town in the 1950s, Cormack also served as a medical physicist in the department of radiology at Groote Schuur Hospital. It was there that he began to think about the possibility of using X rays for diagnostic purposes, particularly in the treatment of cancer patients. X rays are absorbed by dense material, such as bone, hence obscuring the view of the tissue in question. Reasoning that multiple X rays projected at different angles, but in a single plane, would yield a more detailed image, he developed a set of equations to describe the process. However, his findings, published in 1963 and 1964 in the *Journal of Applied Physics*, went largely unnoticed.

Godfrey Hounsfield

Godfrey Hounsfield was born on August 28, 1919, in Newark, Nottinghamshire, England, and raised on a farm. He attributed his interest in mechanical and electrical gadgets, especially experimentation, to his days and experiences on the farm, uncluttered by the distractions of a "larger" and "busier" civilization. He suggested that this was at the expense of his more formal schooling at Magnus Grammar School in Newark, where he claimed to respond only to math and physics with any "moderate" enthusiasm. He joined the Royal Air Force (RAF) as a volunteer reservist at the outbreak of World War II (1939–1945), and became interested in radio and then **radar**. He became a radar mechanic instructor and was moved to the Royal College of Science in South Kensington and then to the Cranwell Radar School.

Godfrey Hounsfield.

After the war, one of his superiors, Air Vice-Marshall Cassidy obtained a grant for him to attend the Faraday House Electrical Engineering College in London, where Hounsfield earned a diploma. In 1951 Hounsfield joined the staff of EMI, Ltd., in Middlesex, England, where he worked on radar and guided weapons. He later became interested in computers, creating drums and tape decks from scratch, experimenting with core memory, and, in 1958, leading a design team to construct the first all-transistor computer built in Great Britain, the EMIDEC 1100.

When this work was finished, he transferred to EMI Central Research Laboratories in Hayes. It was there that he became interested in **pattern recognition**. Through this interest in pattern recognition, he happened upon the work that would eventually lead to computerized tomography.

Hounsfield got the initial idea in 1967, after which he carried on experimentation, finally developing and designing several **prototypes**, some of which went into production. EMI introduced the first commercial scanner in 1972. In this period, 1970 to 1972, Cormack became aware of the developments in CT-scanning and became, once again, more involved in these problems.

Both Cormack and Hounsfield developed interests in biology late in their careers. Cormack died in 1998; Hounsfield continued to work and live in Great Britain. The first heart transplant was performed at Groote Schuur Hospital by Dr. Christiaan Barnard in 1967. This is, of course, where

Cormack worked. Cormack and Hounsfield had worked independently in the same area, and were both honored for the body of their work.

Hounsfield also won the Gardiner Foundation Award for achievement in biomedical research in 1976, and the Lasker Award for research in the biological sciences in 1975. He was knighted in 1981. The two scientists met for the first time in Stockholm, as Nobel Prize laureates. SEE ALSO GRAPHIC DEVICES; IMAGE ANALYSIS: MEDICINE; MEDICAL SYSTEMS.

Roger R. Flynn

Internet Resources

Nobel e-Museum. <http://www.nobel.se>

> **CAT EXPLAINED**
>
> Computer-assisted tomography is a means of taking X-rays of difficult to observe portions of the body. This is achieved by taking multiple images from various angles and then combining the results.

Cray, Seymour

American Computer Designer
1925–1996

Seymour Cray, widely regarded as the father of **supercomputers**, was born in Chippewa Falls, Wisconsin, on September 28, 1925. He died on October 5, 1996, after a car accident. A man of unerring focus, Cray maintained a single goal throughout his lifetime—to build the fastest computer possible.

After obtaining a bachelor's degree in electrical engineering and a master's degree in applied mathematics from the University of Minnesota, Cray started his career with Engineering Research Associates, which became Remington Rand, then Sperry Rand. Here Cray designed his first computer, the ERA 1101. He also helped design the UNIVAC (Universal Automatic Computer) 1103. When the UNIVAC shifted its focus away from supercomputers, Cray did not. Instead, he left to start Control Data Corporation (CDC), leading the first design team to abandon **vacuum tubes** and produce the first commercial **transistor**-based computer, the CDC 1604, in 1958.

Within a few years, Cray decided that the administrative duties associated with running a successful business interfered with his concentration on computer design. With CDC's blessing, he left for home and solitude in Chippewa Falls. CDC built Cray's laboratory close to his home. His time there proved productive, and in 1963, CDC released the Cray-designed CDC 6600. To reduce heat build-up in the compact unit, Cray installed a **freon** cooling system inside the computer. This machine was not only three times faster than its IBM counterpart, but was also smaller and a bargain at $7.5 million each. Customers for the 6600 included the U.S. Atomic Energy Commission, which used it to to study thermonuclear explosions, and the U.S. Weather Bureau, which used it to to assist in weather predictions.

In 1969 CDC released the Cray-designed 7600, which could perform twenty megaflops, or twenty million calculations (**floating point operations** or FLOPS) per second. Many believe the 7600 was the first supercomputer.

When CDC declined to market Cray's next machine (the 8600), instead expanding into other commercial ventures, Cray again chose to focus on supercomputer design. He started Cray Research in 1972. The Cray 1,

supercomputers very high performance computers, usually comprised of many processors and used for modeling and simulation of complex phenomena, like meteorology

vacuum tubes electronic devices constructed of sealed glass tubes containing metal elements in a vacuum; used to control electrical signals

transistor a contraction of TRANSfer resISTOR; a semiconductor device which has three terminals; can be used for switching and amplifying electrical signals

freon hydrocarbon-based gases used as refrigerants and as pressurants in aerosols

floating point operations numerical operations involving real numbers where in achieving a result the number of digits to the left or right of the decimal point can change

MORE POWER

The evolution of supercomputers has continued along divergent paths. Less than five years after Cray's death in 1996, Apple Computer's G4 series of supercomputers became the first desktop systems to deliver a sustained performance of more than one gigaflop, with a theoretical peak performance of 5.3 gigaflops. The G4 Cube takes up less than eight square inches of desk space, and costs less than $2,000. By 2001, the world's most powerful supercomputers, from companies like Cray, Inc. and NEC, could deal with trillions of calculations per second and MPPs (massively parallel processors). They cost millions.

vector processing an approach to computing machine architecture that involves the manipulation of vectors (sequences of numbers) in single steps, rather than one number at a time

scalar processor a processor designed for high-speed computation of scalar values

integrated circuits circuits with the transistors, resistors, and other circuit elements etched into the surface of single chips of semiconducting material, usually silicon

gallium arsenide a chemical used in the production of semiconductor devices; chemical symbol GaAs

silicon a chemical element with symbol Si; the most abundant element in the Earth's crust and the most commonly used semiconductor material

released in 1976, was the first computer to master successfully **vector processing** and at the time was the fastest **scalar processor** in the world. This single-processor, 160 megaflop computer had 1 million, 64-bit words of central memory, and used three types of **integrated circuits**. The computer itself was an 8 × 6 foot (about 2.4 × 1.8 meter) cylindrical structure. With a maximum wire length of 4 feet (1.2 meters), it still required a total of 60 miles (18.3 meters) of wire. Each unit cost $8.8 million. Cray Research went public in 1976, a month before its first sale (to Los Alamos National Laboratories in New Mexico). The sale of stock raised $10 million, helping the company to survive.

By 1984 Cray Research owned 70 percent of the supercomputer market. Cray himself was worth $17 million. In November of 1981, Cray resigned as CEO of Cray Research to become an independent contractor. Again, he sought solitude to build what he called "simple, dumb things." While he worked on the Cray 2, Cray Research, led by Steve Chen, revised the Cray 1. Chen's resultant Cray X-MP was the first multi-processing computer, able to perform 500 megaflops. The resultant rivalry between Cray and Chen eventually led to Cray's departure from the company in 1989. Cray then founded Cray Computer Corporation of Colorado Springs.

Cray wanted the Cray 2 to be four to six times more powerful than the Cray 1. When finished in 1985 with four processors, the Cray 2 doubled that expectation. This supercomputer had the largest internal memory capacity of any computer (two million bytes) and 256 million words of central memory. It could perform 1.2 gigaflops (or 1.2 million FLOPS per second). Cray fit the entire structure in a C-shaped cabinet 53 inches (136 centimeters) across and 45 inches (115 centimeters) high. To diffuse heat, he immersed the circuits in the coolant Fluorinert. Its cost was $17.6 million. What the Cray 2 accomplished in one second had taken a year to accomplish by hand in 1952. This computer was used to study intense magnetic fields associated with fusion reactors and to help design heat shields for space exploration.

In 1985 Cray began work on the Cray 3, using 16 processors. This machine was based on **gallium arsenide** instead of **silicon**, but the design was eventually dropped due to its high development cost. He then began work on the Cray 4, which would have had 64 processors. This project, too, was dropped. Cray Computer filed for bankruptcy protection in 1995.

Still, Cray was convinced that he could design a high performance, low cost system. By the time of his sudden death in 1996, he had established another new company, SRC Computers, toward this goal.

Two factors are cited in the decline of the supercomputer market. First, competition with cheaper and increasingly powerful microprocessors, and the ability for minicomputers to be networked, helped reduce the demand for very expensive machines. Second, with the end of the "Cold War," military budgets were slashed. New supercomputers for military use were no longer a practical consideration, reducing the already exclusive market. SEE ALSO MINICOMPUTERS; PHYSICS; SUPERCOMPUTERS.

Mary McIver Puthawala

Bibliography

Markoff, John. "Seymour Cray, Computer Industry Pioneer and Father of the Supercomputer, Dies at 71." *New York Times*, October, 6, 1996, p. 1.

Slater, Robert. "Seymour Cray: The Hermit of Chippewa Falls and His Simple, 'Dumb Things.'" In *Portraits in Silicon.* Cambridge, MA: MIT Press, 1987.

Internet Resources

Breckenridge, Charles W. "A Tribute to Seymour Cray, SRC Computers, Inc." <http://cgl.ucsf.edu/home/tef/cray/tribute.html>

A History of Cray. Cray Inc. <http://www.cray.com/company/>

"Power Mac G4 Cube." Apple Computer, Inc. <http://www.apple.com/powermaccube/>

Data Processing

Everyone is familiar with the term "word processing," but computers were really developed for "data processing"—the organization and manipulation of large amounts of numeric data, or in computer jargon, "number crunching." Some examples of data processing are calculation of satellite orbits, weather forecasting, statistical analyses, and in a more practical sense, business applications such as accounting, payroll, and billing.

Since the beginning of time people have sought ways to help in the computing, handling, merging, and sorting of numeric data. Think of all the labor that Bob Cratchit performed when keeping track of Ebenezer Scrooge's figures and accounts (in Charles Dickens' *A Christmas Carol*). Certainly Cratchit wished for an easier approach and undoubtedly Mr. Scrooge longed for a more accurate method to keep track of his accounts.

The story of the development of the computer reveals that for centuries people were creating and utilizing various mechanical devices to simplify the calculation and processing of numeric data. Perhaps one of the most relevant occurrences in the development of the computer was the work done by American engineer Herman Hollerith in 1889. In seeking to develop an easier and quicker method to count the U.S. Census, he decided to use **punched cards** to record the data and then use the cards as input into a calculating machine designed to tabulate the data. The technique worked and Hollerith eventually founded the Tabulating Machine Company. In the 1920s, this company became the IBM (International Business Machines) Corporation.

Another important phase in the computer's development also involved seeking a simpler solution for calculations involving large amounts of numeric data. During World War II, the accurate targeting of large artillery guns required frequent solutions of many complex mathematical formulae. The first all-electronic digital computer was developed to produce such calculations. The ENIAC did eventually lead to the development of the UNIVAC (Universal Automatic Calculator) series of computers that for many years rivaled those produced by IBM in the field of data processing.

Subsequently, computers have been the mainstay of data processing, particularly for the business world where they long ago replaced tabulating machines. Computers now allow for the automation of functions such as payroll and billing that previously required an army of clerks and a room full of filing cabinets. Indeed the data processing needs of the business world were as influential in the development of computer technology as were the government's need for accurate census enumeration and the military need for faster ballistic trajectory calculations.

punched cards paper cards with punched holes which give instructions to a computer in order to encode program instructions and data; now obsolete

THE ENIAC

The Electronic Numerical Integrator and Computer (ENIAC) was developed by J. Presper Eckert Jr. and John Mauchly. It was first used in ballistics testing for the military following World War II. The huge ENIAC was nothing like a personal computer as it weighed about thirty tons and contained about 18,000 vacuum tubes.

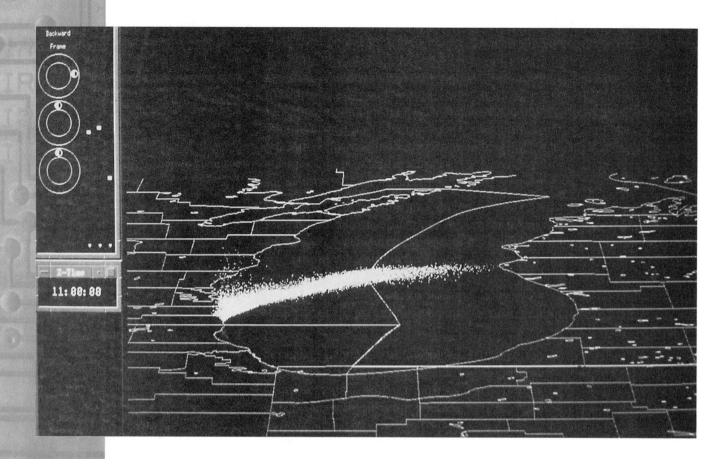

A computer's ability to store and manipulate large amounts of data helps humans to predict weather fluctuations. Here, accumulated data on a toxic gas cloud resulted in a prediction of where the cloud would impact Earth and enabled visual representation of the cloud's position.

relational database a collection of records that permits logical and business relationships to be developed between themselves and their contents

One of the most significant developments in data processing that came about in response to business needs was computer data storage and retrieval, or databases and database management systems. A database is an organized collection of logically related data, which can be shared by different computer programs known as application programs. A database management system (DBMS) is a computer program that creates, maintains, and accesses the database. The database approach has many advantages over simply storing data directly in computer programs. Database systems originated in the late 1950s and early 1960s, largely by research and development personnel at IBM in response to the needs of the business community. Today, one of the most popular database and program combinations is the **relational database** and the relational database management system (RDBMS).

With today's personal computers, many data processing applications developed for business use are now routinely available to everyone. Some examples include spreadsheets, database programs, and personal finance software. Although they can be used in other ways, spreadsheets were developed for accounting and are basically automated ledger books. They utilize columns and rows to display numbers and text, and allow calculations to be performed on the data. Some typical software packages include Excel, Lotus 1-2-3, and QuatroPro. Database and database management systems are valuable data processing tools. Oracle, MySQL, and Access are database programs readily available today. Personal finance software such as Quicken or Money can help people manage money and budgets as well as aid in calculating taxes.

Data processing is a vital function of business and personal computers, and the desire to find easier ways to handle large amounts of numeric data was one of the major driving forces in the development of the digital computer. Indeed, numeric calculations are the backbone of computer operations since all operations are based on binary digits (0,1), or simple numbers. Consequently even when an application is functioning as a "word processor," or a user is playing games, the computer is, in fact, doing data processing. SEE ALSO ABACUS; HOLLERITH, HERMAN; OFFICE AUTOMATION SYSTEMS; TABULATING MACHINES.

Robert D. Regan

Bibliography

Austrian, Geoffrey D. *Herman Hollerith: Forgotten Giant of Information Processing.* New York: Columbia University Press, 1982.

McCartney, Scott. *ENIAC: The Triumphs and Tragedies of the World's First Computer.* New York: Walker, 1999.

Data Visualization

"A picture is worth 1,000 words." Data visualization is based on this old adage, pointing out the value of displaying quantitative information as images or graphs. The idea is to convey the meaning of the data in a simple and intuitive manner. This is achieved by mapping quantity into geometric attributes, length, area, color, symbols, positions, curves, or other visual cues. Common graphs are *histograms* or *bar charts*, displaying quantity as length; *pie charts* for presenting parts of a whole; *time series*, which show the development of a variable over time; and *scatterplots* showing the relationships between two variables by marking pairing quantities. These graphs are abstract, but use real-world properties to support intuitive understanding. A pie diagram makes associations to bakery goods, time series to mountains and valleys, and scatterplots may be discussed using terms such as position, closeness, distance, groups, and outliers or individuals.

The physical connection is more direct in maps, where the information space itself is a real-world representation. Maps are an ideal information space for displaying any type of geographically based data, using concrete or abstract symbols. Depths and heights may be converted into color, for example, on a scale from dark blue, to shades of greens, to dark brown to symbolize the highest mountains. Other geographical data may be presented in different layers on the same map, as when lines represent borders, arrows visualize winds and currents, and symbols show the presence of hospitals or churches. More abstract data can be displayed by positioning pie and bar charts on the map or by using color-coding or shading of areas.

Although the first geographical maps were drawn on clay tablets more than 5,000 years ago, data maps and other visualizations were first created in the seventeenth century. With a few exceptions, such as seismograms from earthquake detectors and electrocardiograms from heart monitors, the graphs had to be made by hand, and handled separately from text through the printing process. This changed with the advent of the computer, which made it easy to collect and organize large amounts of data, to create graphs automatically through spreadsheet programs, and to integrate text and

---

WHAT IS A HISTOGRAM?

A histogram reveals statistics in the form of a bar graph. It is used to indicate variations in the topic being studied. Histograms can provide data on the success or failure of a product, process, or procedure. For example, by studying the sales revenue of a new computer system over the course of several years via a histogram, the manufacturer can determine the success of the product.

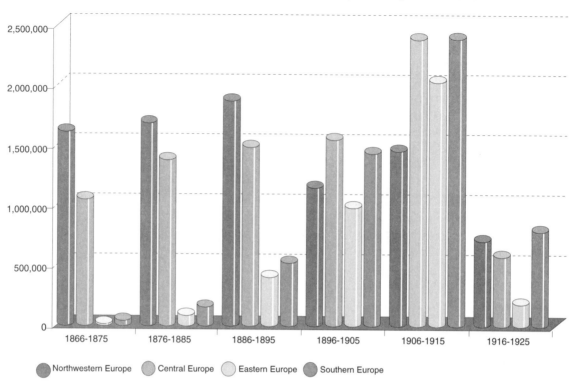

TOTAL EUROPEAN IMMIGRATION TO THE U.S., 1866—1925

● Northwestern Europe ● Central Europe ● Eastern Europe ● Southern Europe

Source: Historical Statistics of the United States, Series C-89-119.

Graphs, like this one charting the total European immigration to the United States from 1866 to 1925, provide a shorthand method for analyzing large amounts of related data.

filter queries queries used to select subsets from a data collection, e.g., all documents with a creation date later than 01/01/2000

graphics in modern word processing software. With laser printers, copying machines, and offset technology, graphics can be printed as easily as text. Data visualization has therefore become an important part of many documents, whether a student paper, scientific journal, or newspaper.

For online presentations, it is possible to create dynamic visualizations. Here the user may set up **filter queries** that select the data to be displayed, choose display methodology, select values to be presented on different axes, and so on. The most advanced systems may also present simulations, showing how data sets change over time. In online systems the visualization may act as an interface to an underlying database, for example by letting the user retrieve an object by clicking on its representation on the display.

Visualizing More than Two Dimensions

Most common visualization techniques are based on one or two variables, but different techniques can be used to visualize higher dimensions. For instance, shadowing techniques may give depth to the display, adding a third axis, or the user may be able to rotate a multidimensional display, looking at it from different viewpoints. VIBE (Visual Information Browsing Environment), an experimental system, uses a different approach based on relative position of data objects with regard to a user-defined visualization space. The metaphor behind this system is a bookshelf, for example where books on geography may be stacked to the left, books on history to the right. A book on historical geography may then naturally be inserted in the middle.

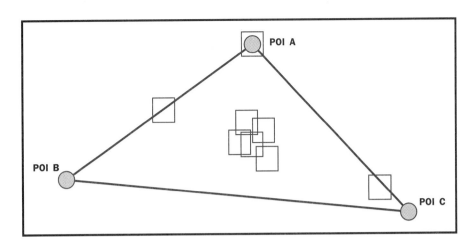

Figure 1. VIBE display space with three POIs.

A VIBE display space is shown in the accompanying figure. It is defined by three POIs (Points Of Interest), shown by circles in the diagram. Data objects are represented as rectangles and will be positioned according to the score they have on each POI. For example, an object that gets a score on A only, will be positioned on top of A; an object that gets a score on A and B, but a zero score on C is positioned between A and B, closest to the POI with the highest score; an object that get a similar score on all three POIs will be positioned in the middle of the space. The coordinates for the documents are calculated as an average of the POI coordinates, weighted by the POI scores. See Figure 1 above.

VIBE works with any type of data. A manufacturer, for example, may use VIBE to display its products in a space defined by POIs such as a price, weight, or volume, while a student may wish to present readings in a space with POIs defined by terms such as "history" or "geography." In the latter case, a function will be needed to map the concept into a numerical score, which may be as simple as counting the frequency of the POI terms within each document. VIBE allows for any number of POIs in a multidimensional display. However, with more than three POIs, the display may become ambiguous, and the user may need to assign colors to POIs or move POIs around to see the correlation between the objects. An advantage with visualization over statistical methods is that all data objects will be shown. VIBE has been used with as many as several thousand objects. The display may then show clusters, positions where most of the objects fall, but still be able to present icons for individual data objects.

Pitfalls with Visual Displays

A picture does not always say more than 1,000 words! Graphs may use so many visual effects that they become confusing for the reader, hiding the meaning of the data. Ideally, the size of the effect shown in the graphic should be similar to the size of the effect in the data. Typical distortions are found in time series of monetary data, where values are not adjusted for inflation or where a special scale is not made apparent to the reader. In a three-dimensional pie chart, the sector in front may look bigger than the one in the back, even if the quantities are identical. It is interesting to see that publications that take accuracy very seriously often fail in their graphics. In addition to controlling the effects of the graphic, it is important to consider if a graphic is needed at all! A few numbers may often be presented better directly in the text or as a table than in a pie chart. SEE ALSO DATABASE MANAGEMENT SOFTWARE; IMAGE ANALYSIS: MEDICINE; SCIENTIFIC VISUALIZATION.

Kai A. Olsen

Bibliography

Kraak, Menno-Jan, et al. *Cartography: Visualization of Spatial Data.* Boston: Addison-Wesley, 1996.

Korfhage, Robert R. *Information Storage and Retrieval.* New York: Wiley Computer Publishing, 1997.

Morse, E. L., M. Lewis, and K. A. Olsen. "Evaluating Visualizations: Using a Taxonomic Guide." *International Journal of Human-Computer Studies* 53 (2000): 637–662.

Tufte, Edward R. *The Visual Display of Quantitative Information.* Cheshire, CT: Graphics Press, 1992.

Database Management Software

Databases are software applications designed to store and retrieve information. Databases have long been employed as a vital tool by government and business to store, organize, and locate information. Modern database management systems are complex software applications that combine information from discrete sources, allowing information to be quickly located and displayed to the user. Perhaps the most elementary example of a database is a simple list of names and their associated phone numbers.

Databases are used for problem solving by all types and sizes of organizations, as well as by consumers, often also referred to as end users. Businesses commonly employ electronic databases to store and retrieve lists of customer names, addresses, phone numbers, billing information, and other data valuable to the organization. Databases are used to solve problems and to answer important questions, such as how much money the company owed, to whom, and to flag when the account becomes past due for payment. They can be also used for **data mining** to query large knowledge bases, making them vital in helping organizations achieve financial goals, increase customer satisfaction as well as efficiency, and reap profits.

data mining a technique of automatically obtaining information from databases that is normally hidden or not obvious

With the advent of the personal computer, database software has become standard in business, government, and even private individuals' work to store, sort, and retrieve information. The Internet has proven to be a valuable backbone for allowing users to access vast databases from remote locations using a personal computer equipped with a modem and communication software. Business and government organizations rely on computer networks and the Internet to distribute databases to their workers and customers. Consumers utilize stand-alone personal computers to create and access databases to store and retrieve information. Common consumer database applications include storing lists of names, addresses, phone numbers, recipes, videos, compact discs (CDs), digital versatile discs (DVDs), etc. Databases can be used to store a wide variety of information in various formats and can also be used to store and retrieve graphics, sounds, text, or a mixture of these formats.

Database Structure

Databases are computer files that store information. These data can be of many different types and formats, depending on the mission. All databases store data in tables or groups of tables. Each table consists of rows and columns, not unlike a grid or graph. Vertical columns of a table are called fields, and the horizontal rows are called records. Each field has a label at the top, and each record has a number at the left margin. An example of a table with two fields and three records follows. The fields are "name," and "phone number."

	Name	Phone Number
1	John Smith	617–555–1212
2	Jane Doe	413–555–1212
3	Cindy Smith	508–555–1212

Relational Databases

When two or more tables are related in a database, it is known as a "**relational database.**" Relational databases allow records from more than one table to be searched and displayed. The two or more tables must share a common field, like name, phone number, etc. If two tables contain a field that is common to both tables, then the data from two tables can be searched in a single query.

relational database a collection of records that permits logical and business relationships to be developed between themselves and their contents

SQL

SQL stands for Structured Query Language and is becoming the standard dialect for accessing database management systems. SQL permits users to perform a wide variety of functions, including creating databases, adding information, updating or altering information stored in the database, deleting data, searching for specific information, and displaying that information once it has been located by a query. SQL can be utilized to search more than one table at a time and can then construct new tables of information. SQL also permits users to change the structure of an existing database and to modify security settings.

SQL command statements are entered via the keyboard and are executed like a software program. Assume that a company has a database table called "employees." This table contains the complete list of all employees with their name, address, city, and phone number. If a list is needed of all the names and phone numbers in this table, one would write the SQL statement as follows:

Select FirstName, LastName, Phone

From EmployeeTable;

The preceding statement tells the database to display all the entries in the table because no specific search condition is specified. If the scope of the search is limited to employees living in a specific city, then one would write the following SQL statement using the Where command.

Select FirstName, LastName, Phone

From EmployeeTable

Where City = "Boston";

Commercial Database Products

There are numerous database development software packages on the market, and they meet a wide variety of end user and commercial applications. These packages support a wide variety of operating systems and computer platforms, including Windows, Macintosh, Linux, and others. Each is intended either for commercial or consumer applications.

Microsoft produces the Access database development software. This package runs under the Windows operating system and is intended for both business and consumer applications. It also offers SQL Server for large database projects. Oracle is a database development software package for creating powerful applications for large-scale database applications in sizable organizations and government agencies. File Maker Pro is a Macintosh-based database development package for commercial and consumer sized applications.

Security

The security and integrity of information systems is of vast importance to organizations, and significant resources are often deployed in this area. The overall integrity and security of the database is the joint responsibility of the network administrator and the database administrator.

If the database resides on a network, which is typical, network security is the first line of defense to protect the database and the information stored within it. Network administrators can limit access to the directory or files where the actual data and program files are stored. This denies access to those who would delete, modify, or corrupt these files.

Working in concert with the network administrator, the database administrator is responsible for ensuring that the database system is secure from unauthorized use and access. Additional responsibilities include modifying the database and upgrading or maintaining the system. The database administrator secures the database application by applying the security settings offered by the particular database package to prevent unauthorized access. The administrator accomplishes this by assigning user names and passwords to everyone in the organization.

Such a system forces users to log onto the system with a valid user name and password before gaining access. The user name and password tell the database software what type of access to grant to the user. This prevents data stored in the database from being altered, deleted, or copied without permission. Access rights are arranged in a hierarchy, with some users having limited access, while trusted users have expanded access. Groups of users can be confined to a "read only" mode that allows them to read information stored in the database but prevents them from making any alterations.

Database management software systems have created the ability to store and retrieve large quantities of information. They have allowed data from widely dissimilar sources to be correlated in order to solve problems and answer questions. They allow companies to maintain lists of their customers, suppliers, inventory, financial records, trade secrets, and other valuable information. Databases can be used to store and retrieve information in many different formats: graphics, sound, text, and mixed modes. The Structured Query Language (SQL) allows databases to be created, populated, updated, and searched. Database management systems can be accessed using stand-alone computers, office networks, and the global Internet, and are undergoing constant evolution and expansion. SEE ALSO COMPUTER SUPPORTED COOPERATIVE WORK (CSCW); PRODUCTIVITY SOFTWARE; SQL; SQL: DATABASES.

Joseph J. Lazzaro

Bibliography

Ramakrishnan, Raghu, and Johannes Gehrke. *Database Management Systems,* 2nd ed. Boston: McGraw-Hill, 2000.

McFadden, Fred R., Jeffrey A. Hoffer, and Mary B. Prescott. *Modern Database Management,* 6th ed. Upper Saddle River, NJ: Prentice Hall, 2001.

Decision Support Systems

Computer systems that provide users with support to analyze complex information and help to make decisions are called decision support systems (DSSs). In some cases, such systems may predict the impact of decisions before they are made.

Decision support systems are an advancement of management information systems, whose main purpose is to supply information to managers. Although the functions of management information systems are limited mostly to control of storage, organization, retrieval, and maintaining the security and integrity of data, decision support systems include model building and model-based reasoning capabilities. Decision support systems do not have the problem-solving competence of expert systems, however, which are programmed with the knowledge of human experts and can make some final decisions without human intervention. Decision support systems generally help human beings solve complex problems, and provide data that can lead to non-predetermined solutions that are beyond the limitations of expert systems.

The concept of decision support systems originated in the late 1950s and early 1960s, when researchers at Carnegie Institute of Technology located in Pittsburgh, Pennsylvania, conducted pioneering studies of organizational decision-making. Some time later Tom Gerrity and a team of scientists performed research on interactive computing at the Massachusetts Institute of Technology. One of their projects was dedicated to supporting investment managers in the administration of their clients' stock portfolios. These original studies were mostly done by graduate students and professors at leading engineering and business schools who had access to the most advanced computer systems of that time. It became obvious at the time that the emerging computer technology could serve as an excellent tool for the development of decision support systems.

Later on, scientists and computer programmers applied analytical and scientific methods for the development of more sophisticated DSSs. They used mathematical models and **algorithms** from such fields of study as **artificial intelligence (AI)**, mathematical simulation and optimization, and concepts of mathematical logic.

In recent years, decision support tools like **data warehousing** and on-line analytical applications have enhanced the capabilities of decision support

algorithms rules or procedures used to solve mathematical problems—most often described as sequences of steps

artificial intelligence (AI) a branch of computer science dealing with creating computer hardware and software to mimic the way people think and perform practical tasks

data warehousing to implement an informational database used to store shared data

systems. Joint efforts of scientists and programmers resulted in the development of the DSS generator—software for the building of decision support systems customized to the user's requirements.

Applications

Over the years DSSs have gained popularity in such areas as business management, medicine and health care, the military, environmental policy, and other areas that involve risk management, proper resource allocation, and similar tactical and strategic decisions. Decision-making is particularly important in the areas of business and finance. Very often, distribution of valuable resources and large sums of money are based on human intuitive judgment. DSSs provide aid in such tasks as cash flow analysis, break-even analysis, scenario analysis, and inventory techniques. The number of working DSSs demonstrates the necessity of such systems. The Taxpayers' Assistant System of the U.S. Internal Revenue Service helps its personnel give correct tax information to taxpayers. Also, DSS programs assist credit card company employees in allowing or disallowing certain charges, and advise bank officers regarding loans and mortgage approvals.

In manufacturing, decision support systems are solving design problems by using analytical, statistical, and model-building software, especially in the car- and aircraft-making industries. Such giants of automotive industry as General Motors and Ford Motor Company use comprehensive decision support systems.

Systems for scheduling and customer support are universally available for use in different fields. Their use helps bring down costs and increase service efficiency. American Airlines developed a system to schedule airplanes for required maintenance. As people deal with increasingly complex machinery and sophisticated instrumentation, DSSs become an important component in service and customer support, particularly providing expertise in troubleshooting and systems operation.

Decision support systems are also widely used in environmental science, particularly in air quality impact analysis. For example, a model developed by the Stanford Research Institute computes hourly averages of carbon monoxide for any urban location, while a program developed by the Argonne National Laboratory of Illinois provides **meteorological** data and classifies sources of emission for the Federal Aviation Administration (FAA).

Health-care professionals are assisted by decision support tools in determining the prognosis of individual patients based on an analysis of clinical data, and in determining whether a patient is eligible for clinical research based on the patient's clinical history. Applications such as alerting systems, critiquing systems, and diagnostic suggestion systems are utilized in hospital operating rooms, intensive care units, laboratories, and other medical facilities. Implementation of these tools can significantly improve the quality and reduce the cost of health care.

These and other DSSs may work actively or in a passive mode. Passive systems are mostly used by physicians for reference purposes, while active systems give advice in certain situations, such as alerting medical personnel when a parameter being monitored in a patient—such as temperature or heart rate—exceeds its designated threshold value.

XPLAINING ONE'S OPTIONS

Decision support systems provide people in various trades and occupations with data to help them make informed judgments. In the field of medicine, DXplain is one such system. Culling data from a depository of 2,000 diseases and 5,000 clinical probabilities associated with those ailments, DXplain offers information on symptoms and treatment options. The system is used at hospitals and in medical schools as a reference tool.

---

meteorological pertaining to the study of the atmosphere and weather phenomena

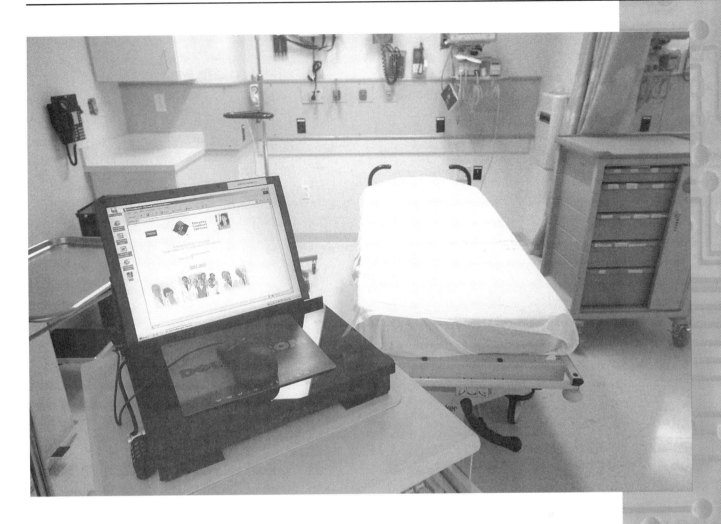

Whether they are active or passive systems, health care decision support systems are limited to the role of advisor to clinicians and other health care professionals. They do not act as expert systems. Only physicians themselves are responsible for decisions made concerning human health; DSSs act as information tools in this and other circumstances.

The emergency room at Boston's Beth Israel Deaconess Medical Center includes a laptop computer, which is used by staff in making medical diagnoses.

Components

An effective decision support system requires reliable data and usually includes an interactive user **interface**, a knowledge base, and an inference (reasoning) engine.

The knowledge base is the component of a DSS that contains both well-established facts and results obtained by trial-and-error methods. It may include such different elements as formulas (algebraic, logical, or statistical expressions), guidelines, and knowledge of risk and cost of operations. Often knowledge is presented in the form of rules.

The inference engine is a complex computer algorithm, which uses the data in the knowledge base to obtain a solution to a problem. There are two approaches for decision-making systems: under certainty and under uncertainty. Decision-making under certainty most often utilizes a mathematical model that gives an unambiguous response. On the other hand, decision-making under uncertainty uses statistical approaches, such as **Bayesian networks**, **neural networks**, and other methods of AI.

interface a boundary or border between two or more objects or systems; also a point of access

Bayesian networks structures that describe systems in which there is a degree of uncertainty; used in automated decision making

neural networks pattern recognition systems whose structure and operation are loosely inspired by analogy to neurons in the human brain

The advancement of decision support systems would be impossible without its interaction with a number of related fields. Business analysts and mathematicians develop mathematical models for use in DSS, software engineers provide tools for knowledge maintenance and data mining, and psychologists assist in DSS design by conducting behavioral decision-making research.

As the need for more sophisticated decision-making will increase in the future, it is probable that decision support systems will become more intelligent and user friendly, and applicable to a broader spectrum of professions. SEE ALSO INFORMATION SYSTEMS; INTEGRATED SOFTWARE; MEDICAL SYSTEMS.

Marina Krol and Igor Tarnopolsky

Bibliography

Berner, Eta S., ed. *Clinical Decision Support Systems: Theory and Practice*. New York: Springler-Verlag, 1999.

Krol, M., and D. Reich. "Development of a Decision Support System for Detecting Critical Conditions During Anesthesia." *Journal of Medical Systems* 24, no. 3 (2000): 141–146.

Marakas, George M. *Decision Support Systems in the 21st Century*. Upper Saddle River, NJ: Prentice Hall, 1999.

Turban, Efraim, and Jay E. Aronson. *Decision Support Systems and Intelligent Systems*, 6th ed. Upper Saddle River, NJ: Prentice Hall, 2001

Desktop Publishing

Desktop publishing (DTP) refers to the practice of producing high quality printed output, fully paginated and including graphics, using personal computers, page layout software, and printers designed to create near typeset-quality pages. The core technologies (the personal computer, WYSIWYG (what you see is what you get) text processing, page description languages, and high-resolution laser printing) were developed at the Xerox Palo Alto Research Center (PARC) in the 1970s. However the particular configuration that launched the commercial phenomenon of desktop publishing in 1985 consisted of Apple Macintosh personal computers running Aldus Publishing's PageMaker page layout software, connected to Apple's 300 dpi Laserwriter laser printer with the Adobe Postscript page description language.

The emergence of DTP was a major event in the history of publishing technology because it allowed almost any small organization, even individuals, to easily and inexpensively produce hardcopy printed pages suitable for use as printing masters. These had the potential to be nearly comparable in aesthetic appearance and typesetting features to what had previously required far more costly, time consuming, and hard-to-use technologies, expertise, and workflows. Desktop publishing also positioned its users to take advantage of digital inputs, which was important as word processing became the routine method for document creation.

Historical Context of Communication Technologies

The social and technological significance of DTP can be best seen by placing it in historical context as an innovation in communication technology.

Many historians and anthropologists consider the emergence of writing to be an absolutely necessary condition for the legal, commercial, and religious systems that characterize "civilized" societies. Although writing had appeared by 2,000 B.C.E., few important innovations occurred for the next 3,500 years. This was the period of "scribal transmission," when texts were "published" by laboriously copying them by hand. A key advancement during these centuries was the development of phonemic (alphabetic) writing systems that were far easier to learn and use than previous word-based systems or syllabic systems. Other innovations included the development of paper and the codex book (rather than scroll), cursive script, and the development of social organizations to manage copying (such as the "scriptorium" of western medieval Europe). Despite these innovations, by the end of the **Middle Ages** books were still extremely rare and expensive to produce, publishing remained a sophisticated specialist practice, and writing and reading were rather rare abilities.

Middle Ages the time period that lasted from around the fifth century C.E. through the middle of the fifteenth century C.E.

The dramatic emergence of printing press technology in late fifteenth-century Europe made it possible to reproduce texts far more easily, and with greater fidelity, than was possible with scribal transmission. The consequences of this invention radically affected all aspects of our social, political, religious, and cultural lives. Printing is now recognized by historians as perhaps the single most influential technological event for western civilization.

A Walk Through Mid-Twentieth Century Printing

Contemporary life involves an immersion in printed material: newspapers, magazines, textbooks, scientific journals, instruction manuals, technical documentation, charts, tables, contracts, receipts, business proposals, catalogs, junk mail, brochures, flyers, product packaging, and so on. But the production of the visually pleasing pages that support this flow of information has until very recently been an expensive and time-consuming process, requiring specialized expertise of many kinds and very costly equipment.

The steam operated presses and "hot type" of the nineteenth century gave way to phototypesetting and computer composition by the mid-twentieth century. However, the publishing process of the 1970s and early 1980s was still an extremely complicated and expensive process.

Consider for example a relatively simple book with black and white line art. Designers prepared written specifications for typography and layout. These were delivered to editors who, perhaps after several revision cycles, used them to "mark up" typewritten or word-processed manuscripts. The marked up copy then went to a "composition house" where computer compositors entered, usually by hand, texts and formatting commands into computer files in order to implement the instructions expressed in the markup.

Next, in a separate step, these files were **"batch" processed** by composition software to create data files in the specific language used by a particular phototypesetting machine. Samples of the phototypesetting (imaged on film) were sent back to the compositor and editor for approval. Note that with no previewing capability, this was the first opportunity the compositor had to see the actual visual effects of the formatting codes.

batch processed to queue non-interactive programs and run them one after another

When samples finally appeared correct to the compositors, they were sent back to the editor who verified that they met the original design

THE SCRIPTORIUM

In the days before the printing press, copies of books had to be created by hand. To assist in this endeavor, scriptoria (copying rooms) were established. These rooms were often cold and ill-lit, as heat and artificial light from candles were perceived to be fire hazards. In some scriptoria, someone would read the text aloud while others copied it. In monastic scriptoria, monks worked alone.

specifications. Several iterations might be involved, and given the nature of the process, even the purely mechanical part of the iteration could take as long as twenty-four hours, especially if either composition or typesetting were outsourced to another company, which was quite a normal procedure. Moreover, if several computers were involved (e.g., the copyeditor's computer, the composition computer, and the typesetting computer), removable media such as eight-track tapes had to be prepared and delivered physically.

Once the samples seemed to be correct, a complete set of "galleys" (unpaginated formatted text) were produced, along with sets of captions, page numbers, running titles, and other features needed to make up the printed page. All of these, along with needed artwork, were sent to "paste-up" specialists who used razor tools, paste, and hot wax to physically compose each individual page on special "paste-up boards" by cutting the galleys of type into columns and pages, adding the artwork (prepared separately), and adding the individual running titles, page numbers, captions, etc. Indexes, in-text references to pages or numbered figures, variable running titles, and other page-based apparatus could not be constructed until pagination was known, so they could only now be composed by the compositors and processed by the layout artists. The completed paste-up boards (called "mechanicals") were then stacked and transported to the printer. From these boards were created printing plates.

Corrections or changes required time-consuming repetitions of this process, and, in particular, any changes that resulted in a change in pagination were enormously expensive. The final product could not be easily revised, updated, or repackaged for other uses or for other delivery formats, whether analog (anthologies, abridgements, new editions) or digital (CD-ROMS, databases, e-books, web pages).

While it is true that systems were eventually developed that allowed text to be composed into pages interactively and previewed in a WYSIWYG (what you see is what you get) environment by the compositor, these were expensive, typically could not accommodate artwork, and in any case were not widely used, even by the early 1980s.

The Emergence of Desktop Publishing

In the mid-1980s, a revolution occurred which radically changed the publishing process. This change was the result of two things, each itself a combination of recently developed hardware and software:

- WYSIWYG page layout software running on a personal computer;
- a high resolution all-points-addressable matrix printer with high-function page description software.

The revolutionary personal computer was the Apple Macintosh. The page layout software was PageMaker, released by Aldus Publishing. The printer was the Apple Laserwriter, and the page description software was called Postscript, by Adobe. The marketing of these components in 1985 marked the commercial debut of desktop publishing.

Problems with Desktop Publishing

This new, widely accessible, generally affordable technology for mass producing typeset-quality pages, complete with graphics, offered many im-

Desktop publishing has revolutionized the publishing business. Today, small publishers can lay out their own publications rather than send them to large typesetting companies.

provements over previous technologies. However DTP also brought with it some problems.

Quality Concerns. The low cost of equipment and the ease with which software could be learned seemed to suggest that anyone who could acquire and operate the tools could create and produce typeset-quality pages. The graphics specialists who knew how to design pleasing pages were rapidly replaced in many organizations by clerical workers or by professionals in other disciplines whose chief qualification for desktop publishing was their expertise in operating an office computer. Because it was assumed that DTP software could be implemented with little or no training, organizations eliminated whole departments and discarded traditional processes of design and production.

Without a framework of policies and procedures to oversee the use of DTP tools, the result was very frequently a loss not only of visual quality (the "ransom note" effect one gets from ugly combinations of fonts and bad composition practices), but also—and much more importantly—a loss of accuracy and effectiveness of the printed materials. Ironically, many organizations discovered that the money-saving potential of DTP tools actually led to an overall loss of efficiency, as tasks that had once been done by professional designers became time-consuming additions to the workload of people with other primary responsibilities.

Information Management Concerns. During the late 1970s and early 1980s another major revolution in publishing was underway. The "descriptive

markup" approach organized digital documents into structures of logical components (such as chapters, sections, titles, paragraphs, lists, block quotations, and other similar items), and then separately associated formatting rules with each type of component. This approach turned out to have many advantages over directly inserting formatting codes into the document, making it easier to create documents, globally alter formatting, support information retrieval, print on a variety of output devices, convert to different file formats, or customize output for a variety of purposes. Documents created this way could be flexibly repurposed for different products and delivery systems. This way of managing a document as a database is based on fundamental principles of information management.

The creators of desktop publishing systems rarely reflected these insights, however, preferring instead to focus on the intuitive ease-of-use and composition capabilities of the software. As a result, early DTP products were generally far less versatile and functional than they might have been. It was hard to import data easily from other more structured formats. Even more significantly, it was difficult to use content that had been processed by DTP systems for anything other than the original intended printed products: DTP files could not be easily repurposed for delivery on CD-ROMs (compact discs-read only memory) or the web, for instance, or accessed by information retrieval tools, or imported into databases, or integrated with emerging networked information systems.

XML the acronym for eXtensible Markup Language; a method of applying structure to data so that documents can be represented

Today these problems are being addressed. In particular, the descriptive markup approach to creating and managing content is increasingly integrated with DTP tools and practices, due in part, perhaps, to the recent near-universal acceptance of **XML** as the standard language for describing publishing content. It is now recognized that the production of effective high-quality publications requires carefully thought-out processes and compliance with fundamental principles of information management. There is no substitute for expertise and carefully defined systems. And there is no substitution for principles and best practices.

Desktop publishing is now common in business, government, and education. It continues to be based on the same basic components found in the original configuration of 1985: high-resolution all-points-addressable matrix printers, personal computers, interactive page-layout and graphics software, and page description printing software—each easy-to-use, powerful, and relatively inexpensive. The challenge now is to integrate desktop publishing into the wider process of creating, managing, and delivering information in the networked world. SEE ALSO DOCUMENT PROCESSING; INTEGRATED SOFTWARE; MARKUP LANGUAGES; TECHNOLOGY OF DESKTOP PUBLISHING.

Allen Renear

Internet Resources

About Desktop Publishing for All Platforms. <http://desktoppub.about.com/>

"The Ultimate Electronic Publishing Resource." desktopPublishing.com. <http://desktoppublishing.com/open.html>

Distance Learning

The terms "distance learning," "distance education," and "distributed learning" are often used interchangeably, though some authors make sharp distinctions between their meanings. Distance education typically refers to distributed learning resources in academic settings, whereas distance learning is commonly defined as the acquisition of knowledge and skills through mediated information and instruction. The focus of the former term is on the process of teaching and its supporting systems whereas the focus of the latter is on the process of learning.

Distance learning can take a wide variety of forms, but generally it means that the instructor and learners are in different places or the teaching and learning occur at different times. Interaction among participants and with the learning resources usually involves some form of electronic media or mediated communication.

Distance learning has been a feature of higher education in the United States for more than a century. Since 1890, an estimated 130 million Americans have taken distance or correspondence study courses. These courses are not offered exclusively by colleges and universities, but also by businesses, nonprofit organizations, trade associations, and the military, among others. In the mid-1990s, more than 5 percent of the 14.3 million students in American higher education were formally enrolled in distance education courses. Distance learning is also an international phenomenon. For example, the pioneering British Open University estimates it has served more than two million people in its first thirty years.

Technology has played an increasingly important role in the delivery of distance education and in the distribution of distance learning resources. In 1890, distance education equated to correspondence (home) study where students worked through specially prepared self-instructional print materials, submitted assignments, and received feedback from their instructors via mail. This model is still the prevalent form of distance education throughout the world. The advent of radio and television brought another dimension to distance learning, and for a time they were heralded as replacements for the classroom.

During the 1980s, interactive television (ITV) emerged as an effective tool for engaging students studying at a distance. ITV connects multiple classrooms by way of two-way audio and video communication. An instructor teaching a class at the home site can see and talk with students at far site classrooms, as they can with the students in the room at the home site. ITV uses hardware and software solutions to compress the video stream so more information can be sent over relatively low **bandwidth** communications lines. For example, three ISDN (Integrated Services Digital Network) lines can provide 384 Kbps (kilobits per second) of dedicated bandwidth between sites, enabling full-motion (30 fps [frames per second]) video and quality audio transmission.

More recently, the Internet has emerged as the preferred technology to support students studying at a distance. Along with this trend, a new breed of integrated web-based tools supports the creation and delivery of instructional materials and provides a variety of communication capabilities.

bandwidth a measure of the frequency component of a signal or the capacity of a communication channel to carry signals

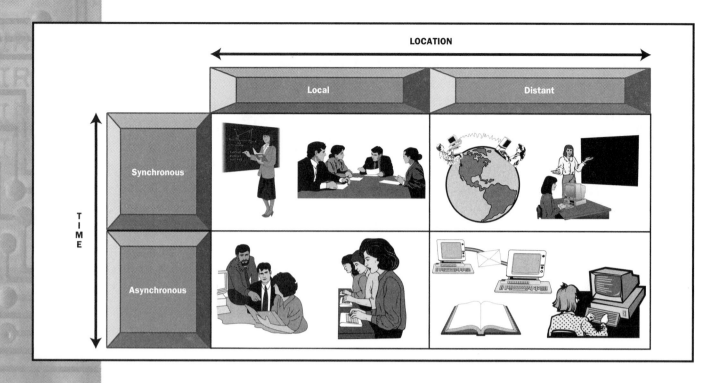

Figure 1. The four quadrants of learning technology.

Products like *Blackboard* and *WebCT* exemplify these course management systems.

Four Distance Learning Models

A wide variety of technologies support learning and the delivery of education. To understand them, consider two dimensions of learning—time and location. Figure 1 divides learning technologies into four quadrants, defined by whether the teacher and learner share the same location (local) or are separated (distant) and by whether the teaching and learning activities take place at the same time (synchronous) or at different times (asynchronous). The case of local/synchronous learning refers to forms of traditional face-to-face instruction and all others refer to distance learning scenarios.

Local/Synchronous. The local/synchronous option is supported by the traditional classroom technologies supplemented with computers, VCRs, DVD players, and data/video projection systems that allow the entire class to view videos, presentations, and demonstrations simultaneously. Educational institutions are increasingly building "smart" classrooms with network access, touch-sensitive display screens (such as *SmartBoards*), and **groupware** to support collaborative work in the classroom. Many instructors also prefer to teach in classrooms that are configured with networked computers at every seat or workgroup and with hardware or software technologies that provide computer input and output monitoring and control capabilities. These allow the instructor to grab any student's screen image and display it on all computers in the class or on the large screen. Many institutions are also supporting laptop use in the classroom, either by providing network ports at each seat or providing wireless network access throughout the campus.

groupware a software technology common in client/server systems whereby many users can access and process data at the same time

Distant/Asynchronous. The distant/synchronous option is supported by technologies like Interactive Television. Satellite downlinks and broadcast television provide a higher level of quality and wider reach, but entail greater costs and allow less interaction, typically providing telephone lines for questions from the recipients. As higher-bandwidth access to the Internet becomes more widely available, desktop video conferencing will become an increasingly effective solution, in either point-to-point or multi-point mode. This option, characterized by software such as *NetMeeting* and *CUseeMe*, provides a video and audio link, along with file sharing, application sharing, chat tools, and whiteboards, allowing multiple attendees to view and edit graphic material simultaneously in a shared space. Synchronous chat tools are common components of web-based course management systems.

Local/Asynchronous. The local/asynchronous option has learners physically present in the same place but performing different learning activities. This is characterized by computer lab and small group activities and is supported by technologies such as streaming video, ported classrooms, wireless network access, and computer-based applications.

Distant/Synchronous. The distant/asynchronous model is the oldest and most common form of distance learning model. It uses self-instructional learning materials in forms ranging from paper and pencil to multimedia content posted on web-based course management systems. Computers are proving to be extremely useful tools in providing active learning experiences, feedback, and communications capabilities. Multimedia enhanced computer-based training (including games and simulations), though difficult and costly to develop, can effectively utilize CD and DVD technologies to great advantage. The Internet has also enabled the effective use of e-mail, list servers, and threaded discussion groups, as well as a host of emerging groupware applications.

Job Demand

While distance learning is greatly enhanced through technology, one should not equate it with technology nor associate it exclusively with a single delivery mode (correspondence, telecourses, computer assisted instruction, ITV, or the web). The essence of distance learning is that it increases dependence on self-instructional course materials and learning activities. This fact has resulted in a dramatically increased job demand for instructional designers (professionals trained in learning and instructional theory and their application) and instructional technologists (professionals experienced in computer, graphics, and multimedia applications). SEE ALSO COMPUTER ASSISTED INSTRUCTION; EDUCATIONAL SOFTWARE; TELECOMMUNICATIONS.

Nicholas C. Laudato

Bibliography

Issue Brief: Distance Education in Higher Education Institutions: Incidence, Audiences, and Plans to Expand. National Center for Education Statistics. February 1998 (NCES 98-132).

"Report on Copyright and Digital Distance Education." *A Report of the Register of Copyrights.* U.S. Copyright Office, Library of Congress. May 1999.

Internet Resources

"1998 Distance Education Survey." *What Is the DETC?* Distance Education and Training Council (DETC), Washington, DC. <http://www.detc.org>

Research Information and Statistics. The United States Distance Learning Association (USDLA). <http://www.usdla.org/04_research_info.htm>

ESSENCE OF DISTANCE LEARNING (DL)

In distance learning, the instructors and learners are in different places or the teaching and learning occur at different times. While it is greatly enhanced through technology, DL should not be equated with technology nor associated exclusively with a single delivery mode. The essence of distance learning is that it increases dependence on self-instructional course materials and learning activities.

Economic Modeling

As computing technologies have become more and more sophisticated, economists have come to rely increasingly heavily on computers for a variety of tasks. Today, economists use computers to analyze large quantities of statistical information, to create simulations or scenarios of what might happen to an economy if a particular economic variable, such as the price of oil, changes, and to solve complex mathematical problems that advance our knowledge of economic processes.

Perhaps the most common use of computers in economics is for the analysis of statistical information. Economists call this type of analysis "econometrics." Using the large amounts of statistical economic information that are now easily available on the Internet and elsewhere, economists can test simple but important questions about economic behavior. For example, based on data for the past two decades for the fifty states in the United States, what can one say about how an increase in the price of a pack of cigarettes will affect the number of packs of cigarettes that people buy? How will this reduce the incidence of such health problems as lung cancer and tooth loss? In order to analyze such questions, economists must have access to information on how many packs of cigarettes are sold at any time, and at what price. They must also know the relationship between the number of people who smoke cigarettes and the number of people who end up getting sick. In addition, they must have powerful computers in order to analyze such large quantities of statistical information. And finally, they must have the methods and software that enable them to answer such questions.

The most widely used method in economics for analyzing relationships between two or more variables (such as the price of a pack of cigarettes and the number of packs bought) is called regression analysis. In a regression, the economist specifies the relationship he or she is trying to analyze. In the preceding example, the regression analysis indicates the effect of the price of cigarettes on their consumption, and the effect of the consumption of cigarettes on the health of populations. Using a regression, the economist is able not only to tell whether or not cigarette consumption falls due to price increases, but also predict the amount by which consumption is decreased due to the price increase. Similarly, the economist may be able to estimate the effect of an increase in the price of a pack of cigarettes on the number of people who develop lung cancer or who lose their teeth as a consequence. Such information is of enormous value to policymakers. In the cigarette example, this information could enable people in the federal or state governments to determine a level of taxation that would reduce the consumption of cigarettes due to an increase in price, without being so large as to be burdensome to cigarette smokers.

Because computers are so integral to the analysis of economic data, a number of software packages are now available that enable economists to run regressions and to answer questions about economic behavior. Microsoft Excel, for example, has a regression tool that allows the researcher to do very basic kinds of economic analysis. Professional economists, however, use more sophisticated statistical software packages for their analyses. Among the most popular packages are SAS and SPSS, which are used by businesses, government agencies, and academic researchers alike for the analysis of eco-

nomic statistics. Depending on the particular kind of analysis to be done, other packages such as RATS, STATA, TSP, Limdep, Matlab, and Gauss are also very useful.

Computers also enable economists to run simulations, in which a possible scenario for the future is created, allowing economists to answer important economic questions about this scenario. For example, an economist might ask what would happen to smoking in the United States if the price of a pack of cigarettes were to triple over the next year. Because this may never have happened in the past, the economist may not be able to use any single example from previous years to estimate the effect of this change in price on the change in consumption. The economist can, however, make an informed guess as to what might happen with the help of software.

Economists use a variety of software packages to simulate scenarios about which there is no prior statistical information. These include the General Algebraic Modeling System (GAMS) and Mathematica, both of which enable the economist to write down explicit relationships between variables that will play a role in the final outcome of the simulation. To extend the cigarette example, we know that a tripling in the price of cigarettes will cause many smokers to cut back on smoking because they have limited income to spend on cigarettes. But perhaps this will only affect casual smokers, for whom it is, presumably, easier to stop smoking. Addicts, on the other hand, may continue to smoke the quantities they did prior to the increase in the

Companies rely on economic modeling to help them analyze the impact of various situations on their businesses. For example, health care organizations can monitor the impact of a rise in prescription costs.

price. Depending on how we think addicts and casual users behave, we may want to model their behavior differently, making the simulation more complex. Fortunately, as computers have become increasingly powerful, economists have been able to analyze increasingly complex economic problems using computers. It is common, for example, for economists at universities and government and policy institutions to simulate the workings of an entire economy using hundreds of mathematical equations written in the GAMS software.

Given the rapid development of economic modeling and the increasing availability of statistical economic information that can be used to understand the way the economy works, it is difficult not be optimistic about the future of economic modeling. While economists have a long way to go before they can be confident about the predictions generated by their simulations, it is encouraging to recall that as recently as the 1970s, weather forecasters were unable to predict the weather with any accuracy. With the development of **supercomputers** and complex models of weather systems, it has now become possible to predict, with a fair amount of accuracy, the weather in the coming week. Perhaps economic modeling today is where weather forecasting was in the 1970s. If so, economists and those who stand to benefit from economic modeling will see many technological advancements in the future! SEE ALSO DECISION SUPPORT SYSTEMS; IMAGE ANALYSIS: MEDICINE; MATHEMATICS; PATTERN RECOGNITION; SIMULATION.

Siddharth Chandra

supercomputers very high performance computers, usually comprised of many processors and used for modeling and simulation of complex phenomena, like meteorology

Bibliography

Pindyck, Robert S., and Daniel L. Rubinfeld. *Econometric Models and Economic Forecasts*. New York: McGraw-Hill College Division, 1997.

Internet Resources

SAS web site. <http://www.sas.com>

Educational Software

Educational software, or computer applications developed for the purpose of teaching and learning, arrived with virtually the first desktop computers. Education professionals recognized this potential early, and many schools acquired computers long before they were found in most American homes. Educational applications then greatly increased.

Educational software encompasses a variety of forms, costs, and purposes. Programs exist to teach individual preschoolers letter names, sounds, and grammar in English as well as other languages. Other programs introduce mathematical concepts for all grades, or are aimed at helping to develop good writing skills. Some programs, such as flight simulators, teach professionals the details of their jobs. Still other programs, called Learning Management Systems (LMSs), are designed for use by certain grades in entire school districts for teaching or evaluation purposes; these often include access to a software company's web site for comprehensive services.

At the college and university level, LMSs are powerful application management systems that offer courses via the Internet for non-traditional students. These tools allow institutions to design entire online courses. The

projects require a team, consisting of the subject-matter expert (usually a faculty member), a graphics artist, a curriculum designer, and a programmer, to put the complete package together.

Selecting Educational Software

Choosing an educational application to integrate into a curriculum can be difficult. Curriculum materials are generally selected for use over the course of several years. One drawback to using educational software programs in this way is that the applications often change from year to year, thus requiring frequent upgrade purchases. Sometimes the latest edition of a program has been modified to run on more powerful computers than a school can afford to use. Sometimes favorite applications are absorbed into other programs or disappear entirely. Another drawback is that there are no universally accepted standards or recognized independent organizations (such as the Food and Drug Administration for medications) for evaluating these programs.

Some LMSs are designed to accommodate hundreds of students. These programs require Internet access, which offers several advantages. Content, such as political maps, can be updated easily when needed. The programs allow individuals to work at their own pace and can be adapted to concentrate

A student uses educational software to learn more about nature and people. Such products give students easy access to a wide variety of information, enhancing traditional study methods.

on an individual's particular weak area. The progress of the students can be evaluated at any time. Most of these programs offer technical support for the faculty if needed, and some offer teacher tutorials.

The cost of these services varies depending on the equipment—for example, are computers supplied by the company or must they be supplied by the school?—the time required per week per student, and how many weeks in total are needed by each student to complete the program. One program designed to help elementary students read costs $30,000 per year, not counting the price of the computers.

Effective Evaluation and Implementation

Educational software is evaluated by many of the same standards used for evaluating other educational materials. Is the program appropriate for the age and development of the user? Are the graphics attractive and do they lead to better learning? Is the depth of the program appropriate? Is the method for teaching effective? Is the software entertaining enough to keep the user interested? Does the program stimulate further learning of the subject?

Once software is selected, it must be effectively implemented. The environment around the computer is important. Is the computer located in a computer lab or is it in the classroom? How often during the week, and for how long, does the student have access to the computer? Is the area inviting? Is it designed to accommodate a single student at a time, or can multiple students access the computer together and learn from each other? Software should be compatible with the environment in which it will be used. If daily use is recommended to meet the learning objectives of a software program, but students will have only weekly access to the program, another program should be selected, or computer access should be increased. Likewise, software designed to be used by two or more students working cooperatively is best used in a setting that comfortably accommodates more than one student at each computer.

Market Issues

Educational software companies, especially ones that produce LMSs, face unique challenges. First, the consumer, generally educators at a school district or a large institution, must be sold on the program. Second, in order for schools to implement the Internet systems mentioned previously, reliable networks must be installed; this takes time and money, especially in older buildings. Third, schools usually have budgets that are conceived well ahead of time and followed strictly. The thousands of dollars that these programs cost must be approved by school boards; financing may need to be found. The entire process of implementing an LMS can take years! Software companies might not have the financial means to survive between the time a school or district agrees to buy a system and the point when the system is actually purchased.

Companies that develop educational software, such as the Learning Company that produces the widely recognized Carmen San Diego and Reader Rabbit series, are easily affected by downturns in the computer software and Internet industries. Some have been sold and resold since the late 1990s, leaving in question the future of both the companies and the content, quality, and variety of their products. The overall number of CD-ROM (compact disc-read only memory) educational software programs available has fallen due to major changes in the software market since 2000.

Software Effectiveness Factors

Surprisingly, many experts agree that the quality of the software is not the most important consideration in how successful it is; the expertise and comfort level of the person helping the student is the single most critical factor. However, by 2000, only half the states in the United States required formal training in computer science for teaching certification, and only twenty percent of teachers felt comfortable including computers in the curriculum. Many software programs offer technical support and tutorials to help teachers become more comfortable with the system. If the software is school-based, another important success factor is the ability of children to access the software from home and the parents' comfort level in assisting the student. Some school districts have started programs that provide laptop computers to students so they can be used outside of school.

There is also controversy about the effectiveness of educational software in general. Many school districts have seen increased test scores after implementing educational software systems. Others claim that the "cool factor" is largely responsible for these results, and that students do at least as well if the same energy is spent in well-planned conventional instruction. Few argue that educational software programs may be a student's first introduction to computers. For those already familiar with computers, educational software prods them to use computers for more than just surfing the Internet. This might prove to be the biggest benefit of all. SEE ALSO COMPUTER ASSISTED INSTRUCTION; INTEGRATED SOFTWARE; LIBRARY APPLICATIONS; OFFICE AUTOMATION SYSTEMS.

Mary McIver Puthawala

Bibliography

Brown, Judy. "From The Trenches." *eWeek*, May 14, 2001, p. 32.

Buckleitner, Warren. "Tightening Up." *Curriculum Administrator* 37, no. 6 (2001): 74.

Fischman, Josh. "New Reading Programs Spell Help for Frustrated Kids." *U.S. News & World Report* 130, no. 15 (2001): 48.

Ratnesar, Romesh. "Learning By Laptop." *Time* 151, no. 8 (1998): 62(2).

Wood, Julie. "Can Software Support Children's Vocabulary Development?" *Language, Learning & Technology* 5, no. 1 (2001): 166.

Internet Resources

All About Learning Technology Standards. Learnativity Web Site. <http://www.learnativity.com/standards.html>

Embedded Technology (Ubiquitous Computing)

Do walls have ears? Not right now, but it will not be long before walls not only have ears, but will also be able to see what we are doing and even tell us things that are relevant to our activities. Traditionally, when people said that walls have ears, they suspected that someone was spying. In the

ubiquitous to be commonly available everywhere

interface a boundary or border between two or more objects or systems; also a point of access

smart devices devices and appliances that host an embedded computer system that offers greater control and flexibility

infrastructure the foundation or permanent installation necessary for a structure or system to operate

prototypes working models or experimental investigations of proposed systems under development

ambient pertaining to the surrounding atmosphere or environment

modern context, the walls will be a lot friendlier. They will sense who is in their vicinity, but only to determine the occupants' needs and to help them by adjusting the room light and the window shades to suit their tastes or by performing similar tasks.

Such service is an illustration of embedded technology (or ubiquitous computing) at work. In simple terms, ubiquitous computing allows computing architecture to be embedded into the environment. Artifacts in the environment can then sense different aspects of their surroundings as well as the user's ongoing activities, reason about them, and act accordingly.

Types of Ubiquitous Computing

Ubiquitous computing can take various forms. A sampling of some of those forms follows.

Portable Computing. Laptops and handheld computers have made computing portable. You can carry your computer with you everywhere, but your experience is only slightly different than in your office—you still must interact with the computer through a more or less traditional **interface**.

Pervasive Computing. **Smart devices** have computing technology in unexpected places. At first this will be in information appliances such as phones, personal digital assistants (PDAs), and pagers. Later, pervasive computing is expected to expand to include more traditional appliances such as toasters, refrigerators, washing machines, ovens, home security systems, and so on. Still later, the **infrastructure** will develop so that smart devices will include equipment like you might find on the road, in an automobile, in a hotel, or in an airport. For example, you might be able to pay tolls or buy airline tickets with your phone-based electronic wallet. **Prototypes** demonstrating such capabilities already exist, but their widespread usage will require a universal infrastructure with increased computing and communications power.

Smart buildings are buildings that are well networked and equipped with smart appliances and have a personal computer based system that can control the **ambient** conditions within the building. The "smarts" are needed to start and stop different appliances to maximize the users' comfort or security and to minimize cost. For example, a smart house could run the water heater whenever energy prices are low; it could select the best times to turn on the heat or air conditioning within the premises, based on which rooms are currently occupied or are likely to be occupied shortly.

Calm Computing. This technology carries out the idea of computing fading into the background. With this technology, the artifacts are intelligent, but do not require focused interaction—we just live with them and they work unobtrusively to make our lives simpler. An example of this is the "dangling string" network monitor. A traditional user interface for monitoring computer network traffic would capture a lot of data and try to present it on a computer screen. By contrast, the dangling string hangs from a hallway ceiling and is controlled by a small motor. Network activity causes the motor to kick the string ever so slightly. Activity in the network is thus presented as the literal hum of the swaying string.

The basic concept behind calm computing is to develop user interfaces that are not based on symbols. Although symbols can convey a lot of de-

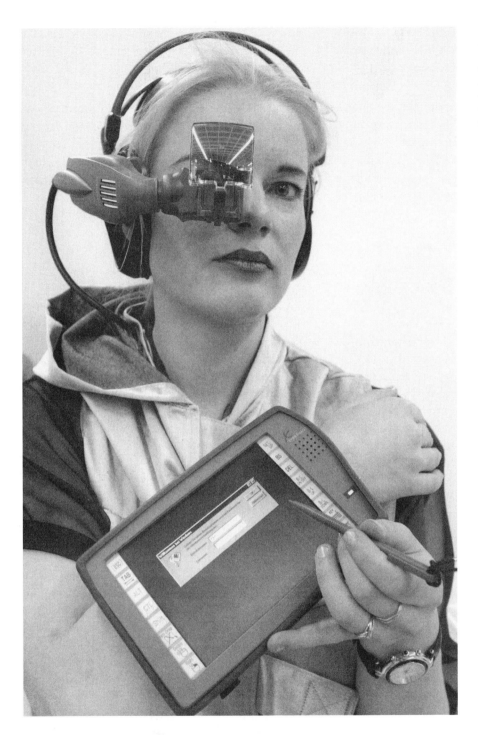

Looking like she stepped out of a science fiction movie, this woman is wearing a futuristic high-tech wardrobe, complete with VR (virtual reality) visor on her head and a touchscreen computer on her forearm.

tailed information, people have to focus on them to extract that information. In contrast, humans can capture a lot of non-symbolic information in a manner that does not require their explicit attention. Although your main current task can be successfully carried out in a symbolic mode, you can be peripherally aware of a lot of other activities without concentrating on them. The hum of a string, the shadows cast by a ceiling fan, the reflections cast by a shimmering pool of water all fall into this latter category. You will probably be aware of the flickering shadows and reflections and how fast they are changing even though you might be concentrating on your word processor or a phone conversation. Now imagine if these shadows and reflections and other changes in environment were used to convey specific meanings such as "All's well in the plant" or "There seems to be a lot of relevant activity in one of the chat rooms I visit" or "Suddenly, the stock market is seeing a lot of trades in the technology sector."

Wearable Computing.   In this opposite of calm computing, instead of having computers embedded in the environment, you carry the computers on your person. One main difference from regular computers is in the user interface. Wearable computers are designed for hands-free operation. Often, the intended user would be walking about or in an awkward posture, such as atop an electric utility pole or inside a narrow submarine engine room. Equipment repair was one of the earliest applications for wearable computing. It allows the user to give commands by voice and view information through a head-mounted display that projects an image on to the user's glasses.

The earliest wearable computers were quite bulky: the user literally had to carry a backpack with a computer in it. However, with advances in technology, it is possible to have wearable computers embedded in wristwatches or pendants or even sewn into clothing. These miniature computers are usually designed for specific applications, such as displaying text and pictures and giving online directions as the user walks about. In another application the wearable computer provides an interface to a three-dimensional information space where the user's head, neck, and eye movements can be interpreted as desires to probe some aspect of the space in more detail. Instead of traditional **virtual reality (VR)**, the user may be engaged in the "real" reality and only occasionally looking into the information space when a specific need requires it.

Related Technology

The techniques involved in ubiquitous computing are as diverse as its applications. Many of these techniques, however, deal with peripheral technologies. We need motors to drive the changes in environment that calm computing requires. We need head-mounted displays for certain kinds of wearable interfaces. For the wearables, we need lightweight processors that consume low power and small batteries that can feed them. Certain kinds of pervasive applications—for instance, those fixed in a tollbooth or a smart home—may have no restrictions on size, power, or communication ability; for applications that entail mobility, all those restrictions apply. For wearable computers, there are significant challenges in materials to weave conducting channels into fabrics. Some researchers are developing techniques to generate power from the normal actions of a human body, such as the impact of the heel on the ground in walking.

Interestingly, although the basic programming required to build ubiquitous applications is the same as programming for other applications, the abstractions involved tend to be quite different. The interface **modalities** of desktop computing are not much use in calm and wearable settings. Another special feature of calm computing is that its effectiveness relies on a lot of reasoning to infer the user's desires. Unlike desktop computing, users do not simply type in or use their mouse to indicate their commands—the system has to figure out if users would like the light to be turned down ever so slightly to adjust to their mood. Thus artificial intelligence (AI) techniques will help here.

virtual reality (VR) the use of elaborate input/output devices to create the illusion that the user is in a different environment

modalities classifications of the truth of a logical proposition or statement, or characteristics of an object or entity

Ubiquitous computing tends to require a significant infrastructure. Depending on the needs of a specific application, the infrastructure should include the ability for different components to communicate on wireline or wireless networks; the components should be able to discover each other's presence as do the Java-based Jini services and other registration services; the components should be able to move around physically while retaining their identity and address as in mobile IP and 3G (third generation) wireless networks. An application might require the ability to authenticate participants through the **public key infrastructure (PKI),** or the ability to make secure payments through SET, the secure electronic transaction protocol. The exact requirements from the infrastructure will vary with the application, but broad-based capabilities are likely to be needed in many cases. For example, buildings should have location sensors so that they can detect users; users' wearable computers should be able to talk to the buildings and to the computers of other users. Computers in automobiles should be able to talk to computers at tollbooths and be able to pay for the privilege of going through the booth.

Most of the technologies necessary for ubiquitous computing exist and the infrastructure is spreading more widely every moment. Although it is still unknown exactly what forms ubiquitous computing will take when it becomes a commercial reality, we can be sure it will be something both challenging and creative. SEE ALSO Ergonomics; Microchip; Operating Systems; User Interfaces.

Munindar P. Singh

public key infrastructure (PKI) the supporting programs and protocols that act together to enable public key encryption/decryption

Bibliography

Ishii, Hiroshi, Sandia Ren, and Phil Frei. "Pinwheels: Visualizing Information Flow in an Architectural Space." In *Proceedings of the Conference on Human Factors in Computing Systems*, Seattle, Washington, March 31–April 5, 2001.

Schilit, Bill N., Norman I. Adams, Rich Gold, Karin Petersen, David Goldberg, John R. Ellis, and Mark Weiser. "An Overview of the PARCTAB Ubiquitous Computing Experiment. Roy Want." *IEEE Personal Communications* 2, no. 6 (1995): 28-43.

Shenck, Nathan S., and Joseph A. Paradiso. "Energy Scavenging with Shoe-Mounted Piezoelectrics." *IEEE Micro* 21, no. 3, May/June 2001.

Expert Systems

Expert systems, also called "rule-based systems," are computer programs or sets of programs that use knowledge of a domain (a specific field or discipline) to act as an expert in that domain. Expert systems have been built for dozens of sub-fields in medicine, business, and science, making this one of the most successfully commercialized branches of **artificial intelligence (AI).**

History

During the early years of artificial intelligence, computer scientists primarily developed programs that solved well-defined, self-explanatory problems (e.g., game playing, machine translation, or symbolic integrations). These programs required clever reasoning techniques to manipulate the logical and

artificial intelligence (AI) a branch of computer science dealing with creating computer hardware and software to mimic the way people think and perform practical tasks

mathematical problems they were presented, but they did not require much knowledge beyond those techniques.

In the 1960s researchers began to realize that to solve many interesting problems, the programs would not only need to be able to interpret the problems, but they would need background knowledge to understand them fully. Through the late 1960s and early 1970s, Bruce Buchanan developed DENDRAL at Stanford University as an attempt to address that problem. DENDRAL was one of the first expert systems written. It was designed to use **mass spectrometry** and other chemical information to deduce the molecular structure of chemical compounds. DENDRAL's knowledge of chemistry consisted of hundreds of rules describing the interactions of chemical compounds. These rules were the result of more than ten years of collaboration between chemists, geneticists, and computer scientists.

mass spectrometry the process of identifying the compounds or elemental particles within a substance

On March 8, 1982, expert systems gained public and corporate attention with a cover story in *Business Week* subtitled "Computers Are Starting to Reason, Make Judgments, and Learn. By 2000, They Will Be Radically Altering Society."

Applications

Users of expert systems are often knowledgeable in the domain of the system, but are not experts themselves. The expert system gathers information by presenting the user with a series of questions. That information is integrated with its stored rules (knowledge) to generate more specific questions. In some cases (e.g., medical diagnosis), the expert system can suggest actions for the user to take (e.g., a culture or blood test) to gather more information. Eventually, the expert system delivers a decision or conclusion, often accompanied by an explanation of how it was reached.

Expert systems allow users to leverage the knowledge of experts without requiring their presence. These systems, though limited to fields where questions can be precisely stated, are useful in any field where experts are rare, expensive, or inaccessible. They can both automate a lengthy decision process and deal with large quantities of data that might overwhelm a human.

Even the broad categories to which expert systems have been applied are too numerous to list, though a particularly comprehensive, if dated, list can be found in the *Expert Systems Catalog of Applications* (1993). In medicine, systems have been applied to ECG (electrocardiography) interpretation, cancer prognosis, athlete health monitoring, infant development, antimicrobial therapy, depression therapy, skin disease diagnosis, and many other domains. Industrial applications include air traffic control, automobile diagnostics, supply chain planning, blast furnace control, power grid management, automobile design, elevator design, locomotive repair, agriculture, and manufacturing facility layout. Scientific systems have also been designed for weather prediction, analytical chemistry, electronic circuit design and analysis, space shuttle maintenance, and hazardous waste management.

While there are many full and partial successes, expert systems have limitations. Though they no longer cost $500,000 to develop as they did in the 1970s, they are still expensive to design. Their development requires the careful, long-term attention of both the programmers encoding the knowl-

edge and the experts providing it. They tend to work only in very narrow domains, and their accuracy can **degrade** without warning if a problem approaches the limits of the system's knowledge. Finally, they are only as good as the experts from whom they were programmed; unlike experts, they cannot advance the state of the art or reach novel conclusions (though they can often reach surprising conclusions that an expert might overlook). If rules are programmed incorrectly, the engine will reach incorrect conclusions or fail without warning and sometimes without indication.

Technologies

Expert systems consist of two primary components: a knowledge base and an inference engine. The knowledge base is a set of rules encoding the expert's knowledge of the field. The inference engine is the set of techniques that manipulates that knowledge with respect to user input.

To develop an expert system, programmers and experts collaborate, often for several years, to develop the knowledge base. The rules are then extensively tested on problems with known solutions and field-tested on new

Auto body mechanics use computerized expert systems to diagnose and evaluate the damage to a car after a major collision.

degrade to reduce quality or performance of a system

problems under an expert's supervision. The team then determines which rules are responsible for problems or errors in the system's conclusions, and corrects those rules. This process is repeated until the system is considered reliable enough to be used by non-experts.

Although the knowledge base must be developed from scratch for any given problem, the inference engine can often be adapted in whole or in part from previous systems. One popular category of tools is the "expert system shell," a pre-packaged engine that is ready to run with the "simple" addition of a rule set. Other tools only provide parts of engines that a programmer can assemble to build a custom engine quickly.

Inference engine techniques have been an active research topic since 1970. In the "brute-force" approach, the engine literally tries every possible answer to the problem until it finds a solution. This only works in domains where a program can list all of the possible solutions (e.g., checkers or certain logical problems) and is often prohibitively slow.

heuristics procedures that serve to guide investigation but that have not been proven

The "heuristic search" method is an improvement that uses **heuristics** to narrow down the list of possible answers before trying them. While this often allows the system to find the solution substantially faster, heuristics are, by definition, not always correct. In some cases, a heuristic will actually eliminate the correct answer. Once the system realizes that the correct answer was eliminated, it will retrace its steps, reversing the narrowing effect of each heuristic it used, until it finds the answer.

In many cases, it is not possible to check an answer for correctness; the only way to find a solution is to show, using strict logic, that the input the user provided proves a conclusion. For these cases, "production systems" are used with rules encoded as if-then statements (e.g., "if it is a bird, then it has wings"). The system can then trigger rules using information provided by the user (e.g., "it is a bird") to reach provable conclusions. By taking those conclusions and using them to trigger other rules, the system can reach more complex conclusions. In some cases, the system can use heuristics to "guess" a possible conclusion. In these cases, the system works backward from the guessed conclusion by trying to find a chain of rules to prove it.

There are many variations on these broad categories of systems. Most current systems keep track of how conclusions were reached so that they can provide plain-English explanations. These explanations assist the user in evaluating the conclusions. Some systems can work with rules that are not always correct by assigning them a certainty (probability of being correct). By combining these certainties as rules are chained, the system can produce a conclusion (or several) and tell the user how certain those conclusions are. **Fuzzy logic** allows a system to deal with qualitative information (e.g., "the fish is large") by interpreting the qualitative statement as several possible quantitative meanings, each with some amount of certainty. For example, the statement "the fish is large" might be interpreted as "there is an 80 percent chance that the fish is larger than 20 pounds, a 90 percent chance that it is larger than 10 pounds. . . ." "Predicate logic" systems can manipulate logical rules far more complex than if-then statements to reach conclusions. Beyond logical rules, more advanced systems can store knowledge as "semantic nets," "frame systems," or "structured objects," among other representations.

fuzzy logic models human reasoning by permitting elements to have partial membership to a set; derived from fuzzy set theory

Current Research

The widespread commercial applications of expert systems have given rise to research topics focusing on both system effectiveness and usability. Better plain-English explanations lead to more reliable systems. Techniques for accelerating the encoding of knowledge into rules reduce the time-consuming process of creating a knowledge base. Alternative methods for representing those rules, even by using multiple methods within a single system, increase the representative power of a rule set. Inference-engines with improved techniques for manipulating rules can reach more complex solutions, and engines that use multiple techniques can use them to complement and check each other. Inference techniques designed for reuse can simplify the complex and labor-intensive process of creating engines. SEE ALSO ARTIFICAL INTELLIGENCE; DECISION SUPPORT SYSTEMS; LISP; NEURAL NETWORKS.

Salvatore Domenick Desiano

Bibliography

Durkin, John. *Expert Systems Catalog of Applications.* Akron, OH: Intelligent Computer Systems, 1993.

Edmunds, Robert A. *The Prentice Hall Guide to Expert Systems.* Englewood Cliffs, NJ: Prentice Hall, 1988.

Jackson, Peter. *Introduction to Expert Systems,* 3rd ed. Harlow, United Kingdom: Addison Wesley Longman, 1999.

Fashion Design

In the high-profile world of fashion design, the emphasis is increasingly placed on selling a dream rather than on describing the cut and construction of garments. The fashion press excels in presenting whimsical creations on models known for their beauty, poise, and exposure. Technological advancements within the field of fashion design are rarely mentioned. When one takes a closer look at the fashion industry, however, one sees how computer technology has changed the landscape and possesses the ability to transform it further.

The design and production of garments usually is the work of a team of individuals, each of whom specializes in a different process. A designer, or design team, will first produce sketches of garments or drape fabric on a dressform to obtain different styles. The artistic rendering of a garment is there to create a mood and is typically supplemented with precise line drawings that are known as "flats." With computer-aided design (CAD) software, a designer can scan a sketch and manipulate the result with image-editing software or draw directly onto the computer's **interface** with a sensor-equipped pen and special tablet.

Although numerous sketches are still done by hand, their precise renderings in line drawings are increasingly achieved through the use of computers. Since software programs can store and project various styles, fabrics, and colors that can be interchanged at the click of a button, the design of clothing is now accessible to many business-minded individuals who may not have the previously required refined drawing skills. As a result, product-development teams and other merchandisers have become more involved in

interface a boundary or border between two or more objects or systems; also a point of access

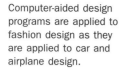

Computer-aided design programs are applied to fashion design as they are applied to car and airplane design.

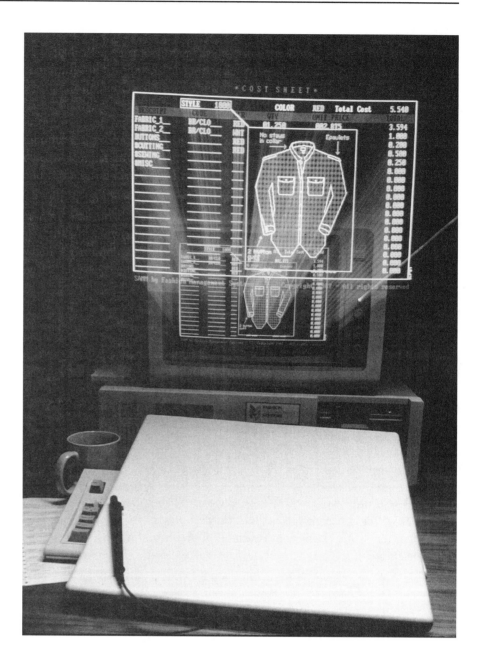

notions small items used in making clothing, like buttons and trims

the design process. The ease, convenience, speed, and versatility offered by image-editing software has thus helped to make it an essential design tool.

In conjunction with CAD software, the business-driven fashion industry also uses computer applications that allow cost-analysis of garments from their earliest stages. Once a garment is sketched, its cost can be projected by using programmed data that estimates the use of fabrics, **notions,** and assembling complexity, depending on stylistic features.

Once the styles are determined, the renderings are given to pattern-makers, who engineer ways to build the garments. Although garments draped on a three-dimensional form can be transposed to paper, the prevalent way to construct a garment is by making a flat pattern that is then cut into fabric and assembled into a three-dimensional sample. Patternmakers use basic pattern shapes that they modify according to design specifications. Essentially, they try to fit a three-dimensional body using a two-dimensional medium. By placing such elements as darts, gathers, and pleats or by breaking down larger flat pieces into several smaller sections, they can improve a garment's fit.

Although the fibers and weave structures influence the drape of a fabric and cannot be easily estimated through computer simulation, the mathematical operations and geometrical nature of the work involved in flat pattern-making make it a perfect candidate for computerization. Basic pattern shapes are now digitized and manipulated directly on the computer. Where the human hand loses precision in cutting and measuring every segment of a pattern, the computer can ensure that all the pieces of the puzzle fit together precisely and conform to the measurements of the body it is to cover quickly and with greater accuracy.

From this pattern, a sample is sewn and adjustments are made to comply with the drape of the fabric and to ensure that proportions are respected. Using the computer, the corrected patterns are positioned in various ways in order to utilize the bolts of fabric with greatest efficiency. Once this placement is determined, the fabric is piled up and the patterns can be cut with a computer-guided laser beam or knife.

Where the fashion industry needs these precision-bound tools to increase productivity and accuracy, the same technology can also allow for greater fit. Although the computerized sector of the industry caters to the masses and produces garments based on standardized measurements, some companies have started offering custom-tailored garments by entering individual customers' measurements into software programs and creating garments according to these specifications.

With the advancement of technology, new applications are devised that offer even greater potential to the field of fashion design. Present CAD software programs for designing and constructing clothing currently use what are called **orthogonal** projections to create patterns. These consist of graphic projections of objects on a grid-like surface or set of perpendicular intersections. These two-dimensional, manually-drawn flat patterns have been around since the eighteenth century, producing a wide range of fashions until settling on our present simple late twentieth century styles.

Orthogonal projection has its limitations and change is in the wind. Already computer tools developed for neuro-surgery, software developed for the aerospace industry, and the newest addition of digitized three-dimensional animation have been adapted by architects who have created a revolutionary approach to CAD design. Although some architects still start with orthogonal projection, others have abandoned it completely or relied heavily on digitized animation in the development and projection of their architectural designs. Providing that the variables found in textiles can eventually be analyzed like those of building materials, this could prove very influential in the cutting and production of clothing.

To advance even further beyond the two-dimensional flat pattern approach to clothing design, the new digital three-dimensional animation could be employed. Even now graphic design programs have become extremely sophisticated and allow designers and retailers to display their products in three-dimensional animated settings that simulate the various body types of online customers.

CUTTING EDGE TECHNOLOGY

Many schools offer coursework in CAD for fashion design majors. As CAD technology improves, more and more potential employers in the fashion industry require applicants to have knowledge of the latest technology available.

orthogonal elements or objects that are perpendicular to one another; in a logical sense this means that changes in one have no effect on the other

More important to the potential use of technology in garment construction, an image of a virtual body could be modeled with the planes of its anatomical structure reduced to simple geometrical shapes. This virtual body could be rotated and draped with the textile of choice. The cut of the garment created could follow the traditional patterns divided into front, back, and side pieces, or explore a new approach that would cover the body's geometrical planes. The pattern piece could cover one plane or be extended to a neighboring plane with which it has a common side. By following a joined series of planes, the seams could be integrated into the design, providing better fit and an endless series of possibilities in terms of design and construction. SEE ALSO ANIMATION; CAD/CAM, CA ENGINEERING; GRAPHIC DEVICES.

Anne Bissonnette and Betty Kirke

Bibliography

Aldrich, Winifred, ed. *CAD in Clothing and Textiles: A Collection of Expert Views*, 2nd ed. Cambridge, MA: Blackwell Scientific Publications, 1994.

Chase, Renée Weiss. *CAD for Fashion Design.* Upper Saddle River, NJ: Prentice Hall, 1997.

Volino, Pascal, and Nadia Magnenat-Thalmann. *Virtual Clothing: Theory and Practice.* New York: Springer, 2000.

Film and Video Editing

When most people think about what makes great movies and television programs, they might consider the importance of a well-written script, or the magical collaboration between a first-rate director and high-powered actors. But many people outside the entertainment business do not know much about the world of post-production, the sophisticated crafts and technologies that turn miles of raw footage into finished products that can teach us, motivate us, and make us laugh or cry.

Computers play a role in many aspects of post-production, including animation and special effects, but one area in which they have brought about enormous change is editing—the art and craft of arranging pictures and sound to tell the story envisioned by the writer, producer, and director.

Background

Moving images were first captured on photographic film in the late nineteenth century, and for decades film—an optical/chemical medium—was the only way to record and preserve moving images. With the delivery of the first practical videotape recorder in 1956, it became possible to capture moving images electromagnetically, eliminating the expensive and time-consuming process of developing and printing film.

Until the early 1980s, film and videotape had separate, well-defined uses in the worlds of news and entertainment. Film's strengths were seen to be excellent picture quality, long shelf life, portability, and a technology that was widely used around the world. Traditionally, film has been used for theatrical presentation, prime-time network TV production, high-end commercials (in 35 mm), and documentary (in 16 mm).

The strength of videotape has been economy, speed of production and post-production, and a "live" look. Originally, tape was used for non-prime television such as soap operas, talk shows, and game shows, and for low-end commercials.

During the 1980s and 1990s, the differences between film and video gradually became less pronounced. As video technology grew more reliable and less expensive, videotape became important in news and documentary production, in corporate communications, and eventually in consumer products. Videotape's picture quality also improved greatly, to the point where low-budget feature films like *The Blair Witch Project* are being shot on video and transferred to film for theatrical distribution. High definition—the highest quality of video—allows image quality that equals that of film. Production costs in "high-def" are lower than in film, and elaborate special effects are easier and less expensive than with traditional film optical effects.

Advanced computer video editing systems eliminate the need to hand-splice film sequences together.

Use of Computers in Editing

For most of the twentieth century, film was cut by hand. Editors were talented craftspeople who worked directly with their material—they assembled scenes by splicing together separate picture and sound rolls, and had great flexibility in rearranging and trimming shots for optimum on-screen impact.

Video editing requires extensive computer resources. High-end professional non-linear editing systems rely on expensive separate video boards with sophisticated video capture chips. All systems require fast processors—the most advanced use multiprocessing to manipulate the torrent of digital data. Video and audio are both best handled in memory-heavy systems with hundreds of megabytes of RAM (random access memory). Editors always want access to more material at higher resolutions, increasing the pressure for more hard drive space. Higher-resolution video requires high-speed interconnections capable of moving data between devices at speeds of between four hundred megabits and one gigabit per second.

The technology was simple, and although the process was labor-intensive, it allowed great creative control.

By contrast, as videotape editing evolved from the 1960s through the 1980s, it was relatively clumsy and needed rooms full of expensive equipment. The process required playing back scenes from two or more video players, and recording them in the desired sequence onto another recorder. Specialist technicians had to operate the equipment, so editors had less creative control over their material. Worse, video editing was "linear"—that is, scenes had to be assembled in order from the beginning of the program, and if a change was desired everything had to be rebuilt from that point on. The technology made the process a lot faster than film editing, but there was less opportunity for subtlety and creativity.

Then came the computer revolution. Starting in the early to mid-1990s, personal computers became powerful enough that production footage (whether it was shot on film or tape) could be transferred to hard disc arrays, and editors working with Mac- or Windows-based editing systems could have the best of both worlds. Computerized systems gave them the precision, random-access ability, and "hands-on" feel of film editing, but, since the systems were electronic, they offered the speed and low cost of the video world.

Use of these computer-based "non-linear editors" or "NLEs"—so-called to distinguish the new style of editing from traditional linear video editing—has totally changed the way content is organized in many media. For example:

- News organizations like CNN use huge amounts of computer storage to keep video materials online, allowing several editors simultaneous access to the footage so they can work on multiple versions of the story for different programs.

- All TV shows and commercials, and most movies, are now edited on NLEs.

- Consumers are buying low-cost, easy-to-use hardware and software to edit their home movies.

The Process

This is how non-linear editing is accomplished on a professional level. The original footage can be shot on film or videotape; footage shot on film is transferred to video in an expensive, carefully controlled process. Then the videotape is digitized, or "loaded in," to the NLE's hard drive.

As the footage is being transferred into the computer, it usually goes through a compression process, so it will need less storage space on the NLE's hard drives. Video files are very large—one minute of "broadcast-quality" picture and sound can consume about two gigabytes of disc storage; high definition footage requires approximately nine gigabytes per minute of material. Editors often need many hours of footage available to them as they edit a project, and digitizing that much footage without compression would require massive and expensive storage systems. But when footage is compressed, at a typical ratio of five to one, a two-minute video clip that might require 4 gigabytes (or 4,000 megabytes) if it is digitized uncompressed will need only 800 megabytes.

The trade-off with compression is that video quality is somewhat reduced (typically, the images are not as crisp and the color fidelity is not as good as the original). But the editors choose a compression ratio that gives them a picture that is good enough to make their decisions. And the reduced quality is temporary—the final product will be made using the high-quality original footage.

As the footage is digitized, the NLE's software helps the editor organize the material. The editor or an assistant "logs in" each shot, writing a description of the shot and what scene it is intended for. The system's visual interface generates a "bin" to hold all the shots that belong in a given scene. A database management system keeps track of where everything is, and allows the editor to sort and retrieve information quickly.

Once the footage is in the system, the creative part begins—building the program scene by scene. That means not just selecting the best shots to tell the story, but also developing a pace and rhythm that propel the story forward, and selecting visual transitions to blend the scenes together. The software provides an easy-to-use graphical display, and gives the editor a variety of tools to arrange the materials, including drag-and-drop, keyboard commands, and placement of scenes on a visual timeline—very much the way word processing software allows a writer to rearrange words.

The NLE's software precisely tracks all the editor's changes, remembers which shots originated where, keeps picture and sound synchronized, and makes an "edit decision list" which describes exactly the portion of each shot that has been selected to be shown in a particular order. The computer plays back the edited scenes in real time, showing the editor, director, producers, and others exactly how scenes will look in the final product. Changes can be made easily, and different ways of organizing the material can be tried out. Because the original material is not being cut or changed during this process—the computer is just displaying the editor's choices of shots in the right sequence—the editing is said to be "non-destructive." The process proceeds over and over, with scenes being continually refined until the creative team agrees that the best possible choices have been made about how to use the materials. This decision point is often called "picture lock."

Once the picture is locked, the process moves in one of three directions. First, if the production originated on film, and the final product is to be a film print (for instance a movie to be shown in theaters), the NLE generates a "negative cut list." The cut list describes exactly what portions of which shots from the original production footage have been selected. Then craftspeople physically cut or "conform" the original negative, splicing it together in the order the editor specified. Finally, traditional optical/chemical film printing techniques are used to make the prints that will be distributed to theaters.

Second, whether the production was originally shot on film or tape, if the final product is to be released on videotape, as television programs are, a "video master" is prepared. This can be done in one of two ways:

- In an "online conforming session," the edit decision list prepared by the NLE software controls a video editing system, using two or more playback videotape machines and one recorder. The high-quality videotapes containing the original footage are automatically played

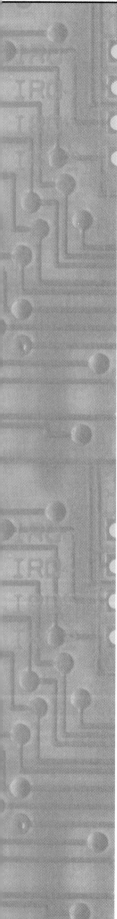

back in sequence on two or more videotape players and assembled onto a new videotape, with transitions and special effects generated by a video "switcher."

• Alternatively, the finished product can be generated completely within an NLE. First, the selected shots—which had originally been compressed to save on storage space—are re-digitized from the original videotapes into the NLE at the full resolution. Then the NLE plays them back in sequence to be recorded on a videotape recorder, with transitions and special effects generated and added by the software on the NLE.

The third way the edited material can be released is directly to broadcast. For instance, once a news story has been edited, it can be transferred immediately from the NLE over a high-speed network to an "air server," from which it is played as often as needed.

Sound Tracks

Audio can be edited within the NLE and released with the video as a final product without any further effort. Often, though, only basic sound editing is done within the NLE, and a separate team of specialists does audio mixing and "sweetening" using a similar computer-based system that is optimized for audio work.

In an audio-editing computer, multiple sound tracks are constructed for dialog, narration, music, and sound effects. The sound mixing team listens to these tracks while watching the edited picture, and carefully blends and enhances the separate tracks to tell the audio portion of the story in the most effective way. Once the sound track is finished, it can be "laid down" on digital audio tape or it can remain within the audio computer; either way it is synchronized by computer with the picture from the NLE as the final video master is produced.

What is the result of all this creativity, effort, and technology? A movie or a television program that—the creative team hopes—is so skillfully prepared that it will entertain us for a little while, or even teach us something about ourselves and our world.

The Future

Technology and economics are driving the evolution of film and video editing. Computer-based video editing at all levels will continue to become less expensive, more powerful and easier to use. This process lowers the barriers to entry for the novice filmmaker, the enterprising journalist, and the consumer who just wants to make better home movies.

The Internet is only beginning to have an effect on editing, but the possibilities are intriguing. Accessing the same materials from anywhere in the world, multiple editors will be able to collaborate on a program. Producers, directors, and executives will screen and comment on the work in progress from anywhere, and highly specialized work like sound mixing and effects generation will have no geographic limitations.

On the high end, both broadcast television and theatrical features are moving away from film and toward high-definition video—a process that will push technical requirements higher as editing systems are built to handle the extreme demands of high-def. Next up is the replacement of traditional 35 mm film projection in theaters with high-definition video taken directly from satellite or fiber optic cable—one more major step in the journey from the film medium to the electronic one. SEE ALSO ANIMATION; GRAPHIC DEVICES.

John Cosgrove

Bibliography

Ohanian, Thomas A. *Digital Nonlinear Editing*, 2nd ed. Boston: Focal Press, 1998.

Geographic Information Systems

Many difficult decision-making processes in geographic planning, environmental, and social studies arise because they require the manipulation and integration of large volumes of spatially-indexed data. Computerized geographical information systems (GIS) provide the key to the efficient use of such data sets because they can efficiently perform such functions on vast quantities of spatially addressed data. These powerful systems acquire data from many sources; change the data into a variety of useful formats; store the data; retrieve and manipulate the data for analysis; and then generate outputs required by a given user.

Underlying each GIS is a powerful spatial database management subsystem that provides such functions as efficient data storage, retrieval and updating, as well as security, integrity, and redundancy control. Within the database, a variety of mappable characteristics associated with any given geographical location are organized as a series of spatially-registered maps, or "overlays." Each of these overlays describes a single theme of geographical features (such as water features, geology, or vegetation), and is stored as a separate data layer. Each feature in a map layer is described by the linking of two components: geometry and attributes.

For example, a road is represented geometrically as a line linked with attributes describing road type, name, and conditions. A land parcel has an interior and a boundary, and is represented by a **polygon** associated with attributes describing ownership, value, and tax. Additional topological or metric information (such as neighborhood, connectivity, distance, and directions) may also be computed from geometry and stored for fast response to topology-related queries.

polygon a many-sided, closed, geometrical figure

A GIS can integrate information from a variety of sources and formats. Common geographical feature maps that describe administrative boundaries, **hydrologic** features, land use, parcels, transportation, and population data, are widely available from government agencies and private data vendors. Additional data can be captured through field measurement, use of GPS (global positioning system), and direct interpretation of remotely sensed images. There are also common data standards for sharing digital geographic data among users and producers. In order to answer queries that require combinations of multiple data inputs, source data must be pre-processed—converted for consistent format and scale and errors corrected—to achieve consistency

hydrologic relating to water

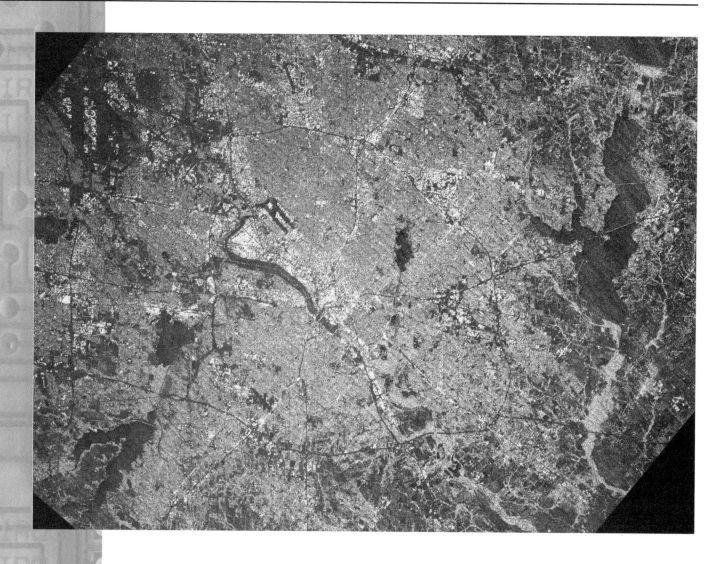

Topographic data and images (like this C-band radar image of the Dallas-Fort Worth area in Texas) are used to create geographic information systems maps. The image was taken by cameras aboard the space shuttle *Endeavor.*

and compatibility in data types, scales, spatial reference systems, spatial units, and coverage.

A typical GIS is capable of performing a variety of data analysis procedures that involve access to both spatial and non-spatial information of one or more geographical feature classes. As a generic spatial analysis engine, a GIS provides a number of primitive operations that can be combined to implement a given analytical procedure.

Map *reclassification* operations merely repackage information from an existing map layer into a new one that has feature classes and attribute categories different from the original one. Map *overlay* operations involve the creation of a new map layer from two or more existing map overlays. It begins by finding point-by-point or region-based spatial coincidence among input maps, and then assigns a new value to each location based on the spatial coincident values of input overlays. An overlay operation requires that input map layers must be compatible in scale, coordinate systems, error characteristics, and data coding methods.

Other analytical functions of GIS include buffer zones, neighborhood characterization, and connectivity measurement. A particular feature of GIS is the ability to calculate more realistic distance measures among objects based on actual geometry, travel time, and cost, rather than straight-line distance. The trend in developing GIS analytical functions is to better integrate GIS with other software in statistical analysis, operations research, and **artificial intelligence (AI)** tools.

In the forty years since their first appearance in the 1960s, geographical information systems have experienced phenomenal growth in sophistication, size, and popularity. Today, GIS is a multi-billion dollar industry and has become part of a basic information infrastructure for private enterprises, government agencies, and academic institutions. The majority of the operational GIS are used for thematic mapping, handling spatial queries, and decision-making support.

Thematic mapping involves making special purpose maps that provide appropriate content, context, symbolization, and illustrations. Geographic information systems provide utilities to make all stages of map-making faster, more accurate, and easier to do. *Spatial query* processing selects objects based on the combination of their locational, topological, and descriptive attributes. *Decision-support* functions of GIS allow users to ask "what if"questions to evaluate alternative actions.

In terms of practical applications, GIS programs assist with resource inventory, administrative recordkeeping, communication or transportation infrastructure and facility management, emergency response, and environmental monitoring preservation. Examples of GIS applications include understanding the process of water and nutrient flows over the land surface; identifying potential markets for a product in the local area; and deciding on the fastest route over which to send a fire truck to a downtown restaurant. All these tasks utilize the functionalities of a GIS to deal with complex spatial data sets.

Geographical information systems represent a **synergistic** development of multiple technical fields, including computer **cartography**, computational geometry, spatial and **relational databases**, and information visualization. Fast retrieval of spatial data is made possible by using efficient indexing schemes such as **quadtrees** or R-trees. The processing of spatial queries (e.g, point-in-polygon) relies on computational geometry **algorithms** such as line sweeping, Voronoi diagrams, and convex hulls. The increasing trend to build spatial data types and spatial operators in database engines make it possible to model the complexities of spatial data with object-relational or object-oriented approaches. Computer graphics and visualization techniques have increased the effectiveness of communicating spatial information to users.

Looking into the future, geographical information systems will likely become more user-friendly. With the development of web-based GIS, there is an evolution from single-user systems to more open, multiple-user systems. There has been much cross-fertilization between the fields of artificial intelligence and spatial information systems due to increased needs to deduct new information from retrieved data. Knowledge-based geographic information systems that incorporate deductive reasoning and learning facilities will be more powerful in modeling human spatial intelligence in the environment. An object-oriented, intelligent, dynamic, multimedia geographical information system will revolutionize people's views

RESEARCH SHARING

The *International Journal of Geographical Information Science* is a scholarly publication that brings together the latest information on GIS technology from around the globe. The publication is geared to professionals involved in GIS applications, and is available online for a fee.

artificial intelligence (AI) a branch of computer science dealing with creating computer hardware and software to mimic the way people think and perform practical tasks

synergistic relating to synergism, which is the phenomenon whereby the action of a group of elements is greater than their individual actions

cartography map making

relational databases collections of records that permit logical and business relationships to be developed between themselves and their contents

quadtrees data structures resembling trees, which have four branches at every node (rather than two as with a binary tree); used in the construction of complex databases

algorithms rules or procedures used to solve mathematical problems—most often described as sequences of steps

of the spaces and worlds in which we live. SEE ALSO EMBEDDED TECHNOLOGY (UBIQUITOUS COMPUTING); SATELLITE TECHNOLOGY; TELECOMMUNICATIONS.

Guoray Cai

Bibliography

Berry, J. K. "Fundamental Operations in Computer-assisted Map Analysis." *International Journal of Geographical Information Science* 1, no. 2 (1987): 119–136.

Laurini, R., and D. Thompson. *Fundamentals of Spatial Information Systems.* London: Academic Press, 1992.

Longley, P. A., et al. (eds.). *Geographic Information Systems: Principles, Techniques, Applications and Management.* London: John Wiley & Sons, 1999.

Gross, Alfred J.

American Inventor
1918–2001

Alfred J. Gross was the inventor of several handheld communication devices, including the first walkie-talkie. Gross began his life-long romance with wireless communications at age nine during a cruise on Lake Erie. While exploring the ship, Gross met the radio operator and was invited into the radio room to listen to the transmission. The sound of wireless telegraphy fascinated him so much that he begged his parents to buy him a crystal set, an early radio.

Shortly thereafter, Gross began to build a **ham radio** from scavenged junkyard materials. By age fifteen he was fabricating his own metal radio chassis in a metal working class. A year later he earned his amateur operator's license. He was now a ham radio operator. The next step for Gross was to build a handheld device—the walkie-talkie—to communicate. He wanted to talk with other ham operators while on the move.

His hobby began to develop into a potential career. By 1938, while a student in electrical engineering at Case Western Reserve, in Cleveland, Ohio, Gross had succeeded in inventing a two-way handheld radio using miniaturized components. He then started exploring ways to use frequencies above 100 MHz. By the end of the 1930s, he had built two models that operated at 300 MHz and could transmit a distance of 38 kilometers (30 miles). As World War II began, Gross' invention would take on a critical function.

In 1941 Gross was invited to demonstrate his walkie-talkie to the Office of Strategic Services (OSS), the forerunner of the U.S. Central Intelligence Agency (CIA). That meeting resulted in citizen Gross becoming Captain Gross and the initiation of the Joan/Eleanor project, a two-way ground to air radio system for military and espionage use. This system would enable personnel on the ground and behind enemy lines to communicate with high-flying airplanes. These transmissions could not be intercepted by the enemy as the radios operated at higher frequencies then the standard available transceivers. This feature enabled undetected gathering and reporting of enemy military movements.

Alfred J. Gross.

ham radio a legal (or licensed) amateur radio

Long after the war, Gross received recognition for his work. His contribution was cited as significantly shortening the war through the successful gathering of intelligence. The net result was the saving of countless lives. This "Top Secret" project was not declassified until 1976.

After the war, Gross set up two companies: Citizens Radio Corporation, which focused on the designing, development, and manufacture of personal wireless transceivers; and Gross Electronics, which designed and manufactured other communications products. Both companies were based in Cleveland, Ohio.

For the next twenty years, Gross developed circuitry for various wireless devices. In 1948 the Federal Communications Commission (FCC) approved the two-way radio, "Citizens' Band," for personal use. Initially, these radios were used by farmers and the U.S. Coast Guard. A year later, Gross invented and patented circuitry that responded selectively to specific signals for use as a pocket-sized receiver, the pager. Physicians were his targeted audience for the use of such pagers. However, the initial reaction of the medical community was unenthusiastic because the device beeped. Medical professionals anticipated that the noise would annoy patients and might even interrupt the physician's golf game. However, Gross lived to see his pager not only accepted but also become a necessary device for many professionals and service providers.

Gross's invention also received unexpected fame when it was featured in the Dick Tracy comic book series, developed by Chester Gould. The cartoonist incorporated Gross' idea of a miniaturized two-way radio into the series as a two-way wrist radio. Then, in the late 1950s, the U.S. Navy parachuted an unmanned battery-operated weather station into the Antarctic that was designed and manufactured by Gross Electronics. Gross continued to develop and patent various cordless and portable telephonic devices through the 1960s.

After closing his companies, Gross did not retire but continued to conduct research as a specialist in microwave communications for Sperry Corporation, General Electric, and Westinghouse as well as other large corporations. At seventy-two he became the senior principal engineer for the Orbital Science Corporation while also continuing to work on personal projects. He also continued to give presentations to elementary and high school students on technology and inventions.

Although his numerous patents expired before Gross could realize the full material rewards for his efforts, he is quoted as observing, without rancor, that, "If I still had the patents on my inventions I would be as rich as Bill Gates." For Gross the true reward was the ability to continue being productive throughout his life. He never lost his zest for exploring and expanding wireless technology and sharing his knowledge and enthusiasm with others. SEE ALSO BELL LABS; CELLULAR TECHNOLOGY; INTERNET; TELECOMMUNICATIONS; WIRELESS TECHNOLOGY.

Bertha Kugelman Morimoto

HONORABLE CAREER

Throughout his career, Gross received recognition for his inventions. Among these are a commendation from U.S. President Ronald Reagan, the Institute of Electrical and Electronics Engineers (IEEE) Century of Honors Medal, and the Marconi Memorial Gold Medal of Achievement.

Bibliography

Saxon, Wolfgang. "Al Gross, Inventor of Gizmos with Potential, Dies at 82." *New York Times*, January 2, 2001.

Hacking

For years, "hacker" was a positive term that described computer enthusiasts who had a zeal for computer programming. Those who hacked took pride in their ability to write computer programs that stretched the capabilities of computer systems and find clever solutions to seemingly impossible problems. Although many computer enthusiasts still ascribe to this definition, the everyday usage of the word has changed significantly. Today, "hacking" generally refers to individuals who break into computer systems or use their programming skills or expert knowledge to act maliciously. (Traditional hackers—the good kind—prefer to use the term "cracker" to refer to these individuals.)

Some of the most common types of hacking include:

- Breaking into computer networks;
- Bypassing passwords or copy protection in computer software;
- Defacing and/or damaging Internet web sites;
- Causing a denial of service attack on a web site or network (preventing legitimate users from accessing a web site);
- Stealing valuable information such as passwords and credit card data.

A Systematic Process

Although portrayed otherwise in Hollywood films and in television shows, hacking is a systematic, tiresome process in which the attacker attempts methodically to locate computer systems, identify their vulnerabilities, and then compromise those vulnerabilities to obtain access. Experts have identified six steps that are generally followed in the hacking process. These include (1) footprinting (reconnaissance); (2) scanning; (3) enumeration; (4) penetration; (5) advance; and (6) covering tracks.

Footprinting. The first technique often used by hackers is called footprinting. The objective is to gather information essential to an attack and enable an attacker to obtain a complete profile of an organization's security posture. During this phase, the hacker might gain information about the location of the company, phone numbers, employee names, security policies, and the overall layout of the target network. Often, hackers can perform this work with a simple web browser, a telephone, and a search engine. Unfortunately, humans are often the weakest security link in a corporation. A clever phone call to the technical support department can often compromise critical information: "Hi—this is Bill and I forgot my password. Can you remind me what it is?"

Scanning. Next, hackers perform scanning to gain a more detailed view of a company's network and to understand what specific computer systems and services are in use. During this phase, the hacker determines which systems on the target network are live and reachable from the Internet. Commonly used scanning techniques include network **ping sweeps** and **port scans**. A ping sweep lets the attacker determine which individual computers on the network are alive and potential targets for attack. Port scanning can be used to determine what ports (a port is like a door or window on a house) are open on a given computer, and whether or not the software managing those ports has any obvious vulnerabilities.

TV HACKERS

The U.S. entertainment industry often portrays hackers as heroes, out to reveal corporate or governmental corruption and conspiracies. Some of the most intriguing hackers to appear on television beginning in the 1990s were featured on the *X-Files*. The trio of conspiracy theorists—Byers, Frohike, and Langly—helped FBI agent Mulder with numerous cases by hacking into top secret government systems.

---

ping sweeps technique that identifies properties belonging to a server computer, by sending it collections of "ping" packets and examining the responses from the server

port scans operations whereby ports are probed so that information about their status can be collected

Enumeration. The third phase is the process of identifying user accounts and poorly protected computing resources. During the enumeration stage, the hacker connects to computers in the target network and pokes around these systems to gain more information. While the scanning phase might be compared to a knock on the door or a turn of the doorknob to see if it is locked, enumeration could be compared to entering an office and rifling through a file cabinet or desk drawer for information. It is definitely more intrusive.

Penetration. During the fourth phase, penetration, the attacker attempts to gain control of one or more systems in the target network. For example, once an attacker has acquired a list of usernames during enumeration, he can usually guess one of the users' passwords and gain more extensive access to that user's account. Alternatively, once the attacker has determined that a target computer is running an old or buggy piece of software or one that is configured improperly, the hacker may attempt to exploit known vulnerabilities with this software to gain control of the system.

Advance. In the advance phase of hacking, the attacker leverages computers or accounts that have been compromised during penetration to launch additional attacks on the target network. For instance, the attacker can break into more sensitive administrator root accounts, install backdoors or **Trojan horse** programs, and install network sniffers to gather additional information (for example, passwords) from data flowing over the network.

Covering Tracks. In the final phase of hacking, the hacker eliminates any records or logs showing his malicious behavior. By deleting log files, disabling system auditing (which would otherwise alert the administrator to malicious activities), and hiding hacking files that the hacker has introduced, he can cover his tracks and avoid detection. Finally, the hacker can install a root kit—a series of programs that replace the existing system software to both cover his tracks and gather new information.

Recent Attacks, Countermeasures, and Motivations

Since the late 1990s, the number of hacking attacks has grown dramatically. Both private companies such as Microsoft, Yahoo, Amazon.com, Buy.com, and U.S. government entities like the Federal Bureau of Investigation (FBI) and the White House have been targeted by hackers. In the vast majority of incidents, hackers have attempted to either launch denial of service attacks or deface Internet web pages with inappropriate content. However, some of the attacks are far more insidious. In January of 2000, a nineteen-year-old Russian hacker, using the pseudonym Maxim, threatened to publish more than 300,000 customer credit card numbers (obtained by hacking into a popular e-commerce site) if he was not given $100,000 cash. Beyond these highly publicized cases, it is unclear how many corporations have been hacked successfully; however, from all accounts, the number is definitely large and growing.

A number of technologies are available to companies to prevent hacking attacks. The most popular tools are Internet firewalls, anti-virus software, intrusion detection systems, and vulnerability assessment tools. Firewalls are used to set up a virtual wall between the Internet and the company's internal network to repel attackers. Anti-virus software detects

---

HACKERS AND Y2K

As the millenium approached, concerns about the Y2K (year 2000) bug surfaced. At that time, many computer programs stored dates as two digits (e.g., "99" for "1999"). People worried that a date of "00" might be read by computers as "1900" rather than "2000" and cause computers to malfunction or shut down. As business and government agencies scrambled to patch these programs, concern grew that terrorists would try to take advantage of the situation and hack into such systems. However, corporations and government bodies, including the Federal Bureau of Investigation, took steps to secure programs, preventing hackers from crashing vital services, such as the distribution of social security checks.

Trojan horse a potentially destructive computer program that masquerades as something benign; named after the wooden horse employed by the Acheans to conquer Troy

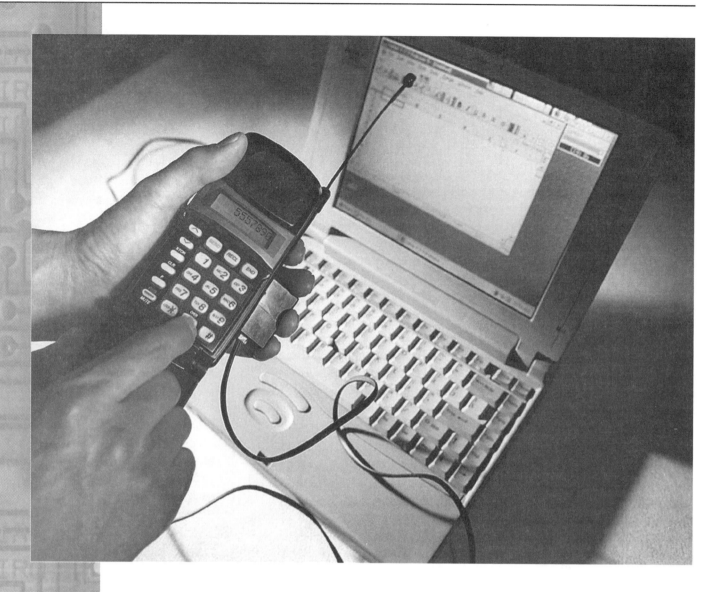

Tools of the trade: Hackers have a variety of tools at their disposal to use in breaching computing and telecommunications equipment. Some hackers meet at conferences to exchange ideas and preview the latest gadgets.

and removes computer viruses, worms, and Trojan horses. Intrusion detection systems watch over critical networks and computers looking for suspicious activities, and can alert administrators in the event of an attack. Finally, corporations use vulnerability assessment tools to inventory their computing infrastructure and better understand the existing vulnerabilities.

Contrary to popular belief, most hackers are not international or industrial spies with evil motives and a desire to rule the world; most hackers have a simpler agenda. Among hackers, one of the most frequently cited motivations is that hacking is fun and is like solving a game or a puzzle. Many hackers perceive their activities to be harmless and they do not believe that they are victimizing anyone. In addition, the thrill of doing something illegal or the ability to access data unavailable to the public can be a tempting motivator. The chance to earn recognition from within a hacker group also offers strong incentive for up-and-coming hackers who have yet to gain a reputation. Finally, many hackers justify their actions by explaining that they are doing a service for other computer users by identifying new security holes.

Judicial, Criminal, and Civil Implications of Hacking

The following federal statutes offer computer crime and hacking protection:

- 18 U.S.C. § 1029. Fraud and Related Activity in Connection with Access Devices;

- 18 U.S.C. § 1030. Fraud and Related Activity in Connection with Computers;

- 18 U.S.C. § 1362. Communication Lines, Stations, or Systems;

- 18 U.S.C. § 2511. Interception and Disclosure of Wire, Oral, or Electronic Communications Prohibited;

- 18 U.S.C. § 2701. Unlawful Access to Stored Communications;

- 18 U.S.C. § 2702. Disclosure of Contents;

- 18 U.S.C. § 2703. Requirements for Governmental Access.

As this list suggests, there is a substantial body of statutory law that applies directly to computer crime and hackers. Hacking of government computers, computers that are used by or for the government, and private computers used "in interstate commerce or communications" can be prosecuted under existing statutes. The existing statutory framework also provides for civil liability for unauthorized interception of communications. Finally, federal statutes exist to protect federal records, property, or public money. Consequently, bank, credit records, and electronic fund transfers are all protected by federal laws.

In recent cases, prosecuted hackers have been incarcerated, sentenced to home detention, and/or ordered to pay restitution. Offenders have been incarcerated for up to two years and some have been ordered to pay thousands of dollars in fines. SEE ALSO HACKERS; PRIVACY; SECURITY; SECURITY HARDWARE; SECURITY SOFTWARE.

Carey Nachenberg

Bibliography

McClure, Stuart, Joel Scambray, and George Kurtz. *Hacking Exposed.* Berkeley, CA: Osborne/McGraw-Hill, 1998.

Internet Resources

Cybercrime. Web site for the Computer Crime and Intellectual Property Section (CCIPS) of the Criminal Division of the U.S. Department of Justice. <http://www.cybercrime.gov>

Manzano, Yanet. "Anatomy of a Hacking Attack." *Policies to Enhance the Forensic of Computer Security.* Computer Science at Florida State University web site. <http://www.cs.fsu.edu/~manzano/research/honorthesis/part2.html>

Hewlett, William

American Executive
1913–2001

William Hewlett teamed with David Packard to create one of the largest and most successful technology businesses in the world, the Hewlett-Packard Company. After an initial investment of $538 to set up shop in a garage,

William R. Hewlett.

oscillator an electronic component that produces a precise waveform of a fixed known frequency; this can be used as a time base (clock) signal to other devices

Silicon Valley an area in California near San Francisco, which has been the home location of many of the most significant information technology orientated companies and universities

Hewlett and Packard worked to see their organization grow into a multi-billion dollar enterprise. The pair also became known for their management style, called "management by walking around," which was copied by other technology companies. In their walks, they made inpromptu visits and talked to employees of all levels, including non-management personnel.

Hewlett was born on May 20, 1913, in Ann Arbor, Michigan, and grew up in San Francisco. Dyslexia prevented him from reading well, so he approached learning by disassembling common objects such as door locks and other mechanical devices and conducting experiments in chemistry. In 1930 Hewlett entered Stanford University, graduating with a bachelor of arts degree in 1934. It was during this time that he and David Packard began a friendship that would last for sixty years.

Hewlett continued his education at Massachusetts Institute of Technology, earning a master of science degree in engineering. The last phase of his education was an advanced degree in engineering from Stanford, which he completed in 1939. That was also the year that he and Packard decided to form an electronics company in Palo Alto, California. With their initial $538 investment, a garage for a shop, and lots of ideas, the Hewlett-Packard Company (HP) was born. The name of the company (i.e., the order of their names) was determined in a coin toss. Hewlett took charge of product development, while Packard assumed marketing duties.

HP's initial products included a tuner for harmonicas, a self-flushing urinal, a shock machine to induce weight loss, and a foul line indicator for bowling alleys. The first successful product, the audio **oscillator**, was based on Hewlett's graduate research at Stanford. The oscillator provided a cheaper, easier way to generate audio frequencies, which made it useful for geological and medical instruments and military equipment. Walt Disney Studios, HP's first customer, used the oscillator to develop the unique sound track for the animated movie *Fantasia*, starring Mickey Mouse. The business was profitable and growing, and by the 1950s HP would become the dominant provider of electronic testing and measurement equipment.

During World War II, Hewlett served on the staff of the U.S. Army's chief signal officer, and then became head of the electronics section of the New Development Division of the War Department Special Staff. In this capacity, he was part of a special team that inspected Japanese industries at the end of the war. One benefit from his military service was meeting first-rate engineers whom he later recruited to work for his company. When he returned to HP at the end of the war, he became vice president of the company.

His military experience gave Hewlett insight into management styles. With Packard, he developed employee-oriented polices. The company pioneered such ideas as profit sharing, flextime, catastrophic health insurance, decentralized decision-making, open offices, and management by objective. When former employees started their own companies in **Silicon Valley**, they often instituted these same practices.

Steve Jobs, cofounder of Apple Computer, credits Hewlett for his own start in life as an entrepreneur as well as for his own management style. Jobs contacted HP as a twelve-year-old looking for spare parts to construct a frequency counter. Not only did Hewlett provide the parts, but he also hired

Jobs for a summer position in the division that produced frequency counters. There are numerous other anecdotes about Hewlett and his generosity with others.

The first HP computer, Model 2116, was an automatic controller for measurement systems. Introduced in 1966, it was redesigned from a free-standing model to desktop size, marketed and sold as a calculator. Hewlett then challenged his engineers to further shrink the size to allow the device to fit into a shirt pocket. The resulting HP scientific calculator quickly replaced the **slide rule** as the computational device for scientists and engineers. Today the company is best known for its laser printers and scanners.

Hewlett's own interests went far beyond engineering. He was a modern-day renaissance man. He and his wife, Flora, established the William and Flora Hewlett Foundation which supports educational, environmental, arts and other programs. After Hewlett's death on January 12, 2001, the foundation was to receive a major portion of his estate in order to continue supporting these causes.

Hewlett was also instrumental in the founding of the Public Policy Institute of California, which researches economic, social, and political issues that impact the state. His interest in conservation led to his purchase of land on the shore of Lake Tahoe (located between California and Nevada) and deeding it to the U.S. Forest Service in order to prevent development along the pristine lake front. Hewlett was also an amateur botanist, and he photographed and catalogued many California wild flowers.

Hewlett held honorary degrees from numerous American colleges and universities, was a member of the National Academy of Engineering and the National Academy of Sciences, and served as trustee for various educational institutions. He also served as a member of the President's General Advisory Committee on Foreign Assistance Programs and the President's Science Advisory Committee during the Lyndon Johnson Administration. In 1985, he was awarded the National Medal of Science by President Ronald Reagan. SEE ALSO COMPUTERS, GENERATIONS; IBM CORPORATION; WATSON, THOMAS J., SR.

Bertha Kugelman Morimoto

slide rule invented by Scotsman John Napier (1550–1617), a device that permits the mechanical automation of calculations using logarithms

DAVID PACKARD

A cofounder of Hewlett-Packard, David Packard (1912–1996) was president of HP from 1947 to 1964. Then he became chairperson of the board and chief executive officer. In 1969 he was appointed as deputy U.S. secretary of defense. In addition to establishing the David and Lucile Packard Foundation, he served on various boards devoted to environment and conservation issues.

Internet Resources

Seipel, Tracy, and Therese Poletti. "Silicon Valley Loses Icon and Philanthropist." *Mercury News.* <http://www.mercurycenter.com>

"William Hewlett 1913–2001." *Hewlett-Packard Company.* <http://www.hp.com/hpinfo/newsroom/hewlett/index2.htm>

Home System Software

One of the principal reasons that the personal computer has become a universally used appliance is that there is a wide array of software designed to support the needs and interests of home users. The personal computer is not only a workstation for word processing, accounting, and Internet access. It is also a reference library providing direct access to atlases, dictionaries, encyclopedias, and other reference works; an entertainment system providing recorded music, movies, and games; and occasionally a medium for controlling other automated home systems.

The software commonly installed on home systems falls into the following categories:

- Productivity applications, including office suites, personal financial management, and HTML composer/editor applications;
- System and disk management utilities;
- Anti-virus software;
- File compression, decompression, and archiving applications;
- Digital document and eBook readers;
- Internet connectivity and web browsing;
- Reference tools;
- Streaming audio and video players;
- CD-RW (compact disc-rewritable) and DVD (digital versatile disc) tools;
- Games.

Office Suites

The office suite is at the core of most home systems. The suite generally consists of a set of applications supporting word processing, presentations, electronic mail, spreadsheets, and database creation, typically outfitted with a common interface, and usually designed to provide inter-application communications. The most popular suite is Microsoft *Office*—there are versions for both Windows and Macintosh operating systems—but there are other commercial suites with modest shares of the market, most notably Corel *WordPerfect Office* and Microsoft *Works*. There is now also competition in the open source software environment, where Sun Microsystems' *StarOffice*, its open source counterpart, *OpenOffice*, and some of the applications included in GNOME *Office*, are compatible with Microsoft *Office* at the output file level.

Personal financial software is another popular productivity application. These programs are designed to manage personal finances—including checking, credit card accounts, and investment accounts—and some enable users to update their personal bank accounts interactively. Banks and investment brokerages have also begun to provide customers with software specially designed to manage personal accounts.

Yet another popular productivity application is the HTML (Hypertext Markup Language) composer/editor. In some cases, the HTML composer/editor is part of an office suite—for example, Microsoft's *FrontPage* is now included in certain versions of Microsoft *Office*, and Microsoft Word is also capable of composing and editing HTML files. Other popular HTML composing and editing tools, such as Macromedia's *Dreamweaver*, are standalone development environments incorporating many other features and utilities, including remote web site management.

System and Disk Management Utilities

Because hard disks grew larger and less expensive in 2001, and the number of programs installed on a home system grew more numerous, utilities aimed

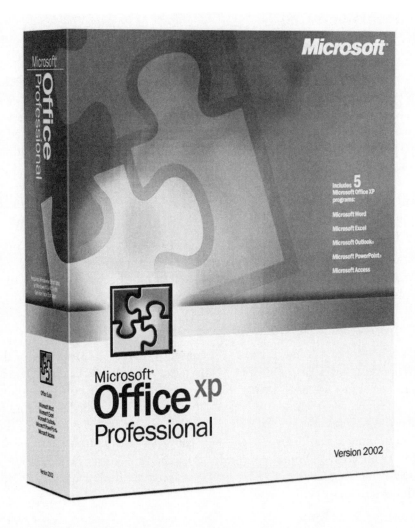

In 2001 Microsoft introduced a new version of Microsoft Office called XP. Among its users are telecommuters who need up-to-date business software in their home offices.

at managing disks and how files are written to disks have become increasingly important.✳ Most of the applications written in this area are designed to scan hard disks for physical defects, detect fragmented files, and reorganize file systems.

✳A new home personal computer in 2002 was likely to have a hard disk of 40-80 gigabytes in capacity.

Disk defragmentation tools re-write the files on a disk to increase the efficiency and reliability with which programs and other files are called from the disk. Tools of this type are important to many users, because disk fragmentation is a common problem on systems that enjoy heavy usage, and because highly fragmented file systems can have a significant and adverse effect on performance of a computer. These programs cannot actually fix physical defects, but most of them are able to preserve the integrity of systems and user data by identifying and marking defective clusters.

Disk management tools are often the core of a much larger set of tools included in a number of popular systems utilities packages. Such sets commonly include utilities intended to correct minor errors in the configuration of the operating system and/or applications, identify and mark redundant files for deletion, clear system and application caches, and restore deleted files.

Anti-Virus Software

Anti-virus software is arguably the most important of the utilities that may be installed on a personal computer. Computer viruses are common, and they can be transmitted in a number of different ways, including infected floppy disks, file transfer, and electronic mail. Most of the viruses that circulate are designed to corrupt and destroy file systems. Some of the newer viruses in circulation are especially dangerous, because they are designed to copy personal information, such as the information in an electronic address book, and then use the data as the basis for propagating the virus and infecting other systems by sending copies of the virus to other users via e-mail. Anti-virus software is designed to scan local file systems, on demand or on a scheduled basis, and check incoming e-mail, with particular attention to the contents of attached files.

A key to the effectiveness of anti-virus software is the frequency and thoroughness with which it is updated. The most effective anti-virus programs are updated as often as several times a week via the Internet.

Adobe Acrobat Reader and eBook Readers

Files rendered in Adobe's Portable Document Format (PDF) are one of the most popular ways of publishing formatted documents, because PDF enables authors to preserve formatting beyond the framework of the application in which the document was created, and because Adobe has elected to make the Acrobat *Reader* available free of charge and for a number of different computer platforms. So, the Acrobat *Reader* is a common part of the software installed on home systems. In addition, Adobe makes available *eBook Reader*, which supports PDF files and the Electronic Book Exchange (EBX) digital rights management standards.

Microsoft makes several document viewers available without charge, including viewers for *Access, Excel, PowerPoint,* and *Word* as well as its *Reader*, which supports Microsoft's own eBook format. The current version of the Microsoft *Reader* supports text, images, and audio. Future versions of the Microsoft *Reader* are expected to support other media, including streaming video.

Archiving and Compression Utilities

Archived and compressed files are a common element of file management, storage, and exchange. There are a number of relevant methods for archiving and compressing (or uncompressing) files in the personal computer environment, distinguished mainly by the efficiency of the underlying **algorithms**, but the most widely used in the personal computer environment are utilities that incorporate the compression/decompression algorithm developed by Phil Katz. Recognizable by the **de facto** standard file extension, *.zip, this archiving and compression format is used to store and transmit programs and documents.

algorithms rules or procedures used to solve mathematical problems—most often described as sequences of steps

de facto as is

Reference Tools

PC vendors recognized early on that they could capture a significant part of the then-lucrative market for home encyclopedia sales if they included CD-ROM (compact disc-read only memory) based encyclopedias and other reference works as part of the installed software bundle that shipped with their systems, or sold reference works of this type as a low-priced addition. As a result, large numbers of systems include a multimedia encyclopedia. (In the beginning, the multimedia encyclopedias were decidedly inferior to most printed encyclopedias, but in recent years, encyclopedias such as Microsoft's *Encarta* have achieved much greater editorial authority.) In addition, such systems often include other reference works, such as an atlas, a dictionary, and a thesaurus, and in many cases these reference works are supplemented by Internet-based updating services.

Internet Connectivity

Tens of millions of personal computer users connect to the Internet from home, and many of them use third-party applications to connect with an **Internet Service Provider (ISP)**, connect to remote systems via telnet, read and send e-mail, and upload and download files. ISPs, most notably America Online, make such software available without charge to customers paying for online access through their services.

Most Internet-connected users are using Microsoft's *Internet Explorer* or Netscape's *Communicator* to browse the World Wide Web. Because web browsers also support various other functions, including remote login, file transfer, and access to remote services, including e-mail services, the web browser is not only an almost-universal application, it is also one that plays a multiplicity of roles on many home systems.

Streaming Audio and Video

In recent years, streaming audio and video have become important sources of information and entertainment for Internet-connected users, particularly users with broadband access (via digital subscriber line or cable modem services). Because there are competing technologies—Microsoft uses technologies based on the WAV file format, whereas almost all of the other application developers in this area rely on relevant aspects of the **MPEG (Moving Pictures Experts Group)** standards— many users have two or more applications to support streaming audio and video installed on their systems. Today, it would not be unusual for a home system to host both Microsoft's *Windows Media Player* and Real Networks' *Real Player*, each of which may be downloaded free-of-charge over the Internet.

CD-R, CD-RW, and DVD

A growing number of home systems are equipped with CD drives that are capable of recording CDs (CD-R) and addressing rewriteable CDs (CD-RW). Such systems include utilities that are designed to write to blank CDs and/or format and read rewriteable discs.

In addition, many new systems are outfitted with drives that support digital versatile discs (DVDs) and an accompanying DVD-ROM player. (DVD is an optical disc technology that holds 4.7 gigabyte of information, and that in an expanded format is expected to hold up to 17 gigabytes of video, audio, or other information. DVD uses the MPEG standards file and compression standard.)

Internet Service Provider (ISP) a commercial enterprise which offers paying subscribers access to the Internet (usually via modem) for a fee

MPEG (Moving Picture Experts Group) an encoding scheme for data files that contain motion pictures—it is lossy in the same way as JPEG (Joint Photographic Experts Group) encoding

Games

Home systems commonly include games of various types. There are many types of games available, but the most popular games fall into the following categories: action; adventure and fantasy; military; and sports simulation. Internet-based games, using Java, Shockwave, or some other distributable media, are increasing in popularity, as are interactive, multi-player games. Computer games are distinctive among the applications installed on home systems because games commonly require more sophisticated or specialized hardware. For example, many games require comparatively more powerful graphics adapters; others require special physical controllers.

The Future

The software discussed earlier is designed to be installed and run locally. But Microsoft, Sun, and other computer industry leaders are now in the process of moving toward a new model for the pricing and distribution of software, under which software will be made available across the Internet and on the basis of renewable subscriptions. The companies that are leading this change believe that the model will generate revenue for them and provide better services for clients. It is not clear, however, whether subscription models served across the Internet will succeed in the short term—customer resistance appears to be significant and the availability of sufficient network **bandwidth** remains a problem—nor is it clear how the new model will influence the configuration of home systems. SEE ALSO Animation; Embedded Technology (Ubiquitous Computing); Integrated Software; Music.

bandwidth a measure of the frequency component of a signal or the capacity of a communication channel to carry signals

Christinger Tomer

Bibliography

Gralla, Preston. *How the Internet Works*, 6th ed. Indianapolis, IN: Que Books, 2001.

Steinmetz, Ralf, and Klara Nahrstedt. *Multimedia: Computing, Communications, and Applications: Media Coding and Content Processing*, 2nd ed. Upper Saddle River, NJ: Prentice Hall, 2002.

White, Ron. *How Computers Work*, 6th ed. Indianapolis, IN: Que Books, 2002.

Image Analysis: Medicine

The evolution of computers has dramatically affected the quality of human life in the field of medicine. Many developments during the last thirty years of the twentieth century have taken place in the field of diagnostic radiology, which is used to diagnose and sometimes treat illnesses. Among the image analysis tools now available that are derived from advances in computer technology are the ultrasound, computed tomography, nuclear medicine, and magnetic resonance imaging.

Ultrasound

Ultrasound is an example of technology that was first developed to serve military purposes. The principle behind ultrasonography was first used during World War II. Called SONAR, it helped detect the presence of underwater submarines. Ultrasound was not widely used in medicine until the early 1970s. Diagnostic ultrasound uses sound waves that are too high for the human ear to detect (between one million and 20 million cycles per second). These sound waves are used to evaluate the soft tissues of the body, such as muscles and organs.

The method is simple. First, a **piezoelectric crystal** is "pulsed" with electricity, making the crystal vibrate in a hand-held unit, called a transducer. The result is a sound wave. When the transducer is applied to the skin with a special "electrophoretic" gel, the sound waves are sent through tissue until they encounter "acoustical resistance." Such resistance makes some portion of the sound wave reflect back to its source. After pulsing, the transducer stops and "listens" for the sound waves reflected back to the crystal. Once that happens, the crystal vibrates again, producing electricity to indicate the pressure, amplitude, frequency, and speed of the returning wave. The computer then records the results. With this information, the computer is able to construct an image of the variety and depth of tissues through which the wave has passed. The use of ultrasound is limited, however. Tissues with too much acoustical resistance, for example bone and air, make this tool useless when the tissue to be examined lies behind a bone or a lung.

Computed Tomography

Computed Tomography, or CT, which became widely used in the late 1970s, would be impossible without computers. In CT, X-rays are transmitted through a body at various angles. The X-rays are then measured on the other side of the body by detectors. Depending on the percentage of X-rays that are successfully transmitted through the body, the computer is able to create a matrix defining the structure of tissues that absorbed the X-rays. The resulting images are usually displayed as slices, however, complex two- and three-dimensional images may be constructed by the computer if additional information is needed by physicians. The CT scanner usually takes multiple slices that are a prescribed distance apart, from millimeters to centimeters.

Modern CT scanners use slices made up of millions of **pixels**. These pixels are assigned a number on the grayscale somewhere in between very black and very white, and given a numerical value. With CT, the computer can adjust the grayscale after the study is complete to allow the trained observer to study a particular tissue density. For instance, the grayscale is adjusted to a very low level to look inside the lung, which is mostly air. With slight differences of grayscale, the image could show subtle differences in lung tissue, but with that particular scale, muscle and bone surrounding the lung would both look white. Conversely, if the goal of the study is to look for a small metal fragment imbedded in the spine, the grayscale would be adjusted to allow the image to differentiate between the density of metal versus the slightly less dense bone. Air, muscles, and other tissues in that study would look uniformly black. Both examinations can be done, without repeating the study, simply by varying the grayscale level of a given result.

Nuclear Medicine

Nuclear medicine is another type of diagnostic study that requires computers. These studies deal with the body's function more than with evaluating anatomy. Special radioactive molecules are tailored to target an

---

EXAMINING THE OCEAN FLOOR

Ultrasound technology (SONAR), first used during World War II to detect enemy submarines, is still used to locate submersed objects. In 1998 a team of scientists, led by underwater archaeologist Robert Ballard, went in search of the USS *Yorktown,* an aircraft carrier that was sunk during the Battle of Midway in 1942. Using a SONAR sled and a robot, the team developed digital images of the Pacific Ocean floor; after analyzing the images, they pinpointed the remains of the ship.

piezoelectric crystal an electronic component that when subjected to a current will produce a waveform signal at a precise rate, which can then be used as a clock signal in a computer

pixels single picture elements on a video screen; the individual dots making up a picture on a video screen or digital image

organ's function. These radioactive materials are usually injected into the patient. After a given period of time, the patient is examined with a special device that measures radioactivity from the body. The computers measure the amount of radioactivity, help determine the source of that activity, and most importantly, are used to filter out misleading radioactivity.

Magnetic Resonance Imaging

Magnetic resonance imaging, or MRI, is very different. A strong magnet is utilized to align protons in the human body. The MRI machine then briefly

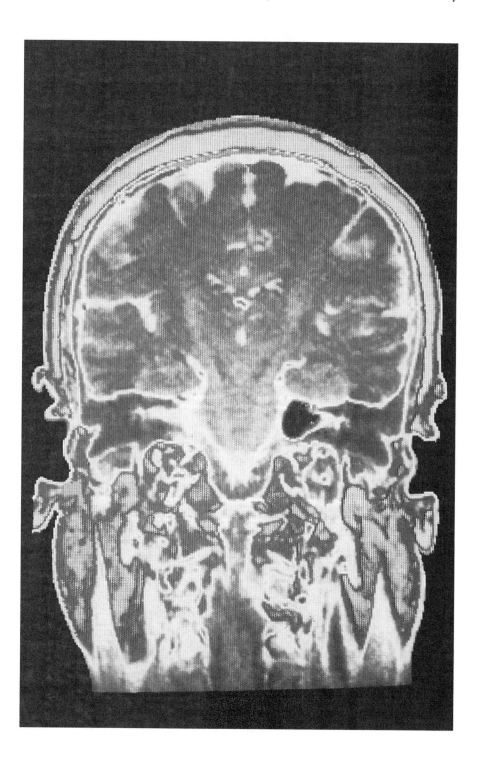

Physicians use magnetic resonance imagery (MRI) scans, like this image detailing the coronal section of the head and brain, to determine the extent of someone's health problems.

sends radio waves through the body, exciting the protons. The unit then "listens" for the radio waves that the excited protons emit. The machine measures the number of hydrogen nuclei, or protons, in a given part of the body. Different body tissues, and even the different chemicals in the tissues, emit different radio waves.

After the study is done using the desired frequency, the information is collected and digitized by the computer, so the information can be presented and analyzed. Since the frequency of the radio waves is chosen for a specific task, the process might be repeated several times using different frequencies in a single study.

Evolution of Medical Technology

All of these techniques would be impossible without advances in both physics and computers. The results from these technologies, as well as regular (called plain-film) X-rays, can be digitized, and therefore analyzed, manipulated, transported, stored, and presented in multiple ways.

When these tools were first introduced, the computers that ran them were **mainframe computers** requiring their own customized room with extensive cooling systems. Over the years, they became smaller as computers became more powerful. By the end of the twentieth century most of these studies were being done with computers only slightly larger than PCs. As with everything else in the computer field, these tools, software applications, and technologies continue to evolve.

mainframe computers large computers used by businesses and government agencies to process massive amounts of data; generally faster and more powerful than desktop computers but usually requiring specialized software

With great technological advances, uses for computer image analysis are limited only by the imagination. Computer color analysis is used to measure the success of bleaching teeth. It is also used to analyze lesion borders in various types of skin cancer as well as to examine the back of the eye through digitized retinal analysis. Image analysis can be used to evaluate wound healing that is undetectable to the human eye. Also, image analysis computer programs are invaluable in guiding surgeons in microscopic surgery.

Outside of medicine, uses for image analysis abound in the sciences, from the development of agricultural products, to the study of the activity and reproduction of plant and animal cells. Image analysis tools are used for the genetic analysis of various living entities. Computer image analysis is also becoming an economical and accurate method in the teaching of biology, microbiology, and other fields of science. SEE ALSO MEDICAL SYSTEMS; MOLECULAR BIOLOGY; SCIENTIFIC VISUALIZATION.

Anwer H. Puthawala and Mary McIver Puthawala

Bibliography

Taveras, Juan M., and Joseph T. Ferrucci. *Radiology: Diagnosis, Imaging, Intervention.* Philadelphia, PA: Lippincott Williams & Wilkins, 2000.

Kistler, Robert A. "Image Acquisition, Processing and Analysis in the Biology Laboratory." *The American Biology Teacher* 57, no. 3 (1995): 151(7).

Integrated Software

Much of the developed world's population now requires computer technology to perform a host of tasks. People rely on computers when they go

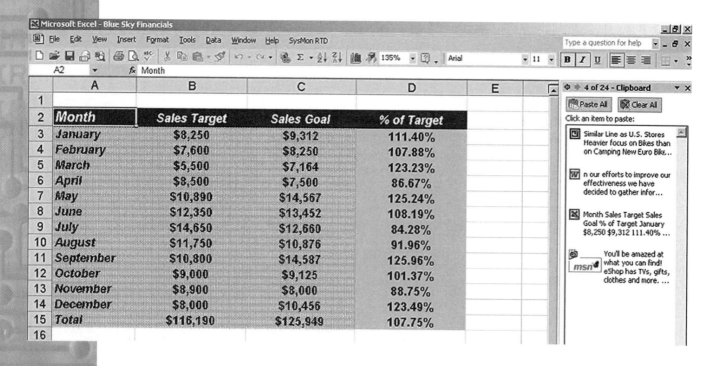

Business office software allows the user to create spreadsheets to track various types of information, including sales targets, expenses, employee attendance, etc. Information captured in spreadsheets can be converted for use in other software programs, including word processing and slide presentation applications.

Hypertext Markup Language (HTML) an encoding scheme for text data that uses special tags in the text to signify properties to the viewing program (browser) like links to other documents or document parts

scripting languages modern high level programming languages that are interpreted rather than compiled; they are usually cross-platform and support rapid application development

shopping, schedule meetings, create presentations, balance checkbooks, make car payments, or seek entertainment. Many Americans use computers at home, at school, at the library, and at work. People expect all computers to "talk" to one another and allow them to transfer documents without errors between computers so that they can share their work with others. Integrated software makes it easy to do that.

One type of integrated software is the business office suite, which is now a staple in many home offices, small businesses, and large enterprises. These suites typically include word processing, spreadsheets, databases, e-mail, appointment scheduling, electronic slide capability, and web browsing programs, all of which can create and exchange information quickly and easily.

Another example of integrated software is the developer's office suite for those who create new software. These packages offer programs including word processing, **Hypertext Markup Language (HTML)** editors, web navigation tools, e-mail, bulletin board managers, application builders, **scripting languages**, directory browsers, help browsers, and program editors.

A suite of programs for home computer use can include software that a home user would find helpful, such as word processing, money management, e-mail, a web browser, an encyclopedia, and a dictionary. A lawyer's office suite typically includes a combination of word processing, proofreading, document assembly, research, web navigation, and e-mail programs.

A variety of manufacturers offer these integrated software packages, and each has its own unique advantages depending on the needs of its targeted customer base. This article describes the typical business office suite.

History

The integration of powerful business software occurred in the late twentieth century. In the early 1980s, Lotus 1-2-3 was the only software available to create spreadsheets; "gopher" was the single application to read e-mail;

and there were only a few word processing options, including WordStar, WordPerfect, or a line editor such as *vi*. Overhead slide presentations could not be created on a computer. Appointment scheduling was done using paper and pencil.

At that time, each piece of office software was an independent entity. Files could not be shared across platforms or combined into one document without expert assistance. Therefore, users could not import WordStar documents into a Lotus spreadsheet, or access files on a UNIX operating system from a DOS (disk operating system). By the 1990s, however, a variety of software manufacturers offered business professionals complex integrated packages that gave them the ability to create complex, format-rich documents.

The first efforts to combine capabilities resulted in integrated programs, such as Microsoft Works and Claris Works. Each was a single program that combined several software functions, such as simplified versions of word processors, spreadsheets, and databases. Early versions of these programs created documents that could not be exported into more sophisticated full-sized word processing or spreadsheet applications. Their primary benefit to the user was that multiple office functions could be accomplished using one piece of software.

Microsoft Office 97 and Lotus SmartSuite 97 are both fully functional integrated software packages of several programs. When they were introduced, they were immediately adopted by many businesses because they allowed several applications to share data easily. Each suite included word processing, spreadsheet, organizer/scheduler, database, graphics, and e-mail programs—all designed to work seamlessly together. They allowed users to create complex documents that incorporated information generated by two or more of the applications, such as a word processing document that included diagrams, graphs, spreadsheets, and hyperlinks.

Pasting, Linking, and Embedding

Integrated software offers users a variety of cut and paste tools to share data among applications. On the simplest level, information can be cut or copied from the source application (for example, a block of cells from a spreadsheet) and pasted into the target application (such as a word processing document). With the paste tool, a user can place a snapshot of the desired section of the spreadsheet in the document. The cutting and copying tools save the desired spreadsheet cells in multiple formats so that the paste process will be successful with a display of the added material in the format that works best. Although the cut, copy, and paste tools are the simplest way to share information, the data in the target document is not kept current if changes are made in the source location. The old data remains until the new data is pasted in its place.

Object Linking and Embedding (OLE) helps resolve this limitation by pasting an embedded link or object in the target application. This process requires the paste link or paste special tools, instead of paste. OLE works only with OLE-enabled applications. When a link is pasted into a target document, it becomes a compound document. All compound documents require the cooperation of all linked applications to create the final product and require that all source applications be kept in their original location. If one of the source applications is moved, or if the compound document is

A WORD ABOUT WORDSTAR

Those who were around when word processing software was in its infancy remember how they marveled when WordStar hit the market. Introduced in 1979, the program allowed the user to generate and manipulate text, store the data for later retrieval and revision, and print out the document. Sound like today's word processing software? It does, but WordStar was the first such program to be a commercial success.

moved, the link is broken and the document remains incomplete until the link is reestablished. As long as the link is intact, all changes made on the source applications are displayed on the compound document.

For example, if the compound document is an analytical paper created on a word processor that includes links to a drawing and a spreadsheet, all three applications (the word processor, the drawing program, and the spreadsheet software) must cooperate to display and print the finished paper. Once the document is created, all subsequent changes made on the spreadsheet or drawing are tracked by a system of reminders. The next time the paper is opened using the word processor, the reminders deliver the changes, which then appear in the document.

A second kind of compound document is one that includes embedded objects, which are created by using the paste special tool. The successful use of embedded objects requires that all source applications remain in their original locations. Embedded objects can be edited directly from within the compound document, without the need to open the source document first. To make changes to an embedded spreadsheet, for example, the user first opens the compound document and then double clicks on the cells that are embedded on the page. This causes a small window to open so changes can be made directly on the page. However, these changes are not transmitted to the source document. Likewise, any changes made to the original spreadsheet are not reflected in the word processing document.

Another option, called paste as hyperlink, creates a hyperlink of the pasted object, such as the cells of a pasted spreadsheet. By double clicking on a hyperlink, the user opens the source application for easy editing. As long as the link remains valid, all changes made on the hyperlinked file are reflected in the compound document. SEE ALSO Database Management Software; Office Automation Systems; SQL; SQL: Databases.

Ann McIver McHoes and Judi Ellis

Bibliography

Blattner, P., et. al. *Using Microsoft Word and Excel in Office 2000.* Indianapolis, IN: Que Corporation, 1999.

Internet Resources

Microsoft Corporate Web Site. <http://www.microsoft.com>

Kemeny, John G.

Mathematician, Educator, and Philosopher
1926–1992

Devoting his career to mathematics and education, John G. Kemeny served as president of Dartmouth College for more than a decade. He also taught at the school for many years and is remembered for his books. Skilled in the field of mathematics, he teamed with fellow professor Thomas E. Kurtz to create the BASIC programming language.

Kemeny was born in Budapest, Hungary, on May 31, 1926. He and his family were Jewish and fled Hungary in 1940 to escape the Nazis. He immigrated to the United States and finished high school in New York City, becoming a U.S. citizen in 1945.

In 1943 Kemeny was admitted to Princeton University, where he majored in mathematics and minored in philosophy. His studies were interrupted when he joined the U.S. Army's **Manhattan Project** at Los Alamos in New Mexico, but in 1947 he graduated from Princeton and began work on a doctorate in mathematics. During his work on the atom bomb project at Los Alamos, Kemeny worked with mathematician John von Neumann (1903–1957). At Princeton his colleagues included physicist Albert Einstein (1879–1955) and mathematician Alonzo Church (1903–1955). In 1949 at the age of twenty-three, Kemeny completed his doctorate and joined the faculty at Princeton. He taught in both the department of mathematics and the department of philosophy.

Manhattan Project the U.S. project designed to create the world's first atomic bomb

Kemeny took a professorship at Dartmouth College in 1953 and served as chairperson of the department of mathematics from 1954 to 1967. In 1964 he and fellow professor Thomas E. Kurtz created the Beginners All-purpose Symbolic Instruction Code (BASIC) programming language. BASIC was designed so that computer novices could quickly become proficient in the writing of computer programs. The BASIC language was adopted by high schools and colleges throughout the world. It is the language that many contemporary computer professionals credit with sparking their initial interest in computers.

Kemeny's *Introduction to Finite Mathematics* sold more than 200,000 copies in the United States and has been translated into several languages. He also wrote *A Philosopher Looks at Science* and *Random Essays on Mathematics, Education and Computers* and is the coauthor of nine other books on mathematics.

In 1970 Kemeny was named president of Dartmouth at the relatively young age of forty-three. His tenure as president was marked by a genuine concern for the teaching mission of the college as well as a clearly liberal political viewpoint.

Kemeny's presidency began during a period of student unrest across the United States, related to the treatment of minorities and U.S. involvement in the Vietnam conflict. When four students at Kent State were killed by National Guard troops during a protest of the war, Kemeny showed solidarity with the antiwar protestors by temporarily suspending all academic activities at Dartmouth.

Kemeny was president of Dartmouth when it first admitted women in 1972. As president he withstood criticism from alumni when he abandoned Dartmouth's Native American mascot, which he found offensive.

By 1981 Kemeny perceived a shift in the political winds. In his final commencement address as president, he warned the students against "a voice heard in many guises throughout history, which is the most dangerous voice you will ever hear. It appeals to the basest of instincts in all of us, it appeals to human prejudice. It tries to divide us by setting whites against blacks, by setting Christians against Jews, by setting men against women. And if it succeeds in dividing us from our fellow beings, it will impose its evil will upon a fragmented society."

Kemeny served as president of Dartmouth for eleven years before returning to the department of mathematics to continue teaching. The

BASIC'S OTHER CREATOR

Thomas E. Kurtz (1928–) was a professor of math and computer sciences at Dartmouth University. He was instrumental in establishing the first time-sharing computer system for use by college students.

John G. Kemeny checks a switch panel in the Three Mile Island nuclear plant in 1979. The reactor caused great concern when it began leaking radiation that year.

mathematician, educator, and philosopher died of a heart attack on December 26, 1992. He was survived by his wife, two children, and two grandchildren. SEE ALSO DECISION SUPPORT SYSTEMS; MATHEMATICS; PROCEDURAL LANGUAGES.

Michael J. McCarthy

Bibliography

Kemeny, Jean Alexander. *It's Different at Dartmouth: A Memoir.* Brattleboro, VT: S. Greene Press, 1979.

Kemeny, John G. *Man and the Computer.* New York: Scribner, 1972.

Knowledge-Based Systems

A knowledge-based system is a computer program that reasons and uses knowledge to solve complex problems. Traditionally, computers have solved complex problems using arithmetic **algorithms** created by programmers. With knowledge-based systems, human knowledge is captured and embedded explicitly within a program in a symbolic format.

algorithms rules or procedures used to solve mathematical problems—most often described as sequences of steps

Expressing knowledge as rules and **heuristics** has two particular advantages over previous software development technology. Not only can explicit knowledge be trapped in the computer, but so can implicit knowledge, which is useful and potentially very profitable. The other advantage is that knowledge that exists in the form of rules can be captured in that form, without having to be converted by teams of analysts and programmers into data definitions and procedures.

Types of Systems

One way that knowledge-based systems can be classified is by the kind of conclusions they produce. Some interpret the available evidence and produce diagnoses—for example, to explain the reason for a machine breakdown. Others interpret the available evidence but offer a prediction, such as the likelihood of a particular applicant for a loan becoming a slow-payer or a defaulter. Some systems address design questions, proposing the form or layout of a product or the configuration of components. Some are related to industrial engineering matters such as the procedure for assembling the components.

However, not all knowledge-based systems are so ambitious. Many merely use the captured rules to determine to which class a particular example belongs. For example, a system might determine whether a particular person is, or is not, entitled to a particular government benefit, an entry visa, or permanent residence.

Development Techniques

During the development of a knowledge-based system, knowledge is extracted from one or more domain specialists, or people who have specialized knowledge in the relevant domain. The knowledge is commonly expressed in the form of antecedent-consequent (IF THEN) rules. In some cases it may be possible for the domain specialist to feed the knowledge directly into the system, but usually an intermediary knowledge engineer captures it using supporting software.

Once the system is developed, a user consults it to find information about some event or situation within a problem domain. The software draws inferences by applying the explicit rules elicited by the expert and the more general implicit rules derived by the system. A result is provided to the user in the form of a diagnosis, prognosis, recommendation, or decision, depending on the nature of the application. In addition, the user may request an explanation of the argument the software used to reach its conclusion.

Knowledge-based systems usually contain three components: a human-computer **interface**, a knowledge base, and an inference engine program. The human-computer interface is where the user formulates queries, which the knowledge-based system uses to solicit further information from the user and explain to the user the reasoning process employed to arrive at an answer. The knowledge of one or more human experts in a specific field or task is stored in the knowledge base. The knowledge base is set up as an intelligent database—it can usually manipulate the stored information in a logical, natural, or easy-to-find way. It can conduct searches based on predetermined rules of defined associations and relationships, as well as by the more traditional data search techniques.

heuristics procedures that serve to guide investigation but that have not been proven

interface a boundary or border between two or more objects or systems; also a point of access

The knowledge base is usually made up of factual knowledge, and sometimes even heuristic knowledge. Factual knowledge consists of information that is commonly shared, found in textbooks or journals, or agreed upon by humans knowledgeable in a specific field or task. Heuristic knowledge, on the other hand, is experiential knowledge of performance; it is the knowledge behind an educated guess.

inference a suggestion or implication of something based on other known related facts and conclusions

The **inference** engine of an expert system is usually set up to mimic the reasoning, or problem-solving ability, that the human expert would use to arrive at a conclusion. The inference engine simulates the evaluation process of relating the information and rules in the knowledge base to the answers to a series of questions given by the operator. Following this model, an expert system will receive propositions, or answers to a certain line of questions, and then try to use its inference engine to process the information into rules. It will compare the propositions to the facts and rules registered in its knowledge base.

Current and Future Uses

The primary goal of knowledge-based systems is to make expertise available to decision-makers who need answers quickly. Expertise is often unavailable at the right place and the right time. Portable computers loaded with in-depth knowledge of specific subjects can bring years' worth of knowledge to a specific problem. The first knowledge-based or expert system, Dendral, was developed in 1965 by Edward Feigenbaum (1936–) and Joshua Lederberg of Stanford University in California and was used to analyze chemical compounds. Since 1965, knowledge-based systems have enhanced productivity in business, science, engineering, and the military. They also attempt to predict the weather, stock market values, and mineral deposit locations; give a medical diagnosis; dispense medication; and evaluate applications and transaction patterns.

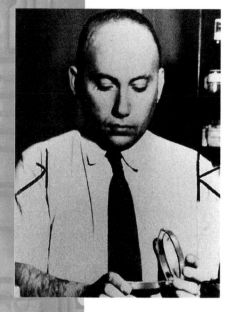

New Jersey-born Joshua Lederberg (1925–) has devoted his career to the study of microbiology and genetics. In 1958 his work was acknowledged with the Nobel Prize in Physiology or Medicine. The Joshua Lederberg Papers, housed at the National Library of Medicine, are being digitized for access via the Internet.

Knowledge-based systems appear to have a great deal of potential, but they also face some challenges. These include the shortage of knowledge engineers with necessary skills; the relative immaturity of many of the available tools; and overly specific problem domains. Most knowledge-based systems deal with very specific problem domains, and therefore do not undertake or support a complete activity, but rather one or two tasks within a sequence or cluster of tasks. The benefit that such software offers is not necessarily to automate the process completely and cut costs drastically, but to assist the user to complete the activity faster, somewhat more cheaply, and probably more accurately. SEE ALSO ARTIFICIAL INTELLIGENCE; NEURAL NETWORKS.

William J. Yurcik

Bibliography

Gonzalez, Avelino J., and Douglas D. Dankel. *The Engineering of Knowledge-Based Systems: Theory and Practice.* Englewood Cliffs, NJ: Prentice Hall, 2000.

Ignizio, James P. *An Introduction to Expert Systems: The Development and Implementation of Rule-based Expert Systems.* New York: McGraw-Hill, 1991.

Jackson, Peter. *Introduction to Expert Systems,* 3rd ed. Reading, MA: Addison Wesley International Computer Science Series, 1999.

Stefik, Mark J. *Introduction to Knowledge Systems.* San Francisco: Morgan Kaufmann, 1995.

Laser Technology

Laser devices use light to store, transfer, or print images and text; they are also used in a wide range of other applications, including surgery and weaponry. The coherent radiation of the laser gives it special strength. The laser (Light Amplification by Stimulated Emission of Radiation) started life as an extension of the maser, or "Microwave Amplification by Stimulated Emission of Radiation." As its name indicates, the maser is an amplifier that was originally used for amplifying weak radio signals from space. Light waves are very much like radio waves but with a much shorter wavelength.

The laser generates light energy by converting the energy states of a material. The energy level of an atom is a function of its temperature. Its lowest energy level is called its "ground state." The application of additional heat, light, or electric field can raise its energy level. The familiar neon sign, which is glass tubing filled with neon gas, works on this principle. Two electrodes are inserted in the ends of the glass tubing and a high voltage is applied to the electrodes to raise the energy levels of the gas atoms.

Neon light results from the gas's natural endeavor to return to its lowest energy state, emitting photons of energy as it does so. A photon is an

Lasers have a vast capacity to create (i.e., printing computer documents, restoring vision through surgery, recording digital information) yet also have the potential to destroy (i.e., advanced weaponry). Scientists continue to find a wealth of uses for the laser.

energy packet of electromagnetic waves. The energy of a photon is inversely proportional to the wavelength of the associated electromagnetic wave, so shorter wavelengths represent the higher energy photons. Small energy transitions emit photons with long wavelengths such as infrared light, while the larger energy transitions produce photons of visible light with blue light.

In the neon sign, the extra energy added is first stored in the atoms of neon gas in the tube by raising them to a higher energy state. As the neon atoms return to lower energy states, the atoms give up the excess energy as photons.

From Neon Signs to Lasers

One form of laser contains a gas, in which the energy level of the atoms in the medium can be increased above their ground state using a high voltage similar to a neon sign. The majority of atoms are forced to an enhanced energy state or a situation called **population inversion**. But, in order to make a laser, the elevated energy state must be *metastable*, as described in the following paragraph.

population inversion used in quantum mechanics to describe when the number of atoms at higher energy levels is greater than the number at lower energy levels—a condition needed for photons (light) to be emitted

In the neon sign, the increased energy state is unstable. The gas returns spontaneously to a lower energy state and eventually to the ground state. A metastable state implies that the atoms will remain in an elevated energy state for a period of time, on the order of one one-thousandth of a second or so, and can be encouraged to change to the ground state by the application of a stimulus. Not all materials have this metastable state and those that do are suitable for lasers. Pure neon is used to generate light in a neon sign, but a mixture of helium and neon can be used to create a laser because the mix has a metastable state.

An atom that has emitted a photon stimulates other atoms to return to a lower energy state from the metastable state. The laser has mirrored ends so the photons bounce between the mirrors and cause other atoms to emit photons. Before long, a large number of photons are bouncing between the mirrors and a very large amount of light energy is generated. One of the mirrors is only half silvered so that some of the photons pass through to form a beam of light instead of being reflected.

Laser Light

In the laser, every atom that releases a photon from the metastable state produces exactly the same color or wavelength of light. Also, the waves associated with the photon are all "coherent" or in step with each other. This produces a light beam that is very pure, having a beam of only one color (that is, a monochromatic beam).

milliwatts a power measurement indicating one-thousandth (or 10^{-3}) of a watt

Laser light can be very intense. Even though a laser has a relatively low total power, the power is concentrated in a very small area. The common laser pointer has a power output of only one or two **milliwatts**, but the power is spread over an area of only about a millimeter in diameter. The intensity of the laser pointer is greater than the intensity of a projected image and is easily visible. Large lasers can produce a total power of more than a kilowatt with an intensity that can cut metal.

Semiconductors and Lasers

A number of materials have been developed that have the necessary characteristics for lasers. Among them are semiconductors, those materials, like silicon, whose electrical conductivity is between that of a conductor and that of an insulator. Many semiconductor diode lasers produce an infrared wavelength longer than the deepest red visible to the human eye. The current state of the art in semiconductor lasers limits the shortest wavelength to the visible red at about 630 **nanometers**. It is generally more difficult to generate shorter wavelengths using a laser of any type.

Semiconductor lasers are particularly useful because they are very inexpensive and are quite small. They are suited for connecting directly to thin optical fibers with little loss of light energy. Special laser diodes are made that produce wavelengths in the infrared that produce the lowest loss in glass fiber. Without the semiconductor laser, long-distance **fiber optic** communications would not be possible.

Harnessing Laser Technology

Just as important as the generation of pure light energy is the detection of light photons. A number of semiconductor devices, diodes, transistors, and **integrated circuits** are capable of sensing light energy. Some of these devices, particularly diodes called photo diodes, can handle very high-speed data and are the receiving end of fiber optic communications systems. The field of generating and detecting light energy is called electro-optics.

When laser light is used for communications, it is necessary to "modulate" or change the light in some way so that it can be used as a carrier of information. The same is true for radio communications. While there are two basic ways to modulate a radio carrier—**amplitude** or angle—in 2001 there were no practical methods of angle modulating a laser, or if angle modulation could be done, there were no practical techniques to gain the advantages that angle modulation produces. This is an area of intense research as many advantages can be gained from angle modulation.

Amplitude modulation can be achieved by changing the electrical power delivered to the laser or by the use of special light modulators. The disadvantage of modulating the electrical power applied to the laser diode is that it causes changes in the wavelength of the light. External light modulators do not cause this change. These modulators are made of non-linear material and are used for very short pulses of light of less than one **nanosecond**.

When laser light is used for producing a display or for scanning an object such as in a checkout counter bar code reader, the laser beam is deflected using mirrors. The mirrors are very small so that they can be deflected without the application of a large force. Special electric motors that turn only a few degrees are used. Deflected laser beams are used to generate images and can generate spectacular light shows. The most intriguing display produced by laser light is the hologram, a true three-dimensional image.

Laser light is used for reading optical discs as well as for scanning bar codes, measuring distances, and detecting objects. The "laser printer" alters the charge on a photoconductive drum to which charged ink particles, called "toner," are applied. High-power lasers can be used for cutting, burning,

nanometers each one is one-thousand-millionth (one billionth, or 10^{-9}) of a meter

fiber optic refers to fiber optics, a transmission technology featuring long, thin strands of glass fiber; internal reflections in the fiber assure that light entering one end is transmitted to the other end with only small losses in intensity; used widely in transmitting digital information

integrated circuits circuits with the transistors, resistors, and other circuit elements etched into the surface of single chips of semiconducting material, usually silicon

amplitude the size or magnitude of an electrical signal

nanosecond one-thousand-millionth (one billionth, or 10^{-9}) of a second

surgery, and even as weapons of war. Lasers are used in any application where an intense, monochromatic, and coherent light source is needed. SEE ALSO INTERNET; TELECOMMUNICATIONS; TELEPHONY.

Albert D. Helfrick

Bibliography

Bromberg, Joan Lisa. *The Laser in America*. Cambridge, MA: MIT Press, 1991.

Hecht, Jeff. *Understanding Lasers: An Entry-level Guide*. New York: IEEE Press, 1992.

Laufer, Gabriel. *Introduction to Optics and Lasers in Engineering*. New York: Cambridge University Press, 1996.

Petruzzelis, Thomas. *Optoelectronics, Fiber Optics, and Laser Cookbook*. New York: McGraw-Hill, 1997.

Stix, Gary, and Miriam Lacob. *Who Gives a Gigabyte: A Survival Guide for the Technologically Perplexed*. New York: John Wiley, 1999.

Svelto, Arazio. *Principles of Lasers*. New York: Plenum Press, 1998.

Legal Systems

As in many areas of business and professional practice, the use of computers in the legal sphere had become widespread by the beginning of the 1990s. In some realms of law practice, such as research and office management, computer automation had a major impact a decade or two earlier. Everything from the way courtroom trials are undertaken to the way lawyers prepare documents has been affected by automated systems. This article focuses on digital technology in six major areas of legal practice. Some topics, like **artificial intelligence (AI)**, that have yet to be developed to the point where they have everyday practical applications are not covered. This does not mean that they do not hold tremendous promise for the future, just that more work needs to be done before they are ready for a commercial market.

artificial intelligence (AI) a branch of computer science dealing with creating computer hardware and software to mimic the way people think and perform practical tasks

Legal Research

The heart of an attorney's work is research. One must be able to locate the primary sources, the cases, statutes, and regulations that make up the law, before clients can be advised, contracts prepared, or litigation brought to trial. This is the area of legal practice that has been most radically affected by the introduction of computer technology.

The earliest experiments with computer-aided legal research were undertaken by John Horty at the University of Pittsburgh in the early 1960s. Horty encoded the text of state public health statutes into a digital form that could be read by a computer. Simple searches could be run by matching language submitted by the researcher against the statutory text using **Boolean logic**.

By the mid-1960s, Horty's research had attracted the attention of several key members of the Ohio Bar Association. They wanted to take automated legal research to the next level by developing a system that would allow massive amounts of legal information to be stored and then retrieved by searching the full text of each document. By 1973 the system, now named Lexis, was ready for commercial marketing. The earliest version of Lexis

Boolean logic a system, developed by George Boole, which treats abstract objects (such as sets or classes) as algebraic quantities; Boole applied his mathematical system to the study of classical logic

was rather primitive; it mostly contained just state and federal case law. Communication problems were frequent and complicated searches were dreadfully slow, often taking longer than thirty minutes.

By 1975 a competing product, Westlaw, was being marketed to attorneys. West Publishing Company, the developer of Westlaw, originally built their product to work solely as an indexed system utilizing the topic and key number indexing employed in their print compilations of cases. Within a few years Westlaw was redesigned as both a full-text and an indexed system.

Today both Lexis and Westlaw are powerful research tools containing hundreds of databases incorporating millions of legal, news, and public record documents. Besides full-text searching, both Lexis and Westlaw now allow for indexed and natural language searching, the latter being introduced as a means to introduce computer-aided legal research to less computer-literate lawyers.

The success of both Lexis and Westlaw has led to several complementary software products. One of these works by extracting case citations from legal documents, such as a brief, and verifying that the cases are still valid law by referencing an electronic citation service. Numerous smaller companies have developed more modest research systems and tools. These CD-ROM (compact disc-read only memory) and online-based products offer relatively low-cost searching compared to Lexis and Westlaw. In addition, with the advent of the Internet, many courts, legislatures, and regulatory agencies have made their documents available via the World Wide Web. Using these Internet-based sources for detailed and comprehensive legal research has drawbacks, however, including the absence of older material, unsophisticated search engines, and the need to consult many different sites.

Document Assembly

The popular image of an attorney is usually based on television characters making heroic gestures in front of a jury. The truth is that many attorneys have never spent a working day in a courtroom. Legal work such as preparing wills, filling out tax forms, incorporating businesses, and handling real estate transactions can at times require shrewd analysis and attention to detail. Just as often, though, they are routine processes that can be automated to save time.

Beginning in the 1980s with the introduction of the personal computer, programs were developed to assist with document assembly. At first these were simple programs, like those to assist in drafting wills, based on word processing software. More sophisticated products, like those to compute taxes, were soon built around database or **spreadsheet** programs. These software packages quickly gained favor with the legal profession and now there are dozens of companies offering a wide range of document assembly products.

spreadsheet an accounting or business tool that details numerical data in columns for tabulation purposes

Case Management

A successful law practice involves more than good research skills and thorough knowledge of the law. There are business components that can be time-consuming, but many of these can be handled with computer technology. Storing client data, keeping track of timesheets, and debt collection are all business functions that are easily automated. One of the most important innovations in this area is software that functions as an electronic calendar or tickler file. These programs allow the busy attorney to track and maintain filing deadlines. The most sophisticated of these are keyed into state or federal court rules and automatically compute the date that a filing or court appearance is due.

Litigation Support

Complicated trials involving large corporations can require enormous numbers of documents. Boxes full of business records and depositions from potential witnesses may have to be examined, indexed, coded, and stored in a manner that allows for rapid retrieval. Up until the 1980s, microfilm was the storage vehicle of choice; computers were relegated to an indexing role. Low-cost scanning technology and cheap, abundant computer memory have allowed the entire process to be automated. It is still a labor-intensive undertaking and generally involves scanning documents onto compact disks as image files. Sometimes, at great expense, these documents are converted to text files using **optical character recognition** software so that they can be retrieved through full-text searching. At the same time, these records are assigned codes that capture identifying information such as date, author, title, addressee, and type of document; each record is also given a unique document number.

Another way computer technology provides litigation support is through the creation of graphics and other visual aids for courtroom use. The most sophisticated of these are simulations that can recreate an accident scene or show the path of a bullet.

Communications

A revolution is currently underway in the court systems of the United States. Fueled by the communications potential of the Internet, courts of all types are developing the capability to allow attorneys to file and retrieve documents in pending cases electronically. The potential is there for all parties in a case to receive filings simultaneously and without delay. Electronic docketing or registration of legal proceedings also allows attorneys to take note of other cases that were filed against a particular party within a specific period of time.

Courtroom Practice

The judiciary, as a whole, traditionally has not been eager to embrace new technology. Little by little changes have been working their way into the courtroom. In many U.S. counties it is now possible to receive real-time transcription of the proceedings of an ongoing trial. The court stenographer utilizes a system that converts shorthand to a transcript format that is distributed through multiple channels in the courtroom. This nearly simultaneous record can benefit deaf or blind jurors and participants.

The paperless trial is another reality that is being played out in a few selected courtrooms around the country. Jurors can view video clips, computer simulations, and exhibits on video screens or monitors in the jury box. The reported advantages have been faster and cheaper trials and the ability

optical character recognition the science and engineering of creating programs that can recognize and interpret printed characters

to focus the jury's attention in a more direct fashion. SEE ALSO INFORMA-TION RETRIEVAL; MEDICAL SYSTEMS; SECURITY.

Marc Silverman

Law students at the College of William and Mary in Virginia test out various computer technologies during a mock trial of terrorists in April 2001. The trial took place in Courtroom 21, which features flat plasma television screens and small LCD monitors on each desk.

Bibliography

Eyres, Patricia. *Smart Litigating with Computers.* Los Angeles: Estrin Publishing, 1992.

Harrington, William G. "A Brief History of Computer Assisted Legal Research." *Law Library Journal* 77 (1984–1985): 543–556.

Leith, Philip, and Amanda Hoey. *The Computerized Lawyer.* New York: Springer Verlag, 1998.

Staudt, Ronald W. *Litigation Support Systems: An Attorney's Guide.* New York: Clark Boardman Callaghan, 1995.

Library Applications

Computers are used in libraries all over the world to provide access to a range of electronic information resources and to manage materials (books, journals, videos, and other media) held in particular collections. For many people, barriers of income, age, gender, or race can limit their access to computer technology and thus to the wealth of information that is available to others. The public library, with its history of providing free information, may offer access to the Internet and make a range of information sources available to everyone. Increasingly, via funds from national governments or from philanthropic agencies such as the Bill and Melinda Gates Foundation in the United States, relevant software, hardware, and network connections are being made available in public libraries so as to minimize this **digital divide**.

digital divide imaginary line separating those who can access digital information from those who cannot

transistors the plural of transistor, which is a contraction of TRANSfer resISTOR; semiconductor device, invented by John Bardeen, Walter Brattain, and William Shockley, which has three terminals; can be used for switching and amplifying electrical signals

The huge size, complexity, and cost of early computers in the 1940s and 1950s meant that they were unsuitable for use in library and information work. However by the 1960s when **transistors** started to replace the original valves, and codes had been developed so that alphabetic characters as well as numbers could be input, stored, and output, work on library applications started. For instance, a study on automation at the U.S. Library of Congress (LC) was undertaken in 1963. A major problem faced was how best to "describe" a book to the computer. Following much debate, which also involved colleagues in Great Britain, a format known as MARC (Machine Readable Cataloging) was developed and is still being used for bibliographic records in libraries all over the world.

Now, the LC not only offers access to printed materials via its reading rooms in Washington but also makes available a wide range of electronic information resources. Many libraries, especially national libraries, digitize material in their collections so that anyone in the world who has access to the Internet can explore the wealth of these collections. Examples of material that could be digitized in a school or college library include past examination papers, previous works of pupils, relevant photographs, college yearbooks, and highly used printed materials. Copyright clearance must be acquired where necessary.

Electronic Library Catalogs

minicomputers computers midway in size between a desktop computer and a mainframe computer; most modern desktops are much more powerful than the older minicomputers

During the early 1970s, many public and academic libraries began using computer systems to help manage and control the basic processes of acquisition, cataloging, and the circulation of items (both books and journals) in their collections. At first programs were written locally, but by the end of the 1970s a number of organizations started to offer integrated software and hardware packages using the **minicomputers** that were then under development. In some instances libraries came together to form cooperatives and to develop shared databases of MARC records so that individual libraries did not have to create their own catalog records.

One example was Online Computer Library Center (OCLC)—a cooperative formed by college libraries in Ohio. OCLC's services expanded; by 2001 they were being used by 38,000 institutions in 76 countries. According to OCLC, its strategy is to develop a "globally networked information resource of text, graphics, sound, and motion" that will be supported by "a set of integrated, web-based tools and services that facilitate contribution, discovery, exchange, delivery, and preservation of knowledge objects and shared expertise of participating institutions."

relational database a collection of records that permits logical and business relationships to be developed between themselves and their contents

client/server technology computer systems that are structured using clients (usually human driven computers) to access information stored (often remotely) on other computers known as servers

Online Public Access Catalogs (or OPACs) started to appear in the 1980s. The OPAC module of an integrated library management system makes use of the techniques developed within online information retrieval systems. Library patrons can search the catalog by entering an author's name, the title of a book, or a subject term on a keyboard and view the results on a screen rather than looking through trays of catalog cards. The OPACs of many libraries in the world can be searched using the Internet. During the 1990s many of these library management systems were developed using software programs based on standard **relational database** management systems (such as Informix and Oracle), standard operating systems (like UNIX), and **client/server technology** using PCs. Among the companies and their li-

brary management products active in 2001 were Endeavor Information Systems (Voyager), Innovative Interfaces Inc. (Millennium), and Sirsi Corporation (UNICORN).

Networks

Computer networks have been used in libraries to link workstations in remote branches to centralized systems, allowing multiple sites to share facilities such as CD-ROM (compact disc-read only memory) drives and printers. Networks are also used to access external services. In the 1970s ARPANET (the forerunner to the Internet) and the commercial **packet-switched network** Tymnet were used by European libraries to access online information retrieval systems in the United States. The rapid developments of the Internet and the World Wide Web greatly influenced the services provided by libraries during the 1990s. Many libraries all over the world provide access to information on the web for their users. In countries where access to information was, or is, strictly controlled, this is a major development. Increasingly **intranets** are being installed in many organizations and library staff members can often provide the necessary information management skills for creating and maintaining information on intranet and Internet web sites.

Online catalogs place a vast amount of bibliographic data at one's fingertips, including what books are available for checkout in that library as well as within its local network.

packet-switched network a network based on digital communications systems whereby packets of data are dispatched to receivers based on addresses that they contain

intranets interconnected networks of computers that operate like the Internet, but serve only a company or organization

Digital Resources

Librarians today still need to select, acquire, and organize quality information resources for their patrons. A new challenge is that much information is published digitally as well as, or instead of, in print. Electronic journals, newspapers, and magazines are common and many books, including student textbooks, are available in electronic form as e-books (electronic books that are available for download onto e-book readers). As "e-learning" and virtual learning environments become more commonplace, the concept of a teacher/lecturer imparting knowledge in a classroom is yielding to less centralized approaches to education. Students are being given more responsibility for managing their educational resources through technology and new media formats. Librarians, in consultation with teachers, are therefore increasingly involved in making appropriate quality learning resources available for students.

Technological developments supporting the collection, management, and preservation of digital materials, the description of digital resources using techniques such as the MARC format, the creation of digital resources, and the implementation of electronic mechanisms for searching a range of resources have given rise to the phrase "digital library" to describe this new world of library science. SEE ALSO Database Management Software; Educational Software; Information Retrieval.

Lucy A. Tedd

Internet Resources

LibDex: The Library Index. <http://www.libdex.com>
Library of Congress. <http://www.loc.gov>
Online Computer Library Center, Inc. (OCLC) <http://www.oclc.org>

Magnetic Stripe Cards

A magnetic stripe card is a card (e.g., a credit card) that contains a stripe of magnetically-encoded data. These cards are paired with readers and writers, and are used in a wide variety of applications for storing information.

Usage

Most identification, credit, automated teller machine, and membership cards have a thin magnetic stripe across one side of the card. By "swiping" the card through or inserting the card into a reader, a computer can read the data on the stripe. Magnetic stripes make card usage much less prone to error because the data are not entered manually. The data cannot be read without a correctly programmed machine, and the cards must be created with special equipment, both of which make cards hard to falsify. The stripes can also contain encrypted information and information not printed on the card which can only be created or read by specialized computers.

Technologies

The magnetic stripe is actually an area of dense microscopic bar magnets, of which there are approximately 200 million per square inch. The magnets can be used to encode the data in an infinite number of ways. High security cards encode the data in proprietary, undisclosed formats that prevent intruders from even reading the data. However, all credit, banking, and automated teller machine cards use the same type of encoding. Most other cards use this encoding as well.

Like larger bar magnets, one end of each microscopic magnet is a north pole (N) and the other a south pole (S). In an empty, horizontal stripe, all of the bars are aligned left to right so that the north poles are facing one direction and the south poles the other. The north pole of each magnet is therefore adjacent to the south pole of the next magnet and, like other bar magnets, all of the aligned magnets act as one larger magnet.

Figure 1: A horizontally aligned row of bar magnets

N – S

Unlike usual bar magnets, these tiny magnets can be made to reverse their polarity. If a single or a continuous group of bar magnets is reversed, the stripe will act like three opposing bar magnets.

Figure 2: A horizontally aligned row of bar magnets with one reversed section

N – – – – –SS– – – – – – –NN– S
　　　　　 ^^^^^^^^^
　　　　　 Reversed Magnets

If several sections of magnets are reversed, the stripe looks like a series of opposing magnets.

Figure 3: A horizontally aligned row of seven sections, each reversed with respect to its neighbors

N – – –SS – – NN– –SS – – NN – – – – –SS– – – – – – – – – – – NN– – – – S

The like poles of two magnets repel each other. This results in a strong magnetic field at those junctions. A magnetic stripe reader has a head, much like the one in an audio tape player, which can detect that field. The head senses the field at a north-north junction as a positive voltage and the field at a south-south junction as a negative one.

Figure 4: The analog signal, with peaks, induced by the magnets in Figure 3.

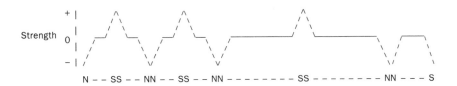

The reader converts the analog signal into a digital one by turning positive peaks into transitions from low to high and negative peaks into transitions from high to low.

Figure 5: The digital signal, created from the analog signal in Figure 4.

Finally, the reader measures the length of each high/low pair. Each pair is interpreted as a bit—a short pair as a binary "1" and a long pair as a binary "0." In this way, the preceding sequence of magnets encodes the bits "110".

The difficulty in this system is that it depends on the reader measuring the distance between the peaks. The card is usually swiped through the reader by a person's hand, and it is difficult or impossible to regulate the specific speed at which the card should be swiped. At a low speed, a single high/low pair will look longer than it actually is. At a high speed, the same pair will look shorter. So, long pairs (zeroes) are exactly twice as long as short pairs (ones). In this way, no matter how rapidly or slowly the user moves the card, so long as the card is moved at a relatively constant speed, the machine reader can differentiate a one from a zero.

These bits are used to represent letters and numbers just as they are in a computer. On most cards, there are actually three independent stripes. The first stripe contains letters in the ANSI/ISO ALPHA format, and can contain a name or other text. The second and third stripes contain credit card or identification numbers, and are in **binary coded decimal (BCD)** format. While the first and second stripe contain "read-only" data, the third stripe is designed to be both written to and read while it is being swiped. This feature is rarely used, however.

These stripes can be made of several different materials, but can all be damaged by strong magnets. A strong magnet will align all of the magnets in the stripe, effectively erasing it.

In 2000 computer chips were added to some credit cards. Though these **"smart cards"** are read in the same way as cards with magnetic stripes—that is, they are swiped through readers—they are capable of holding substantially more information. These chips can also perform calculations, allowing the cards to act "intelligently." SEE ALSO EMBEDDED TECHNOLOGY (UBIQUITOUS COMPUTING); INPUT DEVICES; SECURITY.

Salvatore Domenick Desiano

binary coded decimal (BCD) an ANSI/ISO standard encoding of the digits 0 to 9 using 4 binary bits; the encoding only uses 10 of the available 16 4-bit combinations

smart cards credit-card style cards that have a microcomputer embedded within them; they carry more information to assist the owner or user

Bibliography

ANSI/ISO 7810-7816, Standards for Identification Cards. American National Standards Institute/International Organization for Standardization, 1987-1996.

O'Mahony, Donal, Michael Peirce, and Hitesh Tewari. *Electronic Payment Systems for E-Commerce,* 2nd ed. Boston: Artech House, 2001.

Rankl, Wolfgang, and Wolfgang Effing. *Smart Card Handbook* 2nd ed. New York: John Wiley & Sons, 2000.

Mathematics

The invention and ideas of many mathematicians and scientists led to the development of the computer, which today is used for mathematical teaching purposes in the kindergarten to college level classrooms. With its ability to process vast amounts of facts and figures and to solve problems at extremely high speeds, the computer is a valuable asset to solve the complex math-laden research problems of the sciences as well as problems in business and industry.

Major applications of computers in the mathematical sciences include their use in mathematical biology, where math is applied to a discipline such as medicine, making use of laboratory animal experiments as surrogates for a human biological system. Mathematical computer programs take the data drawn from the animal study and extrapolate it to fit the human system. Then, mathematical theory answers the question of how far these data can be transformed yet still preserve similarity between species. Mathematical ecology tries to understand the patterns of nature as society increasingly faces shortages in energy and depletion of its limited resources. Computers can also be programmed to develop premium tables for life insurance companies, to examine the likely effects of air pollution on forest productivity, and to simulate mathematical model outcomes that are used to predict areas of disease outbreaks.

Mathematical geography computer programs model flows of goods, people, and ideas over space so that **commodity** exchange, transportation, and

commodity raw material or service marketed prior to being used

Scientists and mathematicians use fractal geometry to model a variety of occurrences and patterns found in nature, including coastlines, mountain ranges, seismic patterns, soil erosion, weather patterns, etc. The study of fractals is not limited to Earthly pursuits as seen in this computer-generated model of fractals in outer space.

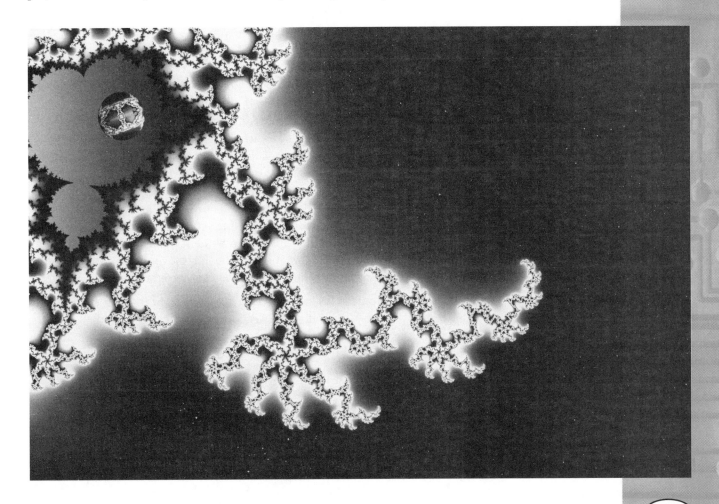

population migration patterns can be studied. Large-scale computers are used in mathematical physics to solve equations that were previously intractable, and for problems involving a third dimension, numerous computer graphics packages display three-dimensional spatial surfaces. A byproduct of the advent of computers is the ability to use this tool to investigate nonlinear methods. As a result, the stability of our solar system has been checked for millions of years to come.

In the information age, information needs to be stored, processed, and retrieved in various forms. The field of **cryptography** is loaded with computer science and mathematics complementing each other to ensure the confidentiality of information transmitted over telephone lines and computer networks. Encoding and decoding operations are computationally intense. Once a message is coded, its security may hinge on the inability of an intruder to solve the mathematical riddle of finding the prime factors of a large number. Economical encoding is required in high-resolution television because of the enormous amount of information. Data compression techniques are initially mathematical concepts before becoming electromagnetic signals that emerge as a picture on the TV screen.

Mathematical application software routines that solve equations, perform computations, or analyze experimental data are often found in area-specific subroutine libraries which are written most often in Fortran or C. In order to minimize inconsistencies across different computers, the Institute of Electrical and Electronics Engineers (IEEE) standard is met to govern the precision of numbers with decimal positions.

The basic configuration of mathematics learning in the classroom is the usage of stand-alone personal computers or shared software on networked microcomputers. The computer is valued for its ability to aid students to make connections between the verbal word problem, its symbolic form such as a function, and its graphic form. These multiple representations usually appear simultaneously on the computer screen. For home and school use, public-domain mathematical software and **shareware** are readily available on the Internet and there is a gamut of proprietary software written that spans the breadth and depth of the mathematical branches (arithmetic, algebra, geometry, trigonometry, elementary functions, calculus, numerical analysis, numerical partial differential equations, number theory, modern algebra, probability and statistics, modeling, complex variables, etc.). Often software is developed for a definitive mathematical maturity level. In lieu of graphics packages, spreadsheets are useful for plotting data and are most useful when teaching arithmetic and geometric progressions.

Mathematics, the science of patterns, is a way of looking at the world in terms of entities that do not exist in the physical world (the numbers, points, lines and planes, functions, geometric figures——all pure abstractions of the mind) so the mathematician looks to the mathematical proof to explain the physical world. Several attempts have been made to develop theorem-proving technology on computers. However, most of these systems are far too advanced for high school use. Nevertheless, the non-mathematician, with the use of computer graphics, can appreciate the sets of Gaston Julia and Benoit B. Mandelbrot for their artistic beauty. To conclude, an intriguing application of mathematics to the computer world lies at the heart of the computer itself, its microprocessor. This chip is essen-

cryptography the science of understanding codes and ciphers and their application

shareware a software distribution technique, whereby the author shares copies of his programs at no cost, in the expectation that users will later pay a fee of some sort

JULIA AND MANDELBROT SETS

Gaston Julia (1893–1978), a French mathematician, studied the iteration of polynomials and rational functions in the early 20th century. A strikingly beautiful picture is produced from function iterations: a, $f(a)$, $f(f(a))$, $f(f(f(a)))$, etc. Mandelbrot sets, named after mathematician Benoit B. Mandelbrot (1924–), are whole families of functions parameterized by a variable. These sets have become something of an art form.

tially a complex array of patterns of propositional logic (p and q, p or q, p implies q, not p, etc.) etched into **silicon**. SEE ALSO DATA VISUALIZATION; DECISION SUPPORT SYSTEMS; INTERACTIVE SYSTEMS; PHYSICS.

Patricia S. Wehman

silicon a chemical element with symbol Si; the most abundant element in the Earth's crust and the most commonly used semiconductor material

Bibliography

Devlin, Keith. *Mathematics: The Science of Patterns.* New York: Scientific American Library, 1997.

Sangalli, Arturo. *The Importance of Being Fuzzy and Other Insights from the Border between Math and Computers.* Princeton, NJ: Princeton University Press, 1998.

Medical Systems

Medical systems help doctors and nurses diagnose and treat patients. Hospitals and clinics rely extensively on computer technology to examine patients, cure disease, advance the science of medicine, and conduct the business of health care.

Embedded Systems

Many visits to a hospital start in the emergency room, which may be filled with electronic devices that look nothing like desktop computers. However, most of these devices rely on an embedded **microprocessor**, the same type of chip that powers other computers. Instead of using a stethoscope, a nurse may depend on an embedded chip in a blood pressure machine to measure a patient's pulse and blood pressure. Another embedded processor may help take the patient's temperature or deliver controlled amounts of a drug through an intravenous tube at regular intervals. These types of systems ease the burden on medical workers and improve the quality of care.

microprocessor the principle element in a computer; the component that understands how to carry out operations under the direction of the running program (CPU)

Other devices tackle more complex tasks such as constantly determining the amount of oxygen in the patient's blood. Some doctors are even using personal digital assistants (PDAs) such as Palm Pilots to help retrieve information about drugs and diseases, as well as to write drug prescriptions and to store information about patients. Even smaller devices known as **smart cards**, which are the same size as a credit card, can store medical information on an embedded chip.

Often, desktop computers are used to consolidate information from embedded systems. For instance, in a critical care unit designed to treat very sick patients, desktop computers may alert a nurse if an electronic sensor determines that a patient is not breathing well. Desktop computers also help people to use smart cards and PDAs.

smart cards credit-card style cards that have a microcomputer embedded within them; they carry more information to assist the owner or user

Desktop Computing and Databases

Health care organizations use desktop computers to accomplish administrative tasks required of any large business, such as routing e-mail, tracking supplies, paying employees, and keeping track of customers—in this case, patients. One of the key tools used to accomplish these tasks is a database. A database is a system that allows an organization systematically to store, process, and retrieve large amounts of data. One can think of a database as

CYBERTHERAPY

Can psychological therapy—also called cybertherapy—be conducted successfully via the Net? The issue is highly debated due, in part, to the fact that psychiatrists need to be licensed in any state in which they practice. Another important consideration is that doctors traditionally consider their patients' facial expressions and body language before making diagnoses. If cybertherapy is conducted via e-mail, those clues are lost. However, some advocates of online therapy suggest videoconferencing as a possible solution.

the nervous system for an organization, because the database provides the information needed to coordinate the actions of its members.

Paper-based databases typically employ standardized paper forms, folders, and filing cabinets. An electronic database is a software program that runs on one or more computers. Electronic databases offer many advantages over paper databases. However, because people are so comfortable with paper forms and because it is difficult and expensive to create an electronic database that can track everything that paper systems track, medical institutions have been slow to change from paper-based systems to electronic databases. Most health care organizations today rely on a combination of paper and computer-based systems.

Medical scientists use databases to conduct research on hundreds or even thousands of patients at a time. For example, to study the effectiveness of a new prescription drug, it is not enough to look at only a small number of patients. Instead, a large number of patients, usually at least 100, must be evaluated. This way, if the patients get better after taking the drug, the scientist can be sure that the drug was responsible for the good results. Databases also help hospital administrators to identify trends and improve the efficiency of health care organizations.

The most important information tracked by a medical database is a patient's medical record. The medical record contains the history of the patient's health and treatments. The medical record may contain prescriptions, doctor's notes, X-ray films, immunizations, and the results of various lab tests. Doctors review the medical record whenever they need to make an important decision about how to treat the patient.

Because electronic systems make it very easy to retrieve and copy information, one of the concerns with electronic databases is patient privacy. Patients expect that their personal medical information will be kept confidential. Hospitals must be sure that each part of the medical record is protected so that only authorized personnel are able to view confidential data.

Computers and databases are also very important when patients are prescribed drugs. One of the important issues with prescription drugs is that some of these drugs can interact, or combine harmfully when taken together. For example, some patients have become sick and even died after taking a combination of prescription drugs that produced harmful side effects. Another problem is that doctors have difficulty remembering the recommended dosage for each of the hundreds of drugs available. With so many prescription and non-prescription drugs on the market and new drugs entering the market constantly, databases help doctors and pharmacists to be sure that they are prescribing drugs in the proper dose and that the drugs will not interact harmfully with each other. The best drug dispensaries require the pharmacist to enter all prescriptions into an electronic database that warns of a potentially harmful drug interaction before the patient receives the medication.

Tele-Health

When a patient far away from a medical facility needs expert medical advice, tele-health technology allows doctors to evaluate patients even though they may be separated by hundreds of miles. Tele-heath is made possible by the

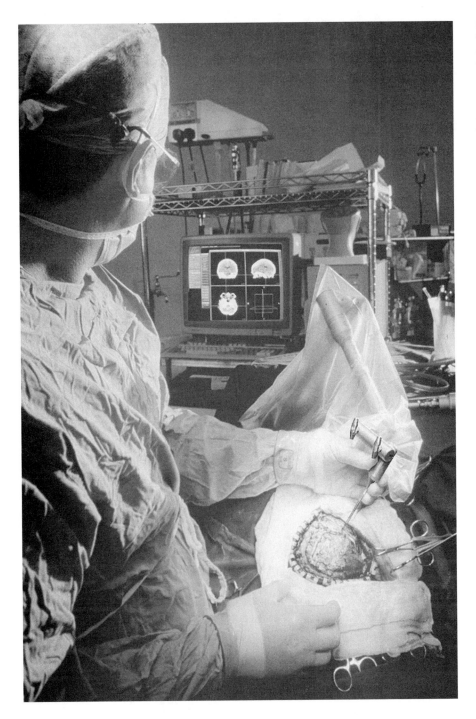

Doctors and nurses use a variety of medical systems to help them treat patients. Computers help medical professionals diagnose health problems and establish effective treatments. Computers can even assist doctors in surgeries by pinpointing or providing detail of the problem area.

same technology that runs the Internet. It could involve the electronic transmission of an X-ray image to a distant radiologist, who can diagnose the patient by examining the X-ray. Tele-health could also involve setting up a computer and camera in a patient's home so that a health care provider can see and talk with the patient without traveling to the patient's home.

Further advancements in tele-health may one day allow a surgeon in one hospital to operate on a patient located in a different hospital. Sophisticated robots could allow the physician to see the patient and even have the sensation of touching him or her. Before this can happen, however, information technology must improve and be extremely reliable so that the electronic connection between the surgeon and the remote control robot will not fail. SEE ALSO BIOLOGY; DATA VISUALIZATION; IMAGE ANALYSIS: MEDICINE.

Maurice McIver

Bibliography

Larkin, T. "Computers May Be Good for Your Health." *FDA Consumer* 18 (Nov. 1984): 8.

Molecular Biology

Deoxyribonucleic acid, better known as DNA, is located in the nucleus of all living cells. DNA dictates which creatures walk, fly, or bore through the soil. Each DNA strand is made up of four nucleotides or "building blocks": adenine, cytosine, guanine, and thymine. These nucleotides, in turn, are made up of a variety of proteins, called amino acids. The strands of DNA, made up of bonded nucleotide pairs, are very long. Molecular biologists have worked toward breaking the genetic code by identifying the nucleotides in order and searching for patterns.

Nature gave scientists one big hint: adenine always bonds with thymine, and guanine always bonds with cytosine. In the past, researchers found fluorescent molecules that mimic the natural nucleotides. When the known fluorescent molecule bonded with an unknown nucleotide, scientists could identify that particular bonded pair of the DNA strand. The process took a decade or more. Researchers hope to speed up this painstaking work with help from computers, so they can accomplish such tasks in hours instead of years.

The challenges are formidable. Scientists must find a way to isolate and copy genes. Sensitive equipment must be developed to allow DNA sequences to be "read" as they are drawn through some kind of microscopic portal. The monitoring equipment must be fast enough, or the process slowed enough, to allow for an accurate identification of these bonded molecules. Finally, researchers must have **algorithms** to help them process the multitude of data they would receive from even one single strand of DNA, which could have 70,000 nucleotides. Computers are then needed to transmit and compare the sequence of the genes being studied with known gene sequence databases, a monumental task for which computers are particularly well suited.

algorithms rules or procedures used to solve mathematical problems—most often described as sequences of steps

The benefits of such research are profound. The study of human genetics is the first most obvious benefit, since these findings will aid research in fields as diverse as inherited diseases and anthropology. Since DNA holds the key to every aspect of the human body, genetic studies could potentially be used to mimic the way different cells work. This would allow researchers to develop and experiment with the effect of medications on the body without using living subjects. Disease processes, such as various forms of cancer, could potentially be duplicated in an electronic model and studied. This kind of understanding would aid in the development of successful treatments. Scientists also hope to use DNA sequences to identify and classify organisms, from the discovery of new bacteria to tracing the evolution of

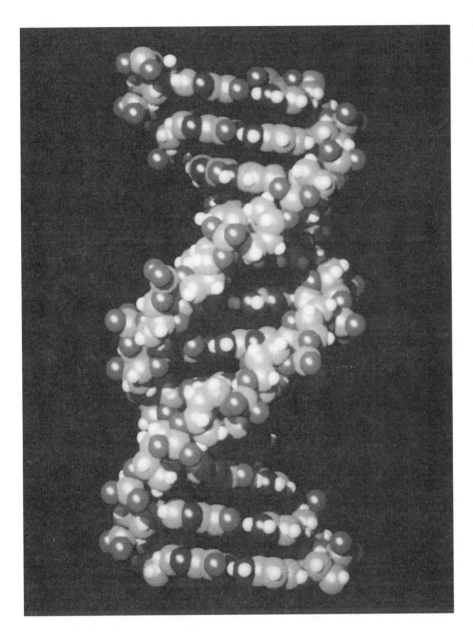

With the help of computer-enhanced graphics, scientists can study DNA molecules and learn more about genetic engineering.

animals. Models of bacterial DNA could help in the study of the spread of diseases.

Gene therapy is a field in which the genes of living things are manipulated and even exchanged with one another to provide a beneficial result. For instance, spider silk, one of the strongest materials on Earth, has been produced by potatoes. Frogs and earthworms have been made to glow in the dark. A type of corn has been modified to fight tooth decay effectively. Vitamin A has been added to rice, making the grain more nutritious. Many of these applications of gene therapy have met controversy, since the long-term effects of gene manipulation in food are unknown.

Bioinformatics is the field in which software is developed to aid in the study of molecular biology. Many of the studies currently being done in molecular biology would be impossible without the help of computers and computer software. This software comes from various places. One researcher developed a basic bioinformatics software application and posted it on the

Linux operating system
an open source UNIX operating system that was originally created by Linus Torvalds in the early 1990s

web for others to download and improve upon, as did the creators of the **Linux operating system**, resulting in a versatile software application. Other firms have hired professionals to develop and copyright applications, which are then sold to researchers and private firms.

The U.S. government has played a pivotal role in the quest for information by establishing the National Center for Biotechnology Information, or NCBI. The NCBI is a division of the National Library of Medicine (NLM), which stores biomedical (such as gene sequence) databases. The NLM itself is a division of the National Institutes of Health (NIH). With all of the resources of the NIH, it is considered the largest biomedical research facility in the world. The NCBI is the result of a cooperative effort. Researchers, academic institutions, and similar agencies from other countries around the world access and contribute to the databases available at the NCBI.

Molecular biology and computers are also finding uses within the medical field. For example, scientists have developed a device that electronically smells the presence of bacterial infections in the lungs. Breath samples are taken from patients and put into an aroma-detection device. The machine measures the electrical resistance of the molecules in the sample of air. The results are then displayed in a two-dimensional "map." Different bacteria produce distinct characteristics on this map. This is a potentially life-saving tool because it allows physicians to treat patients immediately with the correct antibiotic for pneumonia instead of waiting two or three days for sample cultures of the bacteria to be grown and identified.

Although the use of computers is rapidly advancing the field of molecular biology, there is growing evidence that molecular biology is also important to computer science. Researchers at Syracuse University in New York are working with a purple protein called bacteriorhodopsin, produced by a type of bacteria native to salt marshes. This protein is quite stable, readily produced, and easily processed. Many believe it will eventually replace silicon microchips. Bacteriorhodopsin changes shape upon exposure to light. One shape is designated as binary 0, and the other shape is designated as binary 1. Bacteriorhodopsin is suspended in organized layers within a polymer gel. Because an individual protein changes shape upon reacting to different colors of lasers, the shape of an individual protein within the cube can be manipulated.

Floppy drives, CD-ROMs (compact disc–read only memory), and hard drives are different forms of memory that operate on a two-dimensional basis. The bacteriorhodopsin gel would be a type of three-dimensional memory. Researchers believe that one cubic centimeter of this bacteriorhodopsin protein/gel will be able to store between eight and ten gigabytes of information.

Experts agree that future molecular biology studies would be unthinkable without computers. Perhaps in the future, computers will be equally dependent upon molecular biology. SEE ALSO BINARY NUMBER SYSTEM; BIOLOGY; IMAGE ANALYSIS; MOLECULAR COMPUTING; PATTERN RECOGNITION.

Mary McIver Puthawala

Bibliography

Cimino, Daniela. "Modeling a Drug." *Software Magazine* 18, no.1 (1998): 12(1).

Cooke, Robert. "Brave New Bacterial World." *MIT Technology Review* 100, no. 3 (1997): 14(2).

Levin, Carol. "High Protein Computers." *PC Magazine* 14, no. 10 (1995): 29(1).

Music Composition

Computer-assisted music composition is an exciting field. Some of the most interesting possibilities of such composition are depicted in Figure 1, where the possibilities of musical information flows are illustrated. The traditional way of using the computer to compose music is to use software to produce music written in Common Music Notation (CMN), or so-called Western Music Notation, that can be printed and given to human performers who execute music using traditional instruments such as piano, guitar, or violin.

However, the computer can also be used to produce a music score automatically. In this case, the composer becomes a programmer and builds a computer program rather than a music score. A significant example of this may be found in the early work of American composer and teacher Lejaren Hiller (1924–1994), who wrote programs that composed most, if not all, of such scores as the *Illiac Suite for String Quartet* (1956) and *Computer Cantata* (1964).

Another path from the composer to the listener consists in using direct audio synthesis via specific computer programs (e.g., CSOUND, FM synthesis) that integrate the power of a programming language (like "C")

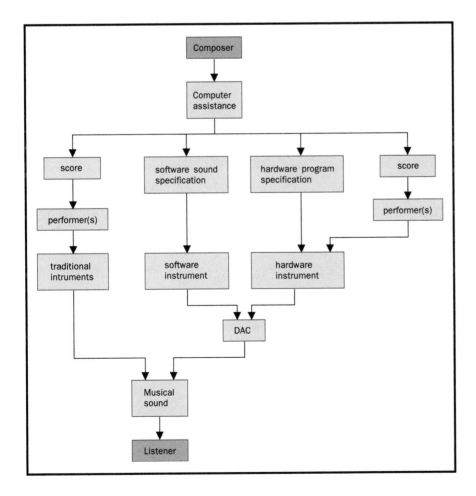

Figure 1. The main paths of computer music composition, from composer to listener.

with specialized functions to treat audio signals. The elaborated signals are played through a Digital to Analog Converter (DAC). Significant examples of this method may be found in works like *Turenas*, by American inventor and composer John Chowning (1934–), that utilize only purely synthesized sounds. This kind of processing on audio data can also be done directly in hardware if real-time interaction is needed. These features can be executed by human performers through the use of computer peripheral hardware, including electronic synthesizers, workstation keyboards, and effect generators. This last option is largely used in popular or light commercial music. These various methods of composing and performing music using the computer can be combined in multiple ways. For example, *Répons*, by French composer and conductor Pierre Boulez (1925–), combines the programmable real-time capabilities of a digital synthesizer with a sizable ensemble of traditional instruments.

Languages for Music Modeling

Music is one of the most complex languages. Many elementary operations are necessary to create a music score; these include editing, saving, loading, visualizing, executing, coding grabbed sounds, printing, and analyzing data. Specific music models and languages have been defined to perform these functions. These can be classified into three main categories: sound-oriented, notation-oriented, and analysis-oriented models.

Sound-oriented models address music modeling by considering the sounds produced, regardless of the visual representation issues of music notation and multiple visualization modalities. Classical examples of sound-oriented models are MIDI (Music Instrument Digital Interface) and CSOUND. Of these, MIDI, first developed in 1982, is the most common. MIDI uses a limited number of music notation symbols (e.g., notes, rests, accidentals, clefs, ties, and dots). MIDI is a **protocol** designed to allow computers and electronic instruments of different manufacturers to work together. MIDI provides a set of common functions such as note events, timing events, pitch bends, pedal information, and synchronization. It is one of the most used languages for the interchange of music information because it allows storing music in a compact form.

Notation-oriented models focus on representing scores on the screen and printing them on paper by using a set of notation symbols. Software examples include Finale, Sibelius, Igor, and Score.

Analysis-oriented models such as EsAC, Humdrum, and MusicData are used to describe music for its further analysis at the level of harmony, style, and melody. These models tend to code music with numbers in order to make metric analysis easier while neglecting several detailed interpretation symbols.

A new category of music languages has been proposed in order to exchange music on the Internet. Samples of this type of language include SMDL, WEDELMUSIC, and Music XML. Some of these are based on the XML (eXtensible Markup Language) programming language currently in use for much Internet content.

Notational Music Composition

Common music editors allow the composer to write music in different ways by using specific input devices such as tables, light pens, or special key-

---

RAPID GROWTH

Music composition technology via computer is rapidly evolving. New paradigms and solutions are now ready to be used by large groups of people.

protocol an agreed understanding for the sub-operations that make up a transaction; usually found in the specification of inter-computer communications

boards. Many allow users to edit with a mouse, import files from other music languages, and use optical music recognition techniques (wherein music information is extracted from a scanned printed or handwritten sheet) or audio recognition (detecting the pitch and rhythm from an audio source). Innovative solutions for music composition have benefited from the increasing presence of distributed systems. For example, MOODS is a cooperative system for editing and manipulating music. The most common input method is using a MIDI keyboard to enter the notes. The composer plays the keyboard, producing the melody for a specific voice or track (typically an instrument) which is translated by the device into MIDI codes and sent to the computer where the codes are converted into music notation. The composer is thus able to see the played notes on the monitor, to store the music, and to print it. Another typical feature is related to the output of music: after the music input phase, the composer can choose the instrument associated with each track and listen to the execution or use it as accompaniment. To do this, the computer sends MIDI commands to drive external (e.g., keyboards, tone and effects generators, controllers) or internal (e.g., software synthesizer) reproducers.

Algorithmic Composition

In algorithmic composition, the composer builds a program rather than a score. This form of composition is totally led by the computer. Two main methods—deterministic or probabilistic—have been developed. The first approach generates notes without random selection. The variables supplied to such a process may be a set of pitches, a musical phrase, or some constraints that the process must satisfy. The other approach integrates random choice into the decision-making process, generating musical events according to probability tables which estimate the occurrence of certain events.

Audio Music Composition

Computer-based audio music composition is based on the elaboration of sound samples. Composers combine synthetic or digitized sounds using specific editing programs (groove machine, audio editing) or hardware instruments (sampler keyboard, sequencer) that provide support for functions such as:

- Multi-track recording or sequencing, to manage several audio tracks simultaneously for playback or recording process;

- Time stretching, which allows for changing the length of audio data duration without affecting the pitch;

- Pitch shifting, in which sound samples are modified in order to transpose the pitch of notes;

- Effect applying, to add reverberation, delay, **modulation**, and dynamics effects.

Audio editor and electronic devices provide the composer with several sound generation techniques like:

- Additive sound synthesis. This common technique merges and filters signals with different wave-forms, different frequencies, phases, and amplitudes to produce new sound signals.

modulation a technique whereby signals are translated to analog so that the resultant signal can be more easily transmitted and received by other elements in a communication system

- Subtractive sound synthesis. In this technique, a complex audio signal is modified through filtering so as to modify the frequency contents.

- Physical modeling synthesis (PhM). This begins with mathematical models of the physical acoustics of instrumental sound production. The equations of PhM describe the mechanical and acoustic behavior of an instrument being played.

- Frequency Modulation (FM) Synthesis. This is based on the theory underlying the FM of radio-band frequencies. This form of synthesis was introduced by Yamaha in 1983 with the DX7 synthesizer. In the basic modulation technique, a carrier **oscillator** is modulated in frequency by a modulator oscillator. This allows the computer to modify amplitude and create harmonics that generate the new signal. SEE ALSO ANIMATION; FILM AND VIDEO EDITING; MUSIC; MUSIC, COMPUTER.

Pierfrancesco Bellini, Ivan Bruno, and Paolo Nesi

oscillator an electronic component that produces a precise waveform of a fixed known frequency; this can be used as a time base (clock) signal to other devices

Bibliography

Bellini, Pierfrancesco, Fabrizio Fioravanti, and Paolo Nesi, "Managing Music in Orchestras." *IEEE Computer*, September, 1999, pp. 26–34.

Roads, Curtis. *The Computer Music Tutorial.* Cambridge, MA: MIT Press, 1998.

Selfridge-Field, Eleanor. *Beyond MIDI—The Handbook of Musical Codes.* London: MIT Press, 1997.

Navigation

Navigation is the art of finding one's way from one location to another. This appears pretty simple in the age of interstate highways and well-marked street intersections: follow the road signs or a map and the task should be easy. But imagine you are in an aircraft or a ship and all you can see is the blue sky above you and the clouds below you or nothing but waves. Now, imagine it is night and you can not see a thing! In our computer-centered society, we have the digital means to use satellite technology and other electronic tools to help us figure out where we are and how to get where we want to go. Long before these were available, however, mathematical navigational systems were devised to guide ship captains and travelers of centuries past; these time-tested tools provide the foundation upon which our sophisticated, electronic navigational tools are built.

Early Navigational Foundations

To aid in navigation and map making, a coordinate system was created using virtual lines of latitude and longitude that cross at 90 degree angles. Latitude is referenced to a circle circumscribed around the Earth called the equator, which is at what is called zero latitude. North of the equator, the latitude lines are parallel to the equator and are called "north latitude." The geographical North Pole is 90 degrees north latitude and the circle at that latitude has such a small radius it is virtually a point. The South Pole is 90 degrees south latitude. The angle of latitude is the angular difference between two lines: one drawn from the center of the Earth to the equator and one drawn from the center of the Earth to the latitude in question.

Longitude lines also run around the Earth but through the North and South Poles. The reference line, the zero meridian, runs through the Royal Observatory in Greenwich, just outside of London, England. Lines of longitude are designated east and west from the zero meridian. Time zones are also a function of longitude and the reference time zone from which all others are measured is called GMT, or Greenwich Mean Time. This brings up an important subject: the inseparable relationship between time and navigation.

Time Zones, Sundials, and Longitudinal Calculations

Nearly everyone is familiar with the sundial, which uses the shadow of its angled center piece, called the *gnomon*, to "tell" time. The sundial tells local time, based on its relationship to the Sun in any given place. As an example, at exactly "high noon" the gnomon produces no shadow as the Sun is precisely midway between sunrise and sunset. But high noon occurs at different times at different places on the Earth. This is why there are time zones.

There are generally 24 time zones corresponding roughly to the one-hour segments of a 24-hour Earth day. There are some odd time zones with half-hour and even smaller increments, but these are rare. The actual time of high noon does not jump in one-hour steps, of course, but changes gradually as one travels around the Earth. If the sundial is adjusted so the gnomon points to true north, the sundial will show true solar time. The difference between true solar time at some location and the true solar time at the zero meridian can be used to calculate longitude.

In order to use the sundial to determine longitude in relationship to the zero meridian, however, a traveler must have an accurate mechanical clock set to precise GMT before traveling. The English government offered a substantial reward in 1761 for the invention of an accurate clock that would operate on a ship for precisely this reason. While the latitude of a ship could be determined by measuring the position of the Sun at its highest point, without a point of reference to time, determining longitude without an accurate GMT reading required lunar observations and time-consuming, difficult mathematical computations. Trade and exploratory ships could travel more safely, accurately, and economically with the use of reliable time-keeping technology.

The requirements for navigation became much more stringent when humans began to travel by air. A ship traveling on open water is relatively slow, so finding a "fix" or position every few hours was sufficient. Even if fog or other bad weather prohibited taking fixes, the ship could slow down or stop until conditions improved. This is not possible with aircraft! Accurate position fixes must be available continuously. Clock and sundial technology could not perform this complex task!

From Radio Beacons to On-Board Computers

One of the first aircraft navigation systems, invented in the 1920s, used radio beacons. The aircraft could hop from one beacon to another on what were called airways. Position could be determined from these airways but this involved tedious procedures that were not only difficult but time-consuming, as well. The beacons were strategically located so that the airways passed

> **UNIVERSAL SKILL**
>
> Animals do it! Humans do it! Do what? Navigate! The ability to travel successfully from one location to another is a skill as old as time itself. Modern navigation has reached such a level of sophistication that aircraft can fly half-way around the globe and land perfectly on a runway using only electronic navigation.

Navigation systems are not limited to aircraft, watercraft, and spacecraft. Cars can be equipped with special navigation systems to help drivers find their destinations more easily.

directly over airports to simplify the navigation. Similar homing beacons were used for ships but only near shore due to the limited range of the beacon's radio signal.

Later, more sophisticated radio navigation systems for both air and sea actually measured the vessel's latitude and longitude, which was plotted on a navigation chart. This was acceptable for ships at sea but unfolding a large navigation chart and plotting a course in an aircraft cockpit was not particularly convenient. However, because it was the best option at the time, it was done.

What would have been ideal would be a computer that took the latitude and longitude information and automatically calculated steering information. Some ship navigators had access to such a computer, which worked with the first long-range radio navigation systems during World War II. These computers were huge mechanical monsters that were acceptable for a battleship but not suited for aircraft.

It was not until small digital computers became available that long-range navigation became commonplace in aircraft. The aircrew could enter the desired final or intermediate destinations, called "waypoints," into the computer, and the computer would calculate the steering information, which was displayed with an indicator. It was even possible to use the steering information in the form of electrical signals to control a ship or aircraft with an autopilot.

Long-Distance Navigation Systems

Since World War II, several improved long distance radio navigation systems have been developed. The first was LORAN, which stands for "long range navigation." Shortly after LORAN was Omega, which was followed by a much-improved LORAN called LORAN-C. Finally, in the late 1970s, the ultimate system was developed, the satellite-based Global Positioning System or GPS. GPS can provide navigation anywhere on Earth within less than one meter (about 3 feet) of error, which is superior to any previous navigation system.

The GPS navigation system consists of a "constellation" of 24 satellites in well-known orbits. A network of ground stations controls the orbits and functions of the satellites. Satellites transmit radio signals that are used to measure the distance from the user to each satellite. A computer solves the geometry problem and determines the user's position.

GPS depends on the very accurate atomic clocks located in the satellites and ground control stations. It is fascinating to realize that the secret to accurate navigation in 1761 was precise clocks, and the same remains true today.

In addition to a radio receiver, the GPS user equipment has a rather extensive computer. It is necessary to separate the signals from the satellites, which are all transmitted on the same frequency and sorted out by the computer. The computer knows which satellites are present and where they are in their orbits. It inserts a number of calibration factors and calculates the position of the user equipment in latitude, longitude, altitude, and precise time. Most GPS receivers used for aircraft have large databases, which include the locations of airports, radio navigation aids, airways, and so on.

GPS products for consumer use have become increasingly popular since the late 1990s. In addition to providing convenience and security to people driving in unfamiliar areas, GPS technology such as the General Motors "OnStar" navigational system, which connects drivers to assistance operators via GPS satellites, can help save lives by directing drivers to hospitals or police stations near where they are, should an emergency arise. SEE ALSO AIRCRAFT TRAFFIC MANAGEMENT; GEOGRAPHICAL INFORMATION SYSTEMS; GLOBAL POSITIONING SYSTEMS; SATELLITE TECHNOLOGY.

Albert D. Helfrick

Bibliography

Clausing, Donald J. *Aviator's Guide to Navigation.* Blue Ridge Summit, PA: TAB Books, 1992.

Hotchkiss, Noel J. *A Comprehensive Guide to Land Navigation with GPS.* Herndon, VA: Alexis, 1995.

Lewis, Ralph. *By Dead Reckoning: Recollections of a Master Navigator.* McLean, VA: Paladwr Press, 1994.

Sonnenberg, G. J. *Radar and Electronic Navigation.* Boston: Butterworths, 1988.

Neural Networks

Since its inception in the 1940s, when it was hailed as "The Electronic Brain," the digital computer has been expected to replicate **cognitive**

cognitive pertaining to the concepts of knowing or perceiving

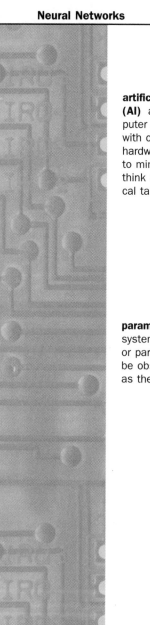

functions. While developments in hardware technology and software techniques have enabled limited successes in this direction, many cognitive capabilities remain uniquely human. The field of **artificial intelligence (AI)** seeks to infer general principles of "intelligence" by analyzing human cognitive processes, and then to encode them in software. The standard approach to AI is grounded in the assumption that human cognition is based on the ability to manipulate symbols using logical operators. An alternative approach, generally known as neural networks, is motivated by the observation that the biological brain is the only device capable of intelligent behavior.

Thus, the neural network framework is rooted in principles abstracted from our knowledge of neurobiological function. Some of these follow:

- Computation is performed by a network of interconnected units, each representing a neuron or a set of neurons.

- Each unit generates an output signal that is a simple **parametric** function of the signals on its input lines, which can be either output signals from other neurons or external signals (environmental input to the network).

- A given unit cannot transmit different signals to different units; its output signal is broadcast to a set of units that can comprise the entire network or any subset.

- Each input line to a neuron has a corresponding weight parameter, a value that determines the influence of that line on the neuron's output.

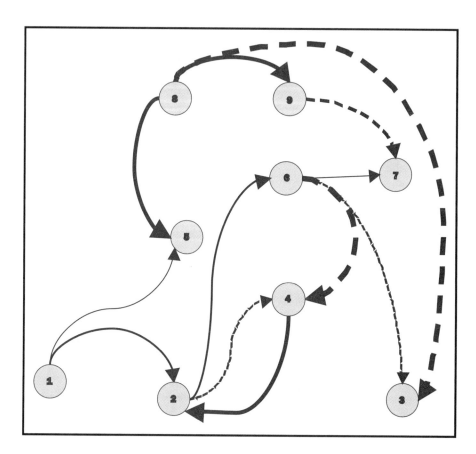

Figure 1. Diagram of a neural network.

- The function ultimately computed by a network is determined by the connectivity of the units, their individual input-output functions, and the weights among them.

A diagram of a neural network is shown in Figure 1. The nine units in the diagram are numbered, and the curved lines with arrows indicate the connectivity of the network. Units 1 and 8 receive no input from other units in the network; their activity values are set by stimuli external to the network, like the light detecting cells in the retina, for example. Similarly, units 3, 5, and 7 are output units; these units do not activate any other units. Generally, output units generate the ultimate result of the network computation. Biologically, they would correspond to *effector* cells in the nervous system; that is, cells that directly influence the environment, like motor neurons that directly stimulate muscle tissue.

The thickness of the links is meant to represent the weight of the connection, and dashed links denote negative values to the links. An N by N matrix is a more precise (and for a computer program, more useful) representation of the connectivity in a network with N units. The table that follows refers to the network depicted in Figure 1. (The weight from unit A to B is the Bth element in row A, where A and B can be 1 through 9.)

	1	2	3	4	5	6	7	8	9
1	0	0.8	0	0	0.3	0	0	0	0
2	0	0	0	-0.2	0	0.9	0	0	0
3	0	0	0	0	0	0	0	0	0
4	0	1.8	0	0	0	0	0	0	0
5	0	0	0	0	0	0	0	0	0
6	0	0	-0.1	-1.1	0	0	0.4	0	0
7	0	0	0	0	0	0	0	0	0
8	0	0	-1.3	0	1.9	0	0	0	1.8
9	0	0	0	0	0	0	-0.7	0	0

The network computation proceeds by computing activity values for each unit according to a function that combines its inputs multiplied by the connection weights. Once the modeler has selected the unit function and set the connectivity of the units, the function computed by the network is determined by the weight values. These values can either be set by the modeler or learned by the network to give a function that is extracted from observations.

Hard-Wired Neural Networks

Consider the task of adjusting several interdependent parameters of a complex system so that its output function is optimal. An example is scheduling classes at a large university, so that conflicts among classroom use, student course choices, and faculty teaching times are minimized. Another is the simultaneous function of the many muscles in the human body in performing a complex task like riding a bicycle or juggling. For a task with multiple simultaneous constraints among the variables, it is often impossible to find a solution that is guaranteed to be optimal (as in, the absolute best). But there are several approaches to finding very good solutions, and for many real-world situations this is sufficient.

A neural network can be designed to approach such a problem by defining each unit to represent the "truth value" of a specific hypothesis. For example, in the class-scheduling task, a unit may represent the plausibility that "English 101 will be taught in Room 312 by Professor Miller from 10 A.M. to 11 A.M. on Monday, Wednesday, and Friday." Another unit would represent another hypothesis, such as "Psychology 400 will be taught in Room 312 by Professor Wu from 10 A.M. to 11 A.M. on Monday, Wednesday, and Friday." Since there is a conflict between these two hypotheses, the connection between them would have a negative value. Thus, a network can represent hypotheses as nodes and constraints among hypotheses as weight values between pairs of nodes. The success of this approach depends on the skills and intuitions of the network designer. While there are some guiding principles to network design, it remains very much an art form.

Neural networks have been applied to many problems of this kind, often providing a better solution than other **heuristic** techniques. A classic example of a difficult (NP complete) problem is the so-called traveling salesperson problem (TSP). Given a set of N locations, the goal of the TSP is to find the shortest path that goes to every point and returns to the starting location. A neural network can be used to find a "pretty good" path; that is, the solution is good, though not guaranteed to be the best. Experiment results published in 1985 by John J. Hopfield and David W. Tank showed that a neural network finds a path that is very close to optimal.

Learning in Neural Networks

One of the most attractive features of neural network models is their capacity to learn. Since the response properties of the network are determined by connectivity and weight values, a learning procedure can be expressed mathematically as a function that determines the amount by which each weight changes in terms of the activities of the neurons. Most neural network learning procedures are based on a postulate put forward by Donald Hebb (1904–1985) in his classic book, *The Organization of Behavior*: "When an axon of cell A is near enough to excite a cell B and repeatedly or persistently takes part in firing it, some growth process or metabolic change takes place in one or both cells such that A's efficiency, as one of the cells firing B is increased."

Various mathematical and computational enhancements to Hebb's original theory have led to many approaches to machine learning. Of these, a technique known as backpropagation, originally discovered by Paul J. Werbos (1974), has been the primary driving force in neural networks since the mid-1980s.

Typically, a network that "learns" is trained to learn the relationship between a set of input and output variables that have been independently measured across many examples. For example, the input might be a set of blood test results and the output might be a binary value that indicates whether the patient was later found to have a particular form of cancer. A learning network could be defined as a set of input units (each representing a blood test result) which activate a set of intermediate units, which then

heuristic a procedure that serves to guide investigation but that has not been proven

PREDICTING STOCK MARKET TRENDS

Can a neural network predict which stocks will rise or fall? Various companies claim success with their systems, which analyze previous trading trends. Some of the factors taken into consideration include current stock values and net change in specific stocks during the previous week.

activate a single output unit (representing the development of a tumor). Initially, the weights are randomly assigned, and so the network output is not useful for medical diagnosis. Training proceeds by presenting input data to the network and comparing the resulting network output to the "target" value (the corresponding output value in the data). The backpropagation technique specifies how to adjust the network weights based on the network error (target minus network output) and the input activation values.

This technique is broadly applicable to problems involving pattern recognition, spanning a broad spectrum of domains. These include military applications, such as detecting submarines from sonar signals; financial applications including stock market prediction; medical diagnosis; and speech recognition. Neural network learning **algorithms** have also shed light onto the neurobiological mechanisms underlying human learning. SEE ALSO ARTIFICIAL INTELLIGENCE; EXPERT SYSTEMS; PATTERN RECOGNITION.

Paul Munro

algorithms rules or procedures used to solve mathematical problems—most often described as sequences of steps

Bibliography

Hebb, Donald O. *The Organization of Behavior.* New York: Wiley, 1949.

Hopfield, John J., and David W. Tank. "'Neural' Computation of Decisions in Optimization Problems." *Biological Cybernetics* 52 (1985): 141–152.

Werbos, Paul J. "Beyond Regression: New Tools for Prediction and Analysis in the Behavioral Sciences." Ph.D. Thesis, Harvard University, 1974.

Open Source

There are three dimensions to the concept of "open source" as it applies to computing. First, open source is a philosophy about computing and sharing programming code to improve the quality of computing. The term "open source" also refers to a wide array of operating systems and applications that have been developed under this philosophy, and, finally, it represents a general approach to the treatment of **intellectual property**, usually in reference to licensing software or related documentation.

Origins of Open Source Computing

The idea of sharing the **source code** for computer programs so that the programs can be debugged, modified, or improved is a practice that began in the late 1950s, when IBM provided programmers employed by their customers with access to the source code for applications running on their **mainframe computers**. The idea of creating source code for the purposes of sharing it can be traced to the early days of the Internet, when programmers wrote and shared source code for the applications that have been fundamental to the development of the Internet. The establishment and workings of the Free Software Foundation (FSF) have also promoted this approach.

The emergence of the Internet provided a global medium through which programmers could exchange source code, documentation, and other information about programming. The Free Software Foundation, which was founded in 1985 and is "dedicated to promoting computer users' right to use, study, copy, modify, and redistribute computer programs," provided

intellectual property the acknowledgement that an individual's creativity and innovation can be owned in the same way as physical property

source code the human-readable programs that are compiled or interpreted so that they can be executed by a computing machine

mainframe computers large computers used by businesses and government agencies to process massive amounts of data; generally faster and more powerful than desktop computers but usually requiring specialized software

not only software (under its GNU Project), but also a social and political framework for advancing knowledge in the field. The foundation promoted the development and use of free software and documentation—not necessarily free of charge, but freely accessible as intellectual property—and campaigned to increase what its members believe to be the ethical and political issues of freedom in the use of software.

The General Public License

One of the key contributions made by the Free Software Foundation has been to establish the legal basis for free software under U.S. intellectual property law, in the form of the General Public License (GPL). Under the GPL, software is licensed for the purpose of making derivative works, may be distributed without charge, and must be disclosed or distributed in source code form. The essential purpose of the GPL is to create a legal environment that is hospitable to the exchange of source code and programs, and which tends to promote efforts to study, change, or improve computer software. Related or variant licensing schemes include the Lesser GPL (LGPL), the Apache license, the Artistic License, the FreeBSD copyright, the Mozilla Public License, the Netscape Public License, the Sun Community Source License (SCSL), and the Sun Industry Standards License (SISL).

proprietary software software created by an individual or company that is sold under a license that dictates use and distribution

There is considerable controversy in regard to the benefits of the GPL. Its proponents argue that software developed and issued under the GPL is less expensive and ultimately more powerful than **proprietary software**, because development and testing are open processes. Critics of the GPL claim that open software diminishes incentives to create better software, because it weakens the business models on which the proprietary software industry has been based.

Because of the connotations of "free software," and owing to the anti-business stance of Richard Stallman, the founder of the Free Software Foundation, a less pejorative term, "open source," was adopted during the 1990s. In order to clarify further the circumstances under which software based on the GPL or related licensing schemes is distributed, a group called the Open Source Initiative has formulated the Open Source Definition, which effectively reconciles different licensing schemes, and the Open Source Certification Program, which is aimed at preventing misuse of the phrase "open source" and identifying software that is developed and/or made available under a license that meets the Open Source Definition.

Open Source Development Models

The open source community is divided, at least philosophically, into two factions. The first faction is united by the belief that there is civic, economic, and moral value in the free development and exchange of software. The second faction is defined mainly by a business model, under which open source development is used to reduce the costs of research and development, accelerate the rate at which systems and applications are developed (and debugged), and create open distribution channels that engender broader interest in the software. For some companies, like Red Hat, open source software is the primary basis of their business. For other companies, such as IBM, open source software is employed to create or maintain a product line while lowering direct investment. For many more firms in the software industry, including Microsoft, public domain and open source software is employed to supplement proprietary products and services.

Open Source Computing and the Emergence of Linux

The Free Software Foundation has exerted considerable influence since its establishment, but the emergence of the Linux operating system is the main reason that open source software has become a significant factor in computing. Developed by a Finnish student named Linus Torvalds (and modeled on the UNIX operating system, but without UNIX source code), Linux was initially released in 1991. Owing largely to continued work by Torvalds on the kernel of the operating system, and an integration of the operating system with a suite of utilities developed by the Free Software Foundation's GNU Project, Linux has matured into a sophisticated operating system that now constitutes a legitimate alternative to proprietary systems on the market for server software. In addition, there are several major open source projects—the most important of them being the GNOME and KDE projects—that are intended to create desktop environments for Linux that will allow it to challenge both Microsoft Windows and the Macintosh OS as an operating system for personal and corporate desktops.

Other Important Open Source Projects

Linux has received more attention, but there are a number of other important open source projects, including the GNU Project's compilers, libraries, and utilities, its Emacs editor, the Perl and Tcl languages, the FreeBSD operating system, the Apache web server, and sendmail. Of these initiatives, the Apache Project—which began in 1995 when a small group of programmers agreed to work collaboratively in order to transform the CERN web server software into a more reliable application—is arguably the most important, because the Apache web server has played a pivotal role in the growth of the World Wide Web, through the continuous development and distribution of a powerful open source application and an array of modular functions and services. Sendmail is the core service for most of the e-mail transported over the Internet.

Richard Stallman (1953–), founder of the non-profit Free Software Foundation, helped create a freely available alternative to UNIX software called GNU (GNU's not Unix).

Open Source Documentation

An important factor in the development of open source computing has been the application of the open source philosophy to the development and distribution of documentation. Commercial developers and vendors have moved to reduce the amount and quality of documentation that is distributed with operating systems and applications, effectively abandoning the provision of documentation for their products to an expensive, but ineffectual "after market." At the same time, the application of the open source model to documentation has led to the widespread availability of guides and manuals that are accurate, thorough, and up-to-date.

For example, the Linux Documentation Project (LDP) has played a key corollary in the development of Linux. The purpose of the LDP is to promote and coordinate the publication of guides and manuals that support both systems administrators and end users. The LDP serves as a central distribution point for a number of independently produced guides. The LDP also promotes the creation and maintenance of so-called "HOWTOs," briefer guides to specific topics, such as disk partitioning, the configuration of proxy servers, and security. SEE ALSO CODES; CODING TECHNIQUES; PROGRAMMING.

Christinger Tomer

Bibliography

Raymond, Eric S. *The Cathedral and the Bazaar: Musings on Linux and Open Source by an Accidental Revolutionary.* Sebastopol, CA: O'Reilly & Associates, 1999.

Young, Robert, and Wendy Goldman Rohm. *Under the Radar: How Red Hat Changed the Software Business—and Took Microsoft by Surprise.* Scottsdale, AZ: Coriolis Press, 1999.

Internet Resources

"The Free Software Definition." *The GNU Project; Free Software Foundation.* <http://www.gnu.org/philosophy/free-sw.html>

Organick, Elliot

Engineer and Pioneering Computer Scientist
1925–1985

Best remembered for his easy-to-understand textbooks about computers, programming, and operating systems, Elliot Organick was a pioneer computer scientist who was also passionate about making advances in technology simple and easy to understand. According to J. A. N. Lee in *Computer Pioneers,* one of Organick's most quoted remarks when hearing about new advances in technology was: "This is great stuff, but does it have to be so complicated?"

Organick was born in Brooklyn, New York, on February 25, 1925. After high school in Manhattan, he began studies in chemical engineering at the University of Michigan in 1941. He graduated in only three years, going on to work as a chemist for the Manhattan Project, the U.S. government's secret effort to develop an atomic bomb during World War II. He returned to academics shortly afterward, however, earning a master's degree from the University of Michigan in 1947 and a doctorate in chemical engineering in 1950.

In those days there were no specialized "computer scientists." Instead, mathematicians, physicists, engineers, and other researchers often used computers to perform numeric computations faster and to get more accurate results. Organick was one of those innovators when he used an IBM Card Programmed Calculator to carry out his chemical engineering **thermodynamic** calculations. He soon became intrigued with using computers to enhance teaching and learning, and by the late 1950s was one of the first true computer scientists.

thermodynamic relating to heat energy

While Organick worked for the United Gas Pipeline Company from 1950 to 1955, his interest in computers helped advance the development of computer applications in the petroleum industry. For a short time after leaving that job, he worked as a consultant in computer applications. However, on the advice of his doctoral adviser, Organick returned to academia and joined the Computing Center at the University of Houston. Within five years he was its director.

In 1959 the Ford Foundation established a major project to induce the engineering faculty of the University of Michigan to use computers in engineering education and teaching. After a nationwide search, the director of the project invited Organick to return to Ann Arbor as associate director. While in Michigan, Organick was able to convince the National Science Foundation (NSF) that all educators needed to know how to use computers. With NSF funding, he organized several courses in 1960, and taught them to engineering faculty and high school science and math teachers during the summers until 1963.

Since good computer science study materials were not available in the early 1960s, Organick undertook to write some himself, with enduring success. His first, *A Fortran Primer*, was initially published in 1961 and later revised in 1966. In 1974 he and L. P. Meissner transformed it into the well known *Fortran IV*. During his stay in Michigan, Organick also explored the Michigan Algorithm Decoder (MAD), which led to his book, *The MAD Primer*. Although this work was not as widely circulated as the Fortran title, programming language designers of that generation admired it.

Between 1968 and 1969, Organick went to the Massachusetts Institute of Technology (MIT) on sabbatical to work on its MAC project. The result of this experience was a textbook on the Multics operating system. In keeping with his reputation as a writer who could explain technical ideas in the computer field clearly and precisely, Organick developed an exceptionally clear description of how the Multics system works.

In 1971 Organick was recruited by the University of Utah as professor of computer science. There, he shaped a ground-breaking undergraduate computer science curriculum. His design was so thorough and farsighted that the program was not restructured until 1985.

By the mid 1970s, Organick had become the leading writer of computer science texts. *Computer Science: A First Course*, which he wrote with A. I. Forsythe, T. A. Keenan, and W. Stenberg, was an immediate success and was translated into five languages. *Programming Language Structures*, authored with Forsythe and R. P. Plummer, was distinctive in its application of comparative linguistic analysis to a wide range of then-current programming languages.

As noted in Lee's book, when Organick was asked how he created so many outstanding texts, Organick replied: "I am such a slow learner that once I understand something, I might as well write it down!"

Organick was deeply committed to education and professional service, which led him to take on a variety of leadership positions in the Association for Computing Machinery (ACM). He served six years on the ACM Education Committee and in 1968 was instrumental in founding the Special Interest Group on Computer Science Education (SIGCSE). He was editor of the education section of the *Communications* of the ACM for two years, and was editor-in-chief of *Computing Surveys* during its first six years, building its circulation to more than 30,000. In 1985 he received the SIGCSE annual award for Outstanding Contributions to Computer Science Education. Organick died of leukemia in Shreveport, Louisiana, on December 21, 1985. SEE ALSO COMPUTER ASSISTED INSTRUCTION; KEMENY, JOHN G.; LOGO; MATHEMATICS.

Ida M. Flynn

MICHIGAN ALGORITHM DECODER (MAD)

MAD was a computer language based on Algol 58 developed at the University of Michigan to teach programming to undergraduate students. It was very efficient, which meant that the programs were returned to the students rather quickly, and it provided good diagnostics, which helped the students find their errors.

MULTICS

Multics (Multiplexed Information and Computing Service) was a general purpose computing system developed by MIT, Bell Labs, and General Electric. The system was meant to support hundreds of timesharing users, which was a significant innovation at that time. Although the system was not a commercial success, its operating system introduced significant concepts in computer design.

Bibliography

Lee, J. A. N. *Computer Pioneers.* Los Alamitos, CA: IEEE Computer Society Press, 1995.

Lindstrom, Gary. "Elliot Organick." *Communications of the ACM* 29, no. 3 (1986): 231.

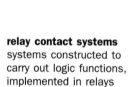

Péter, Rózsa

Hungarian Mathematician
1905–1977

A pioneering theorist of a mathematical discipline with important applications in computer science, Rózsa Politzer was born February 17, 1905, in Budapest, Hungary. Although she never married, Politzer changed her name to Rózsa Péter in 1930. Initially, Péter intended to fulfill her father's wish for her to become a chemist, but lectures by mathematicians enticed her to a course that would change her life as well as the field of mathematics. Through lectures and papers in the 1930s, she promoted the study of recursive functions as a distinct field of mathematics. This aspect of number theory considers functions that are used to study the structure of number classes or functions in terms of the complexity of the calculations required to determine them. Since theories of **relay contact systems**, **cybernetics**, and computer programming are dependent on recursive functions, Péter's work is indispensable to computer science.

After attending the Mária Terézia Girls' School in Budapest, Péter enrolled at Eötvös Loránd University in 1922 to pursue a career in chemistry. Soon after starting, however, she decided to change her field of study to mathematics. Also while in school, she met László Kalmár, with whom she maintained a close, lifelong professional friendship. Kalmár, who became a famous mathematics pioneer in his own right, was the person who later introduced her to recursive functions.

In 1932 Péter wrote a paper on recursive functions. She lectured on the subject at the International Congress of Mathematicians in Zurich in 1932 and again in 1936. At this conference, she was the first to formally suggest recursive mathematics as a field unto itself. In 1935, she received her Ph.D. summa cum laude from Eötvös Loránd University. After publishing several papers on recursive functions, she was invited to join the editorial boards of several international mathematical journals, including, in 1937, the *Journal of Symbolic Logic.*

In 1943 Péter wrote *Playing with Infinity: Mathematical Explorations and Excursions* (not released until 1945 because of World War II), a work intended for the general public. It discussed number theory, geometry, calculus, logic, and Gödel's undecidability theory, all in a manner accessible to nonspecialists. This book successfully attempted to bridge the gap between mathematics and science and the humanities. Péter's work has since been translated into forty languages.

After Germany's 1945 defeat in World War II, Péter enjoyed teaching at Pedagógiai Förskola, a teacher's college in Budapest, for the next ten years. In 1951 she published *Recursive Functions*, the first book on recursive functions. This book was also translated into numerous other languages and

relay contact systems systems constructed to carry out logic functions, implemented in relays (electromechanical switches) rather than semiconductor devices

cybernetics a unified approach to understanding the behavior of machines and animals developed by Norbert Wiener (1894-1964)

became a standard reference. In 1955 the teacher's college was shut down. Péter became a professor of mathematics at Eötvös Loránd University in Budapest. Her interests turned to the use of recursive functions and their relevance to computers. Her first paper on this subject addressed primitive recursive functions and **ALGOL**. After her retirement, she continued her research into recursive functions and their relationship to computer program languages. She published her last book, *Recursive Functions in Computer Theory*, in 1976.

Péter was awarded the Kossuth Prize in 1951 by the state of Hungary for her achievements. She also received the State Award, Silver Degree, in 1970, and the State Award, Gold Degree, in 1973. That same year, she became a corresponding member and the first female member of the Hungarian Academy of Sciences. She was made an honorary president of the János Bolyai Mathematical Association in 1975.

In addition to the study of recursive mathematics, Péter was very active in mathematics education, writing textbooks and teaching both children and mathematics teachers. Péter challenged society, and particularly children, to see mathematics and the sciences as entertaining, joyful, adventurous, and ultimately more than dry, intellectual exercises. She believed mathematics to be an indispensable part of science, and science to be an indispensable part of humanity.

Péter's interests extended beyond mathematics; she enjoyed art and cooking and also wrote theater reviews. She enjoyed literature as well and translated poetry into Hungarian. However, mathematics remained her first love, and in *Playing with Infinity*, she wrote: "I love mathematics not only for its technical applications, but principally because it is beautiful: because man has breathed his spirit of play into it, and because it has given him his greatest game—the encompassing of the infinite." Péter died of cancer on February 17, 1977. SEE ALSO LOVELACE, ADA BYRON KING, COUNTESS OF; MATHEMATICS; PROCEDURAL LANGUAGES.

Mary McIver Puthawala

ALGOL a language developed by the ALGOL committee for scientific applications—acronym for ALGOrithmic Language

PÉTER'S PERSEVERANCE

Péter held no permanent job for eighteen years after graduating from college because, Hungary, as an ally of Nazi Germany, engaged in academic purges aimed at eliminating Jews and others whom the Nazis considered "enemies" from serving on school faculties. Instead, she tutored students and took temporary teaching assignments for financial support. But her lack of employment did not prevent her from establishing herself as a world leader in mathematical logic.

Bibliography

Grinstein, Louise S., and Paul J. Campbell, eds. *Women of Mathematics: A Bibliographic Sourcebook*. New York: Greenwood Press, 1987.

Morris, Edie, and Leon Harkleroad. "Rózsa Péter: Recursive Function Theory's Founding Mother." *Mathematical Intelligencer* 12, no. 1 (1990): 59–61.

Péter, Rózsa. *Recursive Functions*. New York: Academic Press, 1967.

Young, Robyn V., ed. *Notable Mathematicians: From Ancient Times to the Present*. Detroit: Gale Group, 1998.

Physics

In some ways we would not have computers today were it not for physics. Furthermore, the needs of physics have stimulated computer development at every step. This all started due to one man's desire to eliminate needless work by transferring it to a machine.

Charles Babbage (1791–1871) was a well-to-do Englishman attending Cambridge University in the early 1800s. One day he was nodding off over a book containing tables of astronomical phenomena. He fancied that he would become an astronomical mathematician. The motion of heavenly bodies was, of course, governed by the laws of physics. For a moment, he thought of having the tables calculated automatically. This idea came up several times in succeeding years until he finally designed a calculator, the Difference Engine, that could figure the numbers and print the tables. A version of the Difference Engine made by someone else found its way to the Dudley Observatory in Albany, New York, where it merrily cranked out numbers until the 1920s. Babbage followed this machine with a programmable version, the Analytical Engine, which was never built. The Analytical Engine, planned as a more robust successor to the Difference Engine, is considered by many to be the first example of a modern computer.

In the late 1800s, mathematician and scientist Lord Kelvin (William Thomson) (1824–1907) tried to understand wave phenomena by building a mechanical **analog** computer that modeled the waves on beaches in England. This was a continuation of the thread of mechanical computation applied to understand physical phenomena in the 1800s.

In the 1920s, physicist Vannevar Bush (1890–1974) of the Massachusetts Institute of Technology built a Differential Analyzer that used a combination of mechanical and electrical parts to create an analog computer useful for many problems. The Differential Analyzer was especially suited for physics calculations, as its output was a smooth curve showing the results of mathematical modeling. This curve was very accurate, more so than the **slide rules** that were the **ubiquitous** calculators in physics and engineering in the first seven decades of the twentieth century.

Beginning during World War II and finishing just after the war ended, the Moore School of the University of Pennsylvania built an electronic **digital** computer for the U.S. Army. One of the first problems run on it was a model of a nuclear explosion. The advent of digital computers opened up whole new realms of research for physicists.

Physicists like digital computers because they are fast. Thus, big problems can be figured out, and calculations that are boring and repetitive by hand can be transferred to computers. Some of the first subroutines, blocks of computer code executed many times during the run of a program, were inspired by the needs of physics.

Even though digital computers were fast with repetitive tasks, the use of approximation and **visualization** has the largest effect on physicists using electronic computers. Analog machines, both mechanical and electronic, have output that models real world curves and other shapes representing certain kinds of mathematics. To calculate the mathematical solution of physical problems on digital computers meant the use of approximation. For example, the area under a curve (the integral) is approximated by dividing the space below the curve into rectangles, figuring out their area, and adding the small areas to find the one big area. As computers got faster, such approximations were made up of an ever-increasing number of smaller rectangles.

Visualization is probably the physicist's task most aided by computers. The outputs of Lord Kelvin's machine and the Differential Analyzer were drawn by pens connected to the computational components of the machine.

analog a quantity (often an electrical signal) that is continuous in time and amplitude

slide rules invented by Scotsman John Napier (1550–1617), they permit the mechanical automation of calculations using logarithms

ubiquitous to be commonly available everywhere

digital a quantity that can exist only at distinct levels, not having values in between these levels (for example, binary)

visualization a technique whereby complex systems are portrayed in a meaningful way using sophisticated computer graphics systems; e.g., chemical molecules

Physics researchers use computer-generated models, like this image of the neon atom, to explore the boundaries of the science.

The early digital computers could print rough curves, supplemented by cleaner curves done on a larger scale by big plotters. Interestingly, the plotters drew what appeared to be smooth lines by drawing numerous tiny straight lines, just like a newspaper photograph is really a large number of gray points with different shades. Even these primitive drawing tools were a significant advance. They permitted physicists to see much more than could be calculated by hand.

In the 1960s, physicists took millions of photographs of sub-atomic particle collisions. These were then processed with human intervention. A "scanner" (usually a student) using a special machine would have the photographs of the collisions brought up one by one. The scanner would use a trackball to place a cursor over a sub-atomic particle track. At each point the scanner would press a button, which then allowed the machine to punch the coordinates on a card. These thousands upon thousands of cards were processed to calculate the mass and velocity of the various known and newly discovered particles. These were such big jobs that they were often run on a computer overnight. Physicists could use the printed output of batch-type computer systems to visualize mentally what was really happening. This is one of the first examples of truly large-scale computing. In fact, most of the big calculations done over the first decades of electronic digital computing had some relationship to physics, including atomic bomb models, satellite orbits, and cyclotron experiments.

The advent of powerful workstations and desktop systems with color displays ended the roughness and guessing of early forms of visualization.

IT BEARS REPEATING

Physics calculations are often large, but repetitious. As such, they are perfect motivators for the development of computers, which handle such calculations extremely well.

Now, many invisible phenomena, such as fields, waves, and quantum mechanics, can be modeled accurately in full color. This is helping to eliminate erroneous ideas inspired by the poor visualizations of years past. Also, these computer game–quality images can be used to train the next generation of physics students and their counterparts in chemistry and biology classes, making tangible what was invisible before.

Finally, the latest and perhaps most pervasive of physics-inspired computer developments is the World Wide Web. It was first developed as a way of easily sharing data, including graphics, among researchers in the European cyclotron community and also for those outside of it with appropriate interests. So whenever a browser is launched, 200 years of physics-driving computer development is commemorated. SEE ALSO ASTRONOMY; DATA VISUALIZATION; MATHEMATICS; NAVIGATION.

James E. Tomayko

Bibliography

Merrill, John R. *Using Computers in Physics.* Boston: Houghton Mifflin Company, 1976.

Process Control

Process control encompasses the means by which tasks are accomplished by industries, machines, or organisms. Process control mechanisms are found in all complex systems, whether they are mechanical, electrical, or biological—human-made or natural. Major applications of process control are found in such continuous production industries as energy, oil refining, pulp and paper, and steel, and in such complex machines as cars, planes, computers, and robots.

In the context of computer science, process control is defined as the use of a computer system to automate and regulate the operations or processes of a system. One of the challenges in the industry regards the fact that processes often proliferate faster than they can be identified, defined, and managed using high-quality, reliable standards. Because of this, process control has increasingly come to include the coordination and accumulation of human expertise ("organizational memory") as well as the use of machines and computerized control mechanisms.

Process control is generally a continuous, "24/7" working effort; people responsible for process control are organized into round-the-clock staff shifts. Continuous process control is typical of the energy industries. It is also standard in crisis management, air and train control, military forces, hospitals, police and rescue services, and communications. The global economic value of these sectors is huge. All are centrally interested in avoiding operational interruptions while simultaneously improving their processes. All express the need to include, as part of process control, the sharing of information between shifts, the coordination of work processes, and the development of expertise and learning. Business culture issues, the need for high standards of quality and reliability, and time- and safety-critical concerns can prevent easy adoption of new or experimental tools, however.

SHIFTING FOCUS

Process control of continuous production is being revolutionized. The energy, oil refining, pulp and paper, steel, car, and computer industries used to concentrate on automated control of complex physical machines. This is now just one layer, and the focus has moved to supporting human activity and organizational memory.

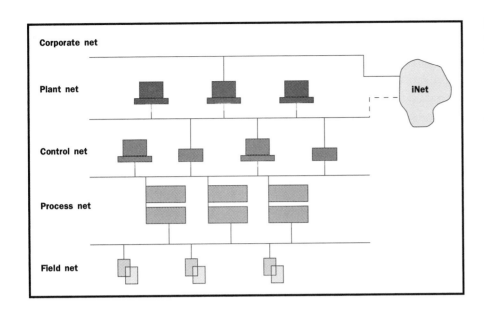

Figure 1: A generic control system architecture.

Process Control Structures

An understanding of information technology (IT) architectures is necessary to comprehend the available variety of control mechanisms and processes, the ways in which they are embedded, and how they need to interrelate. Process control consists of numbers of different information systems. There are multiple ways to categorize them because different concepts are interpreted flexibly. Usage varies according to vendor, user, product, or even continent. The semantics can be confusing. Most traditional ways of defining plant system architecture divide it into technical layers, as in Figure 1.

Figure 1 is an illustration of a generic system architecture. Information systems for immediate process control are contained in the bottom three layers, which are the field net, the process net, and the control net. The field net manages input and output equipment. The process net defines PID (Proportional-Integral-Derivative) controllers, motor controls, interlocking and basic logic, and calculations. It usually contains advanced features such as sequences, batches, and optimizing. The control net is where section- or department-wide control is implemented. The various functions of process control are the responsibility of different departments of an organization. Areas of process-control responsibility can usually be divided into production management, automation/process control, maintenance, quality, laboratory, repair, service, spare parts, raw material, stock, and materials.

Interconnectivity of Process Control

Each department is responsible for a variety of actions, each of which has its own information needs and handling mechanisms, but these are also interconnected. Interconnection is usually expedited by different systems. These include general purpose systems, process information systems, automation systems, logic systems, and special purpose systems (e.g., machine condition monitoring and diagnosis systems). These systems are responsible for a variety of activities including process monitoring, predefined tasks, disturbance control, information exchange, knowledge management, continuous development, and learning. Hardware and information systems have to span information needs at the field, process, control, plant, and corporate levels. Furthermore, these systems need to be interconnected in a user-friendly way. A challenge for IT personnel is to maintain system architectures and prevent them from becoming too complex for end-users.

The work of operating crew personnel can be illustrated on the control-net layer. They routinely monitor processes and perform predefined tasks such as starting batches or accomplishing sequences. When a disturbance occurs, operators concentrate on recovering a normal state as soon as possible. A large amount of information is handled, usually, in a short time. Sometimes process interruptions may last for weeks, and much expertise and information exchange is needed. When a solution is found, staff members have usually learned something; ideally, they share this experience with others. Based on accumulated expertise, the process continuously evolves. The development of higher levels of process control in this field of "organizational memory" is still in its infancy.

Organizational Memory and Process Control

The nature of automation has changed radically. Whereas earlier systems mainly followed process developments, new methods are now revolutionizing process management. Open information systems architecture has become an essential part of automation. Advanced control methods, such as **fuzzy logic** and **neural networks**, are combined with information and knowledge tools, memos, and reports. The so-called "knowledge network" is a new dimension that plays a vital role in increasing production line efficiency. When combined with history and real-time process data, it is a powerful decision-making asset for those responsible for handling disturbance management or production optimization.

The challenge is to be able to select, save, and distribute the right information to the right person at the right time with a process control system that uses standardized user interfaces and tools for collecting and storing process data. It also makes the collected data available to other systems through standard database interfaces within an overall architecture. SEE ALSO CAD/CAM, CA ENGINEERING; EMBEDDED TECHNOLOGY (UBIQUITOUS COMPUTING); ERGONOMICS; USER INTERFACES.

Mike Robinson and Mikko Kovalainen

fuzzy logic models human reasoning by permitting elements to have partial membership to a set; derived from fuzzy set theory

neural networks pattern recognition systems whose structure and operation are loosely inspired by analogy to neurons in the human brain

Bibliography

Ashby, W. R. *An Introduction to Cybernetics.* London: Chapman & Hall, 1956.

Bertalanffy, L. V. *General System Theory.* New York: George Braziller, 1969.

Paunonen, H., and J. Oksanen. *Information Process Control Systems—Knowledge-Based Operation Support.* 7th IFAC/IFIP/IEA Symposium on Analysis, Design and Evaluation of Man-Machine Systems, Kyoto, Japan, 1998.

Schmidt, K., and L. Bannon. "Taking CSCW Seriously: Supporting Articulation Work." *CSCW* 1, no. 1 (1992): 7–40.

Wiener, N. *Cybernetics.* Cambridge, MA: MIT Press, 1965.

Productivity Software

Computer software consists of programs that control computer hardware (systems software) and programs that help users solve problems (application software). System software consists of operating systems (e.g., DOS, Windows 98, Linux), device drivers, utilities, and programming languages. Application software consists of a variety of programs that help individuals or groups perform tasks effectively. Application software is divided into different categories based on how it is used. These categories include word processing, spreadsheet software, data management, entertainment, education, and many others. One of the ways to categorize application software is to group word processing, spreadsheets, data management software, and presentation software into a category called *productivity software*.

Word Processing Software

Word processing software has replaced the typewriter to manipulate text. It can be used to produce documents, such as letters, reports, papers, and manuscripts. Word processors are the most widely used type of software. Word processors are used by students to write reports and papers, by business people to produce memorandums and reports, and by scientists to write research papers and grants.

Word processing software allows users to edit, revise, store, format, and print documents. With a word processor, a user can easily delete, insert, and replace text, use the search-and-replace feature to make global changes to a document, and highlight areas of text (block) on which to perform actions such as "move" or "copy." Informative tables can be created, and images from clip art files or other sources can be incorporated to add clarity or drama to a document. Once the content of a document is set, the user can change the layout and style of the printed page using formatting features of the word processor such as margins, page orientation (landscape/portrait), justification, and line spacing. Spelling and grammar checkers allow the document to be checked for misspellings and grammatical errors. A thesaurus helps the user pick alternate words, and the word count feature provides a quick way to know how many words a document contains. Many word processing programs contain mail-merge options to print customized form letters. Common word processing software includes Microsoft Word, Corel WordPerfect, and Lotus Word Pro.

Spreadsheet Software

Spreadsheet software applications, sometimes called electronic spreadsheets, perform calculations based on numbers and formulas entered by users. The data can be presented in a traditional accounting format or transformed into graphics such as pie charts, bar graphs, and other visual representations of the information.

Traditional, non-electronic spreadsheets consisted of grids of rows and columns printed on special green paper used by accountants to produce financial projections and reports. In 1978 Daniel Bricklin, a student at Harvard Business School, created the first electronic spreadsheet (Visi-Calc). It allowed users to create tables and financial information by entering data into rows and columns arranged as a grid on a computer screen. Spreadsheet software like VisiCalc and its successors, which automated many functions of financial record keeping and data analysis, helped build the popularity of microcomputers as business tools. Electronic spreadsheets are also used by individuals to track household budgets and balance

Many types of software are available to track productivity. Businesses can use the data to make projections about future needs, trends, or ventures.

checkbooks, by business people to create budgets, and by educators to track student grades.

To use an electronic spreadsheet, numbers are entered in cells (the intersection of a row and a column). Cells are given a name consisting of the column letter (such as A-Z) and the row number (such as 1–100). The user indicates how these numbers are to be manipulated using formulas or functions. For example, on a household budget spreadsheet, a formula can be created to add the household monthly expenses and store the results in cell B20. The formula, =SUM (B1:B19), would sum the values stored in the range of cells starting in B1 and through cell B19. Another formula, =B21-B20, could be created to subtract the expenses (in cell B20) from the income (in cell B21) on a household budget spreadsheet. Most spreadsheets also offer a variety of pre-defined formulas called functions that provide powerful mathematical calculations. Typically, these functions are divided into a variety of categories including financial functions (e.g., depreciation, future value, net present value), date and time functions, mathematical and trigonometric functions (e.g., absolute value, sine, cosine, pi), statistical functions (e.g., average, median, variance, standard deviation), and database functions (e.g., average or count the values in a column), to name a few. In 2001 the most popular spreadsheet software packages included Lotus 1-2-3, Microsoft Excel, Quicken, and Quattro Pro.

Database Software

Database software provides a flexible way to join and summarize information from more than one file. Databases are designed, built, and populated with data for a specific purpose and for an intended group of users. Databases help people keep track of things. For example, a high school has a database with information about its students—names, identification numbers, addresses, years in school, grade point averages, and so on. These data are used by the school administration to know how many students are enrolled in the school and determine what kinds of classes are needed for these students. Databases are designed, built, maintained, and queried using a set of tools called a database management system (DBMS). Some common database software packages include Microsoft Access, Oracle, FileMaker Pro, and Microsoft SQL Server.

Desktop Publishing, Graphics, and Presentation Software

Desktop publishing software expands the capabilities of word processing software by incorporating graphic design techniques. These techniques enhance the format and appearance of a document to produce professional-quality newspapers, newsletters, brochures, books, and magazines. Common desktop publishing software includes Adobe PageMaker, Microsoft Publisher, Quark Xpress, and Corel Ventura.

Graphics software helps users to create, edit, and manipulate images. Graphics software can be classified into two major types: (1) presentation graphics used to communicate or make a presentation of data to others, and (2) analytical graphics used to make numeric data easier to analyze (e.g., bar charts, line graphs, pie charts). Common graphics software packages include Adobe Illustrator, Harvard Graphics, Crystal Graphics, Macro Media Flash, and Corel Draw or Painter. Many graphics packages specialize in manipulating photographs (e.g., Adobe Photoshop, Microsoft Picture It, or Corel Photo-Paint) or business charts and graphs, such as flowcharts (e.g., Microsoft Visio, Smart Draw). Other graphics packages allow the creation of 3-D graphics and wireframe models or images that resemble paintings or sketches.

Presentation software provides the tools that users need to combine text, graphics, animations, and sound into a series of electronic slides. Many executives or public speakers rely on presentation software such as Microsoft PowerPoint or Lotus Freelance Graphics to create interesting and informative speeches. Educators use this software in the classroom. Researchers use electronic slides to present their research results at conferences. Business people use slides to make reports or give sales presentations. Both Power-Point and Freelance contain collections of images and sounds to enhance

WHAT IF?

In addition to providing standard calculating formulas and functions, electronic spreadsheets provide modeling capabilities that allow users to describe real-world situations and then test a variety of possible outcomes using different numbers. This ability to perform a what-if analysis is a useful tool. Users can investigate what would happen if sales increase by 10 percent or decrease by 5 percent, or students can determine the semester grade implications of earning an "A" grade on the next examination—or a "B" or "C."

presentations and provide features to animate both text and graphics. Once a set of slides has been created, it can be viewed as a computer slide show or printed as overhead transparencies, paper copies, or 35mm slides.

Integrated Productivity Software

Integrated productivity software packages combine features of several applications programs into one software package that is sold as a unit. Best-selling integrated packages in 2001 included Lotus Works, Microsoft Works, and WordPerfect Works. The benefit of using an integrated package is that the individual applications are designed to work well together, and a user can easily exchange files created in different parts of the integrated package. In addition, the user interface of the package has been integrated so that the user does not need to learn different ways of interfacing with each individual application. Software suites also integrate different applications into one software package. However, the amount of cohesiveness among the applications in a software suite may not be as complete as in an integrated package. Some common software suites are Microsoft Office and Lotus SmartSuite.

Groupware

Another type of application software program that is growing in popularity is groupware. This software provides a way for more than one person to collaborate on a project by maintaining a pool of data that can be shared by members of a workgroup. Typically, groupware software combines single-user applications such as calendars, word processors, and databases into a multi-user application along with an electronic meeting system (EMS). The scheduling component of the groupware system helps to coordinate coworkers' electronic date books or appointment calendars. Groupware can also contain workflow software that helps workers understand and redesign the steps that compose a particular process. In general, groupware is thought to improve productivity by keeping members of a group in contact with one another via calendars and documents. One groupware system, Lotus Notes, uses a very large database containing work records, memos, and notations, and combines it with a multi-function messaging system.

Ironically, whether these productivity tools actually make their users more productive is questionable. While many researchers believe that these software applications actually decrease productivity, others are convinced that people are more productive when using productivity software. SEE ALSO DATABASE MANAGEMENT SYSTEMS; HOLLERITH, HERMAN; OFFICE AUTOMATION SYSTEMS.

Terri L. Lenox and Charles R. Woratschek

Bibliography

Parsons, June Jamrich, and Dan Oja. *New Perspectives on Computer Concepts*, 4th ed. Cambridge, MA: Course Technology, 2000.

Project Management

To understand project management, it is necessary to have a clear understanding of what a project is. A project exists to achieve some goal and once that goal has been achieved the project is finished. Projects do not carry on indefinitely; they have a start, a life-time, and an end. Projects can range from such challenging undertakings as sending a person to the Moon to more everyday tasks such as building a house. A complex project may involve thousands of people working over a number of years to achieve a goal; a simple project may involve only a single person working for a short time.

Project management involves organizing the actions needed to achieve the project goal. The two primary aspects of project management are project planning and project tracking. Project planning involves defining how you will achieve the goal, including listing the specific tasks required. Project tracking means looking at how the project is progressing and comparing that to the plan that describes how you expected things to happen.

Project Planning

The first step in project planning is to define very clearly what the goal of the project is. A clear goal is necessary so that everybody involved can agree on what constitutes a finished project. For example, the goal of a project to build a house could be that the house has everything necessary for living in it except for the furniture. This implies that the house includes plumbing, electricity, and decorations. Exactly what is required to meet the goal must then be spelled out in detail.

Once the project has a clear goal, the next step in project planning is to define the tasks that need to be completed to achieve this goal. For example, the project to build a house includes the following general tasks:

1. Lay the foundation
2. Build the structure (walls, floors etc.)
3. Put on the roof
4. Install plumbing
5. Install electricity
6. Decorate the house.

Ideally, a project plan would include these general categories, plus the sub-tasks that must be accomplished within each category to constitute a finished task. Without a detailed list of the necessary tasks and sub-tasks, it is very difficult to plan a project accurately.

Once tasks are identified, they must be organized to reflect the dependencies between them. Some tasks depend on the output of others. For example, decorating the house cannot be started until the structure has been built and the roof has been put on. In our example we have defined six tasks but a complex project may have hundreds of interdependent tasks. To help manage this complexity, a technique called Program Evaluation and Revue Technique (PERT) was developed by the U.S. Navy for its Polaris missile project. Project planning using PERT involves drawing a diagram, called a PERT chart, to show the dependencies between the tasks. On a PERT chart, the tasks are represented as arrows and events are represented as circles. One event that will appear on all PERT charts is the end of the project. The time order of the tasks on a PERT chart is from left to right, so the end of the project event will be the rightmost, however, the PERT chart

Figure 1: PERT chart showing dependencies between tasks.

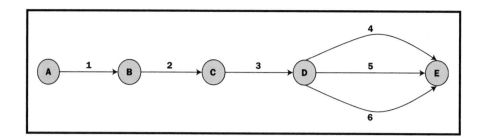

does not say anything about the actual duration of the tasks. Figure 1 shows a PERT chart for our build-a-house project. Event A is the start of the project and event E is the end of the project. This PERT chart shows the dependencies between the six general tasks we have defined.

As well as identifying the tasks to be performed, it is necessary to estimate how much work it will take to complete the task. Table 1 shows estimates for how long each of the house building tasks will take.

Based on the time estimates for the tasks and the list of dependencies between tasks, a schedule can be created. The schedule maps the project tasks to time, indicating when individual tasks will be completed and ultimately when the complete project will be finished. Just as the PERT chart is a good way to identify and track dependencies between tasks, Gantt charts are useful for representing project schedules in a graphic format. The Gantt chart displays a list of tasks. For each task, it shows when in time it will be performed. Figure 2 shows a Gantt chart for the build-a-house project. As shown on the PERT chart, tasks 1, 2 and 3 are scheduled sequentially, due to dependencies among them, while tasks 4, 5, and 6 are scheduled simultaneously, because there are no dependencies between them.

Project Tracking

While the project is underway, the project manager must focus on tracking the progress of the project. Project tracking involves comparing the actual progress of the project against the plan for the project. While the project is running, the project manager may modify the plan to take account of unexpected events that happen during the project.

Planning and Tracking Tools

Many software tools are available to support project management. These tools typically support a number of graphical descriptions of the project including PERT and Gantt charts. The software tools will check that the various representations of the project are consistent, highlighting any inconsistencies. Although software tools can be very helpful in managing a

Table 1. Chart showing estimated time needed for each task.

Task Number	Task Name	Estimate (in weeks)
1	Lay the foundation	8 weeks
2	Build the structure (walls, floors etc.)	6 weeks
3	Put on the roof	3 weeks
4	Install plumbing	2 weeks
5	Install electricity	4 weeks
6	Decorate the house	3 weeks

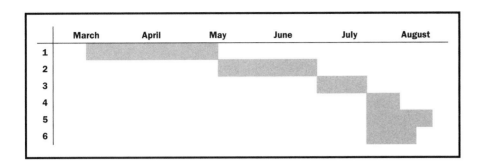

Figure 2. Gantt chart showing project schedule.

project, it is important to remember that the software will not manage the project for you. The project manager must do the project planning and tracking; the software is only a tool to support the project manager.

Project management is about organizing actions to achieve some goal. The principles of project management are the same no matter what the goal of the project is. The example we have used is of building a house but the same principles apply to other types of projects including the development of computer hardware and software. SEE ALSO DECISION SUPPORT SYSTEMS; INFORMATION SYSTEMS; OFFICE AUTOMATION SYSTEMS.

Declan P. Kelly

Bibliography

O'Connell, Fergus. *How to Run Successful Projects II: The Silver Bullet*. New York: Prentice Hall, 1996.

Railroad Applications

To increase the safety and reliability of its trains and railways, railroads have integrated computer controlled information management systems. Some have even moved to satellite tracking. With each upgrade, however, the railroads struggle with the inherent difficulties of automating an old **infrastructure**.

The need for automation is significant. To run an efficient railroad, the company must monitor each locomotive, car, maintenance crew member, train crew member, passenger, railway switch, crossroad signal, and piece of cargo. It even needs to monitor bad weather.

From Telegraphs to Satellites

In 1851 the railroads discovered that the newly invented **telegraph** gave engineers and train station operators a new ability to communicate among themselves. For the first time, the arrival and departure of trains could be coordinated safely, which was especially important when multiple trains shared a single track. Later, when the telephone was invented, train management improved even more.

The first computers bought by the railroads, in the 1970s, were **minicomputers** that recorded and stored critical information in databases. Although the databases represented a significant improvement over paper records, they worked independently of each other: one was for scheduling

infrastructure the foundation or permanent installation necessary for a structure or system to operate

telegraph a communication channel that uses cables to convey encoded low bandwidth electrical signals

minicomputers computers midway in size between a desktop computer and a mainframe computer; most modern desktops are much more powerful than the older minicomputers

BULLET TRAINS

Japan's *Shinkansen* or bullet trains, inaugurated in 1964, were the world's first high-speed trains. Today, they can reach speeds of 300 kilometers per hour and are enormously popular. On average, more than 16 million passengers per day use the bullet trains in the eastern Honshu and Tokyo areas alone.

global positioning system (GPS) a method of locating a point on the Earth's surface that uses received signals transmitted from satellites to accurately calculate position

crews, one for planning cargo shipments, one for moving locomotives, and so on. The databases could not communicate with each other, and most were updated only on a nightly or sometimes weekly basis.

In the 1980s companies adopted a new train-tracking system using bar codes painted on the sides of rail cars. As the trains passed by, the bar codes were scanned and the data was sent to the local computer. In actual operations, however, the bar codes got dirty or the paint wore off so scanners could not read them at high speeds.

Credit-card-sized electronic tags, called transponders, replaced the bar codes. Each one sent out a radio signal that could be read as the train passed by a reader placed along the railway. The technology worked successfully at speeds exceeding 130 kilometers (80 miles) per hour, but the data were collected in local databases, which were not networked together.

In the mid-1990s, railroad companies began linking their databases. The trackside readers became part of an electronic data interchange network that collected data in a worldwide database for the entire rail industry. With these new tools, analysts could spot trends and plan solutions for improved service.

Some railroads consolidated their trackers and analysts in a central operations room, from which they could quickly control almost every aspect of the entire railway. With the aid of these computerized systems, the operators controlled every locomotive, train, signal, and switch on the system.

Satellite tracking was adopted by some railroads in 2000. For example, the CXS Railroad equipped 3,000 locomotives with **global positioning system (GPS)** technology so the company could track the fuel data and location of each car to within 100 meters (110 yards). Although GPS technology works successfully, its use was still controversial as of 2001. Critics say that the system's high cost rules out widespread application throughout the industry.

Conversion Challenges

Operating a railroad is so complex that when something goes wrong, the effects ripple throughout the company and the communities it serves. For example, in June of 1999, Norfolk Southern Railroad attempted to create a single combined computer system to replace its primary train control system and that of the newly acquired part of Conrail, the Consolidated Rail Corporation. The switch from the old systems to new ones—called a *conversion*—took place on a single day, but the difficulties lasted for many months.

The first problem became evident immediately when, on conversion day, the wrong magnetic storage tape was loaded onto the new system. The tape held old data ("test data") instead of real information, which tracked real-life trains, crews, and shipments.

The system began creating incorrect waybills, or instructions, which sent trains and cars to the wrong destinations. In some cases, trains filled with cargo sat idle in train yards waiting for crews that never arrived. Several cars held loads that were never emptied as the cars moved undetected back and forth between terminals. Other trains traveled successfully to their intended destination but were empty of cargo. Crews worked overtime and

certain crew members, who by law cannot work overtime, had to wait for fresh replacements.

Average train speed dropped from 32 kilometers (20 miles) per hour to 26.9 kilometers (16.7 miles) per hour causing widespread congestion and even slower shipments. Extra trains were added for extraordinarily important shipments, which added to the delays. In Ohio, rail cars blocked a traffic intersection causing emergency vehicles to take a 34-kilometer (21-mile) detour around them.

As the delays increased, shippers pulled their cargo from the railroad, choosing instead to send shipments by truck. Even the Norfolk Southern Railroad was forced to spend millions of dollars ($29 million in June of 1999 alone) to ship cargo for its best customers by alternative means.

In time, the problems receded. Six months after the conversion, the new computer system was operational and experiencing only a few glitches. Although the company was still losing millions of dollars' worth of business, it said the integrated system was facilitating its rail operations.

Positive Train Control

The Positive Train Control (PTC) project, run by the U.S. Department of Transportation's Federal Railroad Administration (FRA), promotes the use of computerized technology to manage and control railroad operations in the United States and Canada.

Using magnetic levitation, Japan's "Bullet Trains" are known for their high speed capabilities.

The project's primary goal is to reduce the probability of collisions. In addition, project planners hope to reduce train delays, increase running-time reliability, increase track capacity, and improve the use of crews and equipment. The project consists of a series of program tests conducted in cooperation with railroad companies.

For example, the Michigan PTC project began in 1995 on Amtrak's 114-kilometer (71-mile) corridor linking Chicago and Detroit. Its centralized computer system monitors operations throughout the railroad. As a train moves down the track, the wayside signal system radios the status information to the locomotive's onboard computer. The onboard system keeps the engineer informed of permitted speeds and limits of operation, and it stops the train if unsafe operation is attempted.

The PTC project in Alaska, launched in 1998, uses computer-aided dispatching to help the Alaska Railroad manage a vast network of track that stretches for many miles without signals through rugged wilderness territory. The centrally controlled computer system enforces critical factors, such as mandatory stops and speed changes, but it has no provisions for detecting broken rails or the position of rail switches.

Not everyone applauds the PTC projects. In December of 1999, the Brotherhood of Locomotive Engineers warned that with too much reliance on technology, engineers could lose their situation awareness and their finely tuned operational skills. The union made several recommendations, including simulator training, to help locomotive engineers keep their skills sharp. SEE ALSO Aircraft Flight Control; Astronomy; Display Devices; Navigation.

Ann McIver McHoes

Bibliography

"CREWS_NS: Scheduling Train Crews in the Netherlands." *AI Magazine* 19, no.1, p. 25(16).

"Merged Railroads Still Plagued by IT Snafus." *Computerworld.* January 17, 2000.

"Railroads Hot for Satellite Monitoring." *Computerworld.* April 3, 2000.

Wormser, Richard. *The Iron Horse: How the Railroads Changed America.* New York: Walker and Company, 1993.

Internet Resources

"Federal Railroad Administration Announces Positive Train Control Project." U.S. Department of Transportation web site. <http://www.dot.gov/affairs/1998/fra0298.htm>

Scientific Visualization

The term "visualization for scientific computing," shortened to "scientific visualization," refers to the methodology of quickly and effectively displaying scientific data. Once a computer experiment has been performed, the results must be interpreted. As the volume of data accumulated from computations or from recorded measurements increases, it becomes more important to analyze data quickly. It is also important to design future experiments focused on examining interesting relationships. While looking at statistics can provide insights, it is difficult for the human mind to comprehend large volumes of numbers. Visualization techniques are another approach for interpreting large data sets, providing insights that might be missed by statistical methods.

Scientific visualization is the process of representing raw data output as images that can aid in understanding the meaning of the computer experiment results. However, the purpose of scientific visualization is insight. The pictures provide a vehicle for thinking about the data. Scientific visualization is an external aid to enhance human cognitive abilities for discovery, decision-making, and exploration. Emphasizing parameters of interest using color and highlighting may be necessary to draw attention to particular features. Animation can draw out features dependent on time and help clarify the size and relative position of features.

This technique of converting data into static graphical pictures or dynamic animations works because human beings are inherently better at analyzing information if it is in visual form. The two sides of the human brain function differently. The left side of the brain helps with analytical calculations, verbal communications, and abstract symbols. In contrast, the right side of the brain emphasizes spatial, intuitive, or holistic thinking. It allows the scientist to view an entire complex situation. Graphical representations of data stimulate this part of the brain. Using this approach, a scientist is able to get an overall picture of the data. Later a scientist may use a more analytical method to examine certain anomalies or patterns in the data.

Applications

The main reasons for using scientific visualization are the following: it compresses large volumes of data into a limited number of pictures; it can reveal the correlation between different quantities both in space and time; it can furnish new space-like structures beside the ones which are already known from previous calculations; and it opens up the possibility to view the data selectively and interactively in "real time." By following the motions of structures in time, one can gain insight into complicated dynamics. It is also very useful to have the possibility to change parameters interactively and to immediately see the effect of this change. This process is called computational steering. It increases the effective use of **central processing unit (CPU)** time.

Scientific visualization is used in business to organize, identify, and communicate trends in market and customer data that are obscured or too small to see without amplification. Scientific visualization is used in astronomy to visualize objects known to exist but not directly observed such as black holes, gravitational waves, and collisions of neutron stars. Scientific visualization is used in medicine to visualize cell growth, assist in medical diagnosis, and prepare surgeons for operations. A common example of scientific visualization is the combination of atmospheric data with color, placement, illumination, and texture for use in television weather programs. Two notable scientific visualizations are the visualization of ash plumes from volcanic eruptions, and the visualization of the Visible Man from microtomed traversal and computed **tomography** scans.

Related Domains and Techniques

Scientific visualization uses techniques from the fields of computer animation, computer graphics, image processing, computer vision, computer-aided

central processing unit (CPU) the part of a computer that performs computations and controls and coordinates other parts of the computer

tomography the process of capturing and analyzing X-ray images

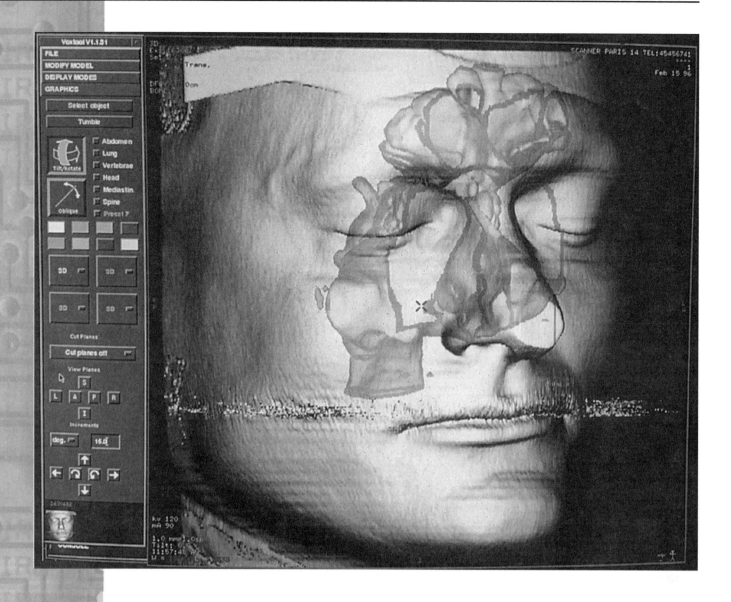

The sinus passages of a patient are rendered in 3-D through the use of computer tomography.

data mining a technique of automatically obtaining information from databases that is normally hidden or not obvious

algorithms rules or procedures used to solve mathematical problems—most often described as sequences of steps

design, human-computer interaction, and signal processing. Scientific visualization is closely related to the new field of **data mining**. While scientific visualization seeks to illuminate known relationships within data, data mining seeks to uncover previously unknown relationships within data.

Software Tools

Images have long been a part of science. In the Renaissance period, Italian astronomer Galileo (1564–1642) interspersed his writings with drawings of the moons of Jupiter and anatomical sketches. Today, more powerful computers and new graphic tools are creating opportunities to visualize events previously too small, too far, or too obscure for a human to see.

Scientific visualization tools range from custom software built specifically for handling certain classes of **algorithms** to general-purpose visualization systems that support a variety of techniques and handle a wide variety and range of data types. Graphical software tools used in scientific visualization include self-organizing maps, charts, graphs, scatterplots, zoom, sort, overview/detail, fly-throughs, and hierarchies. It is important to differentiate between scientific visualization and presentation graphics. Not all computer graphics packages qualify as visualization systems. Presentation graphics are primarily concerned with the communication of information and results in ways that are easily understood. In scientific visualization, one seeks to better understand the data. However, the two methods are often intertwined.

The two most common underlying approaches to transforming data into visual representations are graphical primitives and data sampling. Graphical primitives involve filtering data to extract information and map these data using geometric primitives such as points, lines, or polygons. Data sampling involves moving data into structured grid fields of different types (uniform, rectilinear, irregular) using interpolation and extrapolation.

Research on New Uses

Scientific visualization has already had a great impact on scientific work by making the evaluation of computer experiments easier and helping the scientist to gain more insight into unknown aspects of scientific problems. Datasets are growing at a substantial rate as researchers explore science in greater detail. Effectively visualizing volumes of data using only one million **pixels** in the average computer display requires new methods of visualization. Current scientific visualization research focuses on combining data from multiple sources in the same visualization, developing new tools to help users find what they are looking for using visual search engines, and providing collaborative visualization between geographically remote sites. SEE ALSO DATA VISUALIZATION; PATTERN RECOGNITION; PHYSICS.

William J. Yurcik

Bibliography

Earnshaw, R. W., and N. Wiseman. *An Introductory Guide to Scientific Visualization.* New York: Springer Verlag, 1992.

Nielson, Gregory M., et. al. *Scientific Visualization: Overviews, Methodologies, and Techniques.* Los Alamitos, CA: IEEE Press, 1997.

Pickover, Clifford A., and Stuart Tewsbury, eds. *Frontiers of Scientific Visualization.* New York: John Wiley & Sons, 1994.

Internet Resources

Annotated Bibliography of Scientific Visualization Web Sites. NASA Ames Research Center. <http://www.nas.nasa.gov/Groups/VisTech/visWeblets.html>

Security Applications

Security applications programs are designed to protect computer files, operating systems, and program software, particularly on computers that are connected to networks or are otherwise subject to attack from outside locations. Security programs may be designed to detect the effects of intrusive activity, identify intrusive activity while it is occurring, look for vulnerabilities that might be exploited by an intruder, or help prevent intrusive activity.

Intrusive activity can take place directly, as in the case of an unauthorized user sitting down at an unattended computer and taking some action

---

GALILEO

Galileo, the seventeenth-century astronomer and mathematician, was the first to see the moons of Jupiter. Using a telescope that he developed, Galileo observed four moons orbiting the planet. This discovery was not well received by the scientific community, as most believed that all objects in the heavens revolved around the Earth. Galileo also plotted the phases of Venus and observed sunspots.

pixels single picture elements on a video screen; the individual dots making up a picture on a video screen or digital image

that affects the data, system, or program software in some way. More commonly, however, computer intruders gain unauthorized access through network or online connections. An intruder may alter programs or data contained in the computer, either as an end in itself or to allow future break-ins. An intruder may also install processes on the attacked machine to use in attacking other computers. **Distributed Denial of Service (DDoS)** tools that flood a victim with large amounts of network traffic are an example of the latter.

The best known tool for detecting modified program or data files is Tripwire. Tripwire computes a cryptographic **checksum** for each file that is to be protected and stores this information in a safe place, preferably on write-protected removable media. Periodically, and especially when an intrusion is detected, Tripwire is used to recalculate the file checksums. A change in the checksum indicates a change in the file. If an intrusion has occurred, it may be necessary to examine disks and run Tripwire from a clean copy of the operating system because clever intruders can replace programs, including Tripwire, with versions that have been designed to hide their tracks.

Intrusion detection systems are programs that examine a network or a computer for signs of intrusive activity. Signature-based systems have a built-in model of intrusive activity; they attempt to detect activity known to be intrusive. Anomaly-based systems, by comparison, use a model of normal activity; abnormal activities then become a trigger for suspecting an intrusion. Either form of intrusion detection system (IDS) may rely on a variety of sources of information.

Network-based IDSs examine the **packets** that flow over a segment of a local network. Host-based IDSs get their information from system logs or from information supplied by individual applications. Each approach has strengths and weaknesses. Network-based systems cannot see inside encrypted packets such as those used by **Secure Sockets Layer (SSL)** or **Virtual Private Networks (VPNs)**. In addition, network-based systems have difficulty in keeping up with the high speed (100 base T and gigabit) networks that are becoming common.

Host-based systems cannot easily detect activities such as probes that attempt to discover which hosts are on the network and which ports they support. Signature-based systems can, in general, only detect attacks that are both known and encoded into the program's model of intrusive activity. Anomaly-based systems can only report unusual activity, but there is no assurance that unusual means intrusive. False alarms and missed attacks are problems for both kinds of programs. Signatures that are too general will trigger alarms for non-intrusive activities, while signatures that are too specific will miss minor variations on known attacks. Similarly, an inadequate characterization of "normal" may lead to excessive false alarms, missed intrusions, or both. In addition, intrusion detection programs may be attacked, causing them to miss attacks or issue false alarms.

Virus detection programs are another form of security application that detects intrusive activity. The original virus detection programs looked for the artifacts of infections, examining files for the signatures of known viruses. Modern virus detection programs retain this functionality but also act like host-based intrusion detection systems, checking newly imported files, in-

Distributed Denial of Service (DDoS) an attack in which large numbers of messages are directed to send network traffic to a target computer, overloading it or its network connection; typically, the attacking computers have been subverted

checksum a number that is derived from adding together parts of an electronic message before it is dispatched; it can be used at the receiver to check against message corruption

packets collections of digital data elements that are part of a complete message or signal; packets contain their destination addresses to enable reassembly of the message or signal

Secure Sockets Layer (SSL) a technology that supports encryption, authentication, and other facilities and is built into standard UNIX communication protocols (sockets over TCP/IP)

Virtual Private Networks (VPNs) a commercial approach to network management where privately owned voice and data networks are set up on public network infrastructure

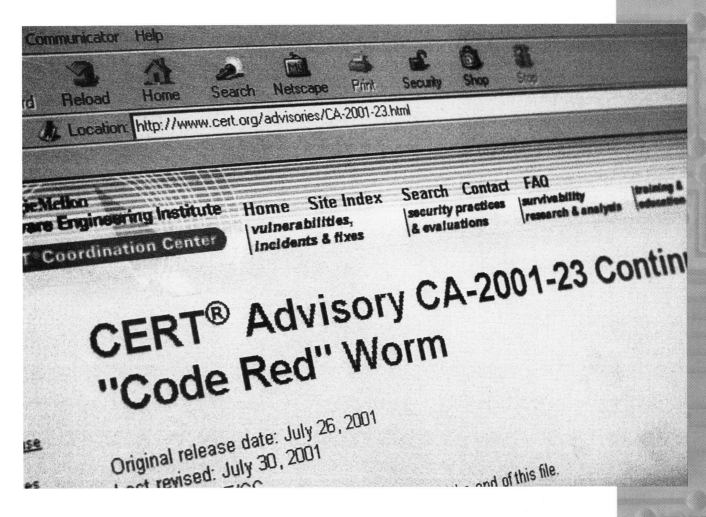

cluding e-mail attachments, for known viruses and removing them before they can be executed and do damage.

There are a number of security applications that examine a system for vulnerabilities that might be exploited by an attacker. One of the first was the program COPS, developed at Purdue University. COPS is a suite of security applications that checks a **UNIX** system for common security vulnerabilities. Most of these involve inappropriate permission settings on system files that might allow an ordinary user to obtain root or "superuser" privileges. Other vulnerabilities detected include poorly formatted group and password files, individual login scripts that could be modified by others, and weak passwords.

Good systems administrators regularly run tools such as COPS and CRACK against their systems to detect security problems and patch them; however, such tools are two-edged swords since they could help a potential intruder find system weaknesses. While COPS and CRACK are host-specific, security applications such as SATAN and NMAP are intended to discover vulnerabilities in machines that are connected to the network. SATAN looks for a set of known problems and offers suggestions for fixing them. NMAP is capable of exploring a **subnet** and reporting on the computers that are present. It will attempt to identify the operating system and services offered by each computer. Both SATAN and NMAP are useful to systems administrators but may be even more useful to potential attackers since the information

In an effort to thwart hackers who spread Internet worms, viruses, and Trojan horses, organizations like the Computer Emergency Response Team at Carnegie-Mellon University in Pittsburgh, Pennsylvania, spring into action to warn computer users of pending threats.

UNIX operating system that was originally developed at Bell Laboratories in the early 1970s

subnet a logical section of a large network that simplifies the management of machine addresses

TAKE A CRACK AT IT

CRACK, a UNIX utility developed by Alec Muffett, efficiently compares a password file containing encrypted passwords with large dictionaries (encrypted lists of words that might be used as passwords). It is fairly easy to add new dictionaries, so choosing a password from, for example, the Klingon dictionary, does not provide security.

provided may identify an attack that is likely to succeed. As a result, considerable controversy has surrounded their public release, and their developers have been both praised and criticized for their actions.

Firewall programs are examples of protective security applications. Firewalls restrict the network traffic that can pass between a computer and the network by limiting the addresses with which the computer can communicate and by identifying the protocols that can be used for communication. Firewalls can be implemented on their own hardware platforms (typically the case when an enterprise is being protected), made part of a network interface component such as a cable or DSL modem, or deployed directly on the protected computer. Personal firewalls of the latter sort are sold as a component of security packages that include virus protection. SEE ALSO INTERNET; SECURITY HARDWARE; SECURITY SOFTWARE.

John McHugh

Bibliography

Branstad, D. *Security Aspects of Computer Networks*. Proceedings of the AIAA Computer Network Systems Conference, Paper 73-427, Huntsville, AL, April 1973.

Farmer, Daniel, and Eugene H. Spafford. *The COPS Security Checker System*. Purdue University Technical Report CSD-TR-993, September 1991.

Kim, Gene, and E. H. Spafford. *Monitoring File System Integrity on Unix Platforms*. Purdue University Technical Report Coast TR 93-02, July 1993.

Internet Resources

Farmer, Dan, and Wietse Venema. "Improving the Security of Your Site by Breaking Into it." <http://www.fish.com/satan/admin-guide-to-cracking.html>

Muffett, Alec. *CRACK*. <http://www.users.dircon.co.uk/~crypto/>

NMAP: The Network Mapper. <http://www.insecure.org/nmap/>

Software Piracy

When someone buys a commercial piece of software, such as Microsoft Office, he or she is bound by a copyright license that specifies how many machines the buyer can load with the software. Thus, a license agreement for a single user allows the buyer to load the software onto one machine (including laptop if the person has one), and to make a back-up copy just in case something happens to the original disk or CD-ROM (compact discread only memory).

Business and Personal Concerns

Companies that want all of their employees to use a particular software must buy a site license. Often, a site license allows the buyer to network the software, so that each user can log on to the company network and access the program. Each user on a network is called a client; a software package such as Microsoft Office cost each client about $50 in 2001. A company with 1,000 employees, therefore, will need to pay around $50,000 to enable all of its employees to use Microsoft Office.

If a person with a single user license loads the software onto a friend's machine, or if a company loads a software package onto each employee's machine without buying a site license, then both the single user and the company have broken the terms of the software license agreement and are

therefore guilty of software piracy. Software piracy involves the unauthorized use, duplication, distribution, or sale of commercially available software.

Types of Piracy

Software piracy is often described as **softlifting**, counterfeiting, Internet piracy, hard-disk loading, **OEM** unbundling, and unauthorized renting.

Softlifting.   This involves installing software with a single-user license on multiple machines, and is the most common type of software piracy within companies. The Business Software Alliance (BSA), a consortium of software developers, reports that from 1993 to 1998 it collected $35 million in settlements of copyright infringement claims against U.S. companies. California and Texas were the states with the highest number of offenders. In most cases, companies cited for copyright infringement attributed illegal downloading to insufficient management control over their employees.

Counterfeiting and Internet Piracy.   These are similar acts and involve the unauthorized duplication, distribution, or sale of commercial software. A person who makes copies of Microsoft Office CDs and sells them is engaging in **counterfeiting**. Internet piracy involves selling the counterfeit products online, often on Internet auction sites. Reviews of these auction

Based in Tel Aviv, Israel, Software Police Ltd. developed a program to stop the illegal copying of software products. Software theft costs companies billions of dollars.

softlifting the act of stealing software, usually for personal use (piracy)

OEM the acronym for Original Equipment Manufacturer; a manufacturer of computer components

counterfeiting the act of knowingly producing non-genuine objects, especially in relation to currency

sites have suggested that up to 90 percent of the software for sale is counterfeit, although such sites try to keep illegal merchandize from entering their auctions.

Hard-disk Loading, OEM Unbundling, and Unauthorized Renting. These are perhaps less well-known examples of software piracy since they can appear to be legitimate practices. Hard-disk loading involves loading software onto new computers when they are sold to a customer. OEM unbundling involves selling a component of a multi-application package as a stand-alone application.

Unauthorized renting involves hiring out software in violation of single-user licenses. Most buyers have purchased PCs with pre-loaded software; however, a person buying small component software, or renting items such as videos and even computer games, would have to know something about particular software licensing agreements to realize whether the software has been pirated.

Piracy Rates

The software piracy rate can be estimated by comparing the number of personal computers sold with the number of software packages sold. Based on the assumption that for each new PC, a standard set of software would also be sold, the software piracy rate is calculated as the percentage shortfall in software sales. The financial loss is then the cost of these missing software sales.

Using this method, the Software and Information Industry Association (SIIA) and the Business Software Alliance (BSA) estimate that the software industry lost $12.2 billion in revenue in 1999 due to the pirating of business software. This is an increase from the 1998 figure of $11 billion and brings the estimated losses since the surveys began in 1994 to a total of $71.4 billion.

The world's highest software piracy rates are in Eastern Europe and the Middle East, with rates of more than 60 percent, suggesting that six out of every ten software packages used are pirated. Fourteen countries are estimated to have a software piracy rate above 80 percent, with Vietnam (98 percent), China (91 percent), Russia (89 percent), and Oman (89 percent) at the top of the list.

Because of the size of their respective software markets, however, the greatest financial losses occur in the United States, Japan, the United Kingdom, France, China, and Germany. These six countries accounted for $6.7 billion, or more than half of worldwide lost sales in 1999. Although the United States had the lowest piracy rate in the world at 25 percent for 1999, the United States alone accounts for more than $3 billion in lost sales.

Countering Piracy

The SIIA suggests a three-pronged attack on software piracy—using legislation, effective enforcement, and public education. This approach is based on the conviction that buying and selling pirated software is essentially **trafficking** in counterfeit goods. Indeed, most countries provide legal protection for software by extending copyright, patent, contract, and trade secret legislation. They also recognize software as **intellectual property**, just like

trafficking transporting and selling; especially with regard to illegal merchandise

intellectual property the acknowledgement that an individual's creativity and innovation can be owned in the same way as physical property

---

PIRATING ABOUNDS

In some countries, more than ninety percent of the software in use is pirated. When legal copies of office suites such as MS Office XP Professional cost around $550 while pirated versions cost less than $10, the economic motivation is clear. But pirated software costs the U.S. software industry more than $10 billion a year.

literary creations and works of art, which are all subject to intellectual property right (IPR) protection.

Recent legislation enacted by the United States to combat digital theft includes the 1997 No Internet Theft Act (NET Act) and the 1998 Digital Millenium Copyright Act (DMCA). The 1999 Digital Theft Deterrence and Copyright Damages Improvement Act raised the fines that could be applied to software pirates up to $150,000.

Who Is a Software Pirate?

So who is a software pirate and why? Many studies have shown that students are prime software pirates. In November 1999, a twenty-two-year old senior at the University of Oregon was the first person to be convicted under the No Internet Theft Act (NET Act). The student was sentenced to two years of probation for making copies of software available for download from a university web site.

When asked why someone might pirate software, people often cite cost as the key reason. Software can be expensive. The highest piracy rates often occur in some of the poorest countries in the world (e.g., Vietnam, China). Given how easy it is to copy software, such theft will continue to be a major issue for software developers for decades to come. SEE ALSO E-commerce; Privacy; Security.

Trevor T. Moores

Bibliography

"BSA Announces Top Ten States for Software Piracy Settlements." *Business Software Alliance*. December 29, 1998.

Cheng, Hsing K., Ronald R. Sims, and Hildy Teegen. "To Purchase or To Pirate Software: An Empirical Study." *Journal of Management Information Systems* 13, no. 4 (1997): 49–60.

Moores, Trevor T., and Gurpreet Dhillon. "Software Piracy: A View from Hong Kong." *Communications of the ACM* 44, no. 12 (2000): 88–93.

Report on Global Software Piracy, 2000. Software and Information Industry Association. May 24, 2000.

Internet Resources

Business Software Alliance. <http://www.bsa.org/>

Software and Information Industry Association. <http://www.siia.net/piracy/pubs/piracy2000.pdf>

Space Travel and Exploration

Many people believe that the rapid increase in the capability of computers was largely due to the demands of the American Space Program. It is indeed true that the National Aeronautics and Space Administration (NASA) did pressure the computer industry for more speed and more memory in its ground based systems, but the computers in the *Apollo* spacecraft that traveled to the Moon and those flying in the later space shuttles are relics of a by-gone era. This conservative attitude is the result of NASA's unwillingness to risk human lives: old technologies have a known track record while there is implicit risk in an untested technology. However, even the unpiloted spacecraft use mostly obsolete computers, though NASA has allowed chances to be taken with their memory technologies. Nevertheless, NASA

ballistic pertaining to ballistics, which is the science and engineering of the motion of projectiles of various types, including bullets, bombs, and rockets

magnetic tape a way of storing programs and data from computers; tapes are generally slow and prone to deterioration over time but are inexpensive

has been a good customer of the computing industry, demanding new techniques even while using older hardware.

Early Piloted Spacecraft Computers

When astronaut John Glenn rode his *Mercury-Atlas* rocket into orbit and into history in February 1962, not a single computer rode with him. The *Mercury* spacecraft was a **ballistic** object, like a warhead, just going fast enough for a few orbits of the Earth. It could not change its orbit, nor could it maneuver in any way except to fire its retro-rockets to return to Earth. In essence, it did not need a computer.

The Apollo Program was a piloted American space flight effort designed to fulfill U.S. President John F. Kennedy's 1961 promise to go to the Moon and back by the end of that decade. To help develop technologies for the piloted *Apollo* spacecraft, there were several programs involving unpiloted lunar spacecraft. One of them, the *Ranger* series of lunar impact probes, was ground-commanded. The probes were only designed to hit the Moon, taking pictures all the way down. The command to start the camera going was the last command that spacecraft received.

The *Apollo* spacecraft, designed to make a soft landing, was an entirely different matter. The soft landing could not be commanded from the Earth, owing to the fact that radio waves take about three seconds to make a round trip. This is why an on-board computer was necessary. The later decision to use a two-part spacecraft, one part landing and one part staying in orbit around the Moon, and the realization that making a re-entry to Earth at 40,230 kilometers (25,000 miles) per hour would be very difficult with a tired crew, sealed the decision. Several years before the *Apollo* spacecraft flew, the interim Gemini Program, using a *Mercury* spacecraft widened to accommodate a crew of two, had a computer put on board to practice rendezvous and computer-controlled descents that would later be used on the Moon mission.

This computer, designed and built by IBM, was a small, custom-made machine with only 4,000 words of memory. More storage was provided by a **magnetic tape** similar to the ones especially made for the Orbiting Astronomical Observatory flight series. This computer hardly stretched the state of the art, but performed flawlessly.

Nevertheless, if there were any problems, a *Gemini* spacecraft could land in minutes. An *Apollo* spacecraft could take days to get back. NASA was worried about reliability. The easiest way to assure reliability was to carry multiple copies of the same computer, so there is always a spare if one computer fails. However, as in all of aeronautics and astronautics, the biggest considerations are size, power, and weight. A redundant system would negatively affect all three, adding the problems of redundancy management. NASA therefore decided to use only one full-sized computer in each part of the spacecraft. One part would always be in touch with the Earth (except when its orbit passed the far side of the Moon). So, big IBM-built ground computers could back it up. The lander, since it could not be commanded from the ground, would carry a tiny computer as a back up that could only put the lander in a parking orbit. The command module would then have to rendezvous and save the crew.

NASA got away with using one computer by extensive testing and knowledge of the history of the various parts. Early in the program, when the requirements for lunar rendezvous and other maneuvers were levied, Massachusetts Institute of Technology's Instrumentation Lab, the designers, asked NASA if the lab could make the machine more capable by using the first mass-produced **integrated circuit** in its construction. This was a four-logic-gate chip. Initially, NASA balked because this represented new technology, but it relented after assurances by MIT that the actual use of this technology was still years away. There were no in-flight failures of the *Apollo* computer.

integrated circuit a circuit with the transistors, resistors, and other circuit elements etched into the surface of a single chip of semiconducting material, usually silicon

The Space Shuttle

The huge size of the orbiter part of the space transportation system suggested the idea that considerable weight could be saved if digital flight controls were used instead of mechanical linkages. Since this system would be used for active flight control, more than one computer was needed. The failure of the one computer would cause the loss of an expensive spacecraft and its crew. Two computers were not enough either, as it would be difficult to tell, in case of malfunction, which one of the two had failed. Both machines would be indicating that the other one was at fault! Similarly, three machines would devolve to that standoff if one failed. So four computers became the minimum, with a fifth machine added and a sixth carried in a locker as a spare unconnected to anything else.

In the 1970s, after the shuttle design was frozen, a capable airborne computer called the IBM AP-101 was procured for it. This machine is also used in the B-52, B-1, and FB-111 bombers as a navigation and weapons delivery computer. The AP-101 originally had 106,000 words of memory and ran at one million instructions per second, much less capability than a typical desktop computer today.

After the loss of the orbiter *Challenger*, the memory was increased to 256K of CMOS (complimentary metal-oxide semiconductor), and the processor was fit on one chip. By continuing to use the same processor, NASA avoided a prohibitively expensive rewrite of the software. These changes were being developed before the disaster, but were delayed by safety considerations.

Unpiloted Spacecraft

The use of CMOS memories, despite their low power consumption, was a breakthrough in piloted spacecraft, which were limited to the fifty-year old technology of core memories until late in the 1990s. Meantime, the Jet Propulsion Laboratory (JPL), operated by the California Institute of Technology and funded by NASA, had been using CMOS memories since the *Voyager* interplanetary probe, launched in 1977.

Traditionally, NASA had always been more comfortable using innovative computer technology in unpiloted probes rather than in piloted spacecraft. Unpiloted spacecraft operated computers mostly in pairs. The first time real general-purpose computers were used in a probe was the *Viking* lander on Mars in 1976. It contained two command computers and two lander computers. *Voyager* had three pairs of computers: command, attitude, and data formatting. The command computers, with 4,000 words of memory, were a

TOURISTS IN SPACE?

Technological advances have made space travel safer. So safe, in fact, that the Russian space program has allowed one civilian, U.S. businessman Dennis Tito, to travel into space with its cosmonauts. Tito paid approximately $20 million in 2001 for his chance to get a better look at the stars. Internet entrepreneur Mark Shuttleworth of South Africa is scheduled to be the second civilian in space.

The twin spacecraft known as *Voyager* (one of which is pictured here) collectively traveled to Uranus, Saturn, Jupiter, and Neptune.

design similar to those on *Viking*. The attitude control computers, also with 4,000 words, were a little faster, but incomparably slower than computers today. The data formatting computers, which take experiment and camera data and prepare it for transmission to Earth, were designed by a JPL engineer as part of his graduate work in electrical engineering.

Beginning with the *Galileo* Jupiter probe, JPL has gone to distributed systems of processors and larger memories; however, they are usually obsolete by launch time. It seems that NASA's motto for computer applications is "Good Enough Is Good Enough." SEE ALSO NATIONAL AERONAUTICS AND SPACE ADMINISTRATION (NASA).

James E. Tomayko

Bibliography

Tomayko, James E. *Computers in Space Flight: The NASA Experience*. New York: Marcel Dekker, Inc., 1987.

Internet Resources

National Aeronautics and Space Administration. <http://www.hq.nasa.gov/office/pao/History/computers/Compspace.html>

Speech Recognition

Speech recognition is a process that allows people to speak naturally to a computer on any topic and to be understood accurately. Speech is a form of communication we learn early and practice often, so the use of speech recognition software can simplify computer **interfaces** and make computers accessible to users unable to key text using a standard keyboard. However, computer-based speech recognition is more difficult to achieve than one might at first assume.

The speech recognition process is statistical in nature and is based on Hidden Markov Models (HMMs). An HMM is a finite set of states, each of which is associated with a probability distribution. Transitions among the states are governed by a set of probabilities called transition probabilities. The HMM is first trained using speech data for which the associated text is known. Subsequently, the trained HMM is used to "decode" new speech data into text.

The recognition vocabulary and vocabulary size play a key role in determining the accuracy of a system. A vocabulary defines the set of words that can be recognized by a speech recognition system. In addition, a language model is used to estimate the probability of a sequence of words in a particular domain. The language model assists the speech engine in recognizing speech by biasing the output toward high-probability word sequences. Together, vocabularies and language models are used in the selection of the best match for a word by the speech recognition engine. Therefore, speech systems can only "hear" words that are present in the vocabulary; a word that is not in the vocabulary will be misinterpreted as a similar sounding word that is present in the vocabulary.

Since speech recognition is probabilistic, the most probable decoding of the audio signal is output as the recognized text, but multiple hypotheses are considered during the process. Recognition systems generally have no means to distinguish between correctly and incorrectly recognized words. Therefore, during recognition, a "word lattice representation" is often used to consider all hypothesized word sequences. A word lattice representation is an acyclic directed graph that consists of nodes and arcs used to represent the multiple hypotheses considered during recognition. The nodes represent points in time, and the arcs represent the hypothesized word. The path with the highest probability is generally output as the final recognized text. Often, the multiple hypotheses (for example phrases such as "be quite" and "beak white") sound the same and may only be distinguished by higher level semantic knowledge provided by the language model.

Speech Recognition Applications

Speech recognition applications may be classified into three categories: dictation systems, navigational or transactional systems, and multimedia indexing systems. Each category of applications has a different tolerance for speech recognition errors. Advances in technology are making significant progress toward the goal of any individual being able to speak naturally to a computer on any topic and to be understood accurately.

Dictation Applications. Such applications are those in which the words spoken by a user are transcribed directly into written text. Such applications are used to create text such as personal letters, business correspondence, or e-mail messages. Usually, the user has to be very explicit, specifying all punctuation and capitalization in the dictation. Dictation applications often combine mouse and keyboard input with spoken input. Using speech to create

interfaces boundaries or borders between two or more objects or systems; also points of access

text can still be a challenging experience since users have a hard time getting used to the process of dictating. Best results are achieved when the user speaks clearly, enunciates each syllable properly, and has organized the content mentally before starting. As the user speaks, the text appears on the screen and is available for correction. Correction can take place either with traditional methods such as a mouse and keyboard, or with speech.

Transactional Applications. Speech is used in transactional applications to navigate around the application or to conduct a transaction. For example, speech can be used to purchase stock, reserve an airline itinerary, or transfer bank account balances. It can also be used to follow links on the web or move from application to application on one's desktop. Most often, but not exclusively, this category of speech applications involves the use of a telephone. The user speaks into a phone, the signal is interpreted by a computer (not the phone), and an appropriate response is produced. A custom, application-specific vocabulary is usually used; this means that the system can only "hear" the words in the vocabulary. This implies that the user can only speak what the system can "hear." These applications require careful attention to what the system says to the user since these prompts are the only way to cue the user as to which words can be used for a successful outcome.

Multimedia Indexing Applications. In multimedia indexing applications, speech is used to transcribe words from an audio file into text. The audio may be part of a video. Subsequently, information retrieval techniques are applied on the transcript to create an index with time offsets into the audio. This enables a user to search a collection of audio/video documents using text **keywords**. Retrieval of unstructured multimedia documents is a challenge; retrieval using keyword search based on speech recognition is a big step toward addressing this challenge. It is important to have realistic expectations with respect to retrieval performance when speech recognition is used. The user interface design is typically guided by the "search the speech, browse the video" metaphor where the primary search interface is through textual keywords, and browsing of the video is through video segmentation techniques. In general, it has been observed that the accuracy of the top-ranking search results is more important than finding every relevant match in the audio. So, speech indexing systems often bias their ranking to reflect this. Since the user does not directly interact with the indexing system using speech input, standard search engine user interfaces are seamlessly applicable to speech indexing interfaces.

Conclusion

Advances in speech recognition technology have progressed to a point that it is practical to consider speech input in applications. Speech recognition is also gaining acceptance as a means of creating searchable text from audio streams. Dictation applications have the highest accuracy requirements and must be designed for efficient error correction. Transactional applications are more tolerant to speech errors but require careful designing of the constrained vocabulary and cueing of the user. Multimedia indexing applications are also tolerant to speech errors since the search **algorithm** can be adapted to meet the requirements of the application. SEE ALSO INPUT DEVICES; NEURAL NETWORKS; PATTERN RECOGNITION.

Savitha Srinivasan

keywords words that are significant in some context or topic (often used in searching)

algorithm a rule or procedure used to solve a mathematical problem—most often described as a sequence of steps

Bibliography

Karat, C., et al. "Patterns of Entry and Correction in Large Vocabulary Continuous Speech Recognition Systems." Proceedings of *CHI '99: Human Factors in Computing Systems*, (1999): 568-575.

Rabiner, L. "A Tutorial on Hidden Markov Models and Selected Applications in Speech Recognition." Proceedings of *IEEE* 77, no. 2 (1989):257-286.

Schmandt, C. *Voice Communications with Computers.* New York: Van Nostrand Reinhold, 1994.

Wactlar, H., et al. "Lessons Learned from Building a Terabyte Digital Video Library." *IEEE Computer* (1999): 66-73.

Yankelovich, N. "How Do Users Know What to Say?" *ACM Interactions* 3, no. 6 (1996).

Spreadsheets

Traditionally, accountants use a grid of rows and columns printed on special green paper to produce financial projects and reports. An electronic spreadsheet is software that simulates this accountant's paper pad or worksheet. Using spreadsheet software, a worksheet appears on the computer screen as a grid of rows and columns. The software performs calculations based on the numbers and mathematical formulas that users enter into this grid. While the terms *worksheet* and *spreadsheet* are used interchangeably, they really refer to different things. The spreadsheet actually refers to the software itself, whereas a worksheet denotes the actual numbers and formulas that underlie a particular task.

The intersection of a row and a column on the worksheet grid is called a cell. Cells are identified by a name that consists of a column letter (A–Z, AA–ZZ, and so on) and a row number. For example, D10 refers to the cell in the fourth column and the tenth row down on the worksheet, and AB45 refers to the twenty-eighth column and forty-fifth row down on the worksheet. Because a worksheet can have thousands of cells, the software allows the user to scroll through the worksheet horizontally or vertically to view the cells.

Cells on a worksheet can be filled with one of four things:

1. nothing (which means that the cell is blank)

2. labels

	A	B	C	D	E	F
1			INCOME STATEMENT			
2						
3	Units Sold	0	114	228	342	456
4						
5	Revenue	$0.00	$11,395.35	$22,790.70	$34,186.05	$45,581.40
6						
7	Fixed Cost	$9,800.00	$9,800.00	$9,800.00	$9,800.00	$9,800.00
8						
9	Variable Cost	$0.00	$6,495.35	$12,990.70	$19,486.05	$25,981.40
10						
11	Total Cost	$9,800.00	$16,295.35	$22,790.70	$29,286.05	$35,781.40
12						
13	Profit/Loss	($9,800.00)	($4,900.00)	$0.00	$4,900.00	$9,800.00
14						

Figure 1. Spreadsheet showing cells.

3. numeric values

4. formulas.

A label in a cell is a descriptive text. Examples of labels include: Units Sold, Revenue, Total Cost, Name, Address, or City. The labels are used to help organize the worksheet. Numeric values refer to the actual numeric data that are used on the worksheet in calculations. Numeric data can take the form of positive or negative numbers, integer numbers, decimal numbers, fractions, or scientific notations.

Formulas are used to indicate how the numeric values are to be manipulated. For example, on a household budget spreadsheet, a formula can be created to add the household monthly expenses and store the results in cell B20. The formula, =SUM (B1:B19), would add the values stored in the range of cells from B1 through cell B19. Another formula, =B21−B20, could be created to subtract the expenses (in cell B20) from the income (in cell B21) on a household budget spreadsheet. Most spreadsheets also offer a variety of pre-defined formulas, called functions, which effect powerful mathematical calculations. Typically, these functions are divided into a variety of categories, such as financial functions (e.g., depreciation, future value, net present value), date and time functions, mathematical and trigonometry functions (e.g., absolute value, sine, cosine, pi), statistical functions (e.g., average, median, variance, standard deviation), and database functions (e.g., average or count the values in a column).

In addition to these formulas and functions, spreadsheets provide modeling capabilities that allow users to describe real-world situations and then experiment with different numbers. This ability to change numbers involved in calculations and see the immediate results is called "what if" analysis. What-if analysis is a very powerful and useful tool and it is what makes spreadsheet software indispensable. Users can investigate what would happen if sales increase by 10 percent or decrease by 5 percent. Students could examine the implications of an "A" grade on their next examination or a "B" grade. If done manually, each change would require erasing the contents of every cell involved in a formula, changing their numeric data, and then recalculating!

Spreadsheet software also has the capability of charting or plotting data, providing database querying and extracting, and macro building. In 2002 spreadsheet software can chart data in many different ways including area, bar, column, pie, and XY charts. By visually presenting the data in chart for-

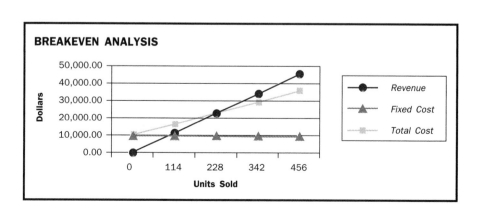

Figure 2. Analysis shown by plotting data.

mat, the data can be readily analyzed and trends spotted. Spreadsheet software in the year 2002 also has elementary database functions. Specific rows or columns of the worksheet can be selected for report production or advanced analysis. A macro is a collection of commands that the spreadsheet software can execute. These commands are written by the user and stored with a particular worksheet. Macros are used to perform repetitive tasks on a worksheet, such as extracting all rows that have an overdue balance and producing a report about it.

History

In 1978 Daniel Bricklin, a student at Harvard Business School came up with the idea for a computerized interactive visible calculator. Bricklin and Robert Frankston created the first electronic spreadsheet software named VisiCalc, short for "visible calculator." VisiCalc and electronic spreadsheets might never have gained acceptance if it were not for a Massachusetts Institute of Technology (MIT) graduate named Daniel Fylstra. He suggested that Visi-Calc should be run on an Apple microcomputer. Bricklin and Frankston programmed the software for Apple microcomputers and Fylstra and his firm, Personal Software, began marketing VisiCalc by placing an ad in *Byte* Magazine. VisiCalc became an almost instant success in the business community.

In the early 1980s, IBM introduced a microcomputer (IBM-PC) that used an Intel microprocessor. However, due to legal problems, Bricklin and Frankston did not develop VisiCalc for this new microcomputer. Rather, Mitchell Kapor developed another electronic spreadsheet named Lotus 1-2-3 that could be used on IBM's new computer. Kapor's Lotus 1-2-3 spreadsheet quickly replaced VisiCalc as the new industry standard. Lotus 1-2-3 was easier to use than VisiCalc and added charting, plotting, and database capabilities to the software. Lotus 1-2-3 was also the first spreadsheet to introduce naming of cells, cell ranges, and spreadsheet macros.

During the 1980s, many companies introduced new microcomputers, while others created new spreadsheet software. In 1984 Apple Computer introduced the Macintosh. The Excel spreadsheet from Microsoft Corporation was written for the Macintosh computer. Excel used a **graphical user interface (GUI)** and the mouse. This interface proved very easy to use, much easier than the command-line interface used by Lotus 1-2-3. In 1987 Microsoft introduced a new operating system for the IBM-PC. This operating system, called Windows, incorporated a graphical user interface. Excel was one of the first software products that ran under Windows. By 1989, when Windows had gained wide acceptance in the microcomputer market, Excel began to dominate the market.

In the late spring of 1995, IBM purchased Lotus Development Corporation. In 2001 Microsoft Excel was the market leader in spreadsheets. SEE ALSO DECISION SUPPORT SYSTEMS; INFORMATION SYSTEMS; PRODUCTIVITY SOFTWARE.

Charles R. Woratschek and Terri L. Lenox

CORE APPLE PRODUCT

The VisiCalc computer spreadsheet software became popular among business and personal computer users, driving the sales of Apple Computers higher. For many, VisiCalc revolutionized how financial data were stored, recorded, and presented.

graphical user interface (GUI) an interface that allows computers to be operated through pictures (icons) and mouse-clicks, rather than through text and typing

Bibliography

Laudon, Kenneth C., Jane P. Laudon, Peter Weill, and Carey Butler. *Solve it! For Windows, Version 2.9 Millennium.* Hudson: Azimuth Corporation, 1992–2000.

Internet Resources

Power, D. J. "A Brief History of Spreadsheets." *DSS Resources.* <www.dssresources
.com/history/sshistory.html>

SQL: Databases

Databases are designed, built, and populated with data for a specific purpose and for an intended group of users. Databases help people keep track of things. For example, one's school probably has a database with information about its students—name, identification number, address, year in school, grade point average, and so on. These data are used by the school administration to keep track of how many students are enrolled in the school and to plan how many and what kinds of classes are needed for these students. Databases like this one (called SCHOOL here) are designed, built, maintained, and queried using a set of tools called a database management system (DBMS). The most common language used with DBMS is called SQL.

SQL (Structured Query Language) is the set of instructions used to define and manipulate data in many **relational databases**. Some people pronounce SQL as "sequel," while others pronounce each letter separately. In the 1980s, SQL become the industry standard adopted by many database vendors including Oracle, Ingres, Informix, RDB, and Sybase.

SQL is used with a particular type of database called relational. Relational databases are easy to understand since they store data in one or more tables. Each table represents a different person, place, object, or event (entity) in a database. For example, in our SCHOOL database there are two tables: STUDENT, with data about our students, and TEACHERS, with data about teachers. Each table has one or more columns representing specific attributes (facts or fields) for each student or teacher. In the STUDENT table, we store student names, addresses, grade point averages (GPAs), class in school, and other related items. Each row in the STUDENT table represents a different student (called a record or tuple). If our school has 1,000 students, the STUDENT table will have 1,000 records. Figure 1 demonstrates an abbreviated set of attributes for one record in the STUDENT table.

SQL statements fall into two major categories: DDL (Data Definition Language) and DML (Data Manipulation Language). The DDL statements

ORIGINS OF SQL

SQL's roots go back to the mid-1970s. At that time, computer scientists at IBM created SEQUEL (Structured English Query Language), a forerunner to SQL.

relational databases collections of records that permit logical and business relationships to be developed between themselves and their contents

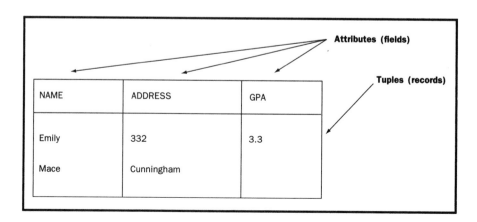

Figure 1. One record in a database.

allow one to create, modify, or delete objects such as tables in a database, and they allow you to restrict access to the database by granting privileges. That is, the administration of a high school could allow students to see their class schedule while preventing them from changing their grades. DDL statements include *create, insert, alter, drop,* and *grant.* The SQL command that follows creates the STUDENT table with eight attributes (FNAME, LNAME, IDNO, BDATE, ADDRESS, GENDER, GPA, and CLASSNO). Attribute names are sometimes cryptic abbreviations of what they represent in the real world. For example, FNAME is a student's first name and LNAME is his or her last name.

> **CREATE TABLE** STUDENT (FNAME VARCHAR(15) NOT NULL, LNAME VARCHAR(15) NOT NULL, IDNO CHAR(9) NOT NULL, BDATE DATE, ADDRESS VARCHAR(30), GENDER CHAR, GPA DECIMAL(6,2), CLASSNO INT NOT NULL, PRIMARY KEY (IDNO) FOREIGN KEY (CLASSNO) REFERENCES CLASS (CLASSNUMBER));

This SQL command creates a table in the SCHOOL database called STUDENT. Each attribute is given a name, a data type, and a size. This tells the database what to expect when we insert actual records into the database, for example, whether the data element is numeric or alphabetic and how much space should be reserved for it. Some of the attributes are labeled with "NOT NULL." This qualifier indicates the attribute must have a value when entered into the STUDENT table. For example, the database will not accept a student's record if the identification number (IDNO) is blank.

Right now the table would be empty; no data about students have been entered. The table can be populated by the SQL command *insert* as shown in the two statements that follow.

> **INSERT INTO** STUDENT **VALUES** ('Eric', 'Mace', 123456789, 1991-8-23, '332 Cunningham Lane', 'M', 3.7, 3); **INSERT INTO** STUDENT **VALUES** ('Lyndsey', 'Vogler', 987654321, 1989-3-5, '104 Golf Club Drive', 'F', 3.8, 4);

Now our SCHOOL database has two records in the STUDENT table—one for Eric Mace and one for Lyndsey Vogler. The *insert* command is one of the DML commands that allow you to manipulate the data in the database. The most common SQL statements are *insert, update, delete,* and *select.* The following three statements show how to see the data stored in our database using the *select* command. We can ask for all attributes or just specific ones. In these examples, only the student's name (last name and first name) is requested.

> **SELECT** LNAME, FNAME **FROM** STUDENT; **SELECT** LNAME, FNAME **FROM** STUDENT **ORDER BY** LNAME; **SELECT** LNAME, FNAME **FROM** STUDENT **WHERE** LNAME = "Mace";

The first statement would list all students in the order they were inserted into the STUDENT table. The second statement sorts the students alphabetically by last name. The final statement retrieves only those records that match a last name of 'Mace'. Since we have just one record with that last name, only Eric Mace is retrieved. However, if we insert a record for Eric's brother, Daniel Mace, and resubmit the third SQL statement, two records will be retrieved.

Another useful SQL command is *update*. This command allows you to change data for a particular record. Suppose another student's GPA has changed. We must indicate the exact record to change (Jon Roberts), the attribute to change (GPA), and its new value (3.9).

UPDATE STUDENT **SET** GPA = 3.9 **WHERE** LNAME = 'Roberts' **AND** FNAME = 'Jon';

Using these SQL commands, we can create a database with multiple tables, populate the database with records, modify the database, and most importantly, query the database to find the information stored in it. The classical database applications track items such as students, orders, customers, jobs, employees, or other items of interest to a business person. Many individuals who like organization create a database to track their CD or book collections, for example. In the 1990s, databases became more readily available and database technology was applied to multimedia (video and sound), geographic information systems (maps, satellite, and weather data), data warehouses (very large repositories of data from a wide range of sources), and Internet-based databases. SEE ALSO CLIENT-SERVER SYSTEMS; DATABASE MANAGEMENT SOFTWARE; OPERATING SYSTEMS.

Terri L. Lenox and Charles R. Woratschek

Bibliography

Abbey, Michael, and Michael J. Corey. *Oracle: A Beginner's Guide.* Berkeley: Osborne McGraw-Hill, 1995.

Date, C. J. *An Introduction to Database Systems.* Reading, MA: Addison-Wesley, 2000.

Elmasri, Ramez A., and Shamkant B. Navathe. *Fundamentals of Database Systems*, 3rd ed. Reading, MA: Addison-Wesley, 2000.

Technology of Desktop Publishing

Desktop publishing (DTP) relies on two primary hardware components: 1) a computer, supplemented by various input devices including scanners and cameras, and 2) a printer that can produce high quality typographical and pictorial output. The process of on-screen DTP page composition is made possible by WYSIWYG (what you see is what you get) page layout software for personal computer use, and page description languages, programming that bridges the gap between the page layout software and the printers that produce pages that match what the user sees on the computer screen.

The DTP Computer

The two key technological features of a DTP computer are an inexpensive personal computer with a **graphical user interface (GUI)** based on windows, icons, menus, and point-and-click actions, and WYSIWYG page layout software.

The personal computer is at the heart of the DTP process. The development of inexpensive, powerful Macintosh computers with easy-to-use graphical user interfaces, based on windows, icons, menus, and pointing (WIMP) provided the driving force behind the development and rapid implementation of DTP applications throughout the 1980s. The key feature of this technology was the graphics (bit-mapped) display that allowed a user

graphical user interface (GUI) an interface that allows computers to be operated through pictures (icons) and mouse-clicks, rather than through text and typing

to manipulate text and graphics on an electronic page, using a combination of the mouse and the keyboard as input tools, and to see an accurate representation of the page on the computer screen as the layout work progressed.

WYSIWYG Software. Composing text on a page has always been a complicated process. Computer software, running on **mainframe computers,** made this somewhat easier, but early programs did not provide for the use of variable width type, specialized formatting, or artwork, or the ability for the user to see a reasonable image of what the page would look like when printed. As specialized systems for publishing were developed, these concerns were addressed, but the programs were complicated to use, requiring mastery of complex formatting instruction language. In addition, the specialized machines were expensive and beyond the means of any but the largest printing enterprises.

Word processing software running on personal computers in the early 1980s was easier to use, and provided some previewing capabilities, but it did not have the functionality required for typesetting, and, without the availability of bit-mapped screens, it could not represent typefaces, exact placement, or art work.

Before long, however, word processors were able to compose variable typefaces and take advantage of emerging powerful graphical user interfaces for previewing and manipulating page layout. The first commercially significant software application for page layout that exploited the graphical user interface and included powerful layout capabilities for arranging and paginating content, was Aldus PageMaker, which was first available for use on the Macintosh computer. Today, other important DTP page layout systems include QuarkXpress, Ventura, Interleaf, and FrameMaker.

The DTP Printer

The two key technological features of a DTP printer are a high resolution, all-points-addressable, matrix marking engine, and a high-function page description language.

High Resolution Printing. The products of late nineteenth- and early twentieth-century printing were aesthetically satisfying, but awkward and time-consuming to produce. The process was based on the use of metal type counters for type and engraving techniques for diagrams and art. Photo-typesetting, which emerged later in the twentieth century, used optical and chemical techniques for typesetting, which improved functionality and maintained high-quality results, but still required very expensive equipment and highly trained operators.

Early computer printing reverted to solid type counters and mechanical inking techniques; these printers were fast, but they had a limited range of typically fixed-width typefaces that resembled typewriter output. Furthermore, they limited the user's ability to place type on the page and so were far below the functionality and quality needed for publishing. Mechanical matrix printers that used a matrix of striking pins—commonly called dot-matrix printers—could more easily create variable-width type-faces and even crude artwork, but the low resolution of the mechanical matrix and the limitation of the mechanism meant that the results, although adequate for

RESEARCH AND DEVELOPMENT

The core technologies at the heart of desktop publishing—the personal computer, WYSIWYG text processing, page description languages, and high-resolution laser printing—were developed at the Xerox Palo Alto Research Center (PARC) in the 1970s. However, the first commercially successful application of desktop publishing hardware and software did not appear until the next decade, with the advent of the Apple Macintosh in 1985.

mainframe computers
large computers used by businesses and government agencies to process massive amounts of data; generally faster and more powerful than desktop computers but usually requiring specialized software

office documents and business communications, were still well below traditional typesetting requirements.

DTP printers, on the other hand, use laser and ink-jet technologies and rely on marking techniques that organize the entire page into a very fine-grained matrix with more definition than is possible with a matrix of mechanical pins. This allows for the high resolution imaging of different typestyles and of both line and gray-scale bit-map graphics.

The first computer printer to use this technique was the Xerox 9700, a 300 dpi ("dots per inch") laser printer released in 1979. The impact of this first commercial laser printer was limited in part by a lack of software that could take advantage of its functionality. In 1979 computer composition was based on **batch processing**, with little support for graphics or printing preview. The 9700's internal software for operating it in **all-points-addressable mode** could not be accessed by most existing composition or text processing software. Finally, the 9700, with a 120-page per minute printing engine and a price of around $350,000, was too expensive to have much impact beyond its intended market of high-volume printing firms.

In the early 1980s, another high-resolution matrix technology appeared commercially as part of a Hewlett-Packard ink-jet printer. Its price was about $6,000. However it was the Apple Laserwriter, a 300 dpi laser printer designed for the Macintosh computer, that ultimately inaugurated the DTP era in 1985. The Laserwriter's incorporation of the Postscript page description language gave it extraordinary functionality that fully exploited the capabilities of the high-resolution matrix engine.

In the early days of DTP, 300 dpi resolution was arguably still well below the visual quality available from traditional typographic printing services. As a result, the expression "near typeset quality" became common to describe output produced by these printers. However when the resolution rose to 600 dpi, and font designs and page description languages improved, many purchasers of typesetting services began to feel that the difference in quality between traditionally printed and DTP-produced pages was slight, and not worth the cost of selecting the more expensive traditional option.

Page Description Languages. Early computer printing typically involved machinery such as physical type counters, each of the same width, which made an ink impression on paper by striking an intervening ribbon. Although the software that composed lines and pages did not need to be as sophisticated as it is now because characters were the same width and relatively few specialized layout features were used, the software that actually operated the printers was even simpler. But while such printing was adequate for data or internal office communications, it did not offer the functionality or quality required by general publishing.

With the development of laser and ink jet printers that could compose high resolution characters and images by placing tiny dots of ink or toner anywhere on the page, both the composition software and the printer software had to become much more sophisticated to utilize the capabilities of such printers more fully. At the same time, a proliferation of printers, each with its own physical requirements, required each word processing or page layout software application to output different kinds of data files for every kind of printer. It was complex and expensive to match user needs with ex-

batch processing an approach to computer utilization that queues non-interactive programs and runs them one after another

all-points-addressable mode a technique for organizing graphics devices where all points (pixels) on the screen are individually accessible to a running program

actly the right combination of computer and printer hardware and software programs that would lead to the desired printed product.

In the 1970s John Warnock, working at Xerox's Palo Alto Research Center (PARC), developed Interpress, a language for the control of high-resolution matrix marking. Warnock became dissatisfied with Xerox's marketing of Interpress and he left the company to form Adobe Systems. In 1984 Adobe released a page description language, Postscript, designed to provide precise programmable and device independent control of page images. This precise programmable control could exploit high-resolution marking engines to produce scaleable high-quality diagrams and artwork as well as aesthetically satisfying typography.

In addition, the possibility of single printer language interface for communication between printers and page layout software simplified the engineering of both. Today almost all publishing systems are Postscript based, with word processing or page layout software producing a Postscript data stream (representing the formatted text), which is then sent to Postscript-based printers, where it undergoes "raster image processing" (RIP), which converts the programming instructions to a bitmap page image.

Beyond the Printed Page

With the advent of electronic publications in CD-ROM (compact disc-read only memory) and World Wide Web formats, DTP page layout systems are now designed to import and export **XML**-encoded content to be integrated with XML-based publishing. Material can be prepared simultaneously for dissemination in multiple formats. With continuing improvement in this area, DTP will continue to play an effective role in the emerging ecology of networked information. SEE ALSO DESKTOP PUBLISHING; DOCUMENT PROCESSING; INTEGRATED SOFTWARE; MARKUP LANGUAGES.

Allen Renear

XML the acronym for eXtensible Markup Language; a method of applying structure to data so that documents can be represented

Internet Resources

About Desktop Publishing for All Platforms. <http://desktoppub.about.com/>

"The Ultimate Electronic Publishing Resource." desktopPublishing.com. <http://desktoppublishing.com/open.html>

Telephony

Telephony is the electronic point-to-point communication of audio signals. At the new millennium, the world has 750 million telephone lines, half of which are in the United States. Half the people in the world have never talked on a telephone! Every telephone "homes on" a *switching office*, either by copper wire or wireless link. Transmission lines, typically fiber or microwave links carrying thousands of simultaneous conversations, connect these switching offices to each other. Starting with Alexander Graham Bell's invention of the telephone in 1876, telephony has become a trillion-dollar-a-year worldwide industry. This industry consists of: (1) the carriers (in some countries, a government branch) that own the networks and provide telephone service and (2) the manufacturers of the switching and transmission equipment that the carriers use. Telephony and computing have had a **synergistic** relationship for about forty years as of 2002.

synergistic relating to synergism, which is the phenomenon whereby the action of a group of elements is greater than their individual actions

A telephone technician (c. 1991) adjusts a switching system for AT&T, one of the world's largest telephone systems.

THE FIRST SWITCHBOARD

The first telephone switchboard was installed in New Haven, Connecticut, in 1878. Operated manually by teenage boys at first, the switchboards connected many telephones through one or two exchanges in large cities. Within a few years, women replaced the boys as operators, as they were considered to be more polite to the callers.

Computing Supports Telephony

In the United States, Bell's company grew into the Bell System, a telephone monopoly that was broken up in 1984. When the Bell System introduced area codes and automated long-distance calling in the 1950s, the cost of modifying the nation's 40,000 switching offices motivated a change from the *wired control* used in electromechanical technology to *program control*. The world's first computer-controlled switching office, now called the "1E," was developed by the Bell System and was installed in 1965. The 1E processor had a 1-MHz clock and no operating system. Now, almost every switching office in the United States, and many of the offices in the world, are program-controlled by huge programs that run on modern processors.

Complicated switching software recognizes off-hooks and on-hooks, processes calls, controls special features and services, implements the numbering plan, routes calls through the carriers' networks, maintains the switching office, manages the network, and communicates with software in other switching offices. Program control not only manages telephony's complexity, but it also enables new features—such as call forwarding, 800 numbers, calling party identification, and mobility—which makes the programs even more complicated. Switching software has become so complicated, and changes so frequently, that only large companies, such as global giants Alcatel, Lucent, or Siemens, can afford the thousands of programmers required to maintain and update the programs.

Computer-controlled switching equipment was common by the 1980s when the world's carriers started using Signaling System 7, a global data network by which switch processors send **packets** to each other for call control and routing. Then, in a 1990s evolution called the "Intelligent Network," the SS7 network added special processors and databases for special service control, translation, and network management. The operation of switching software, the SS7 network, and these IN processors is illustrated by the following three examples.

packets collections of digital data elements that are part of a complete message or signal; packets contain their destination addresses to enable reassembly of the message or signal

Long-distance Busy Tone.   Suppose Dave in Denver calls Alice in Atlanta. Dave dials Alice's number into the USWest switching office on which his telephone homes. This office in Denver sends a packet to the BellSouth switching office on which Alice's telephone homes and requests Alice's busy/idle status. If Alice's telephone is idle, the Denver office determines Dave's default long-distance carrier (MCI, for example), routes the call to MCI's gateway office in Denver, and sends a packet containing the calling and called telephone numbers to this gateway. Then, MCI routes the call through its national network to the BellSouth office in Atlanta, which rings Alice's telephone. If Alice's telephone had been busy, rather than route the call to Atlanta, the USWest office in Denver would connect Dave to a local busy tone.

800-call.   Suppose Dave dials 1-800-555-4567 into the USWest switching office in Denver on which his telephone homes. This office sends a packet to a special database on the SS7 network, which returns a packet identifying AT&T, for example, as the carrier that leases this 800 number. Then, the USWest office routes Dave's call to AT&T's gateway office in Denver and sends a packet containing the calling and called telephone numbers to this gateway. This office sends a packet to AT&T's 800-number translation database, which returns the actual telephone number that AT&T assigned to this 800 number. The call is then routed through AT&T's national network to this real telephone.

Cell Phone Roaming.   Suppose Dave is not home in Denver today; he is in Atlanta and he brought his cell phone. Every cellular carrier's switching office maintains a pair of databases, the *home location register* (HLR) and the *visitor location register* (VLR). Dave's cell phone is registered in his cellular carrier's HLR in Denver. When Dave turns on his cell phone in Atlanta, the telephone communicates with a cellular switching office in Atlanta. This office records Dave's phone number (and home office) in its VLR and sends a packet to Dave's home office in Denver, which records the Atlanta office's ID in Dave's HLR entry. If anyone tries to call Dave's cell phone, the Denver HLR enables the call to be routed to Atlanta. If Dave tries to place a call, the VLR in Atlanta sends billing information to Denver.

It should be apparent that these services, and hundreds of others, would be practically impossible without computers, software, and the SS7 network.

Telephony Supports Computing

The companies that manufacture switching equipment have a long history of innovation in computing. Most notable was Bell Labs, when it was the R&D (research and development) branch of the former Bell System. Bell Labs' scientists built a **prototype** computer in the late 1930s using electromechanical technology, and they developed the UNIX operating system and the C programming language in the 1970s.

More recently, the Internet would be practically impossible without telephone industry resources. Besides using their networks of transmission lines for telephone calls, the carriers also lease channels, typically for use as enterprise private networks for voice and data. Such channels, leased from the various telephone carriers, interconnect the Internet's IP routers, providing its global backbone network. In addition, most residential personal computers get access to Internet service providers by using a **modem** (the word is an abbreviation of *modulator-demodulator*). The PC's modem makes a telephone call to a modem at the ISP. The modems convert computer data (in the PC and ISP) to audio signals, which transmit like voice over the telephone channel.

The relationship between telephony and computing may get even stronger—in fact, the two industries may merge—if "voice-over-IP" becomes practical and universally used. SEE ALSO BELL, ALEXANDER GRAHAM; BELL LABS; INTERNET; SATELLITE TECHNOLOGY; TELECOMMUNICATIONS; WIRELESS TECHNOLOGY.

Richard A. Thompson

Bibliography

McDonald, J. C. *Fundamentals of Digital Switching*, 2nd ed. New York: Plenum, 1990.

Thompson, Richard A. *Telephone Switching Systems.* Boston: Artech House, 2000.

prototype a working model or experimental investigation of proposed systems under development

modem the contraction of MOdulator DEModulator; a device which converts digital signals into signals suitable for transmission over analog channels, like telephone lines

User Interfaces

How do we make computers communicate with humans? The first computers, developed in the 1940s, were no more than huge boxes filled with complex electronics. The computer operators used binary code and primitive peripheral devices, such as punched card readers, to communicate with them. The next generation of computers used the typewriter as an input/output device. Since the end of 1960s, monitors and keyboards have become the standard way of communication between computers and humans. Other input devices, such as touch screen, mouse, joystick, scanner, and voice recognition modules, also became available to users. All these devices have made possible the development of interactive computer systems, which permit users to communicate with computers by entering data and control directions during program execution. A part of an interactive computer system that communicates with the user is known as a user interface.

How Computers and Humans Work Together

Interaction between humans and computers is a two-way communication. To interact effectively, users need appropriate tools that are designed specifically for human-to-computer and computer-to-human links. As in communication with each other, people have a natural desire to be able to use a combination of vision, movements, and speech to communicate with computers. Hence, visual, audio, and physical motion components of user interface are interconnected.

Two different visual interface methods, graphical- and character-based, utilize different kinds of actions. The character-based interface typically requires typing on a keyboard. A graphical interface incorporates the use of a mouse or joystick, which translates physical motion into motion of objects on a computer screen. In addition, visual information may be sent from scanners, digital cameras, and faxes, which are able to translate images into computer code.

Speech also may be used, through voice input devices, to deliver system commands and data directly into a system. It is a complex multi-stage process that involves digital sampling of the acoustic signal, recognition of the elements of speech, and even machine knowledge of the language.

All of these methods and devices can be categorized as human-to-computer communication elements. Prompts, messages, and light and sound signals are examples of computer-to-human interaction. A prompt is a signal on a screen indicating that the computer is waiting for a command or data. In response to users' usually brief commands, computers may provide them with reports, graphics, music, links to Internet web sites, and other digitized information or entertainment resources.

Visual Components

The way information is presented on the screen determines what type of user interface is being used. It could be text for DOS or UNIX commands or a **graphical user interface (GUI)** for a Window-based environment or web-style browser.

graphical user interface (GUI) an interface that allows computers to be operated through pictures (icons) and mouse-clicks, rather than through text and typing

For example, Disk Operating System (DOS) is command-driven and requires a user to know more than fifty commands that the system will accept. All commands are entered at the computer prompt. Although it is a reliable operating system, it is not user-friendly since it is not based on the more familiar concepts of graphics and visual cues, which have subsequently been incorporated into the GUI design of window-based user interfaces.

The names and functions of basic GUI elements, such as files, menus, folders, and wastebasket, were selected to correspond to their familiar counterparts in a physical office environment. GUI requires a mouse to move the pointer or cursor, without a keyboard, and uses a point and click sequence. For instance, to select a menu item, an operator uses a mouse or similar device to move the cursor on the screen and highlights the menu item. Then a click or two on a mouse button indicates and executes the selection. Another technique involves choosing an option by entering a letter or number or simple combination of two or three characters that activate the desired option.

Certain software packages use pictures or icons to speed up the selection process. The user can access the function related to each icon by selecting it with the mouse. In this way the user can create, send, file, or discard documents by simply pointing at the appropriate icon. Data entry of specific information may be executed by filling in the appropriate blank fields on a screen form.

Development of the window-based interface was obviously a step forward compared to DOS but its presentation capabilities are limited to the traditional GUI elements that correspond to the paper world of print and graphic design. The emergence of the Internet and World Wide Web brought multimedia—a combination of text, images, animation, audio, and video—into a format called a web page. Navigation through various electronic environments and possible connections became a very important concept for web users. While in a Windows software environment, all possible links are pre-defined and limited within each application, web users have full control of navigation, and users can access many types of links for almost unlimited "travel" through virtual environments, interactive files, and interconnected sources of content.

Using Multimedia

As computers become more knowledge- and media-oriented, their input and output devices become more sophisticated. In addition to graphics, other forms of data presentation, such as voice, music, and video are also available to users.

In voice input devices, speech produced by an operator is used to enter data or system commands directly into a computer system. Computers may also have speech-generation devices to deliver oral messages in response to signals from a data processing or control system. Messages are created by assembling elements of real speech or by the synthesis of sound waves of certain frequency.

A computer-vision system allows the user to create, save, and reproduce video images. The system consists of a camera connected to a personal computer to create images and software that permits the user to experiment with image processing.

Virtual reality (VR) environments project the user into a simulated three-dimensional space generated by a computer. The illusion of being surrounded by a world of computer-generated images, or a virtual environment, is created by linking the motion of a user's head with changes in the images presented in the visual display. The use of a data glove and head-mounted stereoscopic display allow users to point to and manipulate illusory objects that appear within their view.

Interfaces for Specialized Computers

Making computers widely accessible to people with varying physical abilities requires customization of interactive styles for different user communities. For example, users with fine motor disabilities may utilize alternative

VOICE COMMANDS

Many software companies produce user interfaces for the seeing and hearing impaired. Using speech recognition technology, a user calls out a command to access a particular file or function, such as adding bold to text. Others generate voice instruction coming from the computer itself, allowing the user to know when the bold command is being used. Translators also convert words into sign language for use in teleconferencing.

virtual reality (VR) the use of elaborate input/output devices to create the illusion that the user is in a different environment

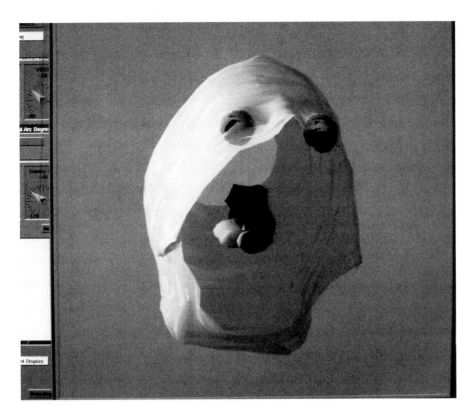

This brain tumor was once considered inoperable. However, with stereotactic radiosurgery, the computer is able to map the exact location of the tumor, helping doctors more effectively deliver radiation therapy. Stereotactic radiosurgery is a one-session treatment that delivers radiation to the target area (a tumor or lesion) and distorts its DNA, causing it to stop growing or expanding.

input devices, such as programmable keyboards, which permit them to operate computers with limited use of hands. They can enter letters, numbers, words, or even phrases by using functional keys. Another way to enter data into the computer is to operate an electronic pointing device, which allows a user to move the cursor on the screen using ultrasound or an infrared beam. Utilizing speech recognition software is another way to make computers accessible to users unable to use manually operated input devices.

A variety of interface systems are widely used by health care practitioners and scientists. Medical doctors are able to study body organs by manipulating three-dimensional digital images. Chemists may observe the progression of simulated chemical reaction in slow motion. Scientists can rotate and resize objects in hypothetical models, and change their angle and point of view. Environmental scientists and geographers may compile, retrieve, and visualize various geographic data, including maps in a three-dimensional format.

Telecommunication devices enable users to transmit text, graphics, video, and voice over a distance using computers. PC users now send electronic- or voice-mail all over the world and can exchange ideas and news in chat rooms and via instant messaging software programs.

Computer interface designers are challenged by the goal of creating an interface that resembles human-to-human interaction as closely as possible. Design considerations should include not only technical aspects but **ergonomic** factors as well. The ideal interface would allow one to concentrate on his or her work without even being aware of the presence of the interface itself. SEE ALSO ERGONOMICS; INTERACTIVE SYSTEMS; WINDOW INTERFACES.

ergonomic being of suitable geometry and structure to permit effective or optimal human user interaction with machines

Marina Krol and Igor Tarnopolsky

Bibliography

Dertouzos, Michael L. *The Unfinished Revolution: Human-Centered Computers and What They Can Do for Us.* New York: HarperCollins, 2001.

Shneiderman, Ben. *Designing the User Interface: Strategies for Effective Human-Computer Interaction.* Reading, MA: Addison Wesley Longman, Inc., 1997.

Weinschenk Susan, Sarah C. Yeo, Pamela Jamar, and Theresa Hudson. *GUI Design Essentials for Windows 95, Windows 3.1, World Wide Web.* New York: John Wiley & Sons, 1997.

Weiss, Elaine. *Making Computers People-Literate.* San Francisco: Jossey-Bass Inc., 1994.

Internet Resources

"Human-Computer Interaction." IBM Research web site. <http://www.research.ibm.com/compsci/hci/>

logarithmic refers to the power to which a certain number called the base is to be raised to produce a particular number

mainframe computers large computers used by businesses and government agencies to process massive amounts of data; generally faster and more powerful than desktop computers but usually requiring specialized software

An Wang.

Wang, An

Chinese-born American Inventor and Entrepreneur
1920–1990

An Wang is remembered for his contributions to the invention of core memory; the accomplishments of his company, Wang Laboratories; and his many inventions, including the world's first commercially successful **logarithmic** calculator and word processing system. Wang's invention of the memory core helped fuel the spread of **mainframe computers** for decades.

An Wang was born in Shanghai, China, on February 7, 1920, the eldest son of a school teacher. His quick intellect became evident at an early age when he finished sixth grade at the age of nine. He studied electrical engineering at Chiao Tung University in Shanghai, an institution comparable to the Massachusetts Institute of Technology (MIT) in the United States. He was ranked first in his class throughout his years at college, graduating as valedictorian in 1940.

In 1944 the Chinese government selected a small group of engineers, including Wang, to travel to the United States at state expense. Their assignment was to learn American technology so they could help rebuild China after the war with Japan, which had begun in 1937 and continued for many years.

Wang enrolled at Harvard University and completed his graduate work with amazing speed. He began his studies in 1946, completing the requirements for a master's degree in applied physics in only two semesters. Thirteen months after starting work on his doctorate, Wang was awarded his Ph.D. in applied physics although graduate students typically study for four or more years before earning similar advanced degrees.

In 1948, with his government funding running out, Wang was reluctant to return to war-torn China and sought employment at Harvard's Computation Laboratory. There Howard Aiken was building the first all-electronic computing machine to be fabricated at Harvard, the Mark IV.

Aiken's first assignment for Wang was for him to find a way to record and read magnetically stored information without any mechanical motion in the machine. Wang worked on the problem for several weeks before discovering the key—a tiny donut-shaped magnetic switch that could be turned on and off electrically in a few thousandths of a second. Wang found that by stringing these switches, called *cores*, in a line, the computer could write zeros and ones to memory and read them back on demand. His invention was stable, fast, and required no mechanical motion. (While Wang invented the fundamental element of core memory, a fellow researcher, Jay W. Forrester at MIT, completed its development by placing the cores in a grid to make memory access faster than ever.) Core memory became a fundamental component of mainframe computers. Wang's patent for the core was the first of forty patents that he would be awarded.

In 1951 Wang took the bold step of quitting Harvard. Using his savings of $600, Wang began his own company, Wang Laboratories, to manufacture and market memory devices and other electronic components. The company grew steadily by manufacturing products for other companies.

In 1964 Wang invented a desktop calculator, called LOCI, his company's first Wang-invented product. For the first time, scientists and engineers could perform mathematical calculations from their desks, without a mainframe computer. When LOCI went to market in 1965, it became a hugely popular tool and company revenues tripled. A series of successful calculators followed, but Wang made a bigger impact with his invention of the commercial word processing machine (1971). The Wang Word Processing System was a revolutionary desktop device with a monitor, computer, and keyboard that was designed to make word processing easy and fast. It was not a **microcomputer**, but each machine had its own microprocessor, freeing it from **minicomputers** or mainframes, a radical idea at the time. By incorporating network functionality in his word processors, Wang was among the first to sell a **local area network (LAN)** that allowed users to share applications, documents, and printers.

When the Wang Word Processing System was introduced in 1976, it catapulted Wang Laboratories to fame, causing company revenues to triple over the next three years. By 1978 the company was the largest supplier of stand-alone word processors in the world; this was several years before IBM entered the market. Other Wang products, including the VS minicomputer and microcomputers, followed.

Wang made several strategic business miscalculations, however. One was not broadening his word processing design to take commercial advantage of a desktop computer until after IBM did so in the 1980s. Later he erred by not making his computers compatible with the newest industry standard—the IBM Personal Computer. In time the huge markets for Wang Laboratories evaporated, and the company tumbled into bankruptcy in 1992.

Wang died of cancer on March 24, 1990, in Boston, Massachusetts. In spite of his humble beginnings in Shanghai, by 1983 he had come to be regarded as the fifth richest man in the world before his company began its slide. A member of the National Inventors Hall of Fame, Wang is still remembered for his contributions to computer science and for the millions of dollars he gave to local arts and educational organizations. SEE ALSO WORD PROCESSORS.

Ann McIver McHoes

THE PHILANTHROPY OF AN WANG

An Wang gained fame for his generous contributions to colleges and universities, hospitals, and arts organizations. In 1983 Wang donated $4 million to rescue Boston's decaying Metropolitan Theatre, which closed when a ceiling collapsed. Today, the facility is known as the Wang Center for the Performing Arts. When asked to explain his philanthropic contributions, Wang said: "In countries or civilizations where one generation has benefited in knowledge, physical faculties, or whatever, it means that you have already profited from the benefits that previous generations lacked. So you should pay back the past and pass other benefits onto the next generation."

microcomputer a computer that is small enough to be used and managed by one person alone; often called a personal computer

minicomputers computers midway in size between a desktop computer and a mainframe computer; most modern desktops are much more powerful than the older minicomputers

local area network (LAN) a high-speed computer network that is designed for users who are located near each other

Bibliography

Kenney, Charles C. *Riding the Runaway Horse*. Boston, MA: Little, Brown and Company, 1992.

An Wang. *Lessons: An Autobiography*. Reading, MA: Addison-Wesley, 1986.

Weather Forecasting

It was not long ago that television weather reports were presented by local personalities standing in front of a marker or chalkboard with a map of the United States drawn on it. To add some spice, small vinyl symbols of the sun and clouds were applied. The local personality was—and for the most part still is—the star. But during the 1980s, a transformation took place. Computers entered the modern television forecast office. This was the beginning of a new era in the forecasting and presentation of TV weather.

In big cities across America, TV weather has become big business. Broadcast **meteorologists** have always known that "the weather" is one of the most important parts of a local newscast. Weather affects everybody, and reports help people answer important questions such as "Should I wear a coat today?" or "Should I carry an umbrella?" Television station managers believed that the more "toys" a TV forecaster had, the more people would watch their station and their forecaster. They were correct for the most part. Weather segments and the associated broadcaster are huge audience draws.

What is the role of a local broadcast weather person? Forecast models and guidance are produced by National Weather Service (NWS) **supercomputers** in various places around the United States. A local TV forecaster has no need or ability to crunch all of those numbers. So, the local weather person receives data in raw form and also obtains prepared forecasts to aid in creating the forecast for the newscasts of the day.

Up to this point, the NWS has done a lot of the work. Measurements, or *soundings*, as they are called, are taken at various cities around the country. These data are sent to the NWS for analysis and forecast model production. The final "products" are then sent to various outlets for distribution. The National Weather Service makes these data available to end users and to private data vendors like Weather Services International (WSI).

From Data to Televised Weather Forecasts

Data supplied by the government (NWS) are sent to a vendor. That private company takes the data and sends the information, either untouched or reconfigured, to television stations via a satellite delivery system. A small dish is placed on the TV station roof to receive the data. The information is then "squeezed" into a Windows-based PC for further distribution at the television station. Many people think that this information and raw data are then analyzed by the local PC to produce an instant five-day forecast, but this is not the case. The data PC only receives and distributes data; it does not "automatically prepare" anything. The role of the local forecaster is to take these data, analyze the information, do a bit of math, and rely on one more element . . . instinct. Only then is a forecast prepared and ready to go to the public. To make this happen, more computers are necessary. The main PC sends data to one or more printers that create printouts of forecasts and

meteorologists people who study weather and weather forecasting

supercomputers very high performance computers, usually comprised of many processors and used for modeling and simulation of complex phenomena, like meteorology

---

HIGHS AND LOWS

A big "H" on a map indicates High Pressure. That means heavy, descending air. Air circulates around a High in a clockwise fashion (in the northern hemisphere). The barometer rises as the High approaches. It is usually difficult for clouds to form. So a High usually brings fair weather. A big "L" on the map signifies Low Pressure. If the big "L" is approaching, a storm is coming! Low Pressure means that air is rising. Rising air is unstable, so clouds form and eventually rain or snow may develop. Hurricanes are intense areas of Low Pressure. The barometer falls as the Low approaches. Fronts usually are connected to Lows. Air circulates counterclockwise around a Low (in the northern hemisphere).

raw data. Local weather bulletins and statements are also printed. The main PC also sends information to other important office-based computers, as well, where it is processed in different ways for several purposes.

Weather Warnings.   One system receiving data is a Windows-based PC that takes weather bulletins, like watches and warnings, and automatically creates informational maps and **crawls** to alert viewers to dangerous or potentially dangerous weather conditions. This First Warning System not only creates the maps and crawls but signals the forecast staff and others in the TV station that severe weather is upon the community and action must be taken. At this point, other TV station staffers, such as engineers in Master Control, can interface with the First Warning System remotely and get the prepared maps or crawls on the air, even if no trained forecaster is on duty at the time.

Weather Maps.   Data are also sent to another computer that handles the production of colorful graphics that can be displayed behind the on-camera weather person. This color graphics computer must be able to prepare and display satellite pictures and other visual aids. It must stand ready to be used as an artistic tool by the forecaster or weather producer. Such a system is rarely a Windows-based PC. Most are manufactured by Silicon Graphics to run various "supercharged" operating systems that can handle the graphic requirements of sophisticated programs quickly and with great detail.

Forecasters use rather dull informational maps behind the scenes. Making these maps look understandable and interesting to the viewer is the challenge of the color graphics system. This system must also monitor or create incoming satellite, radar, and temperature maps. It must present thumbnail shots of each individual map to allow the forecast staff to select easily the ones they want to use. This powerhouse of a graphics system not only acts as a producer but must then become a director as well. Various color graphics ready for broadcast can be displayed in **time lapse mode** or be custom-produced as an animated movie. These animations might show various fronts and features moving across the TV screen behind the on-camera forecaster. The staff also chooses special effects to highlight the display of various graphics. Different "wipes" between frames or movies can add interest to a TV weather segment and make it stand out from the competition.

Radar, Internet Access, and Communication Computers

A TV weather office often includes a PC-based control system for Doppler Radar. The radar system itself might be located miles away from the TV station. But a Windows-based PC acts as the command and control center to determine how many miles out the radar should scan. And the computer can determine which radar maps should be displayed.

Various other PC-based systems exist in most TV weather offices. They might include PCs used for news gathering and scriptwriting. Usually these systems serve many functions. Along with news gathering, they can usually access the Internet and intranet systems for various administrative tasks. These systems can provide backup support to the primary data computer, by acquiring data from the Internet. If the main data PC crashes or experiences a problem receiving signals from the satellite or dish, this backup system can be invaluable. This PC may also be used for sending and receiving e-mail and interoffice communications.

crawls severe weather warnings that are broadcast on the bottom of TV screens

time lapse mode to show a sequence of events occurring at a higher than natural speed so it looks like it is happening rapidly rather than in real time

DOPPLER RADAR

The first weather radar units were taken from old aircraft and adapted for use in forecast offices across the United States. The old aviation radars were looking for other airplanes. The forecast offices were concerned with smaller targets: raindrops or snowflakes. Raindrops are "seen" by radar when the energy from the radar travels through the air and hits a target. The energy then bounces back to the radar unit and displays where the moving target is located. Doppler Radar takes this one step further by "seeing" the rain being blown toward and away from the radar unit. This wind turbulence is then displayed on screen, making it appear that Doppler Radar can "see" and show us the wind.

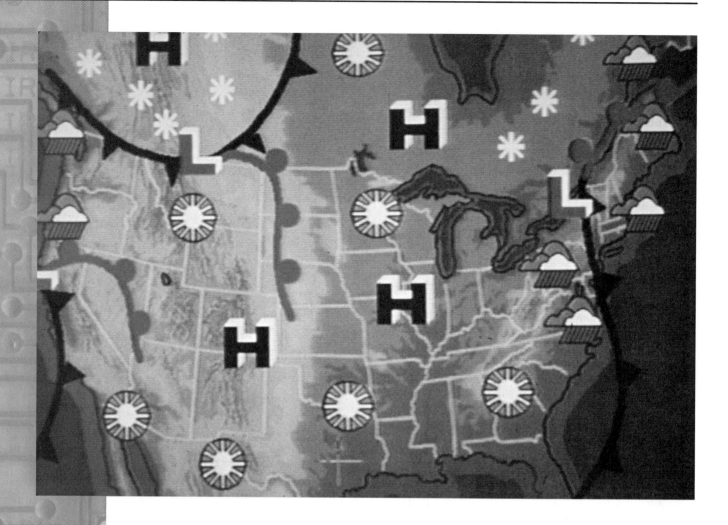

Meteorologists use computer technology to help them predict what weather patterns to expect throughout the world on any given day or even up to a week or more in advance.

In summary, there is no question that computers now rule the local TV weather office. Surge protection and backup generators are used regularly at stations all across the country to safeguard the reliance on these systems. Although the "old days" of markers and chalk bring back fond memories, the computer-based systems in a modern TV weather office offer tremendous data capabilities and provide the on-air weather people with a host of sources to display the very latest weather from down the block or around the world. SEE ALSO AGRICULTURE; AIRCRAFT TRAFFIC MANAGEMENT; DISPLAY DEVICES; SUPERCOMPUTERS.

Chuck Gaidica

Bibliography

Cox, John D. *Weather for Dummies.* Foster City, CA: IDG Books Worldwide, 2000.

Grazulis, Thomas P. *The Tornado: Nature's Ultimate Windstorm.* Norman: University of Oklahoma Press, 2001.

Williams, Jack. *The Weather Book.* New York: Vintage Books, 1997.

Word Processors

How many typewriters are you likely to find in an office today? Probably none, but in the mid-1960s they were plentiful. That was when IBM coined the term "word processing" to market their Magnetic Tape Selectric Typewriter, also known as the MTST. It was very different from other typewriters because it recorded words on magnetic tape and printed them on paper at the same time. Each tape could store many documents, making it possible to retrieve any of them for later printing, or for generating multiple copies of the same document. This was the first device to allow semi-automatic production of personalized letters: after the user typed the names and addresses, the machine took over and completed the task.

The MTST underwent many transformations, and in 1974 it used internal storage along with external storage on magnetic tapes or cards. However, fast typists could not reach their full potential because it was still a mechanical device. It was not until the introduction of **CRT-based** word processing equipment in 1976, with the Wang Computer System, that operators were released from the constraints of mechanical printing devices.

By the mid-1970s customer demand provided the thrust for a new industry: special-purpose computers dedicated to word processing. New vendors of word processors, such as Wang Laboratories, surpassed IBM in sales and product innovation. Word processors have undergone many transformations while evolving from dedicated units to multi-purpose personal computers that can perform several functions, including word processing, database management, and accessing the Internet. "Word processor" now

CRT-based a device using a cathode ray tube (CRT), which is a glass enclosure that projects images by directing a beam of electrons onto the back of a screen

The Wang word processor helped typists make the transition from manual and electric typewriters to computers.

AN WANG, INNOVATOR

In November 1971 An Wang (1920-1990) launched the Wang 1200, which by today's standards was an extremely primitive word processor. The Wang 1200's direct competition was IBM's MTST. In 1975, when Wang was well positioned in the word processing market, the Xerox 800 was introduced. It had a Diablo printer and was twice as fast as the Wang 1200. Wang ordered the design of a system that would offer features specifically requested by users—most of whom were women and secretaries. The result, introduced in June 1976 at the New York Syntopican trade show, was the WCS (Wang Computer System). Its price was $30,000. People came in droves to see text editing done on a screen for the first time. The success of the WCS led to a new division of the Wang company devoted exclusively to word processors.

refers primarily to the software used create and manipulate text documents, rather than to the hardware on which the software is run.

Functions of Word Processing Systems

Most word processing systems provide, in a single software package, all the necessary tools that users need to produce a finished document, from entering and editing text, to formatting and proofreading it, and finally to saving and printing it. Here are the steps one would follow to create a document using a word processing program.

Entering Text. A word processing document starts as an empty window on the computer screen with a flashing cursor bar that indicates your location in the document. As you type, the cursor moves to the right, and the characters are displayed on the screen and stored in the computer's memory. You can fix your typing mistakes at any time by pressing the Delete or Backspace keys. Word processors are equipped with the "word wrap" feature, which automatically moves a word to the next line once a line has reached its full capacity. Therefore, the only time you need to press the Return or Enter key is when you want to begin a new line, such as at the end of a paragraph. On typewriters, a typist had to press the return key to begin a new line of text.

Editing Text. Word processors make it easy for you to change and rearrange your work in many different ways. For example you can easily:

- Navigate to different parts of a document by scrolling;
- Search for and replace specific words or phrases throughout a document;
- Insert text at any point;
- Delete text from any section;
- Move text from one part of a document to another;
- Copy text from one part and duplicate it in another section of the same document or to another document.

Formatting Text. This refers to arranging a document so it will look the way you want it to once it is printed. All word processors allow you to format individual characters, lines, paragraphs, or whole documents. WYSIWYG (What You See Is What You Get) systems also give you a good view on screen of what the final product will look like.

Formatting characters affects the size of the characters (point size), their style (typeface, sometimes called font), and whether they are underlined, written in italic, or displayed in bold, heavy type. The formatting of lines and paragraphs determines the spacing between lines of text, the placement of indents or tabs, and the finished length and position of the lines of type on a page. Document formatting applies to margin settings, as well as headers and footers—blocks of text that appear at the top and bottom of every page.

Other text formatting features give you the ability to:

- Create documents with variable-width multiple columns;
- Perform automatic footnoting;

- Generate table-of-contents and indexing for books and other long works;

- Create and format multicolumn tables;

- Attach hidden text, pop-up notes, or audio notes that can be seen or heard by the user but do not show up in the final document;

- Incorporate graphics created with other applications.

Additional Tools.   Word processing does not end with editing and formatting. Most high-end word processors also include a built-in outliner, spell checker, grammar and style checker, thesaurus, mail merger, and indexer. As word processors become more powerful, they take on many features previously found only in desktop publishing (DTP) software such as merging graphics, tables, and text into one document. Many word processors are capable of producing professional-quality books and periodicals, so the line between word processors and DTP programs is likely to fade with time. SEE ALSO OFFICE AUTOMATION SYSTEMS; PRODUCTIVITY SOFTWARE; WANG, AN.

Ida M. Flynn

Bibliography

Brightman, Richard W., and Jeffrey M. Dimsdale. *Using Computers in an Information Age.* Albany, NY: Delmar Publishers Inc., 1986.

Laudon, Kenneth C., Carol Guercio Traver, and Jane Price Laudon. *Information Technology and Society.* Belmont, CA: Wadsworth Publishing Co., 1994.

Lee, J. A. N. *Computer Pioneers.* Los Alamitos, CA: IEEE Computer Society Press, 1995.

Photo and Illustration Credits

The illustrations and tables featured in Computer Sciences *were created by GGS Information Services. The photographs appearing in the text were reproduced by permission of the following sources:*

Volume 1

Gale Research: **1**; AP/Wide World Photos, Inc.: **4, 35, 39, 44, 60, 82, 91, 136, 148, 190, 209, 219**; Courtesy of the Library of Congress: **6, 25, 52, 58, 83, 98, 103, 126, 150, 193, 211**; Kobal Collection/Warner Bros.: **9**; Kobal Collection: **11**; Archive Photos/Reuters/Sell: **16**; National Audubon Society Collection/Photo Researchers, Inc.: **19**; CORBIS/Bettmann: **22, 41, 73, 86, 165, 201, 221**; AT&T Archives: **28**; U.S. Census Bureau: **33**; Elena Rooraid/Photo Edit: **48**; Photo Edit: **66**; IBM Corporate Archives: **70, 163**; Colin Braley/Reuters/Getty Images: **94**; Adam Hart-Davis/National Audubon Society Collection/Photo Researchers, Inc.: **105**; Michael S. Yamashita/CORBIS: **110**; Reuters NewMedia Inc./CORBIS: **116**; UPI/CORBIS-Bettmann: **118, 176**; Associated Press/AP: **121**; Doris Langley Moore Collection: **122**; Astrid & Hanns-Frieder Michler/Photo Researchers, Inc.: **133**; Microsoft Corporation: **139**; Ted Spiegel/CORBIS: **140**; Prestige/Getty Images: **143**; Richard T. Nowitz/CORBIS: **146**; U.S. National Aeronautics and Space Administration (NASA): **152**; Robert Cattan/Index Stock Imagery/PictureQuest: **156**; Dave Bartruff/Stock, Boston Inc./PictureQuest: **159**; Courtesy Carnegie Mellon University Field Robotics Center/NASA: **172**; Roger Ressmeyer/CORBIS: **179, 184**; Hulton-Deutsch Collection/CORBIS: **187**; Granger Collection, Ltd.: **197**; Larry Chan/Reuters/Getty Images: **204**; Microsoft programs: 213, 214, 215, 216, 217.

Volume 2

Thomas E. Kurtz: **2**; Courtesy of the Library of Congress: **4, 18, 99, 112**; CORBIS/Bettmann: **13**; U.S. National Aeronautics and Space Administration (NASA): **16**; Roger Ressmeyer/CORBIS: **25, 92, 115, 118, 150, 179, 215**; A/P Wide World Photos, Inc.: **31, 36, 40, 65, 73, 89, 110, 133, 136, 143, 161, 165, 167, 171, 199, 205, 212, 221**; UPI/CORBIS-Bettmann: **34, 169, 217, 219**; Courtesy of BT Archives: **46**; CORBIS: **53**; Andrew Syred/National Audubon Society Collection/Photo Researchers, Inc.: **62**; Richard Pasley/Stock, Boston Inc./PictureQuest: **70**; Bob Krist/CORBIS: **77**; Patrik Giardino/CORBIS: **79**; Rob Crandall/Stock, Boston Inc./PictureQuest: **84**; Mario Tama/Getty Images: **94**; AFP/CORBIS: **98**; Custom Medical Stock Photo: **140**; William McCoy/Rainbow/PictureQuest: **147**; Courtesy of Niklaus Wirth: **157**; Reuters NewMedia Inc./CORBIS: **175**; Paul Almasy/CORBIS: **188**; Detlev Van Ravenswaay/Picture Press/CORBIS-Bettmann: **193**; James Marshall/CORBIS: **203**.

Volume 3

Bill Lai/Rainbow/PictureQuest: **2**; Agricultural Research Service/USDA: **5**; Carlos Lopez-Barillas/Getty Images: **8**; A/P Wide World Photos, Inc.: **11, 19, 28, 39, 89, 102, 106, 111, 118, 131**; Laima Druskis/Stock, Boston Inc./PictureQuest: **13**; Bojan Brecelj/CORBIS: **17**; JLM Visuals: **23**; Mediafocus: **24**; Ed Kashi/Phototake NYC: **30**; Reuters NewMedia Inc./CORBIS: **34**; Royalty Free/CORBIS: **42**; Srulik Haramaty/Phototake NYC: **46**; Mark

Antman/Phototake, NYC: **52**;
CORBIS/Bettmann: **55, 206, 211**; Hulton-
Deutsch Collection/CORBIS: **56**; Walter A.
Lyons: **60, 210**; Smith & Santori/Gale
Group: **62**; Darren McCollester/Getty
Images: **69**; Richard Palsey/Stock, Boston
Inc./PictureQuest: **73**; Ed Kashi/CORBIS:
79; Index Stock Imagery: **81**; AFP/CORBIS:
85; Montes De Oca & Associates: **92**; Millard
Berry: **95**; Courtesy of
NASA/JPL/NIMA/Visible Earth: **100**;
Courtesy of the Library of Congress: **108,
124**; Nehau Kulyk/Photo Researchers, Inc.:
116; CORBIS: **122**; U.S. Department of
Education/National Audubon Society
Collection/Photo Researchers, Inc.: **125**; Bob
Rowan/Progressive Image/CORBIS: **133**; Bill
Ross/CORBIS: **137**; Geoff
Tompkincon/National Audubon Society
Collection/Photo Researchers, Inc.: **141**;
Clive Freeman/Photo Researchers, Inc.: **143**;
Roger Ressmeyer/CORBIS: **150**; Free
Software Foundation: **157**; Kenneth
Eward/BioGrafx/National Audubon Society
Collection/Photo Researchers, Inc.: **163**;
Steven McBride/Picturesque/PictureQuest:
168; Michael S. Yamashita/CORBIS: **175**;
Photo Researchers, Inc.: **178**; Chris
Hondros/Getty Images: **181**; David
Silverman/Getty Images: **183**; U.S. National
Aeronautics and Space Administration
(NASA): **188**; Jim Sugar
Photography/CORBIS: **200**; Leif
Skoogfors/CORBIS: **205**.

Volume 4

A/P Wide World Photos, Inc.: **2, 15, 23, 29,
33, 41, 44, 59, 75, 100, 147, 151, 162, 168,
177, 180, 184, 186, 190, 195, 197, 201,**
203; Gene M. Amdahl: **4**; Vittoriano
Rastelli/CORBIS: **7**; Jim Sugar
Photography/CORBIS: **10**; NNS: **22**; John
Maher/Stock, Boston Inc./PictureQuest: **26**;
Kenneth Eward/Photo Researchers, Inc.: **35**;
Steve Chenn/CORBIS: **47**; Christopher
Morris/Black Star Publishing/PictureQuest:
50; Jonathan Elderfield/Getty Images: **54**;
Courtesy of the Library of Congress: **56, 103,
163**; Amy Ritterbush/Stock, Boston
Inc./PictureQuest: **64**; AFP/CORBIS: **66,
113, 125, 131, 134**; Reuters NewMedia
Inc./CORBIS: **70, 89, 108, 120, 194**; Shahn
Kermani/Getty Images: **76**; Associated
Press/AP: **78, 93, 95**; Patricia Nagle/Center
for Instructional Development and Distance
Education/University of Pittsburgh: **85**; Alec
Sarkas/Center for Instructional Development
and Distance Education/University of
Pittsburgh: **87**; Kobal Collection/MGM/UA:
106; Space Imaging: **115**; Courtesy of USGS
Landsat 7 Team at the Eros Data Center and
NASA's Visible Earth: **116**; Reuters/News
and Observer-Jim/Archive Photos, Inc.: **122**;
Reuters/Getty Images: **128**; Oleg
Nikishin/Getty Images: **139**; Netscape
Communicator browser window (c) 1999
Netscape Communications Corporation—
used with permission (Netscape
Communications has not authorized,
sponsored, endorsed, or approved this
publication and is not responsible for its
content): **155, 156, 157, 159**;
YBSHY/CORBIS: **165**; James King-
Holmes/Science Photo Library/The National
Audubon Society Collection/Photo
Researchers, Inc.: **171**; Carnegie Mellon
University: **173**; Microsoft Visual Basic
program: 209, 210, 211.

Glossary

abacus: an ancient counting device that probably originated in Babylon around 2,400 B.C.E.

acuity: sharpness or keenness, especially when used to describe vision

address bus: a collection of electrical signals used to transmit the address of a memory location or input/output port in a computer

aerodynamics: the science and engineering of systems that are capable of flight

agents: systems (software programs and/or computing machines) that can act on behalf of another, or on behalf of a human

aggregate: a numerical summation of multiple individual scores

ailerons: control surfaces on the trailing edges of the wings of an aircraft—used to manage roll control

ALGOL: a language developed by the ALGOL committee for scientific applications—acronym for ALGOrithmic Language

algorithm: a rule or procedure used to solve a mathematical problem—most often described as a sequence of steps

all-points-addressable mode: a technique for organizing graphics devices where all points (pixels) on the screen are individually accessible to a running program

alpha beta pruning: a technique that under certain conditions offers an optimal way to search through data structures called "trees"

alphanumeric: a character set which is the union of the set of alphabetic characters and the set of single digit numbers

ambient: pertaining to the surrounding atmosphere or environment

ambiguity: the quality of doubtfulness or uncertainty; often subject to multiple interpretations

amortized: phasing out something in until it is gradually extinguished, like a mortgage loan

amplitude: the size or magnitude of an electrical signal

analog: a quantity (often an electrical signal) that is continuous in time and amplitude

analogous: a relationship of logical similarity between two or more objects

analytic simulation: modeling of systems by using mathematical equations (often differential equations) and programming a computer with them to simulate the behavior of the real system

Analytical Engine: Charles Babbage's vision of a programmable mechanical computer

animatronics: the animation (movement) of something by the use of electronic motors, drives, and controls

anthropomorphic: having human form, or generally resembling human appearance

anti-aliasing: introducing shades of gray or other intermediate shades around an image to make the edge appear to be smoother

applet: a program component that requires extra support at run time from a browser or run-time environment in order to execute

approximation: an estimate

arc tangent: the circular trigonometric function that is the inverse of the tangent function; values range from $-\Pi/2$ to $\Pi/2$

artificial intelligence (AI): a branch of computer science dealing with creating computer hardware and software to mimic the way people think and perform practical tasks

ASCII: an acronym that stands for American Standard Code for Information Interchange; assigns a unique 8-bit binary number to every letter of the alphabet, the digits (0 to 9), and most keyboard symbols

assembler: a program that translates human-readable assembly language programs to machine-readable instructions

assembly language: the natural language of a central processing unit (CPU); often classed as a low-level language

asynchronous: events that have no systematic relationship to one another in time

attenuation: the reduction in magnitude (size or amplitude) of a signal that makes a signal weaker

authentication: the act of ensuring that an object or entity is what it is intended to be

automata theory: the analytical (mathematical) treatment and study of automated systems

automaton: an object or being that has a behavior that can be modeled or explained completely by using automata theory

autonomous: self governing, or being able to exist independently

autonomy: the capability of acting in a self-governing manner; being able to exist independently or with some degree of independence

axioms: statements that are taken to be true, the foundation of a theory

Bakelite: an insulating material used in synthetic goods, including plastics and resins

ballistics: the science and engineering of the motion of projectiles of various types, including bullets, bombs, and rockets

bandwidth: a measure of the frequency component of a signal or the capacity of a communication channel to carry signals

bar code: a graphical number representation system where alphanumeric characters are represented by vertical black and white lines of varying width

base-2: a number system in which each place represents a power of 2 larger than the place to its right (binary)

base-8: a number system in which each place represents a power of 8 larger than the place to its right (octal)

base-10: a number system in which each place represents a power of 10 larger than the place to its right (decimal)

base-16: a number system in which each place represents a power of 16 larger than the place to its right (hexadecimal)

batch processing: an approach to computer utilization that queues non-interactive programs and runs them one after another

Bayesian networks: structures that describe systems in which there is a degree of uncertainty; used in automated decision making

Bernoulli numbers: the sums of powers of consecutive integers; named after Swiss mathematician Jacques Bernoulli (1654-1705)

binary: existing in only two states, such as "on" or "off," "one" or "zero"

binary code: a representation of information that permits only two states, such as "on" or "off," "one" or "zero"

binary coded decimal (BCD): an ANSI/ISO standard encoding of the digits 0 to 9 using 4 binary bits; the encoding only uses 10 of the available 16 4-bit combinations

binary digit: a single bit, 1 or 0

binary number system: a number system in which each place represents a power of 2 larger than the place on its right (base-2)

binary system: a machine or abstraction that uses binary codes

binomial theorem: a theorem giving the procedure by which a binomial expression may be raised to any power without using successive multiplications

bit: a single binary digit, 1 or 0—a contraction of Binary digIT; the smallest unit for storing data in a computer

bit mapped display: a computer display that uses a table of binary bits in memory to represent the image that is projected onto the screen

bit maps: images comprised of bit descriptions of the image, in black and white or color, such that the colors can be represented by the two values of a binary bit

bit rate: the rate at which binary bits can be processed or transferred per unit time, in a system (often a computer communications system)

bit serial mode: a method of transferring binary bits one after another in a sequence or serial stream

bitstream: a serialized collection of bits; usually used in transfer of bits from one system to another

Boolean algebra: a system developed by George Boole that deals with the theorems of undefined symbols and axioms concerning those symbols

Boolean logic: a system, developed by George Boole, which treats abstract objects (such as sets or classes) as algebraic quantities; Boole applied his mathematical system to the study of classical logic

Boolean operators: fundamental logical operations (for example "and" and "or") expressed in a mathematical form

broadband access: a term given to denote high bandwidth services

browsers: programs that permits a user to view and navigate through documents, most often hypertext documents

bugs: errors in program source code

bus: a group of related signals that form an interconnecting pathway between two or more electronic devices

bus topology: a particular arrangement of buses that constitutes a designed set of pathways for information transfer within a computer

byte: a group of eight binary digits; represents a single character of text

C: a programming language developed for the UNIX operating system; it is designed to run on most machines and with most operating systems

cache: a small sample of a larger set of objects, stored in a way that makes them accessible

calculus: a method of dealing mathematically with variables that may be changing continuously with respect to each other

Callback modems: security techniques that collect telephone numbers from authorized users on calls and then dial the users to establish the connections

capacitates: fundamental electrical components used for storing electrical charges

capacitor: a fundamental electrical component used for storing an electrical charge

carpal tunnel syndrome: a repetitive stress injury that can lead to pain, numbness, tingling, and loss of muscle control in the hands and wrists

cartography: map making

cathode ray tube (CRT): a glass enclosure that projects images by directing a beam of electrons onto the back of a screen

cellular automata: a collection or array of objects that are programmed identically to interact with one another

cellular neural networks (CNN): a neural network topology that uses multidimensional array structures comprised of cells that work together in localized groups

central processing unit (CPU): the part of a computer that performs computations and controls and coordinates other parts of the computer

certificate: a unique electronic document that is used to assist authentication

chaos theory: a branch of mathematics dealing with differential equations having solutions which are very sensitive to initial conditions

checksum: a number that is derived from adding together parts of an electronic message before it is dispatched; it can be used at the receiver to check against message corruption

chromatic dispersion: the natural distortion of pulses of light as they move through an optical network; it results in data corruption

cipher: a code or encryption method

client: a program or computer often managed by a human user, that makes requests to another computer for information

client/server technology: computer systems that are structured using clients (usually human driven computers) to access information stored (often remotely) on other computers known as servers

coaxial cable: a cable with an inner conducting core, a dielectric material and an outer sheath that is designed for high frequency signal transmission

cognitive: pertaining to the concepts of knowing or perceiving

collocation: the act of placing elements or objects in a specific order

commodity: raw material or service marketed prior to being used

compiled: a program that is translated from human-readable code to binary code that a central processing unit (CPU) can understand

compiled executable code: the binary code that a central processing unit (CPU) can understand; the product of the compilation process

compilers: programs that translate human-readable high-level computer languages to machine-readable code

computer-aided design (CAD): the use of computers to replace traditional drawing instruments and tools for engineering or architectural design

computer-assisted tomography: the use of computers in assisting with the management of X-ray images

computer peripheral: a device that is connected to a computer to support its operation; for example, a keyboard or a disk drive unit

concatenates: the joining together of two elements or objects; for example, words are formed by concatenating letters

concentric circles: circles that have coincident centers

conceptualization: a creative process that is directed at envisaging a structure or collection of relationships within components of a complex system

concurrency control: the management and coordination of several actions that occur simultaneously; for example, several computer programs running at once

concurrent: pertaining to simultaneous activities, for example simultaneous execution of many computer programs

configuration files: special disk files containing information that can be used to tell running programs about system settings

cookie: a small text file that a web site can place on a computer's hard drive to collect information about a user's browsing activities or to activate an online shopping cart to keep track of purchases

copyrights: the legal rules and regulations concerning the copying and redistribution of documents

cosine: a trigonometric function of an angle, defined as the ratio of the length of the adjacent side of a right-angled triangle divided by the length of its hypotenuse

counterfeiting: the act of knowingly producing non-genuine objects, especially in relation to currency

crawls: severe weather warnings that are broadcast on the bottom of TV screens

cross-platform: pertaining to a program that can run on many different computer types (often called hardware platforms)

CRT: the acronym for cathode ray tube, which is a glass enclosure that projects images by directing a beam of electrons onto the back of a screen

cryptanalysis: the act of attempting to discover the algorithm used to encrypt a message

cryptanalyst: a person or agent who attempts to discover the algorithm used to encrypt a message

cryptography: the science of understanding codes and ciphers and their application

cryptosystem: a system or mechanism that is used to automate the processes of encryption and decryption

cuneiform: in the shape of a wedge

cybercafe: a shop, cafe, or meeting place where users can rent a computer for a short time to access the Internet

cybernetics: a unified approach to understanding the behavior of machines and animals developed by Norbert Wiener (1894-1964)

cycloids: pertaining to circles, in either a static way or in a way that involves movement

dark fiber: a fiber optic network that exists but is not actively in service, hence the darkness

data mining: a technique of automatically obtaining information from databases that is normally hidden or not obvious

data partitioning: a technique applied to databases (but not restricted to them) which organizes data objects into related groups

data reduction technique: an approach to simplifying data, e.g. summarization

data warehousing: to implement an informational database used to store shared data

de facto: as is

de jure: strictly according to the law

debug: the act of trying to trace, identify, and then remove errors in program source code

decimal system: a number system in which each place represents a power of 10 larger than the place to its right (base-10)

decision trees: classifiers in which a sequence of tests are made to decide the class label to assign to an unknown data item; the sequence of tests can be visualized as having a tree structure

deformations: mechanical systems where a structure is physically misshapen, e.g., dented

degrade: to reduce quality or performance of a system

delimiters: special symbols that mark the beginnings and/or endings of other groups of symbols (for example to mark out comments in program source code)

demographics: the study of the statistical data pertaining to a population

densities: measures of the density of a material; defined as the mass of a sample of material, divided by its volume

deregulation: the lowering of restrictions, rules, or regulations pertaining to an activity or operation (often commercial)

die: the silicon chip that is the heart of integrated circuit fabrication; the die is encased in a ceramic or plastic package to make the completed integrated circuit (IC)

dielectric: a material that exhibits insulating properties, as opposed to conducting properties

Difference Engine: a mechanical calculator designed by Charles Babbage that automated the production of mathematical tables by using the method of differences

differential analyzer: a computer constructed in the early 1930s by Vannevar Bush at Massachusetts Institute of Technology (MIT); it solved differential equations by mechanical integration

digital: a quantity that can exist only at distinct levels, not having values in between these levels (for example, binary)

digital certificates: certificates used in authentication that contain encrypted digital identification information

digital divide: imaginary line separating those who can access digital information from those who cannot

digital library: distributed access to collections of digital information

digital signature: identifier used to authenticate the sender of an electronic message or the signer of an electronic document

digital subscriber line (DSL): a technology that permits high-speed voice and data communications over public telephone networks; it requires the use of a DSL modem

digital subscriber loop (DSL): the enabling of high-speed digital data transfer over standard telephone cables and systems in conjunction with normal telephone speech data

digital watermarks: special data structures permanently embedded into a program or other file type, which contain information about the author and the program

digitizes: converts analog information into a digital form for processing by a computer

diode: a semiconductor device that forces current flow in a conductor to be in one direction only, also known as a rectifier

diode tube: an obsolete form of diode that was made of metal elements in a sealed and evacuated glass tube

direction buttons: buttons on a program with a graphical user interface that provide a way of navigating through information or documents

discrete: composed of distinct elements

disintermediation: a change in business practice whereby consumers elect to cut out intermediary agencies and deal directly with a provider or vendor

distance learning: the form of education where the instructor and students are separated by either location or time (or both), usually mediated by some electronic communication mechanism

distributed denial of service (DDoS): an attack in which large numbers of messages are directed to send network traffic to a target computer, overloading it or its network connection; typically, the attacking computers have been subverted

distributed systems: computer systems comprised of many individual computers that are interconnected and act in concert to complete operations

documentation: literature in a human-readable form that is referred to in support of using a computer or computer system

domain: a region in which a particular element or object exists or has influence; (math) the inputs to a function or relation

doping: a step used in the production of semiconductor materials where charged particles are embedded into the device so as to tailor its operational characteristics

dot.com: a common term used to describe an Internet-based commercial company or organization

dragged: to have been moved by the application of an external pulling force; quite often occurring in graphical user interfaces when objects are moved with a mouse

DRAM: the acronym for Dynamic Random Access Memory; high density, low cost and low speed memory devices used in most computer systems

driver: a special program that manages the sequential execution of several other programs; a part of an operating system that handles input/output devices

drop-down menu: a menu on a program with a graphical user interface that produces a vertical list of items when activated

dumb terminal: a keyboard and screen connected to a distant computer without any processing capability

duplex: simultaneous two-directional communication over a single communication channel

dynamic: changing; possessing volatility

dynamic links: logical connections between two objects that can be modified if the objects themselves move or change state

e-books: short for electronic books; books available for downloading onto an e-book reader

EBCDIC: the acronym for Extended Binary Coded Decimal Interchange Code, which assigns a unique 8-bit binary number to every letter of the alphabet, the digits (0-9), and most keyboard symbols

egress: to move out of an object, system, or environment

electromagnetic: a piece of metal that becomes magnetic only when electricity is applied to it; in general, the more electricity applied to metal, the stronger its magnetism

electromagnetic relays: switches that have a high current carrying capacity, which are opened and closed by an electromagnet

electromagnetic spectrum: a range of frequencies over which electromagnetic radiation can be generated, transmitted, and received

embedded computers: computers that do not have human user orientated I/O devices; they are directly contained within other machines

embedded systems: another term for "embedded computers"; computers that do not have human user orientated input/output devices; they are directly contained within other machines

emoticons: symbols or key combinations used in electronic correspondence to convey emotions

enciphered: encrypted or encoded; a mathematical process that disguises the content of messages transmitted

encryption: also known as encoding; a mathematical process that disguises the content of messages transmitted

end-effector: the end piece of a robotic arm that can receive various types of grippers and tools

end users: computer users

enterprise information system: a system of client and server computers that can be used to manage all of the tasks required to manage and run a large organization

entropy: a measure of the state of disorder or randomness in a system

ephemeris: a record showing positions of astronomical objects and artificial satellites in a time-ordered sequence

ergonomic: being of suitable geometry and structure to permit effective or optimal human user interaction with machines

esoteric: relating to a specialized field of endeavor that is characterized by its restricted size

ether: a highly volatile liquid solvent; also, the far regions of outer space

ethernets: a networking technology for mini and microcomputer systems consisting of network interface cards and interconnecting coaxial cables; invented in the 1970s by Xerox Corporation

Euclidean geometry: the study of points, lines, angles, polygons, and curves confined to a plane

expert system: a computer system that uses a collection of rules to exhibit behavior which mimics the behavior of a human expert in some area

fiber optics: transmission technology using long, thin strands of glass fiber; internal reflections in the fiber assure that light entering one end is transmitted to the other end with only small losses in intensity; used widely in transmitting digital information

field searching: a strategy in which a search is limited to a particular field; in a search engine, a search may be limited to a particular domain name or date, narrowing the scope of searchable items and helping to eliminate the chance of retrieving irrelevant data

file transfer protocol (FTP): a communications protocol used to transfer files

filter queries: queries used to select subsets from a data collection, e.g., all documents with a creation date later than 01/01/2000

firewall: a special purpose network computer or software that is used to ensure that no access is permitted to a sub-network unless authenticated and authorized

firing tables: precalculated tables that can give an artillery gunner the correct allowances for wind conditions and distance by dictating the elevation and deflection of a gun

floating point operations: numerical operations involving real numbers where in achieving a result, the number of digits to the left or right of the decimal point can change

flowcharts: techniques for graphically describing the sequencing and structure of program source code

fluid dynamics: the science and engineering of the motion of gases and liquids

Freedom of Information Act (FOIA): permits individuals to gain access to records and documents that are in the possession of the government

freon: hydrocarbon-based gases used as refrigerants and as pressurants in aerosols

frequency bands: ranges of signal frequencies that are of particular interest in a given application

frequency modulation: a technique whereby a signal is transformed so that it is represented by another signal with a frequency that varies in a way related to the original signal

full-text indexing: a search engine feature in which every word in a document, significant or insignificant, is indexed and retrievable through a search

fuzzy logic: models human reasoning by permitting elements to have partial membership to a set; derived from fuzzy set theory

gallium arsenide: a chemical used in the production of semiconductor devices; chemical symbol GaAs

gates: fundamental building blocks of digital and computer-based electric circuits that perform logical operations; for example logical AND, logical OR

Gaussian classifiers: classifiers constructed on the assumption that the feature values of data will follow a Gaussian distribution

gbps: acronym for gigabits per second; a binary data transfer rate that corresponds to a thousand million (billion, or 109) bits per second

geometric: relating to the principles of geometry, a branch of mathematics related to the properties and relationships of points, lines, angles, surfaces, planes, and solids

germanium: a chemical often used as a high performance semiconductor material; chemical symbol Ge

GIF animation: a technique using Graphic Interchange Format where many images are overlaid on one another and cycled through a sequence to produce an animation

GIF image: the acronym for Graphic Interchange Format where a static image is represented by binary bits in a data file

gigabit networking: the construction and use of a computer network that is capable of transferring information at rates in the gigahertz range

gigabytes: units of measure equivalent to a thousand million (billion, or 109) bytes

gigahertz (GHz): a unit or measure of frequency, equivalent to a thousand million (billion, or 109) hertz, or cycles per second

Global Positioning System (GPS): a method of locating a point on the Earth's surface that uses received signals transmitted from satellites to calculate position accurately

granularity: a description of the level of precision that can be achieved in making measurements of a quantity; for example coarse granularity means inexpensive but imprecise measurements

graphical user interface (GUI): an interface that allows computers to be operated through pictures (icons) and mouse-clicks, rather than through text and typing

groupware: a software technology common in client/server systems whereby many users can access and process data at the same time

gyros: a contraction of gyroscopes; a mechanical device that uses one or more spinning discs which resist changes to their position in space

half tones: black and white dots of certain sizes, which provide a perception of shades of gray

ham radio: a legal (or licensed) amateur radio

haptic: pertaining to the sense of touch

Harvard Cyclotron: a specialized machine (cyclotron) developed in 1948 at Harvard University; it is used to carry out experiments in sub-atomic physics and medicine

head-mounted displays (HMD): helmets worn by a virtual reality (VR) participant that include speakers and screens for each eye, which display three-dimensional images

hertz (Hz): a unit of measurement of frequency, equal to one cycle per second; named in honor of German physicist Heinrich Hertz (1857-1894)

heuristic: a procedure that serves to guide investigation but that has not been proven

hexadecimal: a number system in which each place represents a power of 16 larger than the place to its right (base-16)

high-bandwidth: a communication channel that permits many signals of differing frequencies to be transmitted simultaneously

high precision/high recall: a phenomenon that occurs during a search when all the relevant documents are retrieved with no unwanted ones

high precision/low recall: a phenomenon that occurs when a search yields a small set of hits; although each one may be highly relevant to the search topic, some relevant documents are missed

high-speed data links: digital communications systems that permit digital data to be reliably transferred at high speed

hoaxes: false claims or assertions, sometimes made unlawfully in order to extort money

holistic: looking at the entire system, rather than just its parts

hydraulic: motion being powered by a pressurized liquid (such as water or oil), supplied through tubes or pipes

hydrologic: relating to water

hyperlinks: connections between electronic documents that permit automatic browsing transfer at the point of the link

Hypertext Markup Language (HTML): an encoding scheme for text data that uses special tags in the text to signify properties to the viewing program (browser) like links to other documents or document parts

Hypertext Transfer Protocol (HTTP): a simple connectionless communications protocol developed for the electronic transfer (serving) of HTML documents

I/O: the acronym for input/output; used to describe devices that can accept input data to a computer and to other devices that can produce output

I/O devices: devices that can accept "input" data to a computer and to other devices that can produce "output"

icon: a small image that is used to signify a program or operation to a user

illiquid: lacking in liquid assets; or something that is not easily transferable into currency

ImmersaDesks: large 4 x 5 foot screens that allow for stereoscopic visualization; the 3-D computer graphics create the illusion of a virtual environment

ImmersaWalls: large-scale, flat screen visualization environments that include passive and active multi-projector displays of 3-D images

immersive: involved in something totally

in-band: pertaining to elements or objects that are within the limits of a certain local area network (LAN)

inference: a suggestion or implication of something based on other known related facts and conclusions

information theory: a branch of mathematics and engineering that deals with the encoding, transmission, reception, and decoding of information

infrared (IR) waves: radiation in a band of the electromagnetic spectrum within the infrared range

infrastructure: the foundation or permanent installation necessary for a structure or system to operate

ingot: a formed block of metal (often cast) used to facilitate bulk handling and transportation

ingress: the act of entering a system or object

init method: a special function in an object oriented program that is automatically called to initialize the elements of an object when it is created

input/output (I/O): used to describe devices that can accept input data to a computer and to other devices that can produce output

intangible: a concept to which it is difficult to apply any form of analysis; something which is not perceived by the sense of touch

integrated circuit: a circuit with the transistors, resistors, and other circuit elements etched into the surface of a single chip of semiconducting material, usually silicon

integrated modem: a modem device that is built into a computer, rather than being attached as a separate peripheral

intellectual property: the acknowledgement that an individual's creativity and innovation can be owned in the same way as physical property

interconnectivity: the ability of more than one physical computer to operate with one or more other physical computers; interconnectivity is usually accomplished by means of network wiring, cable, or telephone lines

interface: a boundary or border between two or more objects or systems; also a point of access

Internet Protocol (IP): a method of organizing information transfer between computers; the IP was specifically designed to offer low-level support to Transmission Control Protocol (TCP)

Internet Service Provider (ISP): a commercial enterprise which offers paying subscribers access to the Internet (usually via modem) for a fee

interpolation: estimating data values between known points but the values in between are not and are therefore estimated

intranet: an interconnected network of computers that operates like the Internet, but is restricted in size to a company or organization

ionosphere: a region of the upper atmosphere (above about 60,000 meters or 196,850 feet) where the air molecules are affected by the sun's radiation and influence electromagnetic wave propagation

isosceles triangle: a triangle that has two sides of equivalent length (and therefore two angles of the same size)

iterative: a procedure that involves repetitive operations before being completed

Jacquard's Loom: a weaving loom, developed by Joseph-Marie Jacquard (1752-1834), controlled by punched cards; identified as one of the earliest examples of programming automation

Java applets: applets written in the Java programming language and executed with the support of a Java Virtual Machine (JVM) or a Java enabled browser

joysticks: the main controlling levers of small aircraft; models of these can be connected to computers to facilitate playing interactive games

JPEG (Joint Photographic Experts Group): organization that developed a standard for encoding image data in a compressed format to save space

k-nearest neighbors: a classifier that assigns a class label for an unknown data item by looking at the class labels of the nearest items in the training data

Kbps: a measure of digital data transfer per unit time—one thousand (kilo, K) bits per second

keywords: words that are significant in some context or topic (often used in searching)

kilohertz (kHz): a unit or measure of frequency, equivalent to a thousand (or 103) hertz, or cycles per second

kinematics: a branch of physics and mechanical engineering that involves the study of moving bodies and particles

kinetics: a branch of physics or chemistry concerned with the rate of change in chemical or physical systems

labeled data: a data item whose class assignment is known independent of the classifier being constructed

lambda calculus: important in the development of programming languages, a specialized logic using substitutions that was developed by Alonzo Church (1903-1995)

LEDs: the acronym for Light Emitting Diode; a diode that emits light when passing a current and used as an indicating lamp

lexical analyzer: a portion of a compiler that is responsible for checking the program source code produced by a programmer for proper words and symbols

Library of Congress Classification: the scheme by which the Library of Congress organizes classes of books and documents

light emitting diode (LED): a discrete electronic component that emits visible light when permitting current to flow in a certain direction; often used as an indicating lamp

linear: pertaining to a type of system that has a relationship between its outputs and its inputs that can be graphed as a straight line

Linux operating system: an open source UNIX operating system that was originally created by Linus Torvalds in the early 1990s

liquid crystal display (LCD): a type of crystal that changes its level of transparency when subjected to an electric current; used as an output device on a computer

local area network (LAN): a high-speed computer network that is designed for users who are located near each other

logarithm: the power to which a certain number called the base is to be raised to produce a particular number

logic: a branch of philosophy and mathematics that uses provable rules to apply deductive reasoning

lossy: a nonreversible way of compressing digital images; making images take up less space by permanently removing parts that cannot be easily seen anyway

low precision/high recall: a phenomenon that occurs during a search when a large set of results are retrieved, including many relevant and irrelevant documents

lumens: a unit of measure of light intensity

magnetic tape: a way of storing programs and data from computers; tapes are generally slow and prone to deterioration over time but are inexpensive

mainframe: large computer used by businesses and government agencies to process massive amounts of data; generally faster and more powerful than desktop computers but usually requiring specialized software

malicious code: program instructions that are intended to carry out malicious or hostile actions; e.g., deleting a user's files

mammogram: an X-ray image of the breast, used to detect signs of possible cancer

Manhattan Project: the U.S. project designed to create the world's first atomic bomb

mass spectrometers: instruments that can identify elemental particles in a sample by examining the frequencies of the particles that comprise the sample

mass spectrometry: the process of identifying the compounds or elemental particles within a substance

megahertz (MHz): a unit or measure of frequency, equivalent to a million (or 106) hertz, or cycles per second

memex: a device that can be used to store personal information, notes, and records that permits managed access at high speed; a hypothetical creation of Vannevar Bush

menu label: the text or icon on a menu item in a program with a graphical user interface

metadata: data about data, such as the date and time created

meteorologists: people who have studied the science of weather and weather forecasting

metropolitan area network (MAN): a high-speed interconnected network of computers spanning entire cities

microampere: a unit of measure of electrical current that is one-millionth (10-6) amperes

microchip: a common term for a semiconductor integrated circuit device

microcomputer: a computer that is small enough to be used and managed by one person alone; often called a personal computer

microprocessor: the principle element in a computer; the component that understands how to carry out operations under the direction of the running program (CPU)

millisecond: a time measurement indicating one-thousandth (or 10-3) of a second

milliwatt: a power measurement indicating one-thousandth (or 10-3) of a watt

minicomputers: computers midway in size between a desktop computer and a mainframe computer; most modern desktops are much more powerful than the older minicomputers

minimax algorithm: an approach to developing an optimal solution to a game or contest where two opposing systems are aiming at mutually exclusive goals

Minitel: network used in France that preceded the Internet, connecting most French homes, businesses, cultural organizations, and government offices

mnemonic: a device or process that aids one's memory

modalities: classifications of the truth of a logical proposition or statement, or characteristics of an object or entity

modem: the contraction of MOdulator DEModulator; a device which converts digital signals into signals suitable for transmission over analog channels, like telephone lines

modulation: a technique whereby signals are translated to analog so that the resultant signal can be more easily transmitted and received by other elements in a communication system

modules: a generic term that is applied to small elements or components that can be used in combination to build an operational system

molecular modeling: a technique that uses high performance computer graphics to represent the structure of chemical compounds

motherboard: the part of the computer that holds vital hardware, such as the processors, memory, expansion slots, and circuitry

MPEG (Motion Picture Coding Experts Group): an encoding scheme for data files that contain motion pictures—it is lossy in the same way as JPEG (Joint Photographic Experts Group) encoding

multiplexes: operations in ATM communications whereby data cells are blended into one continuous stream at the transmitter and then separated again at the receiver

multiplexor: a complex device that acts as a multi-way switch for analog or digital signals

multitasking: the ability of a computer system to execute more than one program at the same time; also known as multiprogramming

mylar: a synthetic film, invented by the DuPont corporation, used in photographic printing and production processes, as well as disks and tapes

nanocomputing: the science and engineering of building mechanical machines at the atomic level

nanometers: one-thousand-millionth (one billionth, or 10-9) of a meter

nanosecond: one-thousand-millionth (one billionth, or 10-9) of a second

nanotechnology: the design and construction of machines at the atomic or molecular level

narrowband: a general term in communication systems pertaining to a signal that has a small collection of differing frequency components (as opposed to broadband which has many frequency components)

National Computer Security Center (NCSC): a branch of the National Security Agency responsible for evaluating secure computing systems; the Trusted Computer Systems Evaluation Criteria (TCSEC) were developed by the NCSC

Network Control Protocol (NCP): a host-to-host protocol originally developed in the early 1970s to support the Internet, which was then a research project

network packet switching: the act of routing and transferring packets (or small sections) of a carrier signal that conveys digital information

neural modeling: the mathematical study and the construction of elements that mimic the behavior of the brain cell (neuron)

neural networks: pattern recognition systems whose structure and operation are loosely inspired by analogy to neurons in the human brain

Newtonian view: an approach to the study of mechanics that obeys the rules of Newtonian physics, as opposed to relativistic mechanics; named after Sir Isaac Newton (1642-1727)

nonlinear: a system that has relationships between outputs and inputs which cannot be expressed in the form of a straight line

O-rings: 37-foot rubber circles (rings) that seal the joints between the space shuttle's rocket booster segments

OEM: the acronym for Original Equipment Manufacturer; a manufacturer of computer components

offline: the mode of operation of a computer that applies when it is completely disconnected from other computers and peripherals (like printers)

Open Systems Interconnections (OSI): a communications standard developed by the International Organization for Standardization (ISO) to facilitate compatible network systems

operands: when a computer is executing instructions in a program, the elements on which it performs the instructions are known as the operands

operating system: a set of programs which control all the hardware of a computer and provide user and device input/output functions

optical character recognition: the science and engineering of creating programs that can recognize and interpret printed characters

optical computing: a proposed computing technology which would operate on particles of light, rather than electric currents

optophone: a system that uses artificial intelligence techniques to convert images of text into audible sound

orthogonal: elements or objects that are perpendicular to one another; in a logical sense this means that changes in one have no effect on the other

oscillator: an electronic component that produces a precise waveform of a fixed known frequency; this can be used as a time base (clock) signal to other devices

oscilloscopes: measuring instruments for electrical circuitry; connected to circuits under test using probes on leads and having small screens that display the signal waveforms

out-of-band: pertaining to elements or objects that are external to the limits of a certain local area network (LAN)

overhead: the expense or cost involved in carrying out a particular operation

packet-switched network: a network based on digital communications systems whereby packets of data are dispatched to receivers based on addresses that they contain

packet-switching: an operation used in digital communications systems whereby packets (collections) of data are dispatched to receivers based on addresses contained in the packets

packets: collections of digital data elements that are part of a complete message or signal; packets contain their destination addresses to enable reassembly of the message or signal

paradigm: an example, pattern, or way of thinking

parallel debugging: specialized approaches to locating and correcting errors in computer programs that are to be executed on parallel computing machine architectures

parallel processing: the presence of more than one central processing unit (CPU) in a computer, which enables the true execution of more than one program

parametric: modeling a system using variables or parameters that can be observed to change as the system operates

parity: a method of introducing error checking on binary data by adding a redundant bit and using that to enable consistency checks

pattern recognition: a process used by some artificial-intelligence systems to identify a variety of patterns, including visual patterns, information patterns buried in a noisy signal, and word patterns imbedded in text

PDF: the acronym for Portable Document Format, developed by Adobe Corporation to facilitate the storage and transfer of electronic documents

peer-to-peer services: the ways in which computers on the same logical level can interoperate in a structured network hierarchy

permutations: significant changes or rearrangement

personal area networking: the interconnectivity of personal productivity devices like computers, mobile telephones, and personal organizers

personal digital assistants (PDA): small-scale hand-held computers that can be used in place of diaries and appointment books

phosphor: a coating applied to the back of a glass screen on a cathode ray tube (CRT) that emits light when a beam of electrons strikes its surface

photolithography: the process of transferring an image from a film to a metal surface for etching, often used in the production of printed circuit boards

photonic switching: the technology that is centered on routing and managing optical packets of digital data

photons: the smallest fundamental units of electromagnetic radiation in the visible spectrum—light

photosensitive: describes any material that will change its properties in some way if subjected to visible light, such as photographic film

picoseconds: one-millionth of a millionth of a second (one-trillionth, or 10-12)

piezoelectric crystal: an electronic component that when subjected to a current will produce a waveform signal at a precise rate, which can then be used as a clock signal in a computer

PIN (personal identification number): a password, usually numeric, used in conjunction with a cryptographic token, smart card, or bank card, to ensure that only an authorized user can activate an account governed by the token or card

ping sweeps: technique that identifies properties belonging to a server computer, by sending it collections of "ping" packets and examining the responses from the server

piracy: the unlawful copying and redistribution of computer software, ignoring the copyright and ownership rights of the publisher

pixel: a single picture element on a video screen; one of the individual dots making up a picture on a video screen or digital image

pixilation: the process of generating animation, frame by frame

plug-in: a term used to describe the way that hardware and software modules can be added to a computer system, if they possess interfaces that have been built to a documented standard

pneumatic: powered by pressurized air, supplied through tubes or pipes

polarity: the positive (+) or negative (−) state of an object, which dictates how it will react to forces such as magnetism or electricity

polarizer: a translucent sheet that permits only plane-polarized light to pass through, blocking all other light

polygon: a many-sided, closed, geometrical figure

polynomial: an expression with more than one term

polypeptide: the product of many amino acid molecules bonded together

population inversion: used in quantum mechanics to describe when the number of atoms at higher energy levels is greater than the number at lower energy levels—a condition needed for photons (light) to be emitted

port: logical input/output points on computers that exist in a network

port scans: operations whereby ports are probed so that information about their status can be collected

potentiometer: an element in an electrical circuit that resists current flow (a resistor) but the value of the resistance can be mechanically adjusted (a variable resistor)

predicate calculus: a branch of logic that uses individuals and predicates, or elements and classes, and the existential and universal quantifiers, all and some, to represent statements

privatized: to convert a service traditionally offered by a government or public agency into a service provided by a private corporation or other private entity

progenitor: the direct parent of something or someone

propositional calculus: a branch of logic that uses expressions such as "If ... then ..." to make statements and deductions

proprietary: a process or technology developed and owned by an individual or company, and not published openly

proprietary software: software created by an individual or company that is sold under a license that dictates use and distribution

protocol: an agreed understanding for the sub-operations that make up a transaction, usually found in the specification of inter-computer communications

prototype: a working model or experimental investigation of proposed systems under development

pseudocode: a language-neutral, structural description of the algorithms that are to be used in a program

public key information: certain status and identification information that pertains to a particular public key (i.e., a key available for public use in encryption)

public key infrastructure (PKI): the supporting programs and protocols that act together to enable public key encryption/decryption

punched card: a paper card with punched holes which give instructions to a computer in order to encode program instructions and data

quadtrees: data structures resembling trees, which have four branches at every node (rather than two as with a binary tree); used in the construction of complex databases

quality-of-service (QoS): a set of performance criteria that a system is designed to guarantee and support as a minimum

quantification: to quantify (or measure) something

quantum-dot cellular automata (QCA): the theory of automata as applied to quantum dot architectures, which are a proposed approach for the development of computers at nanotechnology scales

quantum mechanical: something influenced by the set of rules that govern the energy and wave behavior of subatomic particles on the scale of sizes that are comparable to the particles themselves

queue: the ordering of elements or objects such that they are processed in turn; first-in, first-out

radar: the acronym for RAdio Direction And Ranging; a technique developed in the 1930s that uses frequency shifts in reflected radio waves to measure distance and speed of a target

radio telescopes: telescopes used for astronomical observation that operate on collecting electromagnetic radiation in frequency bands above the visible spectrum

random access memory (RAM): a type of memory device that supports the nonpermanent storage of programs and data; so called because various locations can be accessed in any order (as if at random), rather than in a sequence (like a tape memory device)

raster: a line traced out by a beam of electrons as they strike a cathode ray tube (CRT)

raster scan pattern: a sequence of raster lines drawn on a cathode ray tube such that an image or text can be made to appear

read only memory (ROM): a type of memory device that supports permanent storage of programs

real-time: a system, often computer based, that ensures the rates at which it inputs, processes, and outputs information meet the timing requirements of another system

recursive: operations expressed and implemented in a way that requires them to invoke themselves

relational database: a collection of records that permits logical and business relationships to be developed between themselves and their contents

relay contact systems: systems constructed to carry out logic functions, implemented in relays (electromechanical switches) rather than semiconductor devices

resistors: electrical components that slow the flow of current

retinal scan: a scan of the retina of the eye, which contains a unique pattern for each individual, in order to identify (or authenticate) someone

robotics: the science and engineering of building electromechanical machines that aim to serve as replacements for human laborers

routers: network devices that direct packets to the next network device or to the final destination

routing: the operation that involves collecting and forwarding packets of information by way of address

satellite: an object that orbits a planet

scalar: a quantity that has magnitude (size) only; there is no associated direction or bearing

scalar processor: a processor designed for high-speed computation of scalar values

schematic: a diagrammatic representation of a system, showing logical structure without regard to physical constraints

scripting languages: modern high-level programming languages that are interpreted rather than compiled; they are usually cross-platform and support rapid application development

Secure Sockets Layer (SSL): a technology that supports encryption, authentication, and other facilities and is built into standard UNIX communication protocols (sockets over TCP/IP)

semantics: the study of how words acquire meaning and how those meanings change over time

semiconductor: solid material that possesses electrical conductivity characteristics that are similar to those of metals under certain conditions, but can also exhibit insulating qualities under other conditions

semiconductor diode laser: a diode that emits electromagnetic radiation at wavelengths above about 630 nanometers, creating a laser beam for industrial applications

sensors: devices that can record and transmit data regarding the altitude, flight path, attitude, etc., so that they can enter into the system's calculations

sequentially: operations occurring in order, one after another

server: a computer that does not deal directly with human users, but instead handles requests from other computers for services to be performed

SGML: the acronym for Standard Generalized Markup Language, an international standard for structuring electronic documents

shadow mask: a metal sheet behind the glass screen of a cathode ray tube (CRT) that ensures the correct color phosphor elements are struck by the electron beams

shareware: a software distribution technique, whereby the author shares copies of his programs at no cost, in the expectation that users will later pay a fee of some sort

Sherman Antitrust Act: the act of the U.S. Congress in 1890 that is the foundation for all American anti-monopoly laws

signaling protocols: protocols used in the management of integrated data networks that convey a mix of audio, video, and data packets

SIGs: short for "Special Interest Group," SIGs concentrate their energies on specific categories of computer science, such as programming languages or computer architecture

silica: silicon oxide; found in sand and some forms of rock

silicon: a chemical element with symbol Si; the most abundant element in the Earth's crust and the most commonly used semiconductor material

silicon chip: a common term for a semiconductor integrated circuit device

Silicon Valley: an area in California near San Francisco, which has been the home location of many of the most significant information technology oriented companies and universities

silver halide: a photosensitive product that has been used in traditional cameras to record an image

simplex: uni-directional communication over a single communication channel

simputers: simple to use computers that take on the functionality of personal computers, but are mobile and act as personal assistants and information organizers

sine wave: a wave traced by a point on the circumference of a circle when the point starts at height zero (amplitude zero) and goes through one full revolution

single-chip: a computer system that is constructed so that it contains just one integrated circuit device

slide rule: invented by Scotsman John Napier (1550-1617), it permits the mechanical automation of calculations using logarithms

smart card: a credit-card style card that has a microcomputer embedded within it; it carries more information to assist the owner or user

smart devices: devices and appliances that host an embedded computer system that offers greater control and flexibility

smart matter: materials, machines, and systems whose physical properties depend on the computing that is embedded within them

social informatics: a field of study that centers on the social aspects of computing technology

softlifting: the act of stealing software, usually for personal use (piracy)

software-defined networks (SDNs): the same as virtual private networks (VPNs), where the subscriber can set up and maintain a communications system using management software, on a public network

sonar: the science and engineering of sound propagation in water

SONET: the acronym for Synchronous Optical NETwork, a published standard for networks based on fiber optic communications technology

sound card: a plug-in card for a computer that contains hardware devices for sound processing, conversion, and generation

source code: the human-readable programs that are compiled or interpreted so that they can be executed by a computing machine

speech recognition: the science and engineering of decoding and interpreting audible speech, usually using a computer system

spider: a computer program that travels the Internet to locate web documents and FTP resources, then indexes the documents in a database, which are then searched using software that the search engine provides

spreadsheet: an accounting or business tool that details numerical data in columns for tabulation purposes

static: without movement; stationary

stellar: pertaining to the stars

subnet: a logical section of a large network that simplifies the management of machine addresses

supercomputer: a very high performance computer, usually comprised of many processors and used for modeling and simulation of complex phenomena, like meteorology

superconductivity: the property of a material to pass an electric current with almost no losses; most metals are superconductive only at temperatures near absolute zero

swap files: files used by an operating system to support a virtual memory system, in which the user appears to have access to more memory than is physically available

syllogistic statements: the essential tenets of western philosophical thought, based on hypotheses and categories

synchronization: the time domain ordering of events; often applied when events repeatedly occur simultaneously

synchronized: events occurring at specific points in time with respect to one another

synchronous: synchronized behavior

synergistic: relating to synergism, which is the phenomenon whereby the action of a group of elements is greater than their individual actions

syntactic analyzer: a part of a compiler that scans program source code ensuring that the code meets essential language rules with regard to structure or organization

syntax: a set of rules that a computing language incorporates regarding structure, punctuation, and formatting

tangible: of a nature that is real, as opposed to something that is imaginary or abstract

task partitioning: the act of dividing up work to be done so that it can be separated into distinct tasks, processes, or phases

taxonomy: the classification of elements or objects based on their characteristics

TCP: the acronym for Transmission Control Protocol; a fundamental protocol used in the networks that support the Internet (ARPANET)

TCP/IP networks: interconnected computer networks that use Transmission Control Protocol/Internet Protocol

TCP/IP protocol suite: Transmission Control Protocol/Internet Protocol; a range of functions that can be used to facilitate applications working on the Internet

telegraph: a communication channel that uses cables to convey encoded low bandwidth electrical signals

telemedicine: the technology that permits remote diagnosis and treatment of patients by a medical practitioner; usually interactive bi-directional audio and video signals

telemetry: the science of taking measurements of something and transmitting the data to a distant receiver

teleoperation: any operation that can be carried out remotely by a communications system that enables interactive audio and video signals

teletype: a machine that sends and receives telephonic signals

terabyte: one million million (one trillion, or 1012) bytes

thermal ignition: the combustion of a substance caused by heating it to the point that its particles have enough energy to commence burning without an externally applied flame

thermodynamic: relating to heat energy

three-body problem: an intractable problem in mechanics that involves the attempts to predict the behavior of three bodies under gravitational effects

thumbnail: an image which is a scaled down copy of a much larger image; used to assist in the management of a large catalog of images

time lapse mode: to show a sequence of events occurring at a higher than natural speed so it looks like it is happening rapidly rather than in real time

title bar: the top horizontal border of a rectangular region owned by a program running in a graphical user interface (GUI); it usually contains the program name and can be used to move the region around

tomography: the process of capturing and analyzing X-ray images

T1 digital circuitry: a type of digital network technology that can handle separate voice and/or digital communications lines

topographic: pertaining to the features of a terrain or surface

topology: a method of describing the structure of a system that emphasizes its logical nature rather than its physical characteristics

trademark rights: a trademark is a name, symbol, or phrase that identifies a trading organization and is owned by that organization

trafficking: transporting and selling; especially with regard to illegal merchandise

training data: data used in the creation of a classifier

transaction processing: operations between client and server computers that are made up of many small exchanges that must all be completed for the transaction to proceed

transducers: devices that sense a physical quantity, such as temperature or pressure, and convert that measurement into an electrical signal

transistor: a contraction of TRANSfer resISTOR; a semiconductor device, invented by John Bardeen, Walter Brattain, and William Shockley, which has three terminals; can be used for switching and amplifying electrical signals

translational bridges: special network devices that convert low-level protocols from one type to another

Transmission Control Protocol (TCP): a stream-orientated protocol that uses Internet Protocol (IP); it is responsible for splitting data into packets, transferring it, and reassembling it at the receiver

transmutation: the act of converting one thing into another

trigonometry: a branch of mathematics founded upon the geometry of triangles

triodes: nearly obsolete electronic devices constructed of sealed glass tubes containing metal elements in a vacuum; triodes were used to control electrical signals

Trojan horse: potentially destructive computer program that masquerades as something benign; named after the wooden horse employed by the Acheans to conquer Troy

tunneling: a way of handling different communication protocols, by taking packets of a foreign protocol and changing them so that they appear to be a locally known type

Turing machine: a proposed type of computing machine that takes inputs off paper tape and then moves through a sequence of states under the control of an algorithm; identified by Alan Turing (1912-1954)

1200-baud: a measure of data transmission; in this case the rate of 1200 symbols (usually bits) per second

twisted pair: an inexpensive, medium bandwidth communication channel commonly used in local area networks

ubiquitous: to be commonly available everywhere

ultrasonic: the transmission and reception of sound waves that are at frequencies higher than those audible to humans

Uniform Resource Locator (URL): a reference to a document or a document container using the Hypertext Transfer Protocol (HTTP); consists of a hostname and path to the document

Universal Product Code (UPC): the first barcode standard developed in 1973 and adopted widely since

UNIX: operating system that was originally developed at Bell Laboratories in the early 1970s

uplinks: connections from a client machine to a large network; frequently used when information is being sent to a communications satellite

vacuum tube: an electronic device constructed of a sealed glass tube containing metal elements in a vacuum; used to control electrical signals

valence: a measure of the reactive nature of a chemical element or compound in relation to hydrogen

variable: a symbol, such as a string of letters, which may assume any one of a set of values known as the domain

vector graphics: graphics output systems whereby pairs of coordinates are passed to the graphics controller, which are interpreted as end points of vectors to be drawn on the screen

vector processing: an approach to computing machine architecture that involves the manipulation of vectors (sequences of numbers) in single steps, rather than one number at a time

vector supercomputer: a highly optimized computing machine that provides high performance using a vector processing architecture

velocities: vector quantities that have a magnitude or speed and a direction

Venn diagrams: diagrams used to demonstrate the relationships between sets of objects, named after John Venn, a British logician

venture capitalists: persons or agencies that speculate by providing financial resources to enable product development, in the expectation of larger returns with product maturity

video capture cards: plug-in cards for a computer that accepts video input from devices like televisions and video cameras, allowing the user to record video data onto the computer

video compression algorithms: special algorithms applied to remove certain unnecessary parts of video images in an attempt to reduce their storage size

virtual channel connection: an abstraction of a physical connection between two or more elements (or computers); the complex details of the physical connection are hidden

virtual circuit: like a virtual channel connection, a virtual circuit appears to be a direct path between two elements, but is actually a managed collection of physical connections

Virtual Private Networks (VPNs): a commercial approach to network management where privately owned voice and data networks are set up on public network infrastructure

virtual reality (VR): the use of elaborate input/output devices to create the illusion that the user is in a different environment

virtualization: as if it were real; making something seem real, e.g. a virtual environment

visible speech: a set of symbols, comprising an alphabet, that "spell" sounds instead of words

visualization: a technique whereby complex systems are portrayed in a meaningful way using sophisticated computer graphics systems; e.g., chemical molecules

volatile: subject to rapid change; describes the character of data when current no longer flows to a device (that is, electrical power is switched off)

waveform: an abstraction used in the physical sciences to model energy transmission in the form of longitudinal or transverse waves

web surfers: people who "surf" (search) the Internet frequently

wide area network (WAN): an interconnected network of computers that spans upward from several buildings to whole cities or entire countries and across countries

wireless lavaliere microphones: small microphones worn around the speakers' necks, which attach to their shirts

wireless local area network (WLAN): an interconnected network of computers that uses radio and/or infrared communication channels, rather than cables

workstations: computers (usually within a network) that interact directly with human users (much the same as "client computers")

xerography: a printing process that uses electrostatic elements derived from a photographic image to deposit the ink

XML: the acronym for eXtensible Markup Language; a method of applying structure to data so that documents can be represented

Topic Outline

JavaScript
LISP
Logo
Markup Languages
Object-Oriented Languages
Procedural Languages
Programming
SQL
SQL: Databases
Visual Basic

HUMAN INTERACTION

Computer System Interfaces
Human Factors: User Interfaces
Hypertext
Integrated Software
Interactive Systems
Speech Recognition
User Interfaces
Window Interfaces

INFORMATION RELATED TOPICS

Information Access
Information Overload
Information Retrieval
Information Systems
Information Theory
Library Applications
Search Engines
System Analysis
Systems Design

INNOVATION

Artificial Intelligence
Artificial Life
Data Mining
Data Visualization
Data Warehousing
Desktop Publishing
Digital Images
Digital Libraries
Embedded Technology (Ubiquitous
    Computing)
Fiber Optics
Global Positioning Systems

Laser Technology
Mobile Computing
Molecular Computing
Nanocomputing
Optical Character Recognition
Optical Technology
Pattern Recognition
Personal Digital Assistants
Robotics
Robots
Satellite Technology
Scientific Visualization

INPUT AND OUTPUT DEVICES

Display Devices
Game Controllers
Graphic Devices
Input Devices
Keyboard
Magnetic Stripe Cards
Mouse
Pointing Devices
Printing Devices
Reading Tools
Sound Devices
Touch Screens
Video Devices
Word Processors

INTERNET

Authentication
Browsers
Credit Online
Cybercafe
E-banking
E-commerce
E-commerce: Economic and Social Aspects
E-journals and E-publishing
E-mail
Electronic Markets
Entrepreneurs
Internet
Internet: Applications
Internet: Backbone

PRECURSORS TO COMPUTERS

PROGRAMMING

PUBLISHING

SECURITY

SOCIAL ISSUES

Compatibility (Open Systems Design)
Computer Scientists
Cookies
Copyright
Credit Online
Cybercafe
Digital Libraries
Digital Signatures
Distance Learning
E-banking
E-books
E-commerce
E-commerce: Economic and Social Aspects
E-journals and E-publishing
E-mail
Electronic Campus
Electronic Markets
Entrepreneurs
Ergonomics
Ethics
Fiction, Computers in
Global Surveillance
Government Funding, Research
Home Entertainment
Information Access
Information Overload
Journalism
Library Applications
Medical Systems
Mobile Computing
Open Source
Patents
Personal Digital Assistants
Political Applications
Privacy
Service Providers
Social Impact
Software Piracy
Technology of Desktop Publishing
Telephony
Urban Myths
Virtual Private Network
Virtual Reality in Education
World Wide Web

SOFTWARE

Agents
Browsers
Compilers
Database Management Software
Geographic Information Systems
Human Factors: User Interfaces
Integrated Software
Office Automation Systems
Open Source
Operating Systems
Procedural Languages
Productivity Software
Search Engines
Simulation
Spreadsheets
User Interfaces
Window Interfaces

STUDY AREAS

Artificial Intelligence
Artificial Life
Expert Systems
Information Theory
Molecular Computing
Nanocomputing

TECHNOLOGY, DEVICES

Abacus
Analytical Engine
ATM Machines
Bandwidth
Bridging Devices
Cache Memory
CAD/CAM, CA Engineering
Cell Phones
Cellular Technology
Central Processing Unit
Communication Devices
Computer System Interfaces
Display Devices
Game Controllers
Global Positioning Systems
Graphic Devices

TECHNOLOGY, TECHNIQUES

TELECOMMUNICATIONS, PEOPLE AND ORGANIZATIONS

TELECOMMUNICATIONS, TECHNOLOGY AND DEVICES

Volume 3 Index